Patronage Copy No. 447

This book was made possible by
the support of Patrons who pre-paid for their
copies. This copy was subscribed for by

NOTTINGHAM
UNIVERSITY

to whom sincere thanks are expressed

Lou Warwick

8 - 3 - 1977

Under the Patronage of the late Allardyce Nicoll

THE MACKENZIES CALLED COMPTON

The Story of the Compton Comedy Company
Incorporated in the history of Northampton
Theatre Royal and Opera House, 1884-1927

Written and Published
by
LOU WARWICK

Obtainable from the Publisher at 54 St. George's Avenue,
Northampton, England, and from
R. HARRIS & SON LTD, 6 Bridge Street, Northampton
KINGSTHORPE BOOKSHOP, 6-8 Harborough Road, Northampton
J. W. McKENZIE, 12 Stoneleigh Park Road, Ewell, Epsom, Surrey
W. MARK, 27 The Drapery, Northampton
F. A. MOORE, 33 Montagu Street, Kettering
MOTLEY BOOKS, Mottisfont Abbey, Romsey, Hampshire
BASIL SAVAGE, 46 Brookfield, Highgate West Hill, London N6 6AT

Affectionately Dedicated
to the Memory of

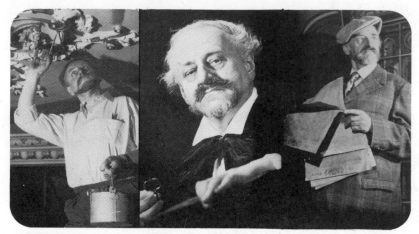

TOM OSBORNE ROBINSON, O.B.E., (1904-76) who served Northampton
Repertory Theatre (the former Opera House) from 1928 to 1975. In the left of
these three pictures by Bryan J. Douglas he is repainting the theatre ceiling. On
the right he is pictured (symbolically he said) against a pawnbrokers in a set of
Lock Up Your Daughters in 1975, this being his last set. He died the following
January. On the opposite page is his drawing of the theatre interior which
appeared in Adventure in Repertory, by Aubrey Dyas, published to mark the
coming-of-age of repertory in Northampton in 1948.

COPYRIGHT 1977 LOU WARWICK
PRINTED IN GREAT BRITAIN BY
BLACKBURN TIMES PRESS LTD.
BLACKBURN, LANCASHIRE
ISBN 0 9503287 2 3

This imagined interior of the Theatre Royal,
Marefair, Northampton, was drawn by Osborne
Robinson for Theatre Un-Royal, the history of that
theatre. It has since been used as the "trademark"
of the Northampton Theatre History series.

RUNNING ORDER

The bill for the first week of the Northampton Opera House in May, 1884, with the Compton Comedy Company inaugurating the new theatre. *(Reproduction supplied by Church's China)*

OPENING

OF THE

NEW THEATRE ROYAL

AND OPERA HOUSE,

NORTHAMPTON.

MANAGER ... ... Mr TARRY

The Manager respectfully informs the Public that the OPENING PERFORMANCES will take place MAY 5th, 6th, 7th, 8th, 9th, and 10th, under the distinguished patronage of

HIS WORSHIP THE MAJOR (M. P. MANFIELD, Esq.,

The Most Noble the MARQUESS of EXETER, K.G. | The Right Honble. LORD BURGHLEY, M.P.
The Most Noble the MARQUESS of NORTHAMPTON | The Honble. C. R. SPENCER, M.P.
The Rt. Hon. LORD BROWNLOW CECIL, | PICKERING PHIPPS Esq., M.P.
The Rev. S. J. W. SANDERS, M.A., President, and the Members of the Northampton Shakspere Society.

Important Engagement for SIX NIGHTS ONLY, of the celebrated

Compton Comedy Company,

FROM THE STRAND THEATRE, LONDON.

MR. EDWARD COMPTON,

ACCOMPANIED BY

MISS VIRGINIA BATEMAN,

(MRS. EDWARD COMPTON) AND FULL COMPANY.

"As a genuine Comedian, Mr. Edward Compton has few equals and no superiors on the English Stage." *The Referee,* Dec. 23rd, 1883.

Stage Managers ... For Mr LEWIS BALL and Mr T. C. VALENTINE
Business Manager Mr EDWARD COMPTON. Mr J. H. SAVILE

SHAKSPERE'S admired Comedy, in Five Acts.

MONDAY.

TWELFTH NIGHT

Or, WHAT YOU WILL.

May 5th,

1884.

Orsino Duke of Illyria	Mr JOHN BURTON	Valentine ... Mr C. H. WORRALL
Sir Toby Belch, Uncle to Olivia	Mr LEWIS BALL	An Officer ... Mr L. J. CLARKE
Sir Andrew Aguecheek, a foolish Knight	Mr J. S. BLYTHE	Viola (first appearance) in Viola Mr STANLEY ROGERS
Sebastian, brother to Viola	Mr WILLIAM CALVERT	... Mr W. J. CONWAY
Antonio a Sea Captain, his friend	Mr W. H. GRIFFITHS	Olivia (a rich Heiress) Miss NELLIE DAMPER
Fabian, servant to the Countess	Mr PERCY F. MACSHALL	Maria, her attendant Miss STELLA BROWN
Malvolio, steward to the Countess	Mr EDWARD COMPTON	Viola, sister to Sebastian, in love with the Duke
(first time of performance)		... Miss VIRGINIA BATEMAN
Clown, Servant to the Countess	Mr T. C. VALENTINE	(Mrs. Edward Compton)

GOLDSMITH'S celebrated Comedy, in Five Acts.

TUESDAY,

SHE STOOPS TO CONQUER

May 6th,

Mr. Hardcastle a country gentleman	Mr LEWIS BALL	Tom Twist ... Mr WHISTON
Young Marlow, a London gentleman	Mr JOHN BURTON	A Slang ... Mr L. J. CLARKE
Hastings, his friend	Mr WILLIAM CALVERT	Mat ... Mr WEATHERBY
Stingo ...	Mr PERCY F. MACSHALL	... Mr STANLEY ROGERS
Sir Charles Marlow	Mr W. H. GRIFFITHS	Roger ... Mr C. H. WORRALL
Diggory ...	Mr T. C. VALENTINE	Miss Neville (niece to ... Hardcastle) Miss NELLIE HALPER
Tony Lumpkin, the young squire, with song		Mrs Hardcastle ... Miss STELLA BROWN
"The Three Jolly Pigeons"	Mr EDWARD COMPTON	Miss Hardcastle ... Miss ... KERNSTAFF
Roger ...	Mr W. GARDINER	Maid ... Miss ... PARKER
Ralph ...	Mr F. EVANS	Miss Hardcastle ... Miss VIRGINIA BATEMAN
Gregory ...	Mr W. F. EVANS	(Mrs. Edward Compton)

SHERIDAN'S Immortal Comedy, in Five Acts. The

SCHOOL FOR SCANDAL

WEDNESDAY,

May 7th,

Sir Peter Teazle	...	Joseph Surface ... Mr W. J. CONWAY
Sir Oliver Surface	...	Sir Harry Bumper ... Mr PERCY F. MACSHALL
Joseph Surface his elder Nephew	...	Sir Benjamin Backbite ... Mr ... BISHOP
Charles Surface his younger Nephew Mr EDWARD COMPTON		Sir Toby ... Mr W. GARDINER
(first time of Master of the House)		Trip (servant to Charles) Mr ... WORRALL
Moses a Jew Money Lender		Lady Teazle Miss VIRGINIA BATEMAN
Careless ... Mr T. C. VALENTINE		Mrs. Candour ...
Sir Benjamin Backbite, his Nephew Mr WILLIAM CALVERT		Maria ... Miss ... RATCLIFF
Rowley ... Mr ...		Lady Sneerwell Miss STELLA BROWN
Servant to Lady Sneerwell		... Miss NELLIE HALPER

VISUAL REPRESENTATIONS

"... *sometimes it seems to me that it is as if amusement were fast becoming the business of life with us.*"

—*Isaac Tarry*

OVERTURE

TWO MISSING PATRONS

Thanking all those who have made the production, and the previous three, possible; announcing a possible return visit; and asking the audience to stand in silence in respect to two seats that are empty. . . .

Professor Allardyce Nicoll, Patron-in-Chief of this book, pictured in the garden of his home, Winds Acre in the Malvern Hills, a few months before his death in April, 1976. His earliest theatre memory was of going with his mother to see the C.C.C. in *The Gentleman In Grey,* in his native Glasgow. At the end of the performance of the play by Compton Mackenzie, he recalled, Edward Compton came on stage with his arm round his author son. But "The house was cold and the play got a poor reception," said Professor Nicoll. *(Nigel Warwick)*

PLEASE
STAND IN
SILENCE . . .

Before ringing up the curtain on The Mackenzies Called Compton I must stop before it to ask the audience to stand for a brief silence in memory of two great men of the theatre, neither of whom were actors, but both of whom were closely linked with this production. First the greatest theatre historian of them all, that humble, modest and approachable man Professor Allardyce Nicoll, who died in April, 1976, and who was the Patron-in-Chief of this volume. Secondly the man whose picture appears on the dustcover, T. Osborne Robinson, O.B.E., scenic designer at Northampton Repertory Theatre for most of his life; to this dedicated artist and sturdy Northamptonian this volume is affectionately dedicated.

It may be asked why a picture of Professor Nicoll does not also appear on the dustcover. The reason is simple; he hated having his photograph taken and submitted only under protest to snapshots taken by the author's then 13-year-old son, Nigel, when the family were invited to the Nicolls' home, called Winds Acre, in the Malvern Hills. One of the resultant "snaps" is included in the book, because the pictures are, for the reasons stated, unique likenesses of the former president of the Society for Theatre Research. It was to have been my greatly anticipated pleasure and honour to motor down to Malvern to deliver his pre-paid copy of the book to Professor Nicoll, but it was not to be. In his last letter in February, 1976, telling me that inoperable cancer had been diagnosed which would "presumably do for me in the not too distant future", he assured me of his continued interest in my project—"although this note is necessarily concerned with letting you know about my affairs please bear in mind that I wish you all success in your tireless endeavours to complete your multi-volumed history." His own "multi-volumed" history of the English drama is, of course, the standard work on the theme. Professor Nicoll was 81. To his widow I extend my deepest sympathy, a sentiment with which I feel sure that all Patrons would wish to be associated.

"Tom" Robinson was to have drawn some new illustrations for me, of the theatre he loved so passionately and to which he devoted almost half-a-century of his useful life; his death has robbed this book of those illustrations which would have been in his inimitable and unmistakable style, though other existing ones have been used. Northampton Repertory Theatre could never be the same after "Tom" had gone and indeed it has not been. Even in the anguished weeks of approaching death he expressed his concern about the theatre's future in increasingly difficult times. His fears have certainly been borne out by events.

This book completes the project of publishing a set of four on the history of theatre in Northampton and the county. It began in 1960 with Death of a Theatre, story of the New Theatre; carried on in 1974 with Theatre Un-Royal, about the 19th century Marefair Theatre; stepped back in time the following year to pre-1806 theatre, in Drama That Smelled; and now concludes with The Mackenzies Called Compton. The series has been made possible financially only by the valiant support of my pre-paying Patrons. The latest list on Pages 295 to 303, is almost exactly the same as the one in the last book and many of these good people also supported me with the second book. The majority of those named were not with me, however, for Death of a Theatre in 1960 and some have therefore asked me how they may complete their set of four books. So far this is impossible, Death of a Theatre being out of print. There is a project, therefore, to produce a limited number of reprint or facsimile copies of that book, with some additions and an Index, which through my inexperience, the original edition lacked. Details appear on Page 306. For those especially interested in the theatre there is a further project, not in the Northampton arena, to publish a Bicentenary life of the 18th century theatre personality Jemmy Whitley; details appear on Page 307.

While this present book represents a farewell appearance for Northampton Theatre History, from where I am standing it seems to be a great shame to demobilise my wonderful army of supporters in book publishing. If any of them care to carry their trust in me so far as to send a pre-payment for a future unspecified book, I shall be delighted to carry on in the hope of producing something worthwhile and something which would not otherwise be published. Again, details on Page 307.

Several Patrons have died since subscribing, or since the last book appeared, among them personal friends. Earl Spencer, who was so helpful with Drama That Smelled, died shortly after handing me his cheque for this book. Mrs. Florrie Driver, who sold Death of a Theatre on Northampton doorsteps, a task which would have daunted me, died in September, 1976, in Rhyl, where she had moved from her native Northampton. The former professional actor Sir Gyles Isham, Bart., who died in the same month as Osborne Robinson, had special connections with the Comptons, as mentioned on Pages 231-2. That noted amateur actor, Fred Tuckley, has passed on as too have Mr. S. G. H. Humfrey, who gave his former opthalmic premises to Northamptonshire Natural History Society, and Mrs. A. C. Finnimore, who was a descendant of Henry Martin who built Northampton Opera House. I note too with regret the death of Sir Spencer Summers, a former Patron of my books. If there are any deceases which have not come to my notice I apologise for not mentioning them.

Apart from the Patrons, there are so many people who have helped me this time that I dare hardly list them, because of the ones I have to leave out. First I must say that I greatly regret not being able to thank Miss Fay Compton, the only survivor of the children of Edward and Virginia Compton (Mackenzie) who could have filled in so much background, provided so much atmosphere, perhaps corrected a few mistakes, had not the fragility of her health precluded an interview. Among those who were able to assist was one who married a Compton, Arthur Howard, whose friendly co-operation was absolutely invaluable. Other descendants of Batemans or Comptons who have helped include Valerie Skardon, of Harrogate, who is a granddaughter of Kate Bateman; and Nicholas Crocker, of Portishead, Bristol, who is a grandson of Edward Compton. At the Theatre Museum and Victoria and Albert Museum Jennifer Aylmer and George Nash stepped far beyond the bounds of duty in granting me facilities to look at the Compton Collection, acquired in 1974. So many helped in so many ways. For instance the editor of the Rochdale Observer published my letter and thus located a picture of the theatre in which Edward Compton gave his very last performance. Rochdale Library and Art Services lent me negatives of the ruins of that theatre, after it had been burned down. Throughout the land librarians and their assistants have been most patient and some very persistent in assisting me with my inquiries, those at Cheltenham (Mrs. Nancy Pringle), Nottingham (Mr. Stephen Best) and Dublin being especially extended in this direction, because of particular associations in those places. As always the staff of Northamptonshire Public Libraries have put up with me very well, notably Miss Marion Arnold, of the Local Room. Harry N. Greatorex, who was Patron-in-Chief of Drama That Smelled, supplied drawings and facts culled from his remarkable theatre collection, Colin Robinson, of Whiston, dug into the archival material among his brother's effects to come up with several relevant items. Kathleen Barker, of Wimbledon, read parts of the text and made such penetrating observations that I rewrote those sections almost completely; she was helpful in more ways than there is room to state here: I don't think the book could have come out at all without the aid of this cheerful theatre historian and, in her role as joint secretary of the Society for Theatre Research, willing servant of other theatre historians. Sister Hilary, of Wantage Convent, clued me up on the former Mother of the establishment who was once an actress, Isabel Bateman. And Alan Burman assisted with photo-copying. As before Ken Nutt and Tony Rowen "looked after the safe keys" by acting as trustees of the money involved.

This time the book has been printed by the litho process as opposed to the hot-metal method and has been produced by the Blackburn Times Press Ltd. who also serve me in printing the Northampton and County Independent magazine. The happy relationship existing in my capacity "at work" has therefore extended into this private activity and I am very grateful to the manager, Mr. John Brown, overseer Mr. Ray Hull, and their team of printers.

In acknowledging with thanks contributions from Northampton Amateur Operatic Company and my employers, Northampton Mercury Co. Ltd., I would like to emphasise that apart from these, it is the Patrons' money alone which has been involved—I have received no "public money" by way of subsidy.

In closing my little Tarry-like homily to the faithful I hope it will not be considered immodest to mention my belief that in terms of quantity Northampton now has more of its theatre history recorded than any other town of its size in the world. On top of my four books there is Aubrey Dyas's Adventure in Repertory, which takes up the story at precisely the time when The Mackenzies Called Compton ends, carrying it up to the 1948 "coming of age" of Northampton Repertory Company. At this moment Aubrey Dyas is working on a further book to bring the story up to the present day, when the company has reached its golden jubilee. When that volume emerges there will be six books on the theatre history of Northampton and the county, plus Ernest Reynold's excellent booklet on the architecture of the Repertory Theatre, published in November, 1976 (50p plus postage, from the theatre).

I sense impatience among the audience and will get on with it.

E. & O. E.

    February 7, 1977

PROLOGUE

DOGS & ACTORS

In the pre-theatre days, dogs—and actors—sometimes performed at Northampton's inns, including the Surprising English Learned Dog at the Angel, Bridge Street, in 1753. But when the Lively Lass came to town in 1747 she appeared at another Angel, a coffee-house in the Drapery. There were also "playhouses" in a riding house and a malting. Finally, in 1806, the town at last acquired a theatre, albeit a very tatty one . . . a Theatre Un-Royal, in fact.

By the Defire of feveral Gentlemen and Ladies,
For the Benefit of the Celebrated Mifs RAYNER,
THIS prefent Evening, being the 30th of November, 1747, at the Angel Coffee-Houfe in the Drapery, Northampton, will be performed the ufual Variety of
Rope-Dancing, Tumbling, Poftures, *and* Ballancing.
With which will be interfperfed feveral new Songs and Dialogues ; alfo a Stage Dance, call'd,
The LIVELY LASS,
By Mifs RAYNER.
To conclude with a New Pantomime Entertainment, call'd,
The Fortune-Tellers ; *or,* Harlequin Diffected.
The Performance to begin exactly at Six o'Clock.
Note, Thurfday Night will be the laft of our playing in Town.

The Lively Lass, alias the celebrated Miss Rayner, appeared at the Angel Coffee-House in the Drapery, Northampton, in 1747. *(Northampton Mercury)*

Prologue

WHEN DOGS & ACTORS CALLED AT THE INNS

Over the centuries Northamptonians have entertained themselves and been entertained in the widest possible variety of ways, from bull-racing to bingo, from throwing stones at cocks tied up in the alleys to making cine films, from playing the viol to learning the electronic organ by numbers. It is a subject about which a full-length book could easily be written, under some such title as How They Were Amused. In fact, at the time of writing the last lines of this book (which are these, the first chancing to be written last) I am at the same time writing the first lines of an enlarged issue of the Northampton and County Independent under the title That's Entertainment, dealing with the many ways in which people have been amused. This issue was to coincide with the golden jubilee of repertory in the theatre with which this present book is concerned.

Entertainers visiting Northampton often performed in inns such as the Angel, Bridge Street, as in November, 1753, when this hostelry was visited by "a dog which reads and writes and casts accounts, answers various questions in Ovid's metamorphosis, geography, English and social history, knows alphabets, reads thoughts."

An advance announcement, which mentioned that the Surprising Learned English Dog was visiting Market Harborough before coming to Northampton, stated that the creature "reckons the number of persons present, sets down any capital or sur-name, solves questions in the four rules of arithmetick, tells by looking on any common watch of the company what is the hour and minute, knows the foreign as well as the English coins. He likewise knows the impenetrable secret or tells any person's thoughts in company and distinguishes all sorts of colours."

During the visit the Mercury noted: "We hear that of all the extraordinary curiosities that have been exhibited to the inspection of the curious none have met with such a general approbation and esteem as the Learned English Dog now at the Angel Inn in this town. He continues in this town until Saturday, November 10, and positively no longer." The word "positive" appears to have had some elasticity in the canine vocabulary for in the issue of the 10th one reads: "The Surprising Learned English Dog begs leave in this public manner to return his humble thanks for the many epistles he has received inviting him to the several towns of the county. Yet tho' to oblige be his principal aim the polite company he has been engaged with for this week past and his prospect of still further favours are circumstances too prevalent with him to admit of his departure from this town before Wednesday next till when he will attend at his lodgings at the Angel Inn in Bridge Street but positively no longer." After taking his delayed departure the sagacious hound made his way to Daventry and Bedford.

As well as animal wonders, inns were the calling place of actors of the pre-theatre days. There are no references to their visits before 1720 because there was no newspaper in the town to record them but 16 months after the Northampton Mercury began in May that year there are mentions of Mr. Toller's Company being at the Talbot Inn in October, 1721, at the time of the races; of an unnamed company performing *The Spanish Fryar,* by the county playwright John Dryden, at the Hind Inn in January, 1723; and four years later one finds the Comedians from Bath (of Mr. Power's Family) at the Hind. A few weeks after this we read of a fire-eater, named Edward Price, who claimed the Royal patronage of George II, performing at the Swan and Helmet, Gold Street, while in July, 1728, the Talbot was the venue for a "Company of Comedians from the Theatre-Royal". It was in the absence of a theatre, even a fit-up one, that these artistes performed in the inns. Later the drama found a home in the town's Riding House in Fish Lane, and then in a former malting round the corner in St. Gyles Street.

The first purpose-built theatre in Northampton was the one opened in Marefair on May 5, 1806, with Mr. Thomas Shaftoe Robertson and his Lincoln Company on the stage in *The Castle Spectre.*

When it came upon the Northampton scene, replacing the previous make-shift facilities in a riding house and a malting, this theatre was thought to be quite splendid but by the time it was in turn supplanted in 1884 no term of disapprobation was too strong for it. In the years following its demise the vocabulary of vituperation grew in volume. It was stuffy, a bandbox theatre, nauseous, a tumbledown shanty, puny, little better than a barn, musty, and a wretched little hole. It might have been thought that all the possible expressions of abuse had been exhausted but in 1974 I managed to coin a new one when my history of the establishment emerged under the title Theatre Un-Royal.

Some of the verbal attacks on it are probably not on record and one might not care to reproduce them if they were. For there is little doubt that some of the managers who lost money in Marefair had their own pet phrases to describe the place. Several either did not make money or lost it, "Empty benches" is a phrase which recurs in reports of performances over the 78 years. In August, 1873, the Northampton Albion stated: "Every manager who is enterprising enough to bring a company is certain to do it at his own personal loss and, of course, the better the company, the greater the loss. Under these circumstances it is to be wondered at that the drama patronises Northampton quite as much as that Northampton does not patronise the drama." On another occasion the Albion said that each time its representative entered the theatre he had a feeling of nausea! But as the Press frequently is when being forthright and trying to gain circulation (the Albion ceased publication after just under two years) the newspaper was guilty of at least some degree of exaggeration. Not every manager lost money by coming to Northampton and there may have been fewer who did so during the last decade up to 1884 than in the 1850s and 60s. The touring system was becoming better established and one such company which did very well indeed was that of Madamoiselle Beatrice. Her Comedy Drama Company visited the town several times both before and after her death at the age of 39 on December 22, 1878.

Facts and figures are hard to come by; even vague remarks "from the horse's mouth" can only be picked up here and there. Alderman Joe Gurney who was for many years a lone Radical reformer on Northampton Town Council dropped out at one meeting that he had been the theatre's secretary for many years and that "it is difficult sometimes to make that pay." Within the period of the theatre's life I came across no figures of losses but in subsequent research for the present book the obituary of a former lessee published in September, 1907, provided one. Henry Nicholson, of Leicester, was the "Prince of English Flautists" and after doing very well in Northamptonshire as a bandleader, providing music for practically every county ball, he made an unprofitable speculation when he tried running the Northampton theatre in 1866. Installing his brother as manager he lost £100 within a year, said the obituary of the 83-year-old flautist.

The obituary columns of 1901 also provided some facts about the last manager at the old theatre who was just a name in Theatre Un-Royal. It transpires that Mr. Joseph Tebbutt was only a part-time theatre manager, being the manager and later proprietor of a Northampton printing works. A member of a family originating in the county village of Earls Barton he had been apprenticed to T. L. and Frank Cordeux, then of Bradshaw Street, Northampton, whose name appears as the printers of many Victorian playbills in the town. When Frank Cordeux retired about 1880 his brother removed the business to Swan Yard, off the Drapery, where Tebbutt was manager for some years before acquiring it. His interest in matters musical and theatrical led him to become manager of the Marefair theatre for eight years before its closure in 1884. Tebbutt, who was a nephew of the Alderman Tebbutt who had been Mayor in 1878, died in December, 1901, at the age of 55. He had an unusual exit from the world for instead of being held at Abington Avenue Congregational Church, where he had worshipped, the funeral service was held at his home, Nestwood, in Abington Park Road. This was because the church was in temporary use as a Board School and the coffin would have had to have been carried upstairs.

Since completing the history of the old theatre I have also been provided (by Miss Kathleen Barker) with an account of an October evening in 1850 when there was a full house—but the audience all had to be sent home, with their money back in their pockets. James R. Anderson described the episode in his Seven Decades of An Actor's Life published in the Newcastle Weekly Chronicle in October, 1887. He related how after returning from a tour in the Isle of Man he visited Leicester "the scene of my early managerial disasters. After this I played an engagement of three nights at Northampton theatre (first and last visit), Mr. H. Jackman manager. October 17, the opening night, was a great disappointment to everyone, more especially for the manager. My theatrical wardrobe had not arrived from Leicester; we could not perform the play announced or any other and he was compelled to return the money taken at the door to a very full house. I thought this cruel contretemps would have ruined our prospects but it didn't. We played to very full houses during the three nights. I should have liked to have gratified the manager's wishes and remained longer, but my Drury Lane affairs were pressing. I promised, however, to play a few nights with him in Gloucester and Cheltenham, in December." This little tale is included here because in the present inflationary situation it seems likely that my hopes of publishing a fuller account of Jackman as a separate volume will be frustrated unless some fairy godmother appears. The incident is interesting because it adds two more towns—Gloucester and Cheltenham—to the tally of 26 Jackman ports of call listed in Theatre Un-Royal. Miss Barker tells me that the dates were in fact played.

In Northampton, advertising must have represented a greater problem from 1880 when daily newspapers began in the town. For many years there had been the Liberal Mercury (1720) and the Tory Herald (1831) slogging it out on political issues and competing for advertising revenue. In 1880 came the Evening Mail which was from neither of these stables but which was published by S. S. Campion, who had previously founded the Northamptonshire Guardian and there followed the Daily Echo (from the Mercury owners) and the Daily Chronicle (from the Herald owners). In its first issue the Evening Mail pointed out that the halfpenny evening journal was becoming a necessary part of the life of every important town. As far as the theatre was concerned the appearance of the daily newspaper had two principal effects. To obtain total coverage an advertiser had to take space in six newspapers instead of three, apart from the fact that the daily papers were published five times a week. Secondly the daily sheet gave a greater immediacy to dramatic coverage. On Tuesday night you could see what the paper had to say about the play given on the Monday, instead of having to wait until Thursday or Friday, when the week was nearly over. The weekly paper might record a more leisurely judgment, the writer having more time to weigh his words, but a review appearing on the Tuesday could be of much more use to the theatre, assuming that it did not advise people to stay away. Not everyone regarded this next day coverage as a boon— one reader wrote to the paper complaining that too much of the plot was being given away.

There were a number of proposals to replace the Marefair Theatre, from as far back as 1861 when Charles Jackman and Frederick Morgan attended a meeting immediately following the end of the Jackman era of 21 years and promised to lease a new theatre which it was planned to erect in the north of the town. The idea got no further than that meeting which was held at the George Hotel. Another abortive scheme was put forward by the actor-manager Henry Dacre. A further project by Mr. Henry Cooper* made some progress but then had to be abandoned, as was reported in the Northamptonshire Guardian in March, 1882. "So the Thespian Temple project had collapsed" wrote a columnist who signed himself Man About Town. "The love of dramatic art in Northampton was not

---

* This Henry Cooper was an auctioneer and valuer and not the Northampton pioneer photographer, as stated in Theatre Un-Royal. A keen Shakespearian and member of the Northampton Amateur Dramatic Club which used to perform at the Marefair theatre he was one of the first 12 men sworn in as members of Northampton Volunteers and was thereafter known as Captain Cooper. A partner also in the brewers, Coles, Allen and Cooper, he moved to Old Laken- ham, Norwich where he died in November, 1908.

equal to a share capital of £5,000 for the erection of a theatre really worthy of the place. I suppose the promises amounted to something like £3,000 but that was manifestly inadequate for the ambitious scheme which had been put forward. We must bide our time and wait until the growth of the population and enterprise justifies the resurrection of this or some similar project." The proposed site on the west side of Guildhall Road had been sold to the Museum and Free Library Committee for a Museum and Reading Room. A plan by the owners of the old theatre to rebuild on the same spot also came to nothing. Probably it was the constricted nature of the site which deterred them.

Before passing on from the negative to the positive, to the plan which did succeed, just a few words about what happened to the old theatre once the new one had outshone it. In January, 1885, it emerged very briefly as the Empire Theatre of Varieties with Mr. Frank Somerville as proprietor and manager. It boasted "new scenery, decorations and renovations" and . . . "the smartest programme out of London." Short-lived too was the effort of Mr. George West to re-open it the following September as the Oxford Theatre of Varieties. For the next couple of years it was used mainly for religious purposes. The Church Army had the help of Canon R. B. Hull, the drama-hating Vicar of All Saints, the civic church of Northampton. He was the only parson to welcome this "Army" the aim of which was to attract to God those who did not normally attend a place of worship. In November, 1885, the Daily Reporter said that the stage was occupied by soldiers of the Army and that scenery and other adjuncts were arranged in seemly order with texts of the scriptures in big letters fixed in conspicuous positions. The services were of a mild Salvation Army type with short snatches of popular hymns interspersed with prayers and recitals of their experiences by the soldiers. By his side the Captain kept a bell which he would ring when he thought the reminiscences had gone on long enough. By the following January, 1886, the old theatre had been booked for a Sunday evening gospel Temperance meeting by the Blue Ribbon movement which, along with the Good Templars and the Band of Hope Union, was of an "all or nothing" persuasion, its more dogmatic members declaring that the moderate drinker was more culpable than the drunkard. The Church of England Temperance Union was the more moderate competitor, allowing the parson his glass of sherry and the working man his glass of beer. Overall the movement was very big business at this time; Mr. Robert Rae's Temperance Annual for 1886 noted that there were 20,000 temperance centres in the United Kingdom and that each week 10,000 meetings were held. I wonder how many of them were in former theatres?

In April, 1886, the old house came alive in an entertainment sense when a benefit concert was given by the Empire Brass Band for the widow and family of Mr. A. S. Deborde, one of their members who had died while skating in the frosty weather early that year. Such benefits were a standard means of aiding dependants in the days before the Welfare State. The Herald used the occasion as another excuse to kick the fallen theatre: "Bless my life! What a change from that tumbledown shanty to the elegant house in Guildhall Road. The one musty, stuffy, faded and lined with cobwebs, the other glittering with gilt, blazing with colour, and flashing with hundreds of gas jets. Exploring its cramped uncomfortable dressing rooms and its puny stage one wonders that the Northampton public tolerated it so long." A month later the same newspaper commented that the "rude forefathers of the Thespian art who played in the old theatre in its young days could never in their wildest dreams have anticipated anything like the 40 tons of scenery and baggage needed for the spectacular *Harbour Lights,* which had a cast of 90 and a stage staff of 40 to handle the elaborate machinery."

The theatre's oak stage and the gates guarding the rear yard, where company horses had pulled in the prop wagons, both found a new home at the windmill in the nearby village of Wootton.

In 1887 when there was a fire at the new theatre the old one came into use for one last week. Then it was taken over by Latimer and Crick, corn merchants, and served for the next 33 years for this and one or two other purposes. In 1908 part of it was being used as a bookshop and the owner used the amusing form of advertisement seen below.

Finally in the early 1920s Northampton Town Council decided to widen Horseshoe Street and therefore bought the place from the Masters and Co-Brethren of St. John's Hospital, the charity and church organisation which owned it. Thus the premises which had served as the town's theatre from 1806-84 were knocked down in the interests of the motor-car. A large quantity of human bones found on the site indicated that up to the time of Henry VIII this was part of the churchyard of St. Gregory's Church. On April 1, 1974, the day that Theatre Un-Royal was published, the Shakespeare public house next door was closed for demolition to allow further road-widening, into the dual carriageway that now exists. So that the spot where the 19th century actors and actresses performed is now well out on the highway.

An advertisement in the Northampton Independent in 1908 for J. S. Billingham's bookshop which occupied part of the former premises of the Theatre Royal, Marefair, forerunner of the Opera House.

Where the "Theatre Un-Royal" was situated in Marefair, Northampton. The theatre, which disappeared in road widening of the 1920s, stood next to the Shakespeare public house as seen above. But in further road-widening of 1974 the public house also disappeared to make way for the dual carriageway seen below. *(Roland Holloway)*

ACT ONE

SO LIKE LONDON

As we sit watching Edward Compton as Malvolio on the first night we can scarcely believe that this is Northampton, so much is the new theatre in contrast with the stuffy old bandbox. The owner is a hotel-keeper, the manager an auctioneer. After nearly three years there's a fire and the pair stand in the circle watching the stage burn down. In 1889 the theatre passes into new ownership—but it's not the Salvation Army. . . .

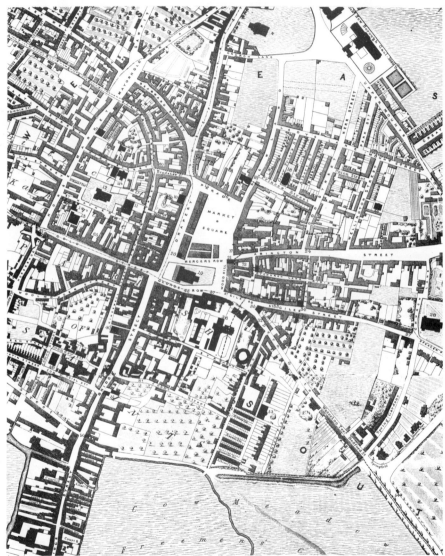

**Guildhall Road, in which Northampton Opera House (now Repertory Theatre) stands,
is the youngest street in the centre of the ancient town and does not appear at all on
this map of 1847. The black circle indicates the site of the theatre. Note behind it Cow
Lane (now Swan Street) down which Northamptonians for centuries drove their cattle to
Cow Meadow (now Beckets Park). The former theatre in Marefair is marked by a white
cross. *(Northamptonshire Libraries)*.**

Scene One: 1884-7

OWNER IS HOTEL-KEEPER, AUCTIONEER IS MANAGER

"Where is it you are thinking of building this theatre I hear about?" a friend asked John Campbell Franklin one summer day in 1883. "I'll show you—it's not far away," replied Franklin.

The pair were in Franklins Restaurant in Guildhall Road, Northampton. It was indeed only a few yards down the road to see the empty site between plots owned by Mr. Goddard and Mr. Blakey on which the front of the theatre would appear, and round the corner via Angel Lane to Cow Lane where the main part of the new building would be, at right angles to the front part.

There Franklin showed his friend the eight cottages he proposed to knock down to make way for the theatre. In a Press interview in February, 1887—seemingly the only interview given by this busy and energetic but unassuming man—he recalled: "When I pointed to the filthy tumbledown ramshackle of old tenements in Cow Lane which were doomed to come down to make way for it he lifted up his hands in grief and said 'What a waste of good property!' adding that whoever built a theatre in Northampton would be ruined in 12 months."

Franklin, who was at this time not a man of the theatre but a hotel and restaurant owner, was reported in July, 1883, to be collecting subscriptions for the purpose of constructing a commodious theatre at an estimated cost of £4,500. Of this £2,500 was to be raised on a first mortgage of the ground and theatre, the remaining £2,000 to be advanced by subscriptions on which 4 per cent would be paid from the date of opening the theatre, which would accommodate 1,500.

John Campbell Franklin was the son of J. E. Franklin who for many years carried on business as a baker and confectioner in part of Leamington House, The Parade, on the north side of the Market Square, premises which also housed the Northampton Mercury newspaper. The son moved from there in June, 1873, being then described as a wine and spirit merchant, to the hotel and restaurant in Guildhall Road built by his late brother Edmund.

While considering the theatre project Franklin did not receive much encouragement from his friends in the business world. At the time, of course, although "the theatre" might have artistic pretensions, it was strictly a matter of business. It was no use whatever having a splendid theatre with plays which were uplifting, edifying or improving if the public did not choose to turn up to be uplifted, edified or improved. Just as pence per square foot philosophies have dictated that the majority of our present day town centres should be occupied by banks, betting shops and building society branches, so in the last quarter of the 19th century the man with capital would weigh up on strictly economic principles the merits of putting up a factory, or a hotel or a theatre. Which would pay the best? It was a question of cash returns.

Or is that too sweeping? Perhaps the men of business might have dual motives—of doing the town a good turn while at the same time making themselves a bob or two. And in some cases, among which is the Northampton example, they would allow themselves to be urged on by artistic friends. The bachelor John Campbell Franklin allowed himself to be urged on by his bachelor friend Isaac Tarry, an auctioneer who loved to play Shylock. Tarry provided the impetus, Franklin the cash.

There was certainly little chance of a Victorian municipality footing the bill for an institution of such arguable value to the community as a theatre. The drama continued to smell in the nostrils of many people, particularly among that element of teetotal Noncomformity on the Town Council, a body which had only just got used to the idea of providing public money for a public library; civic theatres were far into the future.

The site purchased by Franklin was on sloping land situated between streets old and new. Behind it was Cow Lane, the narrow thoroughfare down which Northamptonians had from time almost immemorial driven their cattle to pasture outside the Town Walls in Cow Meadow. In contrast the road at the front of the theatre site had been there less than two decades. Named Guildhall Road it had come about after the erection in St. Giles Square of the new Guildhall or Town Hall, designed by Godwin, in 1864, the new street leading downhill from the hall towards the valley of the river Nene. What is now Guildhall Road remained fields after the new Guildhall was erected. It is almost the only street within a stone's throw of the town centre which is not of great antiquity, an odd one out, among Bridge Street (a parallel street leading down to the bridge over the river), Gold Street, the Drapery, Abington Street, Sheep Street, Fetter Lane, Mercers Row, Horsemarket, Bearward Street, Fish Street (in which was the Riding House, where early drama was accommodated in the 18th century), St. Giles Street (in which was the second make-shift theatre) and Marefair (in which the first permanent theatre was erected in 1806). In fact among all these Guildhall Road is the only one which you will not find on the 1847 map by J. Wood and E. F. Law.

The contract price for building the theatre was £5,015 but this was considerably increased by the extras which were found to be desirable as the work proceeded and the total outlay appears to have been about £10,000. The design for the three-tier theatre included four dressing rooms, all around and over the stage area; supers' rooms; band room, and property room. One bone of contention in planning the house was whether the local authorities would permit the front part of the L-shaped building to be erected right up to the street line or whether it should be set back a few feet. In fact it was allowed to reach out to the pavement.

From that incident between Franklin and his friend of 1883 we move on the appropriate natal period of nine months to the opening night of the Theatre Royal and Opera House, as Franklin had elected to call it (although, for reasons unexplained, the stone carving on the facade was, and remains Royal Theatre and Opera House). As with many theatres the construction work was a rush job in the finish. The hammers of the carpenters were still to be heard on the afternoon of Monday, May 5, 1884.

In imagination we will now arrive for that opening night, stepping out from a line of carriages in which, as requested, we have directed our driver that the horse's head shall face down the street towards St. John's Street railway station. In choosing our seats the choice ranged from paying sixpence for the gallery to a guinea for the private boxes, which are stated to have a capacity of six (which today appears to be an optimistic figure, the explanation being that the boxes were bigger then). As our ladies have intimated that they want to keep on their bonnets for all to see we chose the dress circle at 3s. (bonnets allowed there, we are advised). We could also pay 2s. for the upper circle or 1s. for the benches of the pit. In fact we have reserved our seats previously, not at the theatre, but at Marks Library in the Drapery which acts as a box office for the theatre. As circle patrons we walk in through the long vestibule and "crush room" which the architect has fitted in to make a merit out of the difficulty of the L-shape of the site; pittites enter down the stairs at the side while galleryites climb the stairs up from the back entrance in Cow Lane. The body of the theatre is, we note, at right angles to the approach corridor. Our seats are at the right hand end of the second row of the dress circle. We have no steps to negotiate, the circle being at ground level but we do have to take a dozen paces through a curving corridor before we reach the doors leading into the other side of the circle.

We have come early, at 7 p.m., so there is a full half-hour to sit and take in the scene and discuss the fittings and facilities of the new house. Our first reaction is of being stunned. We can scarcely believe that we are still in Northampton, feeling that some magic carpet has somehow transported us to London. Northampton has never seen anything like this. The old theatre in which shows have just ceased in Marefair is indeed a slum by comparison. Illuminated by the soft glow of a central gasolier, the theatre is 105 feet long, of which 37 feet is occupied by the stage and 68 feet by the auditorium, with an average width of 46 feet. Not vast by any manner or means according to the elevated standards of 1976, but huge and lush in comparison with its predecessor. On this question of size the Reporter has commented: "The conviction has been forcing itself upon the public for some time past that big theatres are big mistakes. Hence all those erected of late in the Metropolis have been of moderate dimensions. The expression of the softer passions is sacrificed in larger theatres. The origin of the ranting, rumbustious style of acting in the English school was doubtless owing to the vast area of our old playhouses."

We note that the house is entirely lit by gas and a 70-year-old member of our party reminisces about how, as a boy of nine, he attended the very first demonstration of gas lighting in Northampton. It was at the old theatre in Marefair. A more youthful and up with the times member of our group says however that he is surprised that electricity was not used to illumine the new theatre, as it was for the new Savoy Theatre in London, opened in 1881. "After all," says our knowledgable friend, "Both theatres were designed by the same architect." This is true and indeed only five years ago the local newspapers reported panic among the gas companies because of the new miracle, first demonstrated in Northampton in 1882. Since then there have been some second thoughts and just three months before this evening the Northampton Mercury predicted that gas would hold its own for a long time to come—"For the moment the prospect of the light of the future seems to be rather dim. Very little progress has been made in the extension of the use of the light for outdoor illumination." Our young friend concedes that he has heard that actors, and especially actresses, do not like the harsher light of electricity.

A free programme was handed to us by the attendant as we entered the circle and we find this very informative indeed, not only about Edward Compton and the Compton Comedy Company who are to present *Twelfth Night** but also about many other things. A full page is taken up with details of people connected with the theatre. We learn that the architect C. J. Phipps was responsible not only for the Savoy Theatre, London, but also for the Gaiety, Haymarket and Prince's theatres, among others. As his representative in Northampton Phipps engaged Mr. Charles Dorman, an architect who came to the town from Uppingham.

We discuss the background of Isaac Tarry who is listed in the programme as "acting manager". Born in 1850 he was the son of a butcher whose shop** was on the corner of the Mounts with Great Russell Street. Tarry trained in a North-ampton auctioneers' offices and became a partner with Mr. John Macquire, the firm being known as Macquire and Tarry, and later, when Mr. Tom Merry joined it, as Macquire, Tarry and Merry. But Tarry's heart was more in the theatre than in auctioneering. He had taken female parts in plays at the Catholic Schools in Woolmonger Street and became a Shakespeare fanatic and secretary of North-ampton Shakespeare Society. His first performance as Shylock had been at the Town Hall in 1877 but he appeared several times in amateur productions at the Marefair Theatre. His stage presence must have come in handy when wielding the hammer on the auctioneer's rostrum.

If it is unusual for a theatre to have an auctioneer as its manager and a hotelier and restaurateur as its owner then it is at least equally as unusual to have a flautist as its musical conductor. The flute is the instrument of William Oates, whom we now see wielding the baton as conductor of the Opera House orchestra. Young William had shown great aptitude for the flute. Joining the Band of the 54th Regiment he had been posted to India, only to be invalided out because the climate did not suit him. Back in Northampton he became a clerk at St. Andrew's (mental hospital, where Northamptonshire's great poet John Clare had been incarcerated) until 1874 when Mr. Richard Phipps found him a berth in the offices of Phipps Brewery and introduced him to the Band of the North-amptonshire Volunteers. His wife is also a brilliant musician playing the harp and piano and teaching music. Mr. Oates also takes advertising space in the pro-gramme to tell us that "all music performed at the Theatre may be obtained of the Musical Director, W. Oates, of Haydn House, Guildhall Road."

The band conducted by the flautist is seven-strong. Playing the two first violins are A. H. Keogh and J. A. Twist while Henry Mason is on second; the viola of George D. Crosland and the double bass of W. Nind complete the strings; there

---

* Not *As You Like It,* as stated in Theatre Un-Royal, a mistake for which I apologise.
** Premises demolished in the 1960s to make way for the new newspaper offices which are being built as this book is published and in which the author hopes to work.

are two woodwinds, J. Duke (clarinet) and J. Shepherd (oboe) and just one brass-man, Mr. Underhill on the cornet.

The contractor for building the theatre, the programme says, is Henry Martin. "Ah, he's come up in the world," says our venerable companion, "since he came to the town from Lutterworth in 1849 as a carpenter." The theatre's own Master Carpenter is listed as Mr. J. Harris while Mr. J. Robins is Property Master.

Other information in the programme is that the ornamental plaster work in the ceiling and box fronts was by Messrs. George Jackson and Sons, of London; the decorations are by Mr. Edward Bell, of London; the Sunlight and Special Stage Gas Works were installed by Strode and Co., London; for the "armchairs" in the dress circle, in which we are seated, we have to thank Mr. C. Wadman of Bath; the act drop and scenery have been painted by Mr. Walter Johnstone, of London; carpets and upholstery are by Phipps and Son; while G. T. Harris of College Street (a firm in existence there until the 1970s) provided the stage furniture. Then there are the paid-for straightforward advertisements. There are a large number of these. Besides being a library Marks also offer tennis raquets, those with a cedar handle for ladies being 3s. 11d. William Mark also diversified as a printer and produced the programmes themselves. John Bingley, "Analytical Chemist" of Northampton, rhapsodises over the merits of one of his products, Bingley's Superior Ginger Ale, which is stocked in the refreshment bars in the theatre.

Franklin uses part of the programme to proclaim the merits of his nearby hotel and restaurant, especially his hot dinners which are available from 12 to 3*. The page with the actual programme and cast lists also draws attention to the fact that refreshments can be obtained in all parts of the theatre at the same prices as charged outside. There are ices and light refreshments, wines, spirits and ales, aerated waters, cigars, cigarettes etc. (though smoking is not permitted and a prominent notice in the gallery draws attention to a triple prohibition–"No Nut-cracking, No Bad Language, No Smoking").

We applaud as the Mayor, Mr. M. P. Manfield, enters and takes his seat. The curtain goes up and so to the play. Edward Compton and his Compton Comedy Company are a little over three years old, but already of high reputation. The programme quotes the comment of the Referee newspaper that "As a genuine comedian Mr. Edward Compton has few equals and no superiors on the English stage." A fuller account of the company appears in the central Interlude of this book. Their opening performance at Northampton is of *Twelfth Night,* a choice which has been criticised by a Philistine local newspaper: "To the bulk of those who frequent theatres it is little known." Such is the magnitude of the task faced by Edward Compton and company in educating their public!

Between the acts Tarry comes on to the stage to make his opening remarks which would be somewhat tedious if we were not still overawed by Northampton's latest acquisition. He does not conceal his pride at what has been accomplished with Franklin's help–"I may perhaps be allowed to congratulate the town

---

* In 1976 there is a project for the theatre to have a restaurant of its own in adjacent converted premises, provided by Northampton Corporation, the present owners of the freehold of the theatre.

upon at last possessing a theatre which, to say the least of it, is some degree more worthy of its patronage that that which it has supplanted. I don't want to be ungenerous or to kick a fallen foe but I think that even those who have vested interests in the little Temple of the Muses in Marefair will be ready to admit that it ceased long ago to be able to supply the wants of an increased and ever-increasing population like that of Northampton." This and much, much more. The voluble Tarry evidently feels that he may have strained our patience for he uses this quotation:

> *As in a theatre the eyes of men*
> *After a well grac'd actor leaves the stage*
> *Are idly bent on him that enters next*
> *Thinking his prattle to be tedious*

Franklin is certainly not tedious. He says far less, mentioning however the great risk the undertaking has involved. Martin, who built the theatre, merely bows when his name is mentioned to cheering.

And so the play resumes. It is so good compared with some of the fare we have endured at Marefair that we immediately resolve to come again before the week is out. Our choice includes Tuesday, *She Stoops to Conquer,* Wednesday, *The School for Scandal;* Thursday, *The Rivals* and *Delicate Ground;* Friday, *The Comedy of Errors;* Saturday, *The Road to Ruin* and *Faithful unto Death.* On the Saturday, following *The Road to Ruin,* a special train to Kettering has been arranged at 11 p.m., calling at Wellingborough, Finedon and Isham.

Asleep in his cot during the performances of that first week was the future novellist Compton Mackenzie, the explanation being that his parents, Mr. and Mrs. Edward Compton, were performing on the stage, their real name being Mackenzie—they were Mackenzies called Compton.

In case we are tempted to look back from the difficult times of the 1970s and regard the 1880s as a desirable period of stability it may be pertinent to recall that during the week the theatre was opened Dr. Buszard, one of its neighbours, declared: "We live in perilous times. The air is full of revolutionary projects and there is no single institution from the Throne downwards which is not threatened." He was a Tory but on the other hand the town's Radical M.P., Charles Bradlaugh, who was being prevented from taking his seat in the Commons at the time, was that week completing a lecture on "Objections to Socialism."

As we depart after being among Franklin's first customers at his theatre we walk a few yards up Guildhall Road and patronise his other establishment. The barmen there already know of our approach for there are wires running from backstage at the theatre, to the bar of Franklins Hotel and Restaurant. As the curtain came down, by this means a bell was sounded warning the bar staff of the rush to come.

Over our pint of beer from the local Phipps brewery we take the programme from our pockets to see what else it has to tell us. There is an "immense attraction" for the following week—the celebrated Charles Majilton Company in the farcical comedy *The Gay City* together with the great burlesque *Brum.* The advance notice draws attention to the fact that the opening scene for *Brum,* set in The

Temple of Nap, "will be used for the first time in Northampton, the stage of the Old Theatre having been too small for it at Mr. Majilton's former visit." Thus (returning to the past tense) the Majilton Company was among a number which were in effect transferring their engagements from one Northampton theatre to its roomier successor. Others during that first 12 months were the companies of Wilson Barrett (his *The Silver King* came for the third week of the theatre's life) and Fred Gould (*The Black Flag* and *All For Her*) but there were others which could not or would not have played in the lowly and tiny theatre in Marefair, especially the more spectacular type of show which, like The Temple of Nap, simply could not be staged there.

In *The Silver King* theatregoers could see a locally born actor, W. L. Abingdon, who was to become the most hated (i.e. popular) villain of the day and to appear in almost every theatre in London. Born as William Lepper Pilgrim in the small Northamptonshire town of Towcester on May 2, 1850, he was managing clerk to Sir Philip Manfield, a shoe manufacturer, before becoming an actor. His first appearance was at Northampton Working Men's Club (believed to be Britain's oldest W.M.C.) but his professional debut was at the Theatre Royal, Belfast, in January, 1881, when he was sacked on the first night for forgetting his lines. He subsequently toured with the company of Kate Bateman (Mrs. Crowe, sister of Mrs. Compton). His father was a tailor, W. Pilgrim, of Wellingborough Road, Northampton. In fact Abingdon was not yet the villain king and in *The Silver King* at Northampton in 1884 he appeared as Samuel Baxter, a detective. The title role was taken by Luigi Lablache, who was on the first of many visits to the theatre. This play by Henry A. Jones and Henry Herman, one of the great money spinners of the era, was also on the first of many visits.

May 26 brought the celebrated nautical comic opera *Billee Taylor!* or *The Reward of Virtue,* with Kate Braham as a member of George Peyton's Company. The Whit Week attraction was "the realistic comedy drama—funnier than a pantomime" *Simon* or *More Ways Than One,* with James Taylor taking the three singing roles of Sidney Cartwright, Joe Steadfast and Sarah Walker; on the Friday and Saturday nights he appeared in *Tempted,* as a joint benefit for him and Miss Ada Alexandra. There followed Harry Granville's Company in *Danites* and then came the first visit to the theatre of a D'Oyly Carte Company (but not to the town—*Patience* had been given in 1882 at the vast Corn Exchange which was preferred to the tiny theatre of the day). *Princess Ida* was for two days only, Friday and Saturday, June 20-21, the theatre being closed from the Monday to the Thursday.

One of the few companies providing a degree of competition to the Compton Comedy Company, in the type of play produced, was the Garrick Comedy Company. Its version of *David Garrick* was the one by G. M. Wood, who took the title role, and it was with "new and magnificent costumes from Paris." Other pieces were *The Heir at Law, The Life of An Actress, The Belle's Stratagem* and *Lost in London.* For the last week of the first season, at the end of June, Haldane Crichton's Company staged *Member for Slocum,* the cast of which included Miss Marie Hassell, later for many years a member of the Compton Comedy Company.

The reopening on July 28 was with a farce from the French, *Three Hats,* with *Crutch and Toothpick* substituted for the Friday night benefit of Mr. George Walton.

Two Orphans was given by Charles Dornton and Company and then came William T. Richardson and Company in *It's Never Too Late to Mend* (on Monday, Tuesday and Wednesday) and Charles Reade's "great moral drama in seven acts" *Drink,* which had a readable sequel in the Letters column of the Daily Reporter: "Mr Editor, all the good effect of the actors portraying most vividly the harrowing and awful effects of strong drink were stultified by the behaviour of habitues of the theatre who had brought in beer in bottles. We had the actors on the stage doing all in their power to let the people see the consequences of strong drink and the young people in the pit and gallery doing all in their power to swallow as much as they could of the demoralising stuff." Nor was the booze the only subject for complaint: "It was also demoralising to hear the filthy slang and swearing that was indulged in by those who drink. A nice predicament for respectable females to have their ears assailed with this bad language. I advise the management to alter it if they expect reasonable people to frequent the pit." People who did frequent the pit regularly resented this affront to their respectability. Was it indeed beer in those bottles? "Pitite" claimed that it was instead "those windy concoctions so dear to the teetotal stomache." Even so, it was a nuisance, he admitted, because"When the pop is finished the bottle is thrown on the floor and rolls about, making a noise." A numerically minded reader had counted the 14 occasions on which he and his wife had had to rise from their seats to allow one individual to get to the bar and also referred to the number of people bringing in pints and quarts in bottles. As the theatre possessed a stage play licence which more or less automatically gave it the right to a drinks licence, it had bars but their existence was not prominently advertised.

At about this time the theatre received its first attack from a religious source. The Rev. Whittaker spoke of the evil influence it had, which prompted a letter to the Daily Reporter claiming that the moral environment of well conducted theatres like the one at Northampton was as irreproachable as any Methodist class meeting. With no touting, no fees and free programmes the Northampton theatre was rated among the best in the country. Such plays as *Recommended to Mercy* and *The New Magdalen* did more for the moral regeneration of the fallen than any amount of goody goody talk, however well meant. At this time Mrs. Kendal (later Dame Madge Kendal, honoured for her acting) read a paper to Birmingham Social Science Society in which she claimed that it was recognised that the progress of a nation depended as much on the diversions as on the education of its people.

Within six months of their opening the theatre the Compton Comedy Company were back on September 15, with a different selection of plays—*Wild Oats, The Rivals, The Comedy of Errors, The Heir at Law, Davy Garrick* and *The Road to Ruin.* There were also some curtain raisers, George Colman's comedietta *Blue Devils* and Compton's own *A Mutual Separation* and also, on the Saturday to close the night, *Faithful Unto Death* a two act drama by E. M. Robson and Compton. On the Monday the manager, Mr. Tarry, gave one of his little homilies from the stage in which he gently complained about the general lack of support in the circle and discussed the problems of a manager in choosing shows—"The advice we receive from time to time is the oddest imaginable; some remonstrate with me because I have not booked Carl Rosa, others because I have not booked Christy's Minstrels; some clamour for Mr. Irving, others for a panorama; some want oratorio, others opera bouffe; no thought of the incongruity of some of the things suggested with the place seeming to enter their minds." There was a difficulty in finding first-rate shows all the time—"I reckon there are only 20, or at the most 30, first-class companies travelling and of course the great cities and towns have the first claim on their attention. You must therefore in the nature of things expect to see now and then a second rate company and not be impatient with your manager because he does not accomplish impossibilities. I have had no companies here but what are regularly engaged for theatres of twice our size, and for towns of thrice our population."

Among forthcoming attractions he listed was *Falka* which he had engaged "in fear and trembling at the enormous outlay involved." It came the following week, this opera with music by F. Chaissaigne and book by H. B. Farnie, and he need not have worried. It did good business, being the second best success of the early years and was still going strong well into the 20th century. The company included Miss Guilia Warwick, Miss Wadman and Mr. J. G. Taylor, all of whom had created the parts in the original production at the Comedy Theatre, London. A notice in the programme stated: "After much anxious consideration the manager has decided NOT to raise the prices, trusting to overflow houses to meet the enormous expense . . . the manager has ventured upon this engagement experimentally, intending if adequate support be given, to follow it up with serious as well as comic opera."

It was the custom in those days, and remained so during the Franklin-Tarry regime, to list in the newspapers not only those who were in the play but the prominent citizens who were in the audience. The Friday night audience for *Falka* included Lord and Lady Erskine, Lord Lewes, Sir T. Grey, the Hon. St. John Jarvis, H. Langham Esq. with a party from Cottesbrooke, and Mrs. J. N. Beasley with a party from Brampton Hall.

The next three shows were Frank Barrett's *Fast Friends* and *The Flying Dutchman* by Alfred Hemmings and Company; George R. Sims' farcical comedy *Mother-in-Law;* and the "great London and Parisian success" *Fedora,* with Laura Villiers.

Then on October 20 came what we might today term the "top of the pops", Minnie Palmer's musical play *My Sweetheart,* by Wynn Miller's Company, with Letty Lind in the title role of Tina and Charles J. Murton as Tony. This was to prove the most popular show of the early years. As with many other shows of the day the programme included a somewhat sickening synopsis:

Act 1, set in Old Hatzell's Farm in Pennsylvania—Mrs. Hatzell takes in summer boarders—Two Innocent Lovers—The Adventuress and Her Scheming Brother—Tony's Accession to Wealth and Title—The False Love.

Act II, in Tony's House in New York—The Fair Devil—The False Friend—Brother and Sister—The Old Sport—Tony's Blind and Forsaken—No, Not blind while Tina has Eyes; Not Forsaken While Tina is by Your Side.

Act III, back again at the Old Farm—Happy Days—The Schemers Defeated—Louisa, Your Loving Husband is Waiting for You Outside—True Love Wins.

This "musical novelty" paid five visits to the Opera House during its first four years. Its London run had twice been patronised by the Prince and Princess of Wales, whose interest in the theatre seems to some extent to have filled the vacuum caused by the withdrawal from theatre patronage of Queen Victoria, following the death of the Prince Consort in 1861.

Woman and The Law, presented by a Wilson Barrett company, was "a play with a purpose . . . to expose the cruelty of Spanish Law which permitted the father of an illegitimate child to take his offspring from the care of its mother by force if necessary, and gives him possession of all property the child might be entitled to . . . further he had the perfect right to withold even the means of existence from the mother and to leave her to starve." After this the Barrett company repeated *The Silver King;* the author Walter B. Payne and his wife, Ada Roby, appeared in the "new and original melodrama" *The Way of The World;* and next came H. D. Burton's bevy of beauties in comedy, ballet and extravaganza, this being a set of plays including *Turtle Doves, Links O' Gold, Bears Not Beasts* (with "exciting champagne dance and chorus, grand prismatic statue ballet"), *The Fire King* and *East Lynne.*

Moralists found some of the scenes depicted in the more sensational pieces, especially those involving crime, to be the opposite of elevating. That moralising London critic Clement Scott had had this to say about the October, 1881, London production of George R. Sims' *The Lights of London:* "The final act opens in the New Cut Market. If anything it is all too real, too painful, too smeared with the dirt of London life, where drunkenness, debauchery and depravity are shown in all their naked hideousness. Amidst buying and selling, the hoarse roar of costermongers, the jingle of the piano organ, the screams of the dissolute, fathers teach their children to cheat and lie, drabs swarm in and out of the public house." In Northampton the piece was presented by a Wilson Barrett company in November, 1884. It was one of several plays which Sims had based on parts of his serial novel Rogues and Vagabonds which had appeared in the Northampton Mercury in 1881, as in other provincial newspapers. "In his inexperience," the newspaper recalled "he had crowded into the one story the threads of at least four or five good plays . . . into one black panorama of avarice and vice." It subsequently provided him with ideas for this play and for *Romany Rye, Harbour Lights* and *In The Ranks.*

It appears to have been during this production that the facility of admission by "Extra Doors" (later and more usually known as "Early Doors") was introduced. The announcement said: "Pe ɔns anxious to avoid the crush will be admitted by the Extra Doors (Gallery, Cow Lane; Pit and Upper Circle, Guildhall Road) which will be opened half-an-hour earlier on payment of 6d. extra (gallery 3d.)" The Early Doors folk had the first choice of seats. This did not, of course, apply to the gentry of the dress circle who could not be expected to join in any scramble.

Miss Alleyn, the celebrated tragedienne, was among Mr. Charles Bernard's Shakespearian Company which appeared early in December with *Romeo and Juliet, As You Like It, The Merchant of Venice,* and some non-Shakespearian pieces including Miss Alleyn's own translation of M. Ohney's drama *Le Maitre de Forge,* which she entitled *A Midnight Marriage.*

After this the theatre closed to prepare for the Christmas show which was not to be a pantomime but "the great Drury Lane drama", Paul Merritt and

Augustus Harris's *Youth,* performed by Messrs. Holt and Wilmot's Company from the Grand Theatre, Islington, under the direction of Mr. C. T. Burleigh. This was in eight tableaux and the programme carried a complimentary letter from General Wolsley to Harris, the great mogul of Drury Lane, praising his "vivid picture of the defence of Hawke's Point—realistic and perfect." For this show there were special late trains at cheap fares, leaving Castle Station for Wellingborough, Rugby, and intermediate stations at 11 p.m. and from the Midland Station at the same time for Desborough, Kettering and intermediate stations. Following *Youth* the same company stayed on to present Paul Merritt's *New Babylon* and *Forces Home* for a few nights each.

The first week of 1885 saw a repertoire of plays by the Fred Gould Company who, as the Mercury recalled, "had occupied the stage of the now dismantled theatre in Marefair again and again and always received an ovation from their many admirers". On this visit they performed *Reckoning Day, All For Her* and *The Black Flag.* They were followed by another troupe which had been seen at the old theatre, William Duck's Company in *Called Back* which was still doing well in London after a transfer from the Prince's Theatre to the Olympic. This was a dramatic version of one of the most popular novels of the day. The Mercury commented: "We note with pleasure that the manager has declined to have anything to do with the many piratical versions although the temptation must have been a great one. In the nature of things much better pecuniary terms might have been made with a company not burdened with the payment of fees to authors etc." Tarry had made his arrangements with the author Hugh Conway and his friend Comyns Carr who had helped with the adaptation. The newspaper noted that unscrupulous people were deluging the country with their own versions not only without the sanction of the author but in the face of his indignant protests.

The ageing tragedian Barry Sullivan was making his first visit to Northampton when he appeared at the Opera House in late January, at the start of his 1885 tour. The previous year's tour had achieved "success beyond measure", noted the Mercury. At Bristol, for instance, he had been met at the railway station by the Mayor and Corporation and a crowd of 10,000 who unharnessed the horses from his carriage and themselves drew him in triumph to his hotel. Uncharacteristically it was a rather more sedate crowd which greeted him at Northampton's Castle Station on the evening of Saturday, January 24. There to say the customary few words was the Mayor (Mr. T. Adams) and he accompanied the actor-manager in a two horse carriage to the George Hotel, where Sullivan in turn spoke a few words from the balcony to the crowd of 2,000 gathered below. At most towns the price was increased for such stellar attractions but not, on this occasion, at Northampton. Nevertheless the Monday night attendance to see him as *Richard III* did not meet expectations. Later in the week came *Richelieu, Hamlet* and *The Gamester.* There were excursion trains from Luton, Wolverton and Rugby.

Another star guest at this time was Edward Terry who appeared as Montague Joliffe in Pinero's *In Chancery,* a role he had created in the initial production at the Gaiety Theatre, London, the previous year. Terry made a speech congratulating the town on having one of the prettiest theatres in the country as well as one of the ablest managers. But I expect he said these things to audiences everywhere.

In February F. A. Scudamore led his company in *Rags and Bones;* C. Garthorne's and Fanny Joseph's Company appeared in *Impulse;* back within six months was *Falka,* presented by Mons. Auguste Van Biene and Horace Lingard; and Mr. Mansell's Company performed *The Unknown,* with a First Act which included "a splendid view of New York Harbour and the Brooklyn Suspension Bridge" and *The Crimes of Paris.*

A winning show which was to prove to have even more durability than *My Sweetheart* and *Falka* was *Les Cloches de Corneville* which was presented in March by Shiel Barry and William Hogarth ("principal baritone from the Royal Alhambra, London"). Shiel Barry was cast as the Miser Gaspard, a role which he had already performed over 1,000 times in London and in which he was to knock up a much greater score.

Then came another money-spinner *The Private Secretary* by the company of C. H. Hawtrey, lessee and manager of the Globe Theatre, London, where the show had reached its 350th performance; it was also playing to crowded houses at the Madison Square Theatre, New York. In its first three years it was to make £100,000 for Hawtrey. At Northampton it was back within 12 months.

After *Twins,* a farcical comedy with Edward Righton in his original character, and Miss Addie Conyer's Company in *Nita's First* the theatre was closed from Monday to Friday of Holy Week, reopening on Easter Eve, Saturday, April 4, with Charles Collette and a company including Mrs. C. A. Clarke whose husband had been one of the few successful lessees of the Northampton theatre in Marefair, as well as operating at Windsor. They performed *My Awful Dad, Micawber, Used Up, The Liar, Paul Pry* and *Cool as a Cucumber.*

For the Race Week Miss Laura Villiers and her "powerful company" appeared in *Fedora* and *Leap Year,* when the programme for the first time listed the music to be played by the orchestra, beginning with two overtures by Auber and Masaniello, La Circassienne and concluding with a galop—presumably played while the audience filed out—entitled Who Goes There?. Next came the "celebrated Milton Rays and Famous Comedy Company" in *Kindred Souls* and Calder's Company in the "great sensational drama" *The White Slave* by Bartley Campbell, in which a troupe of Negro Jubilee Singers were seen.

Wynn Miller's *My Sweetheart* company were back on May 4, with C. J. Murton as Tony again but with a new Tina, Miss Grace Huntley. During that week it was time for Isaac Tarry to report on the first year's operations and this he did from the stage. On that Tuesday night there was a brilliant display of military uniforms in the dress circle to hear him say that the theatre had paid their first dividend out of the profits, not out of capital. Tarry praised especially the Press for their help in founding and maintaining a theatre amongst a people who for lack of opportunity had not been reared in theatre-going and who therefore had to be created, formed and fashioned—in a word, educated up to it. Because of the splendour of the theatre they were able to enjoy better companies than some towns of twice and three times the size of Northampton. But some of the best companies received the worst patronage. Generally speaking support came from a small proportion of the townsfolk—"I see the same faces week after week." The members of the orchestra chose this first anniversary to say thank-you to their conductor Mr. Oates for his "invariable kindness and gentlemanly demeanour", with a gold pencil case, inscribed with his name and address.

Up to this point, at the risk of losing some readers, I have mentioned each and every production staged at the theatre. Clearly it is impossible for reasons both of length and tedium to continue to do so throughout the remaining four decades we have yet to cover and I therefore desist.

At this point Franklin and Tarry must have been staggered if not furious to experience difficulty in getting the theatre licence renewed. It was not, however, that the place was not being properly conducted, but because of a smelly urinal and the situation of the pit bar, to which the magistrates took exception. Mr. Andrews, the solicitor representing the Opera House, was taken aback (or else he was acting the part well, as I suppose a solicitor representing a theatre ought to be ready to do). He said that the old theatre which had existed until 12 months earlier had been a wretched little hole where it was not possible for a decent person to pass yet no complaint was made, yet now that a splendid structure had been erected they went into niceties. From the bench Mr. James Barry was obdurate—a ventilation shaft would not be a satisfactory way of removing the nuisance from the urinal; the object itself must be removed. And the bar must be moved too.

The theatre also had a problem of over-ventilation. The circle suffered from a draught when the wind was in a certain quarter and a letter to the Herald in May, 1885, said that the public had to weigh the enjoyment of a good play against the certainty of a cold in the head.

The provincial premiere of Gilbert and Sullivan's *The Mikado* took place at the theatre on Friday, May 22, 1885. On the Monday and Tuesday the D'Oyly Carte Company had given *Iolanthe*; on Wednesday and Thursday *Patience;* and on the Friday and Saturday "for the first time out of London" came *The Mikado* which had had its premiere at the Savoy Theatre, London, on March 14 that year. At Northampton the Three Little Maids were Bessie Wilkinson (Yum-Yum), Beatrice Young (Pitti-Sing) and Agnes Taylor (Peep-Bo). Albert Christian was Pooh-Bah and Albert Jones was Ko-Ko. In the audience on the Friday were the Marquess of Exeter and officers of the 3rd. and 4th. Battalions of the Northamptonshire Regiment.

Another "first" for the Opera House was a ballad concert given on Tuesday, June 16, 1885, by Northampton Choral Society with the joint aim of swelling the society's own funds and helping to pay for alterations to the organ at the Corn Exchange, where their regular concerts were given.

The last week of the season was billed as "the most important engagement of the year", oddly in view of the recent Gilbert and Sullivan premiere. It was *Rip Van Winkle.*

During the summer break came the first amateur dramatics in the house with Sergeant Major Ansell taking charge of a show in aid of his fellow members of the Royal Antediluvian Order of Buffaloes. It included R. J. Raymond's farce *Mr. and Mrs. White* and T. J. Williams' drama *The Peep Show Man,* together with musical items by a 20-strong band.

A sparse audience turned out for the reopening on August Bank Holiday Monday (which was then at the beginning of the month, it should be remembered) with the Children's Comic Opera Company in *La Fille de Madame Angot.* The cast of 40 was aged from five to 15. There was a children's matinee on the Saturday, with half-price to all parts.

After that single week the theatre closed again for the ordained alterations, with which came a number of improvements, including the fitting of portiere curtains in the circle to cope with the draught problem. It was also proposed— but not I believe carried out at this stage—to heat the circle with water pipes. Moving the pit bar to a situation where it caused less inconvenience proved to be a long job and was not complete until the end of the year; it allowed a pit cloak- room to be provided. The two-foot-thick wall separating the manager's box from the backstage area was pierced to provide an easy means of access for him to reach the stage in the event of having to make an announcement in any emergency, instead of having to fight his way through the crowd in the pit or go outside into the street to reach the backstage. The theatre also acquired at this time a thunder machine, consisting of a wooden tunnel from one side of the stage to the other, with irregular checks and barriers in it down which cannon balls were rolled. The band area was improved with the aim of obviating a loss of sound which had been suffered when the band were half-way under the front of the stage. Stage lighting was improved while in the gallery the removal of a barrier was said to reduce congestion.

Three contrasting actresses who came that autumn were Miss Bateman, Florence Warden and Jennie Lee. Miss (Kate) Bateman, one of the sisters of Mrs. Edward Compton, was described by the Herald as "the most gifted member of the Bateman Family" but this did not prevent them from describing Leah, in which she appeared, as "a funeral dirge from beginning to end." Miss Bateman, who was stated to have previously appeared at the old theatre, was also seen in Mary Warner. An authoress as well as an actress, Florence Warden was seen in her own The House on The Marsh, based on the life of the murdered Charles Peace, and In the Lion's Mouth, which had had its premiere at Nottingham the previous week. The free list was "entirely suspended" for Jennie Lee who, "fresh from her triumphs around the world", appeared in J. F. Burnett's adaptation of Charles Dickens' Bleak House.

Henry Labouchere, one of the town's Members of Parliament (of whom more later) was one of those who were suspected to be the author of The Candidate which was given for three nights only. Other possible authors were stated to be Lord Randolph Churchill and Mr. Justin McCarthy, another M.P. By the time the play paid another visit the mystery had been solved.

During this second year of its life the theatre made what may be termed its first outside broadcast. A group of people in the ancient Peacock Hotel, on the Market Square, listened to the performance of Henry Paulton's musical farcical comedy Lilies, which was being given on the stage of the theatre. This was not done by radio, of course, which had still to be discovered. The transmission was by telephone which would seem to indicate that the theatre was "on the phone" by this time. Paulton himself was appearing in his production and mentioned from the stage that "the frequenters of Mrs. Forth's hotel are listening through the telephone but have promised to patronise the performance tomorrow night." This historic event, which would seem to have involved the use of the telephone as a microphone, occurred on Thursday, September 24, 1885. When Paulton had previously appeared in Northampton it had been at the old theatre and knowing what he did of that old incommodious establishment, he said he had wondered about coming to Northampton again. But having seen the new theatre, he would be very glad to do so.

The first mention of the possibility of booking a seat by telephone did not appear in the Press until December, 1885, and even then the idea was not to ring the theatre itself. All pre-booking at this time was at Marks Library in The Drapery and during the last week of the season, when Haldane Crichton's Company was to perform H. J. Byron's *Not Such a Fool As He Looks* it was stated: "Booking at Marks Library (Telephone No. 12)". As I have been unable to locate any form of early telephone directory I am unable to say just who was and who was not on the phone at this time but not many people were. Public phone boxes were not to appear until the 20th century. It was no use being able to book by phone unless you had access to one of these instruments. The theatre number was 67 and the first time I have come across an invitation to ring this number is in June, 1886, when seats were said to be available by letter, telephone or telegram. By September, 1886, the nearby villages of Kingsthorpe, Hardingstone and Dallington had been connected and there were 93 subscribers. Trunk lines were then being run to Wellingborough, Kettering and Rushden—"It cannot but be beneficial to the staple trade" said the manager of the local department of the South of England Telephone Company.

To return to December, 1885. It was a month which saw appearances on the stage by two managers of the theatre—the present one and the man who was to succeed him. A "regrettably small audience" saw Charles Rider Noble, the future manager, play the part of Sir Henry Auckland in *Impulse,* which was given by C. W. Garthorne's Company, of which Charles Kean Chute was a fellow member. A much greater attraction was provided by the amateur performance of *The Merchant of Venice* in which Isaac Tarry appeared as Shylock later in the month. It was given under the auspices of Mrs. Ratliffe's Blankets for the Poor Fund, for which she organised an annual entertainment. This time there was such a demand for the single performance which had been planned that a second had to be arranged. Two professionals had been engaged to stiffen up the cast, Frank Rodney (Bassanio), and Arthur Felton (the Duke of Venice). Besides Tarry there were two other auctioneers, T. C. Woods (Salerino) and Percy Brain (the gaoler), and a trio of architects, Fred Dorman (Gratiano), George H. Stevenson (Salanio) and Fred Milne (Antonio) who later committed suicide. Miss Alice Ratliffe (Mrs. Ray) was the page to Portia and was clearly a relative of the organiser for as she concluded a Spanish dance in Act II a bouquet was adroitly tossed to her. Portia was played by Miss Carrie Nunnely and others were Charles Kingston (Old Gobbo), Stanley Adams (Launcelot), and Miss Florence Chester (Jessica). We must not omit the name of the man who was in charge of the limes for he was to be the next owner of the theatre—Thomas Phipps Dorman.

The Christmas show of 1885-6 was another play by H. J. Byron, *Weak Woman* starring Edward Terry and including in its cast T. C. Valentine. Terry was to return for a third time in 1886 with Pinero's *In Chancery* and *The Rocket.* Meantime in January, 1886, there was another Pinero play *The Magistrate* about which the Mercury commented that to the staunch upholder of legitimate drama the three-act farce was a "term of the deepest heresy." A farce they would say was a fine thing to fill up the bill but it was all against the tradition of the profession to make it the stock piece. "But London managers know the taste of the public a good deal better than the old-fashioned critics and the success of the new-fashioned farcical comedies is the only justification they need. Three of them are now enjoying long runs at London theatres with no apparent evidence of waning popularity."

Along with *Falka* in February came Auguste Van Biene who was modestly described as "the greatest cello player in the world." This surpassing talent he showed off in the interval by playing Dunkler's Reverie and Drinking Song.

When the Shiel Barry and Hogarth Company brought *La Mascotte* and *Les Cloches de Corneville* the Mercury said it would have anticipated a larger audience for the former "as it has not been presented in Northampton since the suppression of the stuffy little theatre in Marefair."

Isaac Tarry now showed artistic enterprise by organising an exhibition of engravings in the theatre crush room. Art shows of any sort were a rarity in Victorian Northampton and he therefore took steps to arrange that it could be visited by people who did not attend the theatre. The comments on this aspect of the matter clearly reveal the amount of prejudice against the theatre which still existed in 1886. Said the Herald: "We are glad that Mr. Tarry has rendered it accessible to all sections of the public. There are many people who are most anxious to see the collection but who have hitherto been hindered by religious and other scruples which, though we may not understand them, we are bound to respect. Perhaps some of them may discover that judging from the little peep they get it is not quite the abode of sin and wickedness that they have been taught to regard it and that they may be induced to pay a second visit when they can penetrate beyond the crush room." What had Tarry done to allow the Pharisees to visit his Temple of Thespis? During the Holy Week of April 17 when the theatre would have been closed he opened it on Wednesday, Thursday and Saturday to allow non-theatre-goers to see the exhibition. He may have got a secret satisfaction out of making them pay sixpence between 3 and 5 p.m. and twopence from 7 to 10 p.m. The exhibition led to a permanent one including a portrait of Adelaide Neilson, the actress who married the son of a local parson and who died in Paris in the arms of her intended second husband, Edward Compton.

Regarding the anti-theatre attitude reflected in this episode is it not odd that in the more cloistered repertory theatres of today it has often become the respectable and "done" thing to go to the theatre and to be seen doing so?

During that April F. A. Scudamore's *First Class,* with "views of station and train in motion," brought to the theatre J. Pitt Hardacre and Frederick Mouillot who were both to manage many shows at the theatre.

Then came Charles Wyndham as Lord Oldacres in the return visit of *The Candidate* which was now revealed to be the work of Justin Huntly McCarthy M.P. The piece was on a short tour consisting mainly of large cities—it came here from Manchester and left for Birmingham. It came to Northampton presumably because of its local allusions. The Easthampton in the play was really Northampton and the candidate Bradley, "the working man's friend", was a thinly-veiled Charles Bradlaugh, the real-life Radical M.P. for the town who was once, quite literally, thrown out of the House of Commons. Posters advertising the piece appeared on first sight to be election propaganda: "Vote for Bradley, the Working Man's Friend" or "Vote for Oldacres, the Constitutional Candidate." In November that year Wyndham was to revive his *David Garrick* at the Criterion Theatre, London.

In May, 1886, the audience for *Delicate Ground* included Edward William Godwin, that remarkable man with one foot in the world of architecture and the other in that of the theatre. He had designed a gown for Mrs. Mackintosh, a society actress, to wear in this Charles Dance comedietta. Godwin was the architect of that remarkable Guildhall, or Town Hall, which Thomas Phipps Dorman's father had opened when Mayor in 1864. This Northampton visit by the Bristol-born architect came only six months before his death. As a semi-professional critic at that city's Theatre Royal Godwin had singled out for praise a little girl named Ellen Terry who was appearing with her older sister Kate. It was a remarkable twist of fate that in later life, through attending him during an illness, Ellen should be shunned by her husband (and her parents who in true stage manner told her never to darken their door again!) and should set up home with Godwin, she then being 21 and he 35. Some 20 years later Ellen Terry was to sit in a box at the Northampton theatre with her daughter to see a performance by her son, both children having resulted from the liaison with Godwin. Godwin's ambition to design a theatre had never been achieved but he had designed *The Merchant of Venice* for the Bancrofts (he sent the scene painter to Venice to get some local colour) and *Claudian* for Wilson Barrett (when he himself went to Denmark to do the assimilating).

Meantime for the Opera House's second anniversary the Compton Comedy Company paid their third visit to the theatre and in a speech on the actual "birthday" Isaac Tarry reported that the second year had not fulfilled the promise of the first. This need cause no surprise, he said, owing to the length and severity of the depression through which the town's trade had been passing. He looked forward to better things and added that he was sure they "would not like to see this beautiful temple converted into a dry goods store or even a house of prayer, great as is our respect for religion—yet such has been the fate of some theatres, nay of many."

He had a special word for the gods, whose behaviour had been the subject of unsavoury forecasts. They had, on the contrary, vindicated his faith. There seems to have been an element of flattery here for Tarry went on to describe two of their less desirable habits. The first thing he would ask them not to do was to put their fingers in their mouths and give loud piercing whistles (at which one god obliged with a sample) and not, although perched up on high, imagine themselves to be squirrels and sit there cracking nuts. The noise disconcerted the actors, he said.

Tarry also got in a word at the vast numbers of people who expected "orders" (i.e. free tickets) which he described as a growing evil and the despair of many managers. People who would not dream of asking their baker for free bread, their butcher for free meat, or their tailor for a free suit, had no scruples or hesitation in asking for an "order" for a play. Following a controversy in the Letters column, in which some of those who got their free tickets legitimately, for displaying bills, objected to Tarry's comments, he had to mollify them with an explanation that he merely meant to be bantering and quoted the words of Artemus Ward at the door of his tent: "Ladies and gentlemen the show is about to commence. You could not well expect to go in without paying but you may pay without going in. I can say no fairer." People cadging these "orders" had been the bane of the existence of Henry Labouchere, one of the town's Members of Parliament, in his theatre-owning days. "Labby" got so tired of his tailor doing it that one day he returned the compliment by sending a friend round with an "order" for a free suit. Cadging tickets, he said, was the "meanest, most sneaky and contemptible form of beggary."

So presumably Labouchere had paid for the seat he occupied at the Northampton Opera House during the return visit of *The Mikado* in June, 1886. The last week of the season proper the theatre had been closed, in order, it was explained, to make preparations for the return of the opera. On this second visit it coincided with a General Election and that was how Labouchere came to be in the audience on the Thursday night. It was an enormous audience, reported the Herald, and such was the enthusiasm that the number of encores almost amounted to cruelty towards the artists. Seats for the Friday night were said to have changed hands at a premium.

Labouchere, who topped the poll that election with Bradlaugh as the other successful candidate in a field of four, was a millionaire and I consider it surprising that he had not courted local favour by himself building the town a new theatre, during the period when some schemes aborted. Perhaps it was because he had found theatre ownership an unprofitable and at times trying business. Showbiz had figured early in the life of this remarkable character. At 19 he had sailed to America and having lost £250 gambling at cards and fallen in love with a lady of the circus he became a doorkeeper under the big top. With another circus he graduated to doing a barrel-jumping act in pink tights. In the late 1860s he took on the Queen's Theatre, Long Acre, in a partnership with the actor Alfred Wigan which was at first kept secret. Though not by any means consistently successful in financial terms the theatre was a notable theatric nursery, young actors and actresses appearing there including Henry Irving, Ellen Terry, J. L. Toole, Lionel Brough, Charles Wyndham, and Henrietta Hodson, a lively and intelligent young woman who became Mrs. Labouchere. At times Labby ran his theatre as though he was organising a General Election. At each entrance he would put up notices and invite the audience to vote on the piece being presented. Joseph Hatton wrote: "Sometime he brought out plays himself. Occasionally in the course of preparation he would go abroad. When particularly wanted he could not be found. The work went on, however, and so did the losses." The M.P., who also tried his hand at writing plays, said that the Northampton theatre was a model of what a provincial theatre should be.

Besides running a theatre Labouchere ran a newspaper and wrote dramatic criticisms for it. He was no respecter of persons even if they were Henry Irvings: "An actor must, in order to win popularity, have mannerisms and the more peculiar they are, the greater will be his popularity. No-one can for a moment suppose that Mr. Irving could not speak distinctly and progress about the stage after the manner of human beings and stand still without balancing to and fro like a bear in a cage, if he pleased. Yet had he done all this he would—notwithstanding that there is a real touch of genius about his acting sometimes—never made the mark he has. He is, indeed, to the stage, what Lord Beaconsfield was to politics . . . were Mr. Irving to abate his peculiarities, his fervent worshippers would complain that their idol was sinking into the commonplace."

Rated by some to be the finest wit since Sheridan, "Labby" spoke with contempt of those arty-crafty folk who pontificated about what the theatre

Two-way views of the interior of the Northampton Opera House, now usually known as the Repertory Theatre. Above is the drawing by T. Osborne Robinson, who insisted on calling it the "Royal Theatre", while below is a photograph by Eric Lawe, whose father, Arthur Law, used to play the violin in the pit orchestra.

A souvenir of the amateur production of *The Merchant of Venice* given at the Opera House in December, 1885, in aid of Mrs. Ratliffe's Blankets for the Poor Fund, with the manager Isaac Tarry as Shylock. The picture, which is signed Harris Brown, is reproduced by courtesy of Allan Markham, of Wellingborough.

One of the theatre's two boxes *(Bryan J. Douglas)*

The front of the theatre in Guildhall Road is hemmed in by adjacent property. *(Chronicle & Echo)*

A unique feature of the Northampton theatre is that the stage door is on the opposite side of the road from the rear of the theatre, in Swan Street. A tunnel under the road connects it to the theatre. The paint shop is on the "opposite side". *(Bryan J. Douglas)*

Two pictures of Isaac Tarry, auctioneer, amateur actor and first manager of the Opera House. On right he is made up as Shylock. *(Northampton Independent)*

Thomas Phipps Dorman, owner of the Opera House for a decade from 1889. He was a brewer, yachtsman and Free-mason. *(Northampton Independent)*

C. G. Colley-Grattan, the only manager of the Opera House who died in harness, in 1919, was a former manager of the Compton Comedy Company.

Fred Dorman, brother of Thomas Phipps Dorman, was an architect but also had a spell as a professional actor, under the name Fred Doomar.

Charles Rider Noble, manager of the Opera House during the T. P. Dorman regime.

should or should not do but who were not prepared to risk their own money on it—"I never came across one of its votaries, painter, sculptor, author or artist, who was ready to sacrifice one farthing of his own. I was once the owner of a theatre and was perpetually at war with authors and actors who wanted me to ruin myself on the altar of high art but I soon found that this was a term they used for their own fads."

It was after being M.P. for Windsor that he first represented Northampton, in 1880. At one time he lived in the Old Palace Yard, opposite Parliament to which his house was connected by a tunnel. He used to joke about doing a Guy Fawkes.

Edward Terry's Northampton performances of June, 1886, in Pinero's *In Chancery* and *The Rocket* were his last before opening his own theatre in London, then being completed in The Strand. "You'll find me there on St. Valentine's Day," he told his Northampton audiences.

During the August break in 1886 a brass netting was erected round the front of the Opera House gallery to frustrate such efforts as that of the galleryite the previous season who had dropped a bottle on to the head of a gentleman in the dress circle. Backstage a powerful crane was installed to facilitate the movement of heavy scenery and machinery.

If Friday night was "Grand Fashionable Night" as it was frequently billed, especially when a benefit was due, the Saturday night seems to have been "People's Night". Reporting on *A Night Off*, the Daily Reporter said that Saturday night bookings in the aristocratic portion of the house were unprecedentedly good for a Saturday night, "which is supposed as a rule to be People's Night." With the long hours worked by many of the labouring classes, especially those who were shop assistants, it was no doubt either a rush or an impossibility to get to the theatre on most weekdays. Many shops stayed open until 8 p.m. and some until 9.

The theatre reopened on September 6, 1886, with *Diplomacy* by the London critic Clement Scott, presented by Bella Pateman's Company. Two months later the denizens of the gallery were praised for their respectful reception of Shakespeare as presented by the Frank Benson Company. The December week by the *In The Ranks* Company was their last. They broke up, however, after a run of two years in town and three in the provinces which was described as "an almost unprecedented achievement."

By reason of the commercial consideration, no doubt, but also because newspapers were sometimes sued by irate theatre or company promoters, the Press tried to be as kind as possible in its criticisms but when opera first came to the Opera House that December it proved impossible even to be kind, let alone adulatory. There was a large Monday night audience for *The Bohemian Girl* presented by the Balfe Opera Company. The following day the Reporter found it impossible to speak of the production in favourable terms. "The chorus never managed to sing a single number in tune and some of the principal artists were troubled in the same way." Of Mr. Henry Nordblom's Thadeus it was a case of the less said the better. Happily the orchestra was good "and if a little prominent at times, it covered a multitude of sins."

The critic added that he was informed that there were circumstances of a painful nature which prevented the company from doing full justice to themselves. What were those circumstances? The same issue carried a letter from the warm-hearted but distressed manager of the Opera House revealing all. Isaac Tarry recognised that it was an audience's right to express its displeasure but he wished to explain that the company were more to be pitied than blamed. "They had been engaged by a person against whom I will, in charity, bring no worse a charge than utter recklessness. He booked a tour for them, Coventry being the first town to be visited, Northampton the second and Huddersfield and Halifax being the next and it was not until then that it was discovered that he had not the means of carrying out his engagements. The position was a most painful one for all concerned and especially for the members of the chorus who would have starved but for the assistance given them by other members of the company." Tarry himself had also given assistance. Appealed to from Coventry he had footed the bill to bring the company to Northampton.

By Tuesday night things were a little better although,as the Reporter delicately put it: "You cannot of course convert voices with little culture or that have seen their best days into artistic or bright interpretation of classical songs."

During the debate which ensued a sarcastic letter appeared in the paper: "We do not wait to make inquiries whether the performers are suffering from gout or bilious or liver complaint but do there and then open our sacriligious lips and hiss. I am afraid the Northampton public are too bad for words." It was John Dryden, the Northamptonshire-born Poet Laureate and dramatist of the 17th century who asserted that to clap and hiss when at the play was the right of every freeborn Englishman. Abroad the rule was taken very seriously on one occasion; the previous August an actor at Casaie, Piedmont, who was received with hisses shot himself and died on stage.

Back at Northampton there was a further disaster in store. It happened in a scene in which a character named Devilshoof (Richard Lansmere) was seen escaping across a rustic bridge carrying a child. After crossing, the plot called for him to demolish the structure with a hatchet to prevent pursuit. Strictly against Tarry's orders the villain was carrying a live child, borrowed from a man living in Cow Lane. While doing his demolition act he fell, not only bruising himself but breaking the thigh of the child. Ironically the incident was one of the few episodes that night to draw a cheer for its realism.

The following week the theatre had been due to be closed but Tarry gave its free use for a Monday ballad concert by members of the company. Along with the orchestra the entire staff also gave their services to help the 30 broken-down operatics who faced a miserable Christmas after their abandonment in Coventry and their lean week at Northampton. But a mere handful turned up.

A week later it was an entirely different picture and the newspaper commented that the management must have wished that the walls of the Opera House were made of elastic material, as hundreds were turned away from the sensational *Alone in London*. In three nights alone it was stated to have been seen by 5,000 people. "It must cost the manager a pang when he cannot take the money which people are eager to give him. Excitement was at fever heat with the cheering of the virtuous element and hissing and hooting of the villainous characters." That's show business, of course. One week you're up; the next you are down.

In writing previous pieces about the early days of the Opera House I have, in common with other writers—and not all of them mere journalists—tended to over-emphasise the bonnets and the horses' heads. With Macqueen-Pope-like nostalgia we have scrawled merrily away of how bonnets could only be worn in the circle and how carriages were obliged to arrive with the horses' heads pointing down Guildhall Road, towards the Midlands Railway Station in St. John Street, and pick up at the time stated in "Carriages at 10.45". These points are factual but good reporting does not consist merely of writing down facts that are not inaccurate. The really significant point about the first few years is how few bonnets bobbed in the circle and how few horses halted outside the theatre entrance.

If we regard the theatre as a sandwich, with the meat in the higher-priced middle layer of dress and upper circles and the bread in pit and gallery then it was all too often an empty, bread-only sandwich at the Opera House. The gallery up above, where a policeman kept order, may have been crowded to suffocation and the pit down below might be packed out, but all too often there was the merest sprinkling of the gentry and well-to-do in the middle. Time after time one finds references to the scant support here, in comments both from reporters and from the manager. As Tarry put it in one of his speeches from the stage: "From those to whom we looked for most countenance and support we have received the least." During 1886 the Daily Reporter said that the dress circle must be the despair of the management. "The patronage of the occupants of this part of the house is capricious, fitful and uncertain to the last degree. The best part of the house, both for seeing and hearing, is assigned to them and luxurious fauteuils provided for them—in short everything that can be done for their comfort that thought and solicitude can provide—yet it too often proves but 'a beggarly array of empty benches'."

Sometimes the support elsewhere was equally bad. When the T. W. Robertson Company presented Caste, Ours and Home the comment was that "Mr. Tarry might well ask if it was the slightest use to cast pearls before Northampton audiences. You get crowded houses to witness spectacular dramas where acting is subordinate to scenic effects and where every act has its instalment of murder and rapine; or farcical comedies which depend for their success upon broad situations and salacious jests. But when we get a wholesome comedy to which a man may take his wife or sister without one feeling of shame then the manager finds the receipts falling off and is forced to the conclusion that if he is to look after his own interests he must swim with the current and give the people the fleshpots of the Palais Royal or The Alhambra."

In October, 1886, support for On Change was poor everywhere. On the Tuesday night there was, said the Daily Reporter, a bad pit, a worse gallery and no circle at all. "All the greatest London successes are brought to our very doors and we receive them with stolid indifference. One cannot help feeling an involuntary shudder when one reflects that a continuation of the scant support might result in the theatre closing altogether. What a terrible loss this would be. We will not look upon the pessimistic side of things but trust that with more prosperous times for the community at large a more general support will be given to what is, after all, one of the greatest of all educational agencies and, after the pulpit, the greatest and most excellent of moral teachers."

Those who have read my previous book Drama That Smelled can imagine Canon R. B. Hull, the drama-hating parson of All Saints Church, Northampton, choking over his toast as he read that paragraph. For him and for many others the drama still smelled. Its slowness in gaining respectability is indeed why there remained so many empty seats in the middle layer. But as regards the prospect of losing the theatre altogether, loss there was to be but not from lack of support. Within six months of these gloomy thoughts came disaster.

But first I must mention some high jinks in Guildhall Road which resulted not from the drama being there but a new style of religious worship—the Salvation Army, which had since 1880 established a barracks there, as an over-the-road neighbour of the Opera House. That the ructions which occurred resulted from the religious and not the Thespian presence shows just how unexpected life can be.

It was the visit to the town in January, 1887, of the "Army" leader General Booth which led to disorder and riot in the streets. His open carriage had been met on its arrival by torch-bearing soldiers of his army of salvation but also by some of the high spirited hooligans who had "a bit of fun" from time to time. They pelted the General with stones, ice, and other projectiles. In Marefair the crowd made a rush as if to do him personal injury; he was struck on the cheek by a rotten egg, water was hurled from a window in Gold Street, there was howling and hissing, a flag was captured and torn to shreds, instruments were wrested from the hands of the bandsmen, the bass drum being entirely demolished. Policemen fought in vain to keep order but haven in the Guildhall Road barracks was finally attained.

That month Northampton Opera House audiences saw Miss Alleyn, aged 26, as the newly-wed wife of her manager, Charles Bernard, 57-year-old widower and former proprietor of the Princes Theatre, Manchester. They had been married the previous week at Stratford-upon-Avon Church, while playing at Leamington. Part of the marriage service had been conducted over the very spot where Shakespeare lies buried. The only two people attending the ceremony were from Northampton—newspaper proprietor Samuel S. Campion, who gave the bride away, and Mrs. Campion.

The month also brought a return visit from Barry Sullivan, this time in *Richelieu, Hamlet, Richard III, The Stranger* and *Macbeth*.

Critics' opinions have differed ever and it is illuminating to contrast the high praise accorded to the *Jim the Penman* Company at Northampton at the beginning of February, 1887, with the scornful treatment they had just received at Oxford. Said the Oxford Magazine: "A society melodrama is perhaps more difficult for a poor company to act with success than any other kind of play. Possibly the actors themselves are not sufficiently familiar with the precincts of Mayfair to give a true representation of high life and its crimes; possibly they are so careful to make the course of the play clear to a provincial audience that they reduce the tragedy to a farce. At all events it seems plain that as soon as the company which brought *Jim The Penman* to Oxford condescends to attempt work of a less ambitious kind the better it will be for the reputation of the play as well as for that of the individual actors. For since *Called Back* was acted at the Town Hall about a year ago, Oxford has not been doomed to such an example of dramatic incapacity as that which was confidently presented last week. Nature can never have intended either Mr. Theo-Balfour or Mr. Chatterton to become actors. It would not be fair to contrast the former with Mr. Willard or the latter with Mr. Garthorne. But they certainly might have learned something from the London actors, which would have saved them from becoming so persistently ridiculous. The parts of James Ralston and Captain Redwood are, no doubt, difficult to fill adequately; but it needed all the ingenuity of Mr. Theo-Balfour and Mr. Balsir Chatterton to render them completely farcical."

It is difficult to realise that it was the same company in the same play about whom the Northampton Herald said the very next week that they "performed the play to the delight of a very numerous audience," that Theo-Balfour acted James Ralston "with marked ability," while Balsir Chatterton "delineated his part with an elaborate finish which does him immense credit." As regards the play the opinion of the Herald was that "there is little to fear of the degeneracy of the drama."

Who today can judge precisely how good or bad it really was? But it is of some assistance in evaluating the Oxford critique to see what the paper said about the visitors who followed Balfour and Chatterton to the University city. Especially as it chanced to be the Compton Comedy Company who were paying a three-day visit with *She Stoops to Conquer*. The same critic wrote in kindly terms, especially of Compton's own Young Marlow in *She Stoops to Conquer*—"His dash and spirit were as infectious as Charles Wyndham's and it is easy to see why his company is so good as a whole . . . altogether we cannot thank Mr. Compton too much for giving us this play so well. We are getting thoroughly satiated with farces of *The Magistrate* order and the truthful and conscientious spirit in which *She Stoops to Conquer* was given should wake us up to demand more of such treats." This was of course the principal justification for the existence of the Compton Comedy Company. They carried the banner of old English comedy in plays which would otherwise have remained furled as far as the provinces were concerned. The fact that so much rubbish was being put on at the time was a double justification.

At this time Franklin decided to extend his empire of entertainment in Northampton. Upon the death of John Collier of the Melbourne Gardens (named after Lord Melbourne who had had an estate at nearby Duston and who was the first Prime Minister and father figure for Queen Victoria but usually called "Colliers") Franklin purchased the gardens and made extensive improvements. Under his name, Franklins Gardens, they still survive and are the home of the famous rugby team, the Saints.

Unlike Tarry, who would declaim ad lib at the slightest provocation, Franklin was reticent as far as public speaking was concerned and could but rarely be prevailed upon to say a few words, even on such auspicious occasions as the opening and anniversaries of his theatre. Nor, except on one notable occasion, did he allow the Press to interview him. But he was by no means inarticulate as that single interview of February, 1887, reveals. Discussing the merits of Northampton, he commented: "Strangers have an utterly erroneous idea about the town. I have had an exceptional opportunity of observing this through the various dramatic companies which visit us. They evidently expect to find Northampton a counterpart of Hanley, Burslem, Longton and other of the Black Country towns" but "are delighted with its wide, clean and beautiful streets, its noble squares and handsome shops, vying with those of Bond Street, Oxford Street and Regent Street. They are astounded to find that our atmosphere is not charged with smoke and sulphur and that we do not inhale poison with every breath that we draw, that our factories are not begrimed with layer upon layer of filth and soot, that our courts and alleys are not pestiferous dens and that our women and children do not walk about with naked feet, that our artisans do not run the professional chimney sweep close in the race for griminess. The truth is that Northampton needs only to be known to be appreciated. I was born in the town and am proud of it and have a boundless faith in its future. Considering all its railways and other advantages I believe nothing can prevent its becoming a great and important commercial centre—only we must wait until the clouds roll by." The "clouds" were those of depression in trade.

When the Pressman complimented J.C.F. on his theatre he replied: "It is undoubtedly true that the Opera House is the most popular institution in the town. I hope that my conduct of the establishment (in which I owe more than I can say to my friend Tarry) will be taken as a pledge and an earnest of the liberality of my intentions with regard to the Gardens."

The object of his chat with the Press was to enlighten the public on his plans for the Gardens and he was asked whether they were not a large undertaking for him. "No doubt but not more so than the Opera House, indeed they have not cost so much. There were many who shook their heads gravely when I built the Opera House and predicted certain failure. One professional gentleman of high standing in both town and county asked me to show him the proposed site and when I pointed to the filthy tumbledown ramshackle of old tenements in Cow Lane which were doomed to come down to make way for it (and which probably ere now would have been condemned by the authorities as unsafe) he lifted up his hands in grief and said 'What a waste of good property' adding that whoever built a theatre in Northampton would be ruined within 12 months. But I have had no occasion to regret it. Indeed while it seemed the most hazardous speculation of my life it has proved the most remunerative. It's another proof of the old proverb, Nothing Venture, Nothing Win."

As far as the Gardens were concerned Franklin said that he wanted to do some further good for his native town while at the same time doing himself a bit of good—a perfect analysis of the motives of the commercial theatre owner. As it was impossible to prevent the large number of people who wished to from going out of Northampton for amusement and relaxation he hoped to offset this by encouraging a similar influx. His Gardens in the west of the town would be a great boost also to the tramways—"I hope for the shareholders of this hitherto unfortunate speculation 'There's a good time coming'."

Franklin's optimism in the case of the Gardens was not to be justified. Within a short space of time, though not in his ownership, they were to be bankrupt. And within six days of this interview he was sitting in the circle of his splendid theatre watching the stage burn down.

The Enormously Successful Drama of Modern Society.
by Sir C. L. YOUNG, Bart.

JIM THE PENMAN

By arrangement with Mrs BEENARD-BEERE.
Played Two Hundred Nights at the THEATRE ROYAL,
HAYMARKET, LONDON, and now being played at
Madison Square Theatre, New York, to
Crowded Houses.

Mr. BALSIR CHATTERTON'S

COMPANY OF SPECIALLY SELECTED ARTISTES.

The Play produced under the direction of Mr. THEO BALFOUR.

MONDAY, FEBRUARY 7TH,
1887.
AND DURING THE WEEK.

Will be presented the Celebrated Society Romance in Four Acts, by
Sir CHARLES L. YOUNG, Bart, entitled—

JIM

THE PENMAN

James Ralston........	Mr. THEO BALFOUR
Captain Redwood	Mr. BALSIR CHATTERTON
Louis Percival	Mr. W. R. SUTHERLAND
Baron Hartfeld	Mr. CYRIL MELTON
Lord Drelincourt	Mr. M. H. HAY
George Ralston...............................	Mr. CARLON ARNIE
Mr. Clapstone, Q.C.	Mr. WILFORD SELWYN
Mr. Netherby, M.P.	Mr. MURRAY HAWTHORNE
Dr. Pettyaise....................................	Mr. CAPEL POLLOCK
Butler	Mr. ARTHUR HALL
Lady Dunscombe..................................	Miss SWAINE KINTON
Agnes Ralston	Miss CARMEN BARKER
Mrs Chapstone	Miss LILIAN DARRELL

—AND—

Mrs Ralston .... Miss FANNY ENSON

ACT 1.

Morning Room in Ralston's House in
Regent's Park—The Conspiracy.

ACT 2.

The Same — The Diamond Robbery

ACT 3.

Ardleigh Court — — The Detective
Unmasks the Forger.

ACT 4.

The Wedding Breakfast at Ardleigh Court
Retribution.

An Interval of Five Minutes between Acts 1 and 2 : Ten Minutes
between Acts 2 and 3, and Ten Minutes between
Acts 3 and 4.

The Incidental Music Composed and arranged by Mr.
BUCALOSSI, Theatre Royal. Haymarket.

Acting Manager............	} For {	Mr BALSIR	{ Mr WILFORD SELWYN
Representative in advance			Mr ARTHUR GILBERT
Assistant Stage Manager		CHATTERTON	... Mr. ARTHUR HALL

Overcoats, Mackintoshes, Umbrellas, &c., may be left in the PIT
CLOAK ROOM, at a charge of ONE PENNY each Article.

On Monday, February 14th, 1887,

Messrs. Shiel Barry & Hogarth's Comic Opera Company, in

LA MASCOTTE

—AND—

LES CLOCHES DE CORNEVILLE

A faded programme of the week before the fire at Northampton Opera House. The shows announced for the following week, *La Mascotte* and *Les Cloches de Corneville,* were instead performed at the old theatre in Marefair.

LATE ADVERTISEMENT.

OLD THEATRE ROYAL,
MAREFAIR, NORTHAMPTON.
TO-NIGHT AT 8,
Messrs. SHIEL BARRY and HOGARTH'S COMPANY
In the Comic Opera,

"LES CLOCHES DE CORNEVILLE."

Gaspard, as played by him all over } Mr. SHIEL BARRY.
the World .... }

Centre Boxes, 3s.; Side Boxes, 2s.; Pit, 1s.; Gallery, 6d.
Doors open at 7.30; to commence at 8.

Interlude

FIRE!!!

UNUSUAL AUDIENCE, on Sunday the 13th

TALE OF TWO THEATRES, by one Architect

FIERY FACTS & Figures

PANIC—the real Killer

LIGHT, HEAT & SMOKE

DANCERS in Danger

FIGHTERS too Feeble

LAWS too Lax

REFORMERS Shaw, Godwin & Irving

SAFETY & the Amateur

LOSS & occasional Profit

GOING to Extremes

An artist's impression of the fire at its height at Northampton Opera House on Sunday, February 13, 1887, with the flames licking across the proscenium to burn the front benches of the pit and to blister and blacken the paint as far back as the rear of the galley.

UNUSUAL AUDIENCE,

on Sunday the 13th

One o'clock on a Sunday morning was an unusual time for an audience to be in the theatre watching what was happening on the stage. It was also an unusual audience. The proprietor Mr. Franklin and the manager Mr. Tarry were among the small "house", which included some policemen, several reporters scribbling away in their notebooks and a few members of the public. But the majority were firemen. The date was February 13, 1887. The stage was on fire, a wall of flame from basement to roof.

Arthur Hall, who first discovered that there was a fire, was the assistant stage manager and baggageman of the *Jim The Penman* company. After the perform- ance ended at 10.35, he had completed his usual Saturday night chore of packing up the company gear and taking it down to the railway station—in this case the nearby Midland Railway Station in St. John's Street. He had left the theatre at about 11.30 and it must have been around midnight as he made his way back to his lodgings in Cow Lane at the home of Mr. T. C. Smith, one of the theatre employees who took in touring folk to supplement his income.

Cow Lane was at the back of the theatre and as he turned the corner Hall saw smoke coming out of crevices in the stage door and from windows higher up. He ran to Mr. Smith's to give the alarm; Smith in turn ran to Franklins Hotel to tell the owner that his theatre was on fire. At first Franklin would not believe it.

Meantime, shinning bravely up a rainwater pipe Arthur got into the theatre through one of the windows. But the heat and smoke were overpowering and he had to retreat. Given the keys by Franklin, Smith unlocked the stage door with the idea of saving the props and getting the handpipe and hose but the rear of the stage was a mass of flames. The front entrance, on the other hand, was still completely accessible and Franklin and others went in. Tarry arrived and rescued the books from his office which was at that time off the front corridor—it was not yet upstairs in its present position, in what was intended to be a billiard room.

The summons to the Fire Chief was one of the first to be made by telephone. Captain Pilgrim was rung up and the alarm was given to the police and members of both the Town and Volunteer Fire Brigades. Perhaps it was because the system was inefficient, perhaps it was because it was a Saturday night and they were out celebrating something or other, but, as the Mercury reported: "For some cause or other the firemen did not respond to the summons with hardly their usual alacrity."

The second-in-command was Superintendent Lines whose vigour had been questioned two years earlier when he was said to be in a state of health which meant that he was not so active "nor can he stand the fatigue of many hours labour at a fire but tries to do his best." In contrast, on the night of the theatre fire, Captain Pilgrim was reported in the Press to have been a bundle of energy— "He was everywhere, directing here and superintending there." Harris, the stage carpenter, was quickly on the scene and he and Robins, the property master, helped to direct the firemen to the places where danger seemed most imminent.

The firemen used "an immense quantity of hose." The first supply of water came from a hydrant near the top of Cow Lane, the second from one in Guildhall Road, the hose being taken in through the vestibule and into the dress circle. At first it had been thought unwise to open the circle doors and Franklin cut his hand breaking a window in one of these to permit the hose to be pushed through. When the doors were opened it was seen that the stage was a wall of flame from basement to roof. The curtains, including the drop scene of Queen Eleanor's Cross, one of the local historic landmarks, had fed the blaze and the front seats of the pit were ignited by the heat alone; paint on the front of the circle and at the rear of the gallery was blistered and blackened. But nevertheless, throughout the night it was possible for the "audience" to be there, a quite remarkable circumstance.

The roof over the stage was the first part to fall in, great beams crashing down, and later flames took hold of the splendid decorated ceiling over the auditorium and parts of this came down too.

At the top of Cow Lane the steamer was puffing and thumping away as it forced water along the hose. Ostlers and stable boys led frightened horses from the stables of the Swan Inn. Carriages, dog carts and other vehicles were taken out and drawn up outside the Town Hall while the trembling animals were led into the yard of the George Hotel. The Town Hall itself was aglow with the reflection from the burning theatre and nearby buildings were lit up as if it was day.

At the front of the theatre a fire escape was brought into use, up which the firemen scrambled to reach the roof, which they did via the houses of Dr. Buszard and Mr. Goddard. Thus they were able to cut a hole in the roof and pour water through it, by means of which they were gradually able to beat back the fire. On the roof they were seen in dark relief against the flames—which were visible from miles away, so that some thought there were some unusually fiery proceedings at the iron works at Hunsbury Hill.

Some of the people living in adjacent houses were evacuated. "Two children from the house of Dr. Buszard in their night dresses and under the care of a sparsely clad domestic were taken to the Midland Railway Refreshment Rooms further down the street. A fireman took the sobbing children in his arms and a servant girl, also crying, ran behind."

By 1.30 Captain Pilgrim was able to assure Franklin that some of the theatre would surely be saved but many of the firemen were still at work for another six hours, being given food in relays at Franklins Hotel. In the flies buckets still hung "for use in case of fire". The orchestra pit was burned out, all that remained of Mr. Nind's bass viol being the scroll. Several rows of seats in the pit were consumed and others were charred. Yet in the prop room at the rear a primed revolver had not gone off.

The cause of the fire remained a mystery though it was thought to have begun in the ladies' dressing room over the right hand side of the stage. The theatre, which was now stated to have cost £12,000 in all, was insured with the North British and Mercantile office of which the local agent, almost needless to say, was Isaac Tarry.

Though temperamentally overcome by the loss of the theatre which he had done so much to create, Tarry put on a remarkable burst of energy the result of which was that, all obstacles surmounted, the show went on next day, Monday, in the old theatre, which had been given a hasty dust-up. There was a good first night house for *Les Cloches de Corneville,* by Shiel Barry and Hogarth's Comic Opera Company. In one of his little pep talks Tarry announced that he hoped to carry on there until the Guildhall Road Theatre could be repaired.

But during the rest of the week support dwindled away; people were not prepared to put up with the limitations of the "Theatre Un-Royal" and the subsequent bookings had to be abandoned or postponed. As the Mercury put it: "The fact is that the place is so small and the companies Mr. Tarry has booked are so expensive that it could not possibly pay to hold performances there. Besides, the inconveniences of the Old Theatre are innumerable."

[To continue directly with the history of the Opera House, turn to Page 99.]

TALE OF TWO THEATRES,

by one Architect

Within eight months another theatre designed by C. J. Phipps was in flames. In tragic contrast to the Northampton Opera House fire, which was "after hours" and in which there was not a single casualty, the one at Exeter's Theatre Royal the following September was during a performance and 186 lives were lost. This was another comparatively new theatre, the previous one having been burned down on February 7, 1885.

The second season at the new Theatre Royal was only a fortnight old when, on September 5, 1887, scenery caught fire and the curtain was dropped during the third scene of Act IV of *Romany Rye.* Within a very short space of time the place was a holocaust. In the auditorium there was a scramble for survival but in the gallery, which had only one exit, smoke and fumes rose quickly and many of the occupants died where they sat, suffocated. Of those who did manage to get out many perished among a huge pile of bodies at an angle of the steps leading down from the gallery. Some were rescued by fire escape from high windows when hope seemed to be gone; others died trying to jump down to the street. All the musicians escaped even though their route lay under the blazing stage. All the actors and actresses got away too, including Frederick Mouillot who had spoken what were to be the last lines to be heard in that theatre. By the time the blaze was got under control at 1.15 a.m. only the bare walls remained.

The cause of the fire was said to be overcrowding of scenery on the stage. In Northampton the Herald commented that a gallery seating 200 with but one exit, as at Exeter, was bound to be a deathtrap and said that the astonishing thing was that "all preceding experience seems to be lost in such cases." Had the theatre been examined by a duly qualified inspector it would not have been allowed to remain as it was. "It is carrying our English love of liberty and independence too far to insist upon the opportunity of being roasted to death." What was wanted was a direct central authority with power to control the construction of public buildings. At present builders and managers of theatres "really have it all their own way."

At the official inquest it was established that there had been no safety curtain, no proper division of stage and auditorium, no stage lantern, a roof that was too low and exits that were cramped and tortuous. The jury censured the architect for ignoring the safety regulations and the magistrates for licensing the building. Phipps shrugged off all safety obligations as not being the business of the architect!

Some of the evidence concerning him makes highly unsatisfactory reading. My own immediate reaction to it is amazement that a man so casual in his approach to questions of safety should have been allowed to go on building further theatres—he had a tally of about 40 when he died in May, 1897, at which time his Dover theatre was still being erected. Mr. J. T. Pengelly, clerk to the magistrates, said that when the question of the lack of a fire curtain was raised during the justices' tour Phipps replied that there were only two or three in existence and they were "found not to answer, practically of no use." In his own evidence the architect said that to his knowledge there was only one fire curtain in England. He declared that in his opinion the Exeter theatre had been a safe one(!) and when a juror asked whether he considered that it could have been made a safer place had another £2,000 been spent on it he uncompromisingly replied, "No. I do not."

Evidence by the city surveyor, Mr. Cameron, was no more reassuring. revealing that the magistrates were quite unsure just what their powers were in this field. He said that the Town Council had no jurisdiction on the question of exits from public buildings, there being no power under the Public Health Act of 1875: the committee considered that they had no right to order structural alterations in the building except with regard to sanitary matters. While the Metropolitan powers applied only in London a set of their rules had been handed to the directors of the theatre who said that they had been anticipated and observed.

Judging by the testimony of stage staff the fire began when *unbattened* scenery in the flies blew on to gas lighting. People in the gallery, which was an extension of the upper circle, were a mere six feet from the ceiling. It seems likely that "hand grenades" used to fight the fire gave off poisonous fumes which abetted the smoke in suffocating so many where they sat. Police Sergeant Sullock gave evidence of going up a fire escape and trying to pull people through a window, from among a heap of bodies at the foot of the gallery stairs "but they were packed so tightly that the skin came off in my hands." Imagine the looks of hatred directed at Phipps by relatives of those who had perished, as this evidence was heard. On the other hand at the height of the fire half-a-dozen people were found to be drinking in the pit bar, unaware that anything was amiss. The lessee, Mr. S. Herbert-Basing, was away on a professional engagement at Ilfracombe on the night of the fire and read of the disaster in the Tuesday morning papers. But he expressed the opinion that the Exeter theatre had been far and away safer than many he had been in. Summing up to the jury the Coroner said that it was desirable that the Metropolitan powers be extended to all municipalities.

The issue of Era containing the inquest report included a letter from Clark,

Runnett and Co. Ltd stating that iron curtains of their manufacture were in the Prince of Wales Theatre, London; the Royal Opera House, Dundee; and the Royal Lyceum Theatre, Edinburgh.

Not surprisingly there was a reaction among audiences throughout the country, many theatregoers being at least temporarily reluctant to risk their lives by going to the theatre. Many a reassuring speech was made from the stages and many a reassuring article appeared in local newspapers, often claiming that the theatre in their city or town was exceptionally safe. When *Current Cash* was being played at Northampton by J. Pitt Hardacre's Company that same month, immediately post-Exeter, Hardacre made a speech at the end of Act IV in which he described the Opera House as one of the safest theatres in the kingdom. At the Exeter fire, he said, 190 were in the gallery, of whom over 100 died; the previous Monday there had been 500 in the gallery at Northampton, all of whom made their exit within two-and-a-half minutes of the final curtain.

It has to be remembered that audiences used to be packed in far more tightly than people would nowadays tolerate, let alone authorities permit. People were allowed to stand in the gangways—and these were by no means as adequate as they are now, certain seats having since been removed, in some cases because they were behind the pillars. In its present guise as a Repertory Theatre the Opera House seats some 600 (without the gallery) but when Phipps designed it he gave an assurance that it would take 1,500, or 1,700 at a pinch.

Hardacre also observed that even when the Opera House blaze was at its height it was possible to watch the fire from parts of the auditorium. The Herald confirmed this: "Our own reporter stood in the dress circle when the fire was at its height and although the heat was great it was not enough to drive him from his coign of vantage or prevent his taking notes."

Hardacre contrasted the speedy spread of the fire at the Exeter theatre, which he cited as proof of its flimsy construction, with Northampton, where the builder had done his work in a magnificently solid manner. Despite having some time to gain hold before being discovered the flames had not spread beyond the stage. The salvation of the Opera House was in its massive walls—a really splendid piece of masonry between stage and auditorium.

Public concern was mounting and by a remarkable piece of timing when the Exeter fire occurred the London Saturday Review had nearly completed a series of articles on the provision of safety in various places of amusement in London. The series had begun on June 11 and ended on September 10—five days after the Exeter disaster.

The French newspaper Tempo drew a comparison between the Exeter fire and one the previous May at the Opera Comique, Paris, during a performance of *Mignon*. Within two hours of the scenery catching fire from gas jets the theatre was reduced to a ruin and 77 were dead. The journal suggested the use of electric light, the current to be generated in a separate building; the use of non-inflammable scenery and draperies; the multiplication of doors, staircases and balconies; nightly inspection by the police; the setting up of special fire brigades among the theatre staff; and the provision of tip-up seats. But Tempo doubted whether France would benefit by the lessons of the English disaster any more than England had benefited from the French one.

The newspaper's feeling that nothing had been done following the Opera

Comique conflagration was probably not shared by the proprietors of a number of other Parisian theatres, who were having to foot large bills for alterations ordered by the authorities. In August, 1887, a columnist in the Era wrote: "When the catastrophe at the Salle Favart occurred I expressed the opinion that among the victims should be classed the managers of all the Paris theatres. At the time I only took into consideration the falling off in receipts inevitable from the panic with which the public was seized. The losses incidental to that panic cannot yet be estimated, for it is likely to continue for many months to come. But I left out of my calculations the outlay to which managers will be put by the alterations which have been ordained since. A partial glimpse at the expenditure thus entailed has now been afforded us. The cost of alterations at the various houses may be estimated in round figures as follows: Palais-Royal, £4,000; Gymnase, £3,000; Folies Dramatiques, £4,000 (of which a third will be borne by the landlord); Vaudeville, £2,000; Nouveautés, £2,800; Varietés, £1,500; the little Cluny, £800. The Odéon gets off best, having little or nothing to expend. Operations have not begun at the Bouffes, and will not be very costly at the Renaissance, Ambigu and Port-St.-Martin. The Palais Royal has been turned completely topsy-turvy and will be so altered as to be unrecognisable. On and after the 1st January next the electric light is to supersede gas in the following houses: Opéra, Francais, Odéon, Vaudeville, Palais-Royal, Gymnase, Renaissance, Port-St.-Martin, Ambigu, Folies-Dramatiques, Nouveautés, Châtelet and Varietés. At the Theatre de Paris, Bouffes, Cluny and Déjazet gas will still be tolerated. We may estimate therefore, that full £30,000 will go out of the treasuries of the Paris theatres to pay for the alterations necessitated by the terrible warning at the Opera Comique."

FIERY FACTS

& Figures

During the year under discussion there were 17 theatre fires involving the destruction of 14 theatres and the loss of 238 lives. These were:-

January 10	Stadttheater, Gottingen
January 15	Sidoli Circus, Bucharest
January 18	Hebrew Dramatic Club, London
January 28	Theatre Royal, Swansea
February 12	Opera House, Northampton
April 6	Manor House Theatre, Ringwood
May 25	Opera Comique, Paris
June 28	Lafayette Theatre, Rouen
July 4	Teatro Principale, Caceres, Spain
July 12	Aleazar Theatre, Hurley, Wisconsin

February 13, 1887—Fire at Northampton Opera House, designed by C. J. Phipps—No casualties. *(Photo-copy Bryan J. Douglas)*

September 5, 1887—Fire at Exeter Theatre Royal, designed by C. J. Phipps —186 deaths, at least. The final figure could not be exact because "so many bodies were reduced to ashes by the intense heat." *(Courtesy Harry N. Great-orex)*

The theatre where Edward Compton made his last appearance, on March 27, 1915.
It was as Davy Garrick that he took what was to be his final bow, at the Theatre Royal.
Rochdale. The pictures on these two pages show the theatre as it was, at the height of the
fire which destroyed it in November, 1954, and the ruins being inspected by Gracie Fields,
a native of Rochdale. *(Photos by courtesy of Rochdale Libraries and Arts Services Rochdale
Observer, Mr. Bill Lyth and Mr. M. Bentley).*

In this scene from *Lilian* by Christopher Denys when the Fire Chief arrives at the Old Vic to announce that the theatre is to be closed down because fire regulations are not being complied with he finds Lilian Baylis cooking sausages for the chorus on an open gas ring at the side of the stage. She even has the cheek to ask him to hold the pan for a few minutes! This was Mr. Denys's last production at Northampton Repertory Theatre, in October, 1976, after 15 months at the theatre. This part of the episodic play told how Lilian was set to raise £30,000 to pay for the necessary alterations. With the aid of her personal friend, God, to whom she frequently communicates on bended knees, in familiar terms, she managed to do it. Like a number of his presentations in 1976, *Lilian*, which many, including me, thought to be the best production of the year, lost a lot of money and some lines in it proved to be ironically appropriate, such as: "I thought we were here to improve, not amuse"; "Anybody in his right mind would go and do something else"; "I don't know where you think the money comes from"; and "I really must think about stepping down." Picture includes Keith Bartlett, Glynn Sweet, Jacquey Chappell, Susan Colverd, Kay Gallie ("Lilian"), Antony Linford and Arnold Peters (the Fire Chief). *(Bryan J. Douglas)*

August 27	People's Opera House, Stockport
September 5	Theatre Royal, Exeter
September 9	Theatre Royal, Burnley
September 12	Newsome's Circus, Edinburgh
November 2	Renz's Circus, Hamburg
November 13	Lecture Theatre, Cardiff
December 29	Grand Theatre, London

By the nature of their construction and use theatres are singularly prone to conflagration and, once a fire has started, to its quickly spreading. But where theatres are concerned fire has been a common leveller, consuming not only the tawdry, plainly combustible temporary theatre in a barn or makeshift building but also the great, spacious and stately homes of the drama. Not only has it laid low the Daventry theatre in Northamptonshire in a thatched barn, the skating rink "theatre" by Abington Park, Northampton, and a glorified booth of wood in the Northamptonshire town of Finedon, but also the theatre dedicated to Shakespeare at Stratford-upon-Avon and even mighty Drury Lane.

It has not always been the most palpably dangerous theatres which have succumbed. Precautions taken in erecting the Northampton Opera House had been notably absent 78 years earlier in the theatre in Marefair. Writing reminiscently but not nostalgically about that old theatre in 1921, when it was about to be demolished, a journalist stated: "To reach the pit visitors had to tunnel down from the front entrance under the side of the orchestra. Had anything happened to cause a stampede there must have been a terrible catastrophe."

Theatres built of wood would seem to be especially hazardous. Such a theatre was burned down in March, 1888, at Oporto, Portugal. There is a particularly horrific account of what happened at the Baquet Theatre there. The Mercury said that the 66 bodies and 53 heaps of "unrecognisable human remains" after the fire were not entirely the direct product of the flames—"There was a rough attendance of the nautical tide-waiter and deck porter in the second gallery and these were pitiless in crushing down all who were weaker than themselves. They used fists and knives to cuff, kick and slash to the front. Young girls, children and women were literally butchered where they stood." There had not been an empty seat at the performance which was a benefit, in a theatre which was formerly a circus, constructed of wood and declared by architects to be unsafe.

In November, 1910, fire struck the 1,000 seater Empire Theatre of Varieties in the Northamptonshire town of Wellingborough. This was a wooden building on brick foundations, rushed up earlier that year to cater for the short-lived skating craze and then turned into a variety and picture hall. It stood at the corner of Gloucester Place and Park Road and went up in flames an hour after the evening performance. The cause was said to be an electric short circuit and it was by electric bell that the 10 firemen were summoned.

At Christmas time in 1912 there was a fire in a wooden auditorium in the nearby town of Finedon. The Daily Chronicle reported: "At Finedon on Sunday the theatre, a wooden structure, was partly destroyed by fire." Dick Whittington and His Cat had occupied the stage of the theatre which belonged to Mr. Harry de Marr and had been standing for two months in Mr. Knight's paddock at the rear of the Gate Inn. This time a rocket was fired to summon the brigade.

At Johnstown, U.S.A., in December, 1889, there was a blaze at a theatre which had been condemned and which was only in use because floods had six months earlier put other, better, houses out of commission. Stables adjacent to the theatre caught fire and in the panic which followed, with people inside trying to get out and people outside trying to get in to rescue relations and friends, 12 were trampled to death and 70 injured.

To attempt a complete catalogue of theatre fires is beyond the scope of this Interlude and I have room to mention only a few more cases especially deserving examination.

The incidence of conflagrations and of deaths resulting from them follows no regular pattern. Lists compiled by Captain Eyre M. Shaw in 1876 and 1889 showed that 20 fires in 1876 caused the total destruction of 20 theatres and 350 deaths; whereas the following year 14 fires caused the destruction of 13 theatres but a mere two deaths. In 1882 there were 35 fires, 20 theatres were destroyed and two died; whereas the year after that 442 deaths resulted from only one more fire and the destruction of the same number of theatres. The history of theatres is punctuated with death and destruction but it is very much a random punctuation.

The earliest fire I have come across is that at the Globe Theatre, London, erected in Bankside in 1599 for Shakespeare's Company; it was burned down and rebuilt in 1613, only to be pulled down by the Puritans in 1644 as their purge of the drama got into gear. The Cockpit in Drury Lane was converted into a theatre in 1616 but was burned down by an apprentice the following year; it was rebuilt as the Phoenix.

The first musichall to be burned down in London was the Oxford, on February 11, 1868, while the doubtful distinction of being the "youngest" theatre in Britain to go up in smoke may belong to the Grand at Derby, opened in Babington Lane in March, 1886, and burned down in May. Edward Terry's Company which was then in residence had appeared at Northampton a few months earlier. J. W. Adams, who played Tootles in *A Weak Woman* and Lord Leadenhall in *The Rocket,* was suffocated in a dressing room. The theatre re-opened the following November. Also a casualty at three months was the Prague Theatre, which took nearly 10 years to build and opened in May, 1881, on the occasion of the wedding of Crown Prince Rudolph and Princess Stephanie. It burned down in August. Thirty were injured—they were "leaning against a rail which fell down" but there were no fatalities.

One of the most rapid fires was that at the Adelphi Theatre in Edinburgh's Broughton Street on Tuesday, May 24, 1853. Following an afternoon rehearsal the outbreak was discovered at a quarter past five by a carpenter, who rushed into the house of the lessee, Mr. Wyndham, which was part of the building. Mrs. Wyndham escaped with their four-day-old baby, the future theatre magnate F. W. Wyndham, while her husband raised the alarm—significantly it was with the various insurance offices, as well as the police office, that he did so. The fire progressed so rapidly that within an hour only the bare walls remained.

The worst single disaster in terms of human life is usually accepted as the one at the Lehman Theatre, St. Petersburg, on February 14, 1836, with over 800 deaths. Second place in this grim league table is usually accorded to the Ring Theatre, Vienna, where 700 perished on December 8, 1881, after a hanging lamp fell just before the performance was due to begin. The previous year some 150 people had been killed in a Nice theatre following a gas explosion which put the lights out. This had been taken as a warning by the authorities in the Austrian capital, the magistrates resolving to take steps to prevent something similar happening in their city. They instructed the Mayor, Julius von Newald, to get on with it but this he failed to do. As soon as he saw flames coming out of the theatre he drove home exclaiming "I am ruined!". Proceedings were taken against him and others accused of neglect.

In other tables of theatre fires I have seen various claims listed in large round figures but whether they can be authenticated is another matter. Here they are, as listed in the Mercury in January, 1904: May 15, 1845, The Theatre, Canton, China, 1,670 dead; 1872, Theatre, Tientsin, 600; April, 1893, The Theatre, Kanil, 2,000.

Other major disasters include the Saragossa Theatre in 1778, with over 600 deaths; the Berditscheff Circus, Russian Poland, in 1883, 300 dead; Consays Theatre, Brooklyn, New York, in 1876 with 283 dead; and casualties of over 100 dead at the Theatre Royal, Quebec, in 1846, and the Leghorn Theatre, Italy, in 1857.

Bolton is among towns which have had more than their fair share of theatre fires. It has had three. The Theatre Royal was burned down in 1852 and rebuilt three years later. The Temple Opera House, in the former Temple Mill in Dawes Street, was burned down in April, 1882, and not rebuilt. Then in January, 1888, the replacement Theatre Royal was burned too. Casualties this time were a donkey and two pet sheep which had appeared in the pantomime *Red Riding Hood* and a cow belonging to the butcher next door, which presumably did not have long to live anyway. A new foundation stone was laid (by Henry Irving) and a new theatre opened in November, 1888.

Arson seems to have been a rare cause of theatre fires but at Bolton a billposter named Robert Preston was charged with this offence after the 1888 fire.

Arson was suspected as the cause of the destruction of His Majesty's Opera House, London, in December, 1867. The fire was said to have been started by Pietro Carnivalli who led the band and whose wife was a singer there. Some grievance was believed to be the motive of the musician who is said to have made a deathbed confession at Bristol in 1910. On the site of the opera house were erected the Carlton Hotel and His Majesty's Theatre and when the hotel burned down in August, 1911, staff from the theatre rescued 20 ladies over the roof while goods from the hotel were piled on the stage of the theatre. The street barriers led to the cancellation of the performance that night at the nearby Haymarket Theatre, because patrons could not reach it.

Lightning was seen to be the cause of the Reading Theatre going up in flames in August, 1894, but the origin of many theatre fires has not been ascertainable. Some saw the wrath of God in the burning down of the Bath Theatre in 1862. Those who believed that theatres should be closed during the whole of Holy Week pointed out that this was the first time this theatre had departed from the rule. It opened on the Wednesday and caught fire on the Friday—Good Friday.

PANIC
—the real killer

In a fire situation, and sometimes in a non-fire situation, panic was often the real killer: it was more dangerous than the flames. Normally the slightest sign, or even rumour, of an outbreak was the signal for a pell-mell retreat by those in the auditorium. It was the rush to get out which caused injury and death rather than the fire. The simple reason for this is that an audience which has taken up to thirty minutes to assemble tries to leave within as many seconds. If the exits are sufficient and the passages sufficiently wide, given an orderly exodus it can be done but if the corridors are too narrow and the exits too few and there is a panic, people can get trampled to death, and many have been. The mad rush to escape can be highly lethal.

One of the first members of the theatrical profession to try to rationalise the subject of fire was the 18th century actor-manager Henry Lee, who related in his memoirs the story of a false alarm at the Aylesbury theatre in about 1790. The "theatre" stood "very near the yard of one of the principal inns." The innkeeper wanted to get hold of his ostler, whose name was William Squire. Suspecting him to be in the audience he went up the gallery steps shouting "William, William." Getting no response he heeded advice that there might be a dozen Williams in the house and instead shouted "Squire, Squire", thus causing a panic, the words being taken for "Fire, Fire."

In his colourful way Lee described screaming, scrambling from the gallery down into the boxes, from the boxes into the pit; every passage was soon clogged up and, the outward doors being hung on the inner side ("a great error in public places" observed Lee), could not be opened, so that no-one could get out.

While he was undoubtedly right about the door hinges, Lee was less intelligent in his general observations: "As regards theatres, accidents may occur from haste or from pressure but accidents may not occur from fire; it is impossible unless the audience choose to set fire to themselves. The grand safety principle is this: there are so many eyes in all parts of the theatre, at least during a performance, that dangers of this kind are sure of being seen and consequently put an end to." How wrong can you be?

Panic in a crush was the cause of an incident in 1794 out of which political capital was made. At the Haymarket Theatre, London, there was no fire but 15 people were trampled to death at a Royal performance on February 3. A Republican leaflet criticised the lack of Royal mourning for the dead. In 1807 a false alarm at Sadlers Wells led to 18 being trampled to death. In 1858 16 died at the Cobourgh, later Victoria Theatre, following a bogus alarm. Fourteen perished in similar circumstances at the Star Theatre, Glasgow, in 1884.

A tiny fire which required only a couple of buckets of water to put out caused 10 deaths at the Theatre Royal, Gateshead, in 1891. During a pantomime performance a woman noticed something smouldering on the floor and led a rush to get out. The entire audience panicked but all got out except those in the gallery. There the door had been bolted and an attendant who heard the to-do and went up to undo it was at once trampled underfoot. When things died down a bit it was thought downstairs that everyone was safe but two men who went up to check found a heap of dead and dying on the gallery steps.

Following a factory fire in London in 1890 a columnist in the Mercury wrote: "It seems odd that though much fuss is made over theatres and musichalls, and very properly too, in case of fire neither churches nor factories, which people go to to find their way to heaven and to earn their bread on earth, are in any way looked after or interfered with. We could point to more than one London church in which, if a fire broke out, the congregation would be like rats in traps."

In a religious context the finest example I have come across of not panicking was in Northampton in September, 1880, during an early meeting of the Salvation Army in the Corn Exchange (now the Top Rank Bingo Hall). The Evening Mail, then in its first year, reported: "For some time a bunch of religious enthusiasts styling themselves the Salvation Army have occupied an upper storey where what are called religious services are held. The Town Fire Brigade was called to the room to extinguish a fire but the service carried on. The Lady Captain said that their business was to save souls: that of the firemen to save their bodies."

Idealistic perhaps, but if all theatre audiences had been motivated by even a portion of this selfless principle many lives would have been saved, along with their souls.

Arson was said to be the cause of the fire at Bolton's Theatre Royal in January, 1888, in which the casualties were a donkey and two pet sheep appearing in *Red Riding Hood* and a cow belonging to the butcher next door. *(Courtesy of Harry N. Greatorex)*

LIGHT, HEAT & SMOKE

Lighting, heating and smoking are three factors to be considered in discussing the question of fire in the theatre. Lighting because so many fires resulted from the candles once used for illumination and from flames and explosion of the gas which replaced candles; heating because in the days before central heating, blazes could occur when coal or coke fell off open fires; and smoking because of the danger from dropped ash and cigar and cigarette butts, especially when smouldering became flame after audience and staff had gone home, both at the front and back of the stage.

The replacement of candles by gas was not a 100 per cent success. At Covent Garden, where gas had been installed in 1817, it was actually taken out in 1828 because of the smell of the locally manufactured gas. In turn, but for other reasons, some actors did not take kindly to gas being supplanted by electricity. It was considered a harsher light and in respect of the Lyceum Theatre, London, Ellen Terry wrote in her memoirs: "When I saw the effect on the faces of the electric footlights I entreated Henry (Irving) to have gas restored and he did. We used gas footlights and gas limes there until we left the theatre for good in 1902. To this I attribute much of the beauty of our lighting."

Certainly the Northampton Opera House was lit by gas until the turn of the century. In the fields of domestic and street lighting, of course, gas held sway much longer than in the theatre. My grandfather dropped dead of a heart attack in 1948 when he reached up to pull the control turning off the gas lamp in his living room.

Both in respect of candles and gas there was not only the fire danger but also that of the heat generated by the flames and both consumed the oxygen in the atmosphere. Writing in the Mechanic and Chemist in June, 1839, Sir Frederick French said that one wax candle consumed as much oxygen as two men while 240 candles would deteriorate the atmosphere as much as 700 men. The chemist Lavoisier worked it out that the oxygen in a theatre diminished by a quarter from the start to finish of a performance.

Until the late 19th century the auditorium normally remained lit during the performance and in summer this could produce a heat that was quite oppressive. There was also another aspect of the matter. In July, 1881, the Era observed: "This hot weather the lighting of theatres is worthy of more attention than it receives and a rapid decline of the dramatic season is owing more to the temperature of the theatres than to any apathy respecting the performance. The immense heat from the footlights is equal of itself to several fires burning in front of the stage and every breath of air that comes from the stage carries this heated atmosphere into the body of the house. In some houses the auditorium is chiefly lighted and the atmosphere is not oppressive while in others where the auditorium is completely dark it is like sitting in an oven." The Era considered that few audiences were prepared to sit in the dark and "We should not like them to miss the pleasure to ordinary playgoers to see a well dressed and refined audience."

It is surprising that more fires did not result from the old methods of heating. In 18th and early 19th century advertisements there are many references to "fires kept constantly in the pit", as in Henry Jackman's announcement at Daventry, Northants, where special reassurance was needed in the first season of the new theatre in 1836—because of the walls not being dried out. Jackman's solicitor friend Thomas Lewis Gery advised postponement of the opening because "A number of persons would be afraid of going into a building which is so damp until it has had the heat of summer upon it." The following November we find Jackman assuring his patrons that he has had a stove fixed in the pit "where a fire is constantly kept and I trust the theatre will be found perfectly warm and comfortable."

Jackman's theatre did not burn down but a previous Daventry manager was less fortunate. This was Mr. Richards who in February, 1803, went to the ladies' dressing room at about 5 p.m., prior to opening the house, and found it in flames, a hot coal having dropped from the stove on to the mat. "Providentially none of the performers were come to dress nor any of the audience assembled." The fire communicated itself to the canvas which had been used to drape the inside of the building, which was in fact a thatched barn. Soon all was lost, along with the theatrical apparatus, an adjacent barn, and the tools of the carpenter who had fitted up the stage.

The most recent local example of primitive and potentially dangerous heating is at the old Empire Variety Hall, in the grounds of the Plough Hotel. Contemporary Pressmen described the establishment in the usual glowing terms but writing reminiscently in the Independent a journalist recalled Charles Collette singing "in the winter of 1895 in a round of excellent songs at the old hall called the Empire, a primitive building with a corrugated iron roof and warmed by huge braziers of glowing coke in the auditorium."

To smoke or not to smoke has at times been a vexed issue in theatre management, just as it is today in the field of health. Safety was not the only aspect to be considered but clearly it was one. Legally speaking the odd position used to be that you could smoke in the musichall, derived from the concert room of a tavern, but that you could not do so in the legitimate theatre. This was somewhat illogical and indeed completely so when musichall and legitimate theatre operated in the same building, as at the Northampton Opera House with the introduction of twice-nightly variety in 1908. It brought a relaxation of the no smoking rule and at the end of the variety season a reminder that smoking was not now permitted.

One early smoking restriction was of a partial nature, it would appear. At Abingdon, Berkshire, in March, 1827, Henry Jackman's posters (which he printed on his own portable press) carried the amusing injunction: "Gentlemen are requested not to bring Segars to the theatre."

On the reopening night of the old Northampton theatre in 1861, following its being taken over by William Thomas who also ran the tavern musichall on the opposite side of Horseshoe Street, the stage manager Harry Haines announced from the stage that the objectionable practice of smoking would not be tolerated under any circumstances and that any parties violating the regulation would be turned out.

By the following year Thomas's brief reign was over and a report in December, 1862, stated: "Smoking was carried on in all parts of the house and this although it is stated on the bills that smoking is strictly forbidden and that 'Police officers will be in attendance to enforce decorum and order.' " That night we read too that people in the gods were "kicking large lumps of wood off the front of the gallery and hurling them down on the heads of the pit along with lighted bits of paper", a practice scarcely in the best interests of fire prevention.

In 1922 Milton Bode organised a smoking poll at the Northampton Opera House. Voting papers were issued to patrons, a copy of the ballot slip being found among the papers of the late Mr. T. Osborne Robinson. I have not come across an announcement of the result but it was probably a negative for not until three years later does one find an advertisement stating: "Smoking now permitted in all parts."

Today smoking is not allowed in Northampton Repertory Theatre (the former Opera House) but the rule has not applied during the entire 50 years of repertory there and I recall some actors and actresses telling me that they knew they were losing the attention of members of the audience when a red line of glowing cigarette ends appeared.

F. W. Wyndham, the theatrical impresario, was rescued as a four-day-old baby from one of Edinburgh's theatre fires, the one at the Adelphi in 1853. The fire pictured here, however, was at the city's Theatre Royal in 1875. *(Courtesy of Harry N. Greatorex)*

DANCERS
in Danger

In its day gas certainly improved the lighting of theatres, and even when electricity came along, some stayed with gas by choice. But gas also made the theatre a much more dangerous place to be in, especially for women dancers. Dangers there had been when the footlights were candles but gas increased the peril by multiplying the sources. It was used also in lighting effects which had not previously been possible.

The proximity of their muslin skirts to the gas jets caused a number of dancers to be burned, often fatally. Writing in the Mercury in February, 1864, a London correspondent surmised: "I suppose Lord Raynham will now bring in a Bill on the subject of ballet dancers and their skirts. In the meantime the Lord Chamberlain has declared that he can do nothing but make the managers take certain precautions to prevent such accidents as happened the other night to Columbine at the Britannia Theatre. That dresses can be made uninflammable there is no doubt and that managers can be made to supply such dresses is equally certain. But, as Mr. Webster pathetically pointed out the other day, the garments which usually catch fire are undergarments, with which the manager cannot interfere. So I suppose that if the ladies of the ballet will not guard themselves against getting into a blaze, the managers cannot be expected to do more than provide the means to put them out."

At Northampton in April, 1870, Miss Lilly Davis, a dancer, tripped and fell on to the footlights when her light dress became instantly ablaze. She was severely burned and was in bed for weeks.

In his book Victorian Ballet Girl Ivor Guest dealt mainly with the story of Clara Webster who died in 1844 after catching fire on stage but he also gave much grimly relevant background material. Someone had even written a poem on the subject:

> There are perils dire
> Which oft beset the ballet girl and worst of all is fire
> Most deadly of the deadly foes that threaten player folk
> An enemy who never sleeps, whose power ne'er is broke
> While of the groups theatrical the greatest risk who run
> Are lightly costumed ballerinas, escape for them there's none
> A spark upon the muslin dry, then instantly it lights
> Into a blaze like lightning's flash, at sea, on summer nights
> A blazing mass of agony, all maddened which they fly
> Yet fly not from the enemy who dooms them thus to die
> That shrivels up the growing limbs, and face and form alas
> Leaving of female loveliness, a charred and calcined mass
> Ah happy if they die at once, and from life's stage retire
> Than linger on in torment from the all remorseless fire.

In 1868 an article in the Lancet described the risks run by the dancer as scarcely less than those of a soldier in the front line and asked whether Parliament was never going to legislate on the use of non-inflammable material. The immediate cause of the comment was the death of Fanny Smith (real name Frances Ann Higginbotham) whose skirts caught fire in Day's Concert Hall, Birmingham, on Friday, March 20, 1868. A steel pen grinder by day and dancer by night she survived three days. Others, as the poem stated, lingered longer in torment. Such as Emma Livry, the great hope of the French ballet, who caught light at a Paris Opera rehearsal and was for months in agony.

A remarkable example of the show being carried on by an actress despite the fact that she had become ignited was that of Madame Albertazzi who was appearing in *Night Dancers* at the Princess's Theatre, London, in 1846. As Giselle she was about to rise from a bed of roses to warn Albert of his peril when her skirt took flame from one of the blue lamps used to colour a tuft of flowers. She rushed wildly about until backstage staff came to the rescue and tore off the burning robe. A great cheer arose from the audience and continued during the rest of the scene as she carried on "in the skeleton of a skirt." The Sheffield newspaper in which I read the account advised the steeping of such stage dresses in alum.

Ivor Guest mentions numerous other cases including Ernestine Marra, burnt in the last act of *Le Prophete* at Marseilles in 1854; Fraulein Leinsitt in Hamburg in 1856; and the same year Pauline Genet of Niblo's Gardens, New York; Annie Fowler, severely burned as Columbine in pantomime at the Grecian Theatre, London, in 1859; Fanny Julia Power, who died at Liverpool in 1862; a Miss Smith in pantomime at the Princess's Theatre, London, in 1863, Lucia Padovan at Trieste in the same year; Leontine Chatenay at Rio de Janeiro in 1867; Amalia Tromba and Emilia Alsaniello, a double tragedy at Naples in 1868; Topsy Elliott, "cruelly burnt" at the South London Palace in 1877.

A dancer who caught fire in 1855 did not at first realise it. "You're on fire!" shouted members of the Plymouth audience as Madamoiselle Julie (Julie Annie McEwan) stepped back over a row of burners illuminating a backcloth of a fairy lake. The dancer, who was in the role of the Fairy of the Lake, died three weeks later. The Coroner observed: "It is scarcely in my province to interfere with the dressing of ladies or to dictate the material. Dresses steeped in alum and water would not ignite but girls say that it spoils the colour and set of the dresses."

In this field France set an example. When, in 1857, Emperor Napoleon III heard of a flame-proof salt he ordered a demonstration. Two years later a decree made obligatory the treatment of all scenery and costumes used at the opera. One dancer, Emma Livry, put into writing her refusal to wear a dress that was Carteronised (after the inventor Carteron) and was subsequently incinerated.

England's Clara Webster, the main subject of Mr. Guest's book, was burned at Covent Garden in 1844 during a performance of Balfe's new opera *The Daughter of St. Mark*. She became a pillar of flame and died three days later, at the age of 23. The hands of a stage hand who tried to save her were burned to the bone. At the inquest the Coroner gave a demonstration of how material that had been impregnated would not burn.

Being in "drag" may have led to the death of Leading Seaman Arthur Armstrong of H.M.S. Pembroke in a fire at the Garrison Theatre, Chatham, during amateur theatricals by the Blue Jackets in May, 1902. His dress caught fire.

FIGHTERS

too Feeble

At a meeting of Northampton Town Council in December, 1876, Alderman Joseph Gurney, who was for many years secretary of the Marefair Theatre, gloomily predicted that if his house in Kingsthorpe Road ever caught fire it would have burned down before the fire brigade, and adequate water supplies, arrived.

Apart from the availability of water, Victorian Fire Brigades were a Fred Karno affair compared with what we have today, both with regard to their composition and their equipment. In the early part of the century reliance was placed on the private brigades organised by insurance companies to safeguard buildings on which policies had been taken out with them. If a property did not have their "mark" affixed to it, they would show no interest. Following the Covent Garden fire of March, 1856, the London Fire Brigade confined its efforts to protecting insured property surrounding the theatre. When local authorities did start to get organised there was a reluctance for the brigade to go to fires outside its area.

As well as the Town Fire Brigade there was the Northampton Volunteer Fire Brigade, formed in 1864 by Mr. Richard Phipps, a partner in the principal local brewing firm, and in 1878, partly by subscription and partly by grant, Northampton bought its first steam fire engine, which was not to be replaced, by a motor engine, until 1910.

As regards the theatre there was an awareness of the fire hazard for at a meeting of the Town Hall, Survey and Buildings Committee which considered the plans for the new theatre in November, 1883, Councillor Gibbs asked to be reassured on the safety question. He was told by Mr. Charles Dorman, who represented the architect C. J. Phipps, that there were adequate exits and that the staircases were to be of concrete and over 5'6" wide. By means of the duplication of exits the house could be cleared in three minutes.

In 1885, two years before the Opera House fire, Captain Pilgrim confidently predicted that his brigade could deal with any fire which might arise. These words, spoken at the Volunteer brigade's annual dinner at the Stag's Head, Abington Street, were brave indeed considering that this was the town which had almost been wiped out in the Dreadful Fire of September, 20, 1675. He also mentioned that a fire escape was due in a few weeks time. When it duly arrived Councillor Stanton told the Town Council that he did not like the idea of its being kept in Guildhall Road because it would be useless for fires in the north of the town. In fact it was to be handy for the fire at the theatre, which was in that very thoroughfare.

The following April, of 1886, saw fire bells installed in the homes of the firemen so that they could more easily be summoned. Five years earlier a regulation had been made in Berlin that all theatres must be connected by electricity to the nearest Fire Brigade station

It was ironic that during the theatre's summer break of 1886 particular attention was paid to the fire question. A Press account explained that in most theatres the borders, strips of canvas representing sky or ceiling, were divided by parallel wires across the stage, a system used at the Derby Theatre which had recently burned down. At Northampton Mr. Tarry installed wire netting which "puts fire from this cause quite out of the question."

Within months, however, the Opera House stage was in ruins and there followed an inquiry into the efficiency of the fire fighting arrangements. The year 1887 had seen not only the Opera House fire but one much more serious in financial terms. Premises at the corner of Lady's Lane and Wood Street, originally used as a currier's but employed for 13 years as a shoe factory by Henry Randall, burned down in November. Damage was estimated at £15,000.

The "inquest" of 1888 considered dismissing the old Town Brigade and introducing one consisting largely of police officers under the control of the Chief Constable. They would receive suitable training from specially appointed officers but would become firemen only when the bell rang. In a budget for the new set-up it must have appealed to the economically minded councillers of the day when they noted that the cost of the Chief Constable-cum-Fire Chief was set down as: nil. Councillor Manfield, another shoe manufacturer, stated that his firm had found it difficult to get fire insurance because of the inefficient state of the Fire Brigade. Councillor Norman objected to the old brigade being dismissed but Alderman Gurney said that there was no sort of feeling against the brigade or any of its members.

That year fire fighting came in for dramatic treatment on the Opera House stage. In May, 1888, Captain Gilbert Pomeroy's Company performed *The Still Alarm,* in the third Act of which there was "a copy of the Central Fire Station, New York," and the audience saw "the harnessing of horses to the engine and departure to the fire—a faithful replica of the system now in vogue in America's Fire Department, which Captain Shaw, of the London Fire Brigade, has recommended for adoption but which, mainly on account of costs, has not yet been done."

The man who took over as manager of the Opera House the following February was an ex-fireman (as well as a former member of a Lifeboat crew!). He was Charles Rider Noble who a couple of months after his arrival showed a Press representative round the theatre and pointed out new fire apparatus including a complete system of hosepipes and hydrants "so that we could attack and quench a fire at any point either at the back of the house or the front and extinguish it within a very few seconds." The hose was fitted with an attachment "on the new patent principle now used by the London Fire Brigade—if you have seen the Northampton Fire Brigade at work you must have noticed that they are forced to spend many seconds screwing on the hose to the supply pipe. Here nothing of the kind is needed. The pipes are fitted with a spring cap in the simplest possible manner."

The theatre staff were also to be trained. "I am going to drill every man on the staff, flymen, scene shifters and all the lot. Some evening when it is convenient and I have got them properly drilled I intend to ask the audience to keep their seats after the performance and we shall show them the preparations for coping with fire." The theatre, he claimed, was the best protected in the provinces.

The house appears to have been spared further outbreaks apart from a small incident at about the start of the 1939-45 War when smoke was seen coming from the central chandelier. Mr. Harold Nash, who was playing the piano at the theatre at that time and who is a Patron of this book, recalls: "It happened during one of the intervals. The power was turned off and the chandelier was lowered by Mr. Fred Pratt, the stage manager, and attended to."

Luton-born Captain Pilgrim, who led the fire fighters at the 1887 fire, died in May, 1915, aged 70. He had led the volunteer brigade for a dozen years, until its disbandment.

LAWS
too Lax

Meantime what was going on in the legal arena? Safety in theatres was controlled by a section of the Theatres Act of 1843, the law which restored legality to most of the country's theatres. In February, 1864, the Lord Chamberlain wrote to theatre managers in London on the subject and in 1877 a Select Committee of the House of Commons inquired into the best means of preventing fires in the Metropolis, especially in connection with theatres, musichalls, and other places of entertainment.

The Lord Chamberlain at the time was the Marquis of Hertford who expressed the opinion that the only weapon he then had, of being able to withhold licences, was too blunt an instrument. He would like to see a special officer appointed who would be responsible for the construction of theatres and their inspection thereafter. But, he said, it would not be possible for him to control theatres throughout the country as well as in the capital—this would have to be left to the local authorities. As regards the 600 musichalls in London he did not see how they could be brought under his control without a very large staff indeed and the Lord Chamberlain being made Minister of Public Amusements, as was the case in France.

To some extent the Marquis seemed complacent, saying that there had been only three theatre fires in the area under his jurisdiction within the previous 20 years and none within the past decade. No lives had been lost except at the Victoria Theatre in 1858, and those due to panic, not fire. But since the Brooklyn fire (of 1876) he had caused theatres to be inspected regularly. He confessed that some of the smaller houses were so unsatisfactory that the consequences of a panic would be fearful.

A year later came the Metropolis Building and Management Acts Amendment Act which covered London theatres and included 17 regulations dealing with construction, separation, proscenium walls, enclosure of staircases, separate exits, heating, ventilation, separation of scene docks, carpenters' shops, and the provision of fire mains and apparatus etc. While the Act gave full power to the Metropolitan Board of Works to regulate the construction of all new theatres, musichalls etc. its powers over existing buildings were very limited. Defects could be remedied only if it could be done at "moderate expense." Furthermore the Board's powers covered only two-thirds of the theatres in what is generally regarded as Metropolitan London. And the provinces were still left to look after themselves.

In 1881 a return showing means of exit from theatres was called for and an Order was made in the House of Lords that April.

The following February a London meeting of dramatic critics passed a resolution demanding the setting up of a Royal Commission on theatres and places of public amusement from the point of view of public safety.

The safety bolt enabling theatre doors to open outwards under pressure was invented in 1883 by Mr. Arnott of the Lyceum Theatre. The Mercury commented: "One advantage is that being once unfastened it cannot be re-bolted by accident. A disaster similar to that at Sunderland is thus rendered impossible." This referred to a shocking occurrence in June that year in which 183 children were suffocated at a conjuring entertainment. They were in the gallery and at the close of the performance rushed down to claim prizes and piled up behind a door which became closed. One of the first places where the safety bolt was installed was the London Pavilion Musichall where it was among changes made at the instigation of the Board of Works.

REFORMERS
Shaw, Godwin & Irving

Three men were pioneers in trying to get the law tightened up in this field. They were a fire brigade chief, an architect who never himself designed a theatre, and a leading actor. The fire chief was Captain Eyre M. Shaw; the architect was Edward Godwin, who designed Northampton's Town Hall; and the actor was Henry Irving, whose ideas for a safety theatre were translated into a building by Milton Bode and Edward Compton, who were to be joint owners of Northampton's theatre.

Captain Shaw wrote a book on the subject. Forthright indeed was the preface to his first edition of 1876: "Our own country represents a humiliating example of the entire absence of any system or method whatever."

Thirteen years later, in the preface to his second edition, he recalled: "When I first became officially connected with the safety of life and property in 1860 the point most frequently and urgently forced upon my observation was the extreme danger of many buildings in which large numbers of persons were congregated together, including schools, churches, and theatres, and by degrees it became impressed on me that of all buildings theatres were the most dangerous."

Shaw faced a dilemma. Should he, as he put it, cause a panic by making the facts known, or would this compound the danger . . . for of all things in theatres panic itself can be more lethal than flames. But as years went by and little happened he felt impelled to speak out, his special targets being "monstrosities in the way of theatres which have disgraced our cities for years."

Shaw peered and poked into every corner and cranny of theatres in making detailed suggestions as to how the audience might be protected both from the flames and from their own selfish panic. A night watch might save theatres from conflagration he said, though he was far less interested in protecting the property than the persons—although he worked out that between 1867 and 1868 the 15 theatres destroyed in Europe and America represented a loss of £650,000, of which one alone, the Theatre du Sultan, Constantinople, accounted for £240,000. Between 1878 and 1889 a total of 2,215 persons had perished in theatre fires.

Division of theatres into before and behind the curtain was the major single point made by Shaw who saw that it was often across the open door of the proscenium that the flames came leaping. At this point the entire building should be divided into two by means of a firewall starting in the basement and going right through to the roof and above it to a height of from four to six feet. At the "great opening" itself an effective protection could be obtained by means of a metal curtain which could be dropped at a moment's notice, worked by steel or iron chains.

Second in importance he placed the substitution of electricity for gas as the means of illumination. This should be compulsory as it was already in Spain. A Royal decree published in the Madrid Gazette of March, 1888, forbade absolutely the use of gas in theatres. After six months grace all theatres in the city had to be lit by electricity and when applying for a licence the owner or manager had to submit a sample of the wire used. At the time Shaw's second edition emerged every Madrid theatre was thus lit and the enactment was about to be extended to every other Spanish city.

Other points made by Shaw were numerous. They concerned simplicity of exits and the existence of obstruction-free surroundings: he drew attention to the existence in one foreign country of a minimum 13 feet distance between a theatre and other buildings. Handrails should be provided in passages and iron staircases outside emergency exits. There should be a limit on the numbers of audiences "in the same way as steamships, omnibuses etc." and "it should be a misdemeanour here, as on the other side of the Atlantic, to occupy the aisles or passageways between the seats with camp-stools or chairs or to allow persons to stand in the passageways during performance". The placing of carpenters' shops in the roofs of many theatres was a danger, being right over the main gaslight. Internal dressing rooms should be of solid heatproof material not as sometimes happened "a mere collection of apparently temporary fittings."

Adverts covered several pages of Shaw's second edition. Merryweather and Sons recommended high pressure fire mains and automatic sprinklers on stage and in dressing rooms, operating as soon as the temperature reached 150 degrees Fahrenheit. George Jackson and Sons boosted their patent fibrous plaster—"light, easily fixed, and non-inflammable"—and listed theatres where it had been used, including the Northampton one. There was Bell's asbestos paint and stage curtains which had undergone the test of being saturated in paraffin and subjected to the full power of the footlights for one-and-a-half hours without damage. Fireproof doors and panic doors were advertised by John Tann. A. Hutchinsons trumpeted the merits of their india rubber hoses. James Stott had a patent gas governor and escape detector. Fireproof cement was on offer by Joseph Robinson and Co. The Worthington Pumping Engine Company inserted a picture of one of their firepumps—"one of the most reliable in the market.". E. H. Bayley pointed out that they had been sole builders and contractors to the

Metropolitan Fire Brigade for 18 years and that their telescopic and fly ladder escapes had been used at all the big London fires. Iron staircases suitable for fire escapes were offered by the St. Pancras Iron Works.

This was fairly early days for the telephone—invented in 1876—but the United Telephone Co. of Cannon Street, London, took a page to recommend the benefits of a theatre being on the phone so that "instant communication can be obtained—in some instances both night and day—with the Head Fire Brigade Station, whence wires radiate to all the local Fire Stations."

Godwin was a theatre architect manqué—he always wanted to design one but such a commission never came the way of this somewhat unpredictable man. A pity, because otherwise he might have designed the first "safety theatre." His ideas, many coinciding with those of Shaw, appear sound. He compiled detailed reports which he sent to the authorities in 1876 and 1882. Regarding dressing rooms he spoke of the danger of "wood partitions, stairs, and floors rendered very dry by the amount of gas consumed behind the scenes" yet "found in all sorts of places about the stage, sometimes under it, sometimes at the side, sometimes at the back."

After the Exeter disaster Henry Irving consulted Alfred Darbyshire, an architect, who recalls his own reactions in The Art of the Victorian Stage, which he wrote in 1907. One of his ideas was that no opening should be allowed in the wall between front and back stage, other than the proscenium itself; the only means of communication between the auditorium and the backstage area should be external, he advised.

This is a good illustration of how there are two viewpoints to almost every question, for the Northampton theatre had had such an additional opening inserted as a safety measure in 1886! As the Press had reported: "The two feet thick wall in the manager's box has been pierced and a door fixed with a staircase leading down to stage level. By this means the manager can go from front to back of the house easily. This would be an incalculable advantage in case of groundless alarm where it often needs but a few words from one in authority to allay the excitement and remove the danger. Formerly the only communication was through the pit and this was often blocked when the house was very crowded. There was no help for it but to leave the theatre and go via the entrance round Angel Street into Cow Lane and enter by the stage door, involving great loss of time when in the emergency alluded to every moment would be of priceless value."

Ideas put forward by Irving and Darbyshire in the Daily Telegraph in October, 1887, were that the stage must have a fireproof roof and a large smokeshaft with glazed louvres—"in case of fire, the proscenium opening being closed, both flame and smoke will at once make for the shaft."

A footnote in the book states that these ideas were incorporated in Darbyshire's designs for the New Theatre Royal at Exeter and the Palace of Varieties, Manchester, but what was heralded as the first "Safety Theatre" erected on the principles outlined by Irving was the one opened by Milton Bode and Edward Compton at Dalston on July 25, 1898. The architects were Messrs. Wylson and Long, of 10 King William Street, The Strand, London. The Era reported: "It has been many years since Sir Henry Irving suggested a house of this class and called it his patent safety theatre but it has been reserved for Messrs. Bode and Compton to be the first to put the principles then suggested into practice as far as the site and surroundings would allow." The main difference was that the house was on two levels only. There was a part called a gallery but it was not on a separate tier, being instead at the rear of the circle. This obviated the danger of having a gallery higher than the proscenium arch—which was liable to cause fumes from any stage fire to rise and suffocate the gallery occupants, as it did at Exeter.

Undoubtedly the biggest single invention in theatre safety was the safety curtain. One of the earliest of these was at Drury Lane itself where it was fitted in the new theatre of 1794 along with a large water tank in the roof. It did not, however, prevent the theatre being burned down 14 years later.

From Liverpool there were reports of a novel idea in safety curtains. In February, 1882, the Era described an invention by Henry Bennett, of Bennett Brothers, of that city, of a curtain incorporating water pipes two inches in diameter, with holes punched in them at one-eighth inch intervals. When it was demonstrated to the local Watch Committee, the Chief Constable, and Mr. E. Saker, lessee of the Alexandra Theatre, a fire on one side which was constantly stoked up for half-an-hour did not penetrate the curtain. Nearly 30 years later, in 1911, there was a very similar report of the invention by Fred Wilkins and Bros. Ltd., of Liverpool, of a "new" type of curtain which when lowered made contact with the water supply by means of special valves at its two bottom corners. Water flowed up through tubes comprising the frame and returned down the back of the curtain through nozzles placed along the horizontals, thus providing a thin film of water running down it. Thus it kept the curtain cool and absorbed the heat. It could be operated from several points both backstage and in the auditorium, by means of breaking a glass and operating a switch.

Two years earlier a faulty curtain had stopped the show at the Lyceum, London. After being lowered at the end of Act II of *Two Little Vagabonds,* it refused to rise again. The manager could not even go on stage to make his announcement that the performance would have to be abandoned and did so from the orchestra pit.

SAFETY

of the Amateur

While attention was being paid to professional theatre, what of performances by amateurs? The late Victorian period produced a great upsurge of activity in amateur drama, in which middle class and even titled people were to the fore. Good causes of a wide variety were served, such as when Lady Erskine of Spratton Hall, Northants, performed in aid of lighting the village streets. A few of these amateur shows took place in the splendid surroundings of the professional home of the drama, in Guildhall Road, but the vast majority were in make-shift premises fitted up for the purpose.

These were also in the widest possible variety. Members of the Spencer family might perform in the long library of their stately home at Althorp, Northants, as indeed they did in January, 1909 or 1910, when the casts of *The Hat, Foolish Jack* and *The Baffled Spinster* included the Hon. Delia Spencer, Miss Cynthia Spencer, the Hon. Lavinia Spencer, the Hon. George Spencer, the Hon. Cecil Spencer and Viscount Althorp as Mons. Levereur, a mesmerist, dressed in a gorgeous robe, with turban and magic wand.

Lesser amateurs might perform in an old coach house, like the one at Ashby St. Ledgers which in June, 1900, was the scene of performances in aid of church restoration, by permission of Mr. C. H. B. Whitworth.

Many amateur, as well as some professional, performances were given in Northampton Town Hall. This was the scene of the inaugural performance in February, 1895, of Northampton Amateur Dramatic and Musical Society, of which both local Members of Parliament, Henry Labouchere, the Radical, and "Dolly" Drucker, the Dutch-born Conservative, were vice-presidents.

A year later a Northampton Catholic Amateur Dramatic Society was formed with a Roman Catholic priest, Father O'Sullivan, as its president. Three Reverend Fathers were in the audience at the inaugural performance, of *The Irish Tutor* and *A Day At The Fair,* at the Clare Street Schools.

The fashion in minstrel entertainment set professionally by the Matthews C.C.C. Christy Minstrels at the St. James Hall, London, was paralleled in the amateur field so that scarcely any town was without a troupe and many villages had them too. For example we find the Northampton Amateur Minstrels giving a vocal and instrumental entertainment at the Gymnasium, Abington Street, Northampton, in February, 1892, while in the village of Gayton the following April the Sunflower Minstrels performed in aid of a girl whose father had been killed in an accident in the village brickyards. In April, 1898, the parish rooms of Little Bowden, near Market Harborough, were the scene of an entertainment by a "Nigger Troupe" connected with the Church Lads Brigade.

There were military amateur dramatics. The theatre at the R. A. Barracks at Weedon, Northants, was "not a very imposing or commodious memorial to Thespis" but, said the Mercury, it evoked "a laudable desire to foster a taste for amateur theatre among the garrison."

Schoolrooms were a popular venue for the amateurs. In Guilsborough Grammar School in January, 1897, Countess Spencer attended a dramatic performance organised by Mrs. T. M. Jameson for the relief of the "pitiably severe distress in the Metropolis." In April the following year the schoolroom at Brixworth housed an entertainment organised by Lady Erskine and Mrs. Jameson, including two scenes from *The School for Scandal.*

One of the most interesting of Northampton's amateur drama groups was in the paternalistic drapery establishment of Adnitts Brothers, in the Drapery (where Debenhams is today). Its performers were drawn from a staff who largely lived on the premises and the shows were usually given in their own dining room. But when they decided to give a performance for the Good Samaritan Society and the Drapers, Warehousemen and Clerks School, Purley, Surrey, in March, 1896, they moved to the Town Hall. Scenery from the theatre was lent by Charles Rider Noble, and furniture was provided by Jefferys, an establishment still going very strong in Gold Street.

I came across an 1899 reference to Lady Erskine and Mrs. Jameson being members of the Northamptonshire Village Kyrle Society which "has performed in many villages." The society had been formed three years earlier to "organise the musical and dramatic abilities of the neighbourhood in order to provide free entertainments in the local workhouses and villages." The joint secretary and treasurer was Miss C. Pattinson, of Brixworth.

Thus, all over the county there were amateur performances in all sorts of premises, some built partly with entertainment in mind and with some regard to safety for large numbers, but others with no claims in that direction and no supervision by the authorities. Ought they to be brought under the same strictures as were now applied to the professional theatre? That was the question. In April, 1883, a Bill put forward by the Earl of Onslow sought to permit the performance of stage plays in unlicensed premises, if the aim was to assist charity. It was defeated.

In Northamptonshire the answer to the question was yes and it began to be applied rather earlier in the town than in the rural areas. In November, 1890, we find Northampton Watch and Theatrical Committee being rather particular about an application for performances to take place in St. Michael's Schools. The committee sent a sub committee to inspect the place and insisted on three conditions: that lobby doors opening inwards must be taken off their hinges or replaced by doors opening outwards; that gas lights on the stage must be protected; and that a police constable must attend the performance to see that the first two conditions were observed. Not until July, 1898, do we find the County Council discussing a code drawn up after canvassing other counties to see what they did. Councillor Denton thought it quite unworkable—there was not a school in the county with doors opening outwards and with two exits. The chairman said if the rules were to be binding on schools then rural drama would come to an end. Councillor Simpson said amateur theatricals gave a great deal of pleasure during the winter. On the other hand Councillor Gotch warned that if they did not act there might be a disaster before long.

LOSS
& occasional Profit

Who are the losers in theatre fires? Well there are some who lose their lives or are injured. There are the obvious losers of money and property—the owners, managers, permanent staff, companies appearing at the theatre, adjacent businesses relying for custom on the passing trade of patrons going to and from their entertainment . . . and there is also the general public represented by those passing patrons.

The owners may lose their building or its value by being under-insured, especially in times of inflation such as we are now passing through. But even in stable times many owners found themselves under-insured when the unthinkable happened and their theatre was burned down. Even such an important house as the almost brand-new Prague Theatre, which went up in flames in 1881 was insured for only two-fifths of the £100,000 which it had cost to build. When Drury Lane burned down in 1808 the loss was estimated at £250,000 but the insurance cover was only £35,000. The owner, Richard Brinsley Sheridan, play-wright and politician, was thus ruined. The Northampton Opera House was in a more fortunate position at the time of the fire of 1887 because the manager Isaac Tarry had effected the policy through his own auctioneers' office (and probably took a commission on the transaction). Owners may also lose their income, by way of rent.

Managers and staff, both front and back stage, may lose their livelihood, if only temporarily while rebuilding takes place. A company on tour might lose not only its week's work but the apparatus and costumes which it needs for the rest of the tour. Pit musicians may lose instruments, as they did at Northampton where all that was left of Mr. Nind's bass viol was the carved scroll.

Equipment could also be burned in transit between theatres. During Henry Irving's tour which had begun at Northampton in 1903 the theatrical train was en route from Leicester to Halifax when a spark set fire to some of the scenery, including that for *The Merchant of Venice*. In March, 1906, a fire in trucks on a train at Nuneaton destroyed the scenery of several theatrical companies.

Sympathy for those who have suffered in theatre fires has usually been forth-coming in practical form. At Northampton the authorities speeded up formali-ties to allow the old theatre to be brought back into use. Even the drama-hating Vicar of All Saints, Canon R. B. Hull, who had a hand in the old theatre's current use by the Church Army, seems to have been obliging. Props were lent by the authorities of the St. Andrew's (mental) Hospital from its 300-seat theatre opened the previous year. At Northampton, of course, it was only properties and scenery owned by the theatre which were burned because the *Jim The Penman* Company gear had just been removed that incendiary Saturday night and that of the *Les Cloches de Corneville* Company had not yet arrived. In the case of the musicians' loss of instruments it was to a degree a case of self-help for they played at the concert aimed at compensating them. The night the Compton Comedy Company was born at Southport, February 7, 1881, there was a fire in the Worcester Musichall, operating in the Corn Exchange, following a perfor-mance by the American C.C.C. Christy Minstrels. Offers of help in this case were the placing at their disposal of the Theatre Royal by the lessee, Mr. W. Gomersal; aid with props and costumes by the local amateur Christy Minstrels; and the loaning of instruments by local music dealers. In March, 1914, help was extended to the Burgess and Barrett Company who were appearing in *Little Jack Horner* at the Grand Theatre, Chorley, when this wooden building was destroyed by fire. Donations to relieve their straitened circumstances included £5, the proceeds of both houses that night at the Pavilion Musichall, and £2 10s. from a matinee given at the town's New Theatre Royal by Mr. C. Hamilton Baines.

And what of the public? What they lost was the means of being entertained. The degree of loss to any particular community would depend on what alterna-tives were available; where there were two or more theatres the public could turn to the remaining one(s). If the law at any particular time restricted the number of theatres then the loss would be all the more keenly felt. This, of course, was precisely what the repressive Act of 1737 did in London, restricting all legitimate performances to the theatres with a Royal Patent, and this situation obtained, with a few exceptions, until the reforming Act of 1843. The Drury Lane and Covent Garden theatres were the principal "Patents".

The original Drury Lane theatre which had been erected near the site of the old Cockpit opened on May 7, 1663, and was burned down some eight years later, on January 25, 1672. Reopening in 1674 it carried on with alterations until 1791 when it was pulled down.

Conversely, in one or two cases the loss of a theatre by fire has been counted as an advantage and this was the view of some regarding the destruction of the vast theatre which was erected in its stead and had a life of just under 15 years before being burned down in 1809. Sheridan, who was running it at the time as a means of income to support the political side of his career, is said to have stood watching the flames drinking from a bottle of wine—"Cannot a man take a glass of wine by his own fireside?" His was the loss. And the gain? Some felt that the fire was a mercy for the sake of The Drama because the very size of the place had led to ranting and roaring, if only to be heard and seen. To reach the most distant parts of the house performances had to be very much larger than life. Even today the mistake is sometimes made of building theatres that are too big, in which opera glasses are essential in the back row, not to mention hearing aids. Or am I becoming senile? When I saw a National Theatre Company production at Birmingham Repertory Theatre in 1975 there were times when I could not make out who was speaking on stage, let alone hear what was being said.

Covent Garden was destroyed by fire in 1808 and 1856. On the first occasion the cause was said to be a wad fired from a gun in *Pizzaro;* 20 died. The second fire was the result of a bal masque held during a lean period in the theatre's history. The organiser was Professor Anderson, "Wizard of the North" who more than once appeared in Northampton.

In his Annals of the Edinburgh Stage, James C. Dibdin described the burning of the Adelphi Theatre, Edinburgh, on the afternoon of May 24, 1853, as "not altogether an unmixed evil for the theatre as it was, with the stage where the auditorium is now situated, was highly inconvenient, not to say dangerous. If the fire had occurred at night when the house was full it would have been impossible for more than a very few to have escaped, the passages being not only long, but narrow. The building was so unsuitable, in fact, that the proprietors had considered as to the expediency of pulling it down and rebuilding when the fire saved them the trouble of making up their minds." The lessee, R. H. Wyndham, moved on the Theatre Royal but six years later this was pulled down after a final performance on May 25, 1859, the Government having purchased the site for £5,000 for the erection of the General Post Office.

Another instance in which a loss was inverted to become a gain was at Dundee in 1963 when the old theatre went up in flames and the repertory company had to move to a converted church hall. This was situated further from the city centre and nearer the university. In his book, Theatres Outside London, John Elsom recounts how the improvisatory atmosphere attracted the students who demanded a more ambitious policy of play selection. What happened to the old audience? "We killed them off!" said Ronald Sartrain, the theatre's administrator. "Well, it was a little far for them to come!!"

With all the fires that had taken place and the lessons that had been learned it might have been expected that the closing years of the 19th century and the whole of the 20th century would be free of fires. This was not the case, by any means.

Fires continued to occur. In October, 1899, the recently renovated theatre at St. Helen's, Lancashire, suffered some £10,000 damage. The following March Madamoiselle Henriot, aged 35, was suffocated in a dressing room during a fire at the Theatre Francais, Paris. The nine killed in a fire at the Empire, Edinburgh, in May, 1911, included Lafayette, the American illusionist. A lantern had fallen from a position high in the wings and the resulting fire in the scenery threatened to waft across the footlights. The hero of the disaster was a musician who climbed on to the stage and played God Save The King to calm the audience. But when the safety curtain came down, saving the audience, he was on the wrong side of it and lost his life. Bodies were found in three of the dressing rooms.

And three years after the turn of the century there occurred one of the most serious disasters among the scorched pages of theatre history. The mortuary in Chicago was actually turning away bodies after the holocaust in the Iroqouis Theatre, a 1,700 seater built on the lines of the Paris Opera Comique. The mortuary was "house full" following a Wednesday matinee on December 30, 1903.

Panic had been rife at the theatre, the biggest scene of carnage being at the foot of the staircase to the upper gallery. Many of the 587 bodies were those of women and children who had been trampled underfoot. One of the rescue workers was Bishop Fallowes of Chicago who said he had been on bloody battlefields but had never seen anything like it.

The cause of the fire was said to be an improperly covered electric wire—so that electricity could also be a killer. But the real culprit was a safety curtain which refused to come down. Evidently the authorities did not insist on its being used at every performance.

Afterwards it was the usual story of bolting the stable door after the horse has left—19 theatres in the district were closed for not complying with the regulations. The fire even had direct repercussions in Northampton where the Town Council insisted that the Opera House management should begin the regular use of the emergency doors in clearing the theatre. The Press reported that patrons seemed inclined to leave by the usual exits.

A novel fire warning was suggested at a meeting of the committee of the Theatre Girls Club, Soho, in April, 1930, when the treasurer, Mrs. Arnold Glover, suggested that a notice be erected at the foot of the wooden stairs: "In case of fire, escape by the chapel window."

Meantime a new danger had arisen, in a new type of "theatre"—the picture palace which, far from being the luxurious super cinema of later years, was in the early years a make-shift place—an opposite number of the barns and stables which had served as fit-ups in the days of the strolling players. Here there was the added danger of the film catching fire. During one of Northampton's early picture shows, about 1905, the operating room caught fire and all the films were destroyed so that the season came to an immediate end. This was at the Corn Exchange and the report I saw, a reminiscent one of some years later, stated that most of the audience had not realised that there was a fire. The manager seems to have been a cool customer avoiding panic by going on and singing a song before telling the audience to leave.

When legislation on cinematograph shows was being considered in September, 1904, the question arose of whether there should be any differentiation between permanent picture houses and travelling booths in which animated pictures were shown. A cause for special concern was the requirement that 14 days notice should be given to the local authorities. It was pointed out that this would be difficult for a booth owner who might visit half-a-dozen counties within a month.

One of the longest lasting permanent cinemas in the country was the Temperance Hall, Newland, and there a fire occurred in July, 1912, when a vivid flash was seen across the screen. The newspapers reported that "the audience at once suspected something was amiss when one of the operators came rushing out of the operating box carrying a spool of film . . . ladies of the balcony were alarmed at the ominous noises within the box from which dense fumes were emanating." They certainly appear to have had ground for their suspicions! The chief operator, Mr. J. P. Field, smothered the fire with sand and a wet blanket and no-one was hurt. But the following November 54 died in a cinema blaze at Bilbao. At Paisley in December, 1929, a cinema manager was charged with culpable homicide when 70 children died in a rush to locked secondary exits after some film caught fire. There I must leave the question of cinema conflagrations, as being outside my field.

It was in the year of the Chicago theatre fire that a theatre lessee at Bristol was allowed to get away with a legal dodge as a means of avoiding doing some safety alterations. This happened at the Theatre Royal, Bristol, which had been among that select few in the provinces to hold the Royal Patent, which it had first been granted in 1778. This meant, however, that its licence was controlled by the Lord Chamberlain himself and in 1903 he proved rather particular about its fire risks after his surveyor Frank T. Verity had pointed out, among other shortcomings, that "there was absolutely no separation in the fire risk between the stage and the auditorium, the division being a lath and plaster partition, there being a brick wall only between the orchestra and the cellar under the stage." Some of the work required was done, only to meet further demands, following which the lessee Ernest Carpenter quietly dropped the Royal patent and applied to the magistrates for a local licence, which he duly got! The work was only deferred as it had to be carried out some years later.

GOING

to Extremes

No-one would wish "dodges" to be employed as regards safety in places of public resort but one may ask whether in the 1970s things have not perhaps gone rather too far in various directions.

As I write in 1976 well over £20,000 has been spent on making the former Opera House, now Repertory Theatre, at Northampton a safer place. One "improvement" has been the replacement of a metal pass door by two wooden ones, part of the reason being that while metal doors can never burn and wooden ones will, the time taken for the wooden doors to burn is known! It is only fair to add that having two doors allows one to open the first without the possibility of being confronted by a wall of flame. Or so the argument goes.

While some of the architects and planners of today have been erecting schools and old people's homes of dubious safety other experts have been bringing in safety regulations of unparalleled severity and cost. In the days when alumina cement has led to the evacuation of almost new buildings; the construction of the roofs of new old people's homes has led to the rapid extensions of fires and high death tolls; when even the odd skyscraper has been found to be wanting; buildings have begun to be erected in the expansion area of Northampton on unsafe foundations, helping to cause the collapse of local firms; other experts have been devising sets of fire regulations which have laid an immense burden on theatre owners, hotel keepers, and others.

The very day I was writing these lines I opened a newspaper to encounter a headline: "Ceiling crash escape for 200 children." This happened when the children had just finished lunch and left the school dining hall when the ceiling came down.

As regards fire regulations schools not long built have had to have vast sums spent upon them on new fire safety arrangements at a time when they have been cutting down on book supplies. Recreation centres like the Lings Forum at Weston Favell, Northampton (where theatricals are sometimes held) have scarcely been finished before new regulations have made them outdated firewise and additional money has had to be found. Keepers of seaside boarding houses have had to increase their charges to match outlay on "ideal" fire safety modifications.

In the view of some, and not all of them moronic moneygrabbers, things have gone from one extreme to the other, as in so many fields of human activity.

During the early years the "box office" of the Opera House was in a shop premises in the Drapery – Mark's. No picture survives of Mark's at that time but there is this drawing by George Clarke, of about 1840, of Birdsall's Library, their predecessors. In between these two ownerships it belonged to Mark Dorman. *(Northamptonshire Public Libraries)*.

Franklins Gardens Hotel, Northampton, bears the name of John Campbell Franklin, who built the Opera House. He bought the Gardens in 1887, expressing the hope that his planned improvements would bring a boost to the tramways to this western district of the town. Hitherto, he said, the trams had been "an unfortunate speculation." *(Drawing by Ron Mears)*.

An impression by Northampton artist Jim Purvis of the situation in Guildhall Road in the late 1880s, with the Opera House on one side and the Salvation Army Citadel on the other. While being anti-theatre, and especially anti-musichall, Salvationists made use of many theatres for their meetings and when the Opera House came on the market in 1888 there were strong rumours that they were going to buy it and make it their headquarters.

Scene Two: 1887-9

RUMOURS OF AN "ARMY" ASSAULT

Getting the theatre back into action after only 10 weeks brought congratulatory messages from Henry Irving, Charles Wyndham, H. Cecil Beryl (proprietor of the Theatre Royal, Edinburgh, and the Royal Princess Theatre, Glasgow), Clement Scott (the London playwright and critic who enclosed his poem on The Lays of London) and Augustus Harris (proprietor of the Theatre Royal, Drury Lane, who sent a statue of himself). The statue outlasted Harris who died in July, 1896, at the age of 44, after having been knighted; his widow married Edward Terry and when she came to the theatre with her new husband and saw the statue she burst into tears.

Not only had the theatre been restored but also improved. By taking three feet off the dressing rooms at either side of the stage, the flies had been widened six feet, while the former dressing rooms at the rear had been abolished altogether. The largest scenery on tour could now be accommodated without folding, to which some companies objected. Nor had there been an overall loss of dressing rooms because some new ones had been created downstairs, where none had existed before.

The bandroom had also been enlarged. The band instruments had been destroyed and in March a concert had been held at the Town Hall with the object of compensating the musicians. Although he was not to return to the Opera House Mr. Oates conducted and his wife played the piano and harp. Violin solos were given by Mr. J. A. Twist who was to succeed Mr. Oates.

Replacing the old Act Drop of the Queen Eleanor Cross in the vicinity of Northampton, which had been destroyed, was a Royal one without local significance, of Windsor Castle.

The four rows of pit seats damaged by the fire were replaced and all the pit benches were recovered. The wooden barrier dividing the two parts of the circle, formerly painted chocolate, was now covered with Lincrusta leather material. The gallery had been improved by installing a ventilation shaft.

Greeting theatregoers in the crush room were Shakespearian quotations including "A Thousand Welcomes", "Salutations and Greetings to You All" and "Let them Want Nothing that My House Affords."

The 27 × 22 ft. room over the entrance had been intended for a billiard room but was now reallocated as the manager's office, one which, said the Mercury, might be envied by managers of many larger theatres. Yes indeed: in 1976 it still houses without difficulty the 15-strong Board of Directors which controls the theatre's destinies, in times at least as difficult as those during which Tarry coped in his one-man part-time style of management.

Most significant of the new installations were four fire hydrants, placed close to the upper circle, at the stage door, for use on the roof, and in the private boxes—"Those present at the fire will readily understand of what immense benefit a hydrant in this part of the auditorium might have been. Had this been done before, much of the damage might have been saved as both the firemen and the public were able to get into the boxes the whole of the time the fire was burning."

The May week of reopening included the theatre's third anniversary when Miss Lingard and Company appeared in *Sister Mary,* written for her by Wilson Barrett and Clement Scott. The National Anthem was followed by Marche des Comediennes composed by Mr. A. E. Klitz, a Northampton musician, and dedicated to Isaac Tarry, who appeared on stage, again his usual effusive self. Franklin also appeared, bowed, but declined to speak.

Subsequent weeks brought the Lonsdale Company in *Nell Gwynne;* Marie de Grey and Company in *Jane Shore* and one of Frank Harvey's melodramas, *Woman Against The World,* and Mrs. Dawes and Company in *Nancy and Co.*

The theatre now faced increased opposition from two sources. With the first Franklin was not likely to be worried as he owned it himself—the former Melbourne Gardens, renamed Franklins Gardens, a name retained to the present day. The grand reopening on Whit Monday followed the erection of a 200 ft. long Jubilee Hall (this was the year of Queen Victoria's Golden Jubilee). The bear pit had also been drained and cemented and there was a rather well-timed demonstration of the Lewis Hand Fire Extinguisher—"No public building or private house should be without one." The new manager of the Gardens was Mr. W. Lawrence, who had held similar positions at the Castle Hotel, Derby, and the Pleasure Gardens, Isle of Man.

The second form of opposition sounded quite serious—the erection of a variety hall claimed to seat 2,000. The previous October a limited liability company had been formed to take over the Plough Hotel, Bridge Street, the licence for which had a few years earlier been transferred from the Crow, a disreputable tavern musichall in Gold Street. The company had purchased an adjoining garden in which was a former skating rink and on this site they proceeded to build the Plough Hall. In fact it turned out to be a rather primeval sort of place, which was to have a chequered career lasting only 13 years. Open braziers of glowing coke provided the heat but the gardens were lit by electricity—an early use of this form of energy.

What began as the Plough Hall had several transient names and transient managements. Harry Day, of Birmingham, was followed by Mr. Rowlands who at the close of his circus season announced publicly that it had left him out of pocket. Then came Messrs. George Ware, Graham and Co., of London, and after that Gus Levaine, who was unusual for a musichall proprietor, whom we normally visualise as bulbous-nosed, rosy-hued, and whose right hand, when not wielding a gavel, is occupied by a glass.

Following a Saturday matinee he arranged for poor children there was a controversy in the letters columns of the Press during which Gus proclaimed that he was a non-drinker and a practising member of the Church of England. Assailed by a Kettering correspondent who signed himself "Young Christian" and who said musichalls and theatres were the ruin of thousands of young folk, he replied: "Although I don't drink myself I am not such a bigot as to suppose no-one else has a right to. I have no interest in the bars whatever." In fact his Press advertisements had mentioned, "Wines, spirits and cigars" but it appears that these had to be obtained from the nearby hotel. Soon after the exchanges the reference to alcohol was replaced by a mention of tea and coffee at a penny a cup. Gus declared that although 1,000 children had attended the matinee he had lost money. Admission had been 1d. and 2d. so remembering that there were then 240 pence to the £ his takings were probably about £6.

In November, 1888, the Plough Hotel Company themselves took charge of the hall and installed as manager Smythe Cronin, who had been Levaine's deputy chairman. Cronin, a 29-year-old Dubliner, died seven months later. Levaine had moved on to the former Crow in Gold Street, which he renamed the Grand Variety Hall, but he lasted only a few weeks there his closing scene being in the County Court where Marks of The Drapery sued him for the cost of some posters they had printed for him. In April, 1889, the Bridge Street Hall reopened as the Victoria Palace of Varieties, managed by Frank Harold, "well-known London and provincial variety artist."

To return to Guildhall Road and 1887. When Boucicault's The Jilt was given during Whit Week the advertisement noted that as the usual box office at Marks would be closed on the Bank Holiday seats could be booked at the theatre by letter, telephone or telegram.

After a short break in July the theatre reopened for August Bank Holiday week only with Mizpah, after which there was a further break. The Mercury said that some people would like to see the theatre opened all the year round "but the excellent proprietor cannot be expected to carry it on through the dog days at a certain dead loss." The second reopening was on August 29 with Auguste Van Biene's and Lingard's Company in the comic opera Pepita which was about to be staged in London after seven months in the provinces.

After the September fire at the Exeter Theatre, in which 186 died, there was a reaction among audiences throughout the country as they realised how danger-ous a place a theatre could be. In towns which had recently had theatre fires, like Northampton, there was a special awareness. A number of reassurances were forthcoming as I have noted in the Fires Interlude.

There were two first appearances in Northampton that autumn, Kate Santley making her local debut in Indiana and Arthur Dacre doing the same in an acting capacity, with his wife Amy Roselle in Our Joan. Dacre had made an unusual transition—from the theatre of the hospital to the theatre of the drama. Born Arthur Culver James he had first acted as an amateur while a student at Aberdeen University from which he graduated in 1874. The following year he was for a short time a surgeon locum tenens at Northampton General Infirmary. Turning professional he played in the U.S.A. with Dion Boucicault. Returning to England he was with Wilson Barrett at the Court Theatre, London, and in The Old Love and the New met Amy Roselle, whom he married in 1884. It was a significant title for the previous year there had been a divorce case in which he had charged his first wife with multiple adultery and she had accused him of violence.

Born in 1854, the daughter of a Glastonbury schoolmaster, Amy Roselle was not even named on her first visit to Northampton at the age of 10, to the old theatre in Marefair, being merely an also-ran to her infant prodigy brother Percy. Billed as "one of the greatest wonders of the age, possessed of a remarkable memory and no mean histrionic ability" Master Roselle was only 12 but played Hamlet, Macbeth, and Richard Duke of Gloucester. "Master Roselle is accompanied by his sister", said the Press report. But if Amy was outshone by her brother in 1864 she in turn put her ex-doctor husband in the shade in later years. At 15 she had played Lady Teazle and while still in her teens became a member of the Haymarket Company and later accompanied Sothern to the U.S.A.

After becoming an actor Dacre did not forget his old background and was always willing to give free performances in hospitals. On the 1887 visit he and his wife went to Northampton General Infirmary.

November shows of 1887 included an American drama set in New York, *Shadows of a Great City,* with William Calder's Company. Then Frank Benson and his company paid a second visit and in December the bills announced that the "original Tony of *My Sweetheart",* the American actor Charles Arnold, would be featured in *Hans the Boatman.*

In a December audience that year was the editor of The Stage, who commented "I do not think there are many theatres in England, even taking in London, that can compare with this theatre in the matter of management." Praise indeed, considering that the manager was an "amateur"! He noted too that some patrons had travelled 15 miles. "The pit, which Mr. Tarry informed me would seat 900 was filled with an audience as quiet and respectable as that of Mr. Irving's Lyceum pit."

Whatever the behaviour of the pit, there were several incidents exemplifying that the gods were not to be trifled with. They would not, for instance, tolerate songs aimed at their political favourites. Northampton's working class and some other elements were proud of their Liberalism and Radicalism—was not theirs the town which persisted in returning to Parliament Charles Bradlaugh, the man who would not swear a religious oath of allegiance and who was thrown bodily out of the House of Commons? They showed their disapproval on the last Saturday night of 1887 during the performance of *Vetah* starring Kate Santley and advertised as an Eastern comic opera but described in the Press as the Opera House's first pantomime. The trouble came when Henry Ashley, who appeared as a rajah, added some verses of his own to the popular ditty Two Lovely Black Eyes:

> *Mr. Gladstone has gone to the Continent*
> *If he never returned we'd be quite content*
> *The Dover folk snowballed him well ere he went*
> *   Oh what a surprise!*

At once there was a hostile reaction and for several minutes uproar reigned. The Mercury noted that the introduction of politics before a Northampton audience was always risky because the pittites and gods held strong opinions and resented any reflection upon their political idols. But the singer had a surprise in store—a further verse which changed the groans to cheers:

> *But whatever the party to which a man leans*
> *Who'd use any man so are dirty spalpeens*
> *And I'd like to give each of those snowballing beans*
>   *Two Lovely Black Eyes!*

You had to be careful too about playing the National Anthem, Queen Victoria, a recluse since the death of her husband, not being universally popular at that time. The type of Northamptonian who filled the Opera House gallery was probably strongly represented also at the smoking concerts held in the Plough Hotel.

At the close of one of these the chairman, Mr. Herbert C. Tyler, diplomatically affirmed that he admired the Junior Member (Mr. Bradlaugh) very much (Hear Hear!) but he would like before separating to propose the health of the Queen. This was drunk with musical honours, Chairman Tyler sharing the solo verses with Mr. W. Opie Carter.

In January, 1888, the amicable settlement of a strike in the local shoe industry was announced from the stage of the Opera House and celebrated by the singing of Auld Lang Syne.

A pack of foxhounds was among the cast of the musical *Dorothy*. One of its visits, in January, 1888, brought Fred Emney to the theatre and the free list was "entirely suspended". The optimism was rewarded. "Not only were the popular parts full as soon as the doors were open but the manager's White Elephant, the dress circle, also had its full complement of visitors." The crowded house on the fashionable Wednesday night included Mr. Thomas Phipps Dorman, who was to buy the theatre the following year. We know this because the newspaper was in the habit of publishing lists of names of those attending, those of the middle and upper classes that is to say. Despite the comparative splendour of the theatre compared with the "dingy little cupboard" in Marefair filling that part of the house was a continuous headache.

Whatever the shortcomings of the old theatre one company which had never failed there was that of Madamoiselle Beatrice. On visits in 1873, 1876, 1877-8, 1880 and 1881 it had drawn packed houses but in the new theatre it failed to repeat its past successes. Along with a few classics, including *The School for Scandal,* Madamoiselle Beatrice had included in her repertoire many novelettish pieces with names like *Married Not Mated* and *Love and Honour,* written by her right-hand man Frank Harvey, and when she died in December, 1878, she left money to him with a request that the company be carried on under her name. This was done well into the 1890s.

For some reason the company did not appear during the first three years at the Opera House and when it did arrive in January, 1888, the old magic had gone. The Mercury reported: "In the old days when the Thespian cult had a fitful existence in the bandbox-like theatre in Marefair Mr. Frank Harvey was a name to charm with and the Beatrice Company was always sure to draw bumping houses" . . . but "there have not been wanting prophets of evil who predicted that after their greatly enlarged experience of plays and players Northamptonians would not see their old favourite again without an unpleasant feeling of disillusionment. It was pretty clear on Monday that these predictions were not unjustified for though the house was good the performances failed to elicit any enthusiasm and while Mr. Harvey was cheered on his first appearance he was not even called before the Act Drop" (at the end). "The fact is that he is trying to live on the past reputation of the company and is running the risk of losing it altogether . . . he inflicts upon us a constant succession of his own patchwork pieces and relying upon himself and two or three old stagers entrusts the minor parts to indifferent performers."

For a provincial critic this was putting it fairly hot and strong, especially in days when some actors and managers were successful in suing newspapers and writers who had impugned their professional ability or calibre. It was also good criticism, in that it meant something, and still has something to tell us today of changing tastes of this period. A particularly telling thrust was that "he takes no account of the constantly rising standard of stage management." Harvey who continued to churn out turgid stuff similar to *The World Against Her* and *The Wages of Sin* which he presented in Northampton that week—he wrote 24 of them during the last 11 years of his life—died in Manchester in March, 1903.

Harvey's neglect of stage management was in complete contrast from a piece which followed soon afterwards—the provincial premiere of *Pleasure,* which was genuinely "direct from Drury Lane". It was by Paul Merritt and Augustus Harris of Drury Lane, where Harris was on a profitable tenure of spectacular and extravagant shows. The Mercury reported. "In *Pleasure* it would seem that the highest point of realism has been touched. It is a striking example of the modern development of the stage carpenter's craft. Times have indeed changed since the good old days when the scenery was denoted by the primitive device of a board inscribed with 'Scene. A Room In The Palace' or 'Scene: On the Battlements' etc. Now we go to the extremes of realism and stage managers who do not keep up to the advancing standards of public demands cannot hope for popular favour. The earthquake effect is certainly the nearest approach to a genuine convulsion that it is possible to imagine." But to go with the balloons of praise the newspaper provided a pin. "The play itself, it must be confessed, is a very poor sort of thing but the day is long past when 'The play's the thing'."

The design of the theatre's original drop scene had included a peacock and some members of the profession and public had not liked this challenge to the theatrical tradition that the bird means bad luck and that peacocks should not be represented nor should peacock feathers be worn. After the fire, however, it had again been included in the design. Augustus Harris refused to allow his company to appear unless it was painted out and this was done. I am not very superstitious myself (mind you I *never* wear peacock feathers when going to the theatre) but certainly in this case one has to admit that the relegated bird appears to have wrought a belated vengeance, during the run of Harris's *Pleasure*.

Mr. Hamilton Ashley, brother of a London actor manager, was playing the villain. On the Monday night he was slow to pick up cues. On Tuesday, as the Mercury put it, "He betrayed evident signs of incompetency to perform his part arising from his being the worse for liquor. His utterance was indistinct and confused and he was constantly requiring the aid of the prompter so much so that the prompter could be heard in the dress circle before the performer appeared to catch it himself. Early in the second act his utter incompetency to continue became still more painfully apparent. He shuffled towards the wings as if to catch the prompter's voice and at length utterly broke down." The audience booed and he left the stage. The stage manager, Marshall Moore, read the part after making a short apology and offering the audience their money back; none of the gallery left and only one or two from the pit. Perhaps the novelty of an actor performing book in hand appealed to them.

Tarry had not yet arrived but when he did he went on stage to make a further apology and to condemn the "outrageous insult" to the audience and himself. He had just telegraphed Augustus Harris who, he was sure, would share his indignation. Harris not only did so but speedily arranged for Edward Sass, who had been in the London cast, to take the part for the rest of the week. As Sass was booked in London the following week the role was later handed to Charles Eaton. Continuing Tarry promised his audience that no company of which THAT MAN was a member would ever play in the insulted theatre.

There have been many instances in which actors have gone on stage the worse for alcoholic wear. At Northampton there was the precedent of 1863 at the old theatre when the leading actor Gustavus Vaughan Brooke had had to abandon a performance of *Othello* and catch the train back to London, still in a brandy-inspired stupor. But on many occasions audiences have not known that an actor was under the influence, so well can many Thespians hold their liquor. That great Northampton Rep. stalwart of two decades ago Franklin William Davies once told me that at one point in a scene in which he was holding his top hat in one hand he was not quite sure whether he was going to deliver his next line or be sick into the topper. I must not go off into a long rigmarole about one of my favourite subjects but will mention just one more case, showing that the problem is not new. In some early performances it would appear that the drink in those stage glasses was the real stuff not the cordial nowadays used for cheapness as well as sobriety. The premature downfall of Higden's comedy *The Wary Widow* at Drury Lane in 1693 was said to be due to the fact that real punch had been supplied for the drinking scenes in the first half of the play.

But to return to the spectacular side of *Pleasure,* it might be wondered how such vast casts, with such vast amounts of machinery and vast numbers of stage staff could be afforded. Cheap labour is the answer. It was possible to travel very large companies and recruit local extras or supers (supernumeraries) very inexpensively indeed. When another Harris success, *Human Nature,* this time written in conjunction with Henry Pettitt, came to the theatre in April, 1888, it was claimed that the number employed on stage was 200. In this case, 200 was, however, a somewhat bogus figure for it included members of the 48th Regimental Depot who had been drafted for the battle scenes. With them came a brass band and a drum and fife band so that counting the gentlemen of the orchestra pit there were three bands and perhaps 50 musicians. Nor were these pit players overpaid and both nationally and locally there were to be strikes in efforts to get a rise.

Earlier in the year Robert Buchanan's and Harriett Jay's *Alone in London* had been seen "in four acts and nine tableaux. The Press commented. "Nothing better has ever been done on our stage than the triple shift in the third act from the old house at Rotherhithe to the Thames by moonlight and then to the old sluice house and the opening of the floodgates."

Jim the Penman, brought back by Theo-Balfour, did not attract—"The frost without was equalled by the frost within," commented the Mercury.

The second attempt to stage opera was much more successful than the first, which had indeed been a fiasco. It came in March, 1888, with the arrival of the J. W. Turner Opera Company of 60 performers. For such visits many theatres increased their prices but Tarry chose not to do so and seemed proud to be able to claim that even if the seats were full every night of the week he could not show a profit—an artistic pride matching that of some of our spendthrift subsidised producers of today! The band was "doubled" for the week which embraced *Faust, Maritana* and *The Bohemian Girl.* For once Northamptonians did not let the side down and there were good attendances.

March also saw the performance of *The Red Lamp,* "based on Russian life", which had been premiered in Reading the previous week. With it came a curtain raiser, *A Month After Date,* written by a local dramatist W. Jones, alias Sylvanus Dauncey.

A fifth visit was paid by *My Sweetheart* and in May Arthur Dacre and Amy Roselle returned with their own company in Charles Reade's *The Double Marriage,* set in France in 1798. During the week a waltz dedicated to Miss Roselle, called Thalia, was played by the orchestra. In a speech from the stage Dacre said he felt proud of the way the audience had received a far better artist than he could ever hope to be—his wife. He was probably not pleased, however, when the Mercury confirmed this—while she was "superb" he "perhaps scarcely rises to the heights." Instead of visiting the Infirmary the Dacres went along this time to entertain mental patients at St. Andrew's Hospital; he recited from *Hamlet* while she sang The Lost Chord.

On the Monday night, it being the last week of the tour, members of the company presented the couple with a silver travel clock inscribed. "More is thy due; more than all can pay. Presented to Mr. and Mrs. Arthur Dacre by the members of their first provincial company, May 28, 1888." The quotation is from *Macbeth.*

The Saturday performance, a benefit night for Dacre attended by Earl Spencer, coincided with the 69th birthday of Queen Victoria but the playing of the National Anthem "did not pass off without an attempt at a counter demonstration", as the Mercury reported. At the end of the play flowers were lowered from a box on pink ribbons and Dacre made a speech thanking especially the gallery "where the heat must be tropical."

What appeared to be a sensational counter-attraction was presented at the Corn Exchange for three nights from May 31, 1888, in the person of Miss Blanche Belle, an actress who had married the son of Squire Bouverie, of Delapre Abbey, Northampton. But Mr. F. Kenelm Bouverie was a cad. In the chair at the performances was Mr. G. W. Churchley, a solicitor employed by Blanche, alias Mrs. Bouverie. He related how only a week after the marriage the despicable Mr. Bouverie had tried to get his bride to support him by turning to prostitution and when she declined deserted her and went to America. Her appeal to the family had received only sympathy, and she had therefore returned to her old profession as a means of support. A song had been especially written for her by Frank Egerton, including

> They say I was awfully lucky
> To marry so wealthy a nob

but it was not among her repertoire at the Corn Exchange, which consisted of You Can't Do Without Us (Women) and Girls Were Never Better Than They Are Just Now.

In June, 1888, over 100 Franklin employees attended a dinner at Franklins Gardens at which the manager paid tribute to him. Said Mr. W. Lawrence: "In an acquaintance with him from the cradle and school I have never found him angry. He is always the same, friendly, kindly, placid, amiable. His serenity is never disturbed."

On June 30, 1888, the Mercury said that J.C.F. contemplated retiring and three weeks later it announced the sale by auction of most of his property, including the Opera House. Among the buyers rumoured to be after it was the Salvation Army, a possibility on which the Mercury commented: "People will have amusements and they are wise who try to purify and elevate them, not to destroy them."

The idea of the "Army" purchasing the theatre was not as outlandish as it might seem. With Nottingham setting a lead in 1860 theatres had been used widely for religious meetings and some had been held in Northampton's old theatre. In the capital the idea was taken up in February, 1867, by the East London Christian Mission, forerunner of the Salvation Army, which by using the Effingham Theatre, one of the lowest resorts in London, "lifted itself to a position of fame and influence with the unchurched masses of London", as the official history of the "Army" puts it. Subsequently the Salvationists also employed the Grecian Theatre, attached to the Eagle public house; the Oriental Hall, Poplar, "a dirty draughty and comfortless place of the lowest description, with floors covered with nutshells and orange peel, and open communication with cellars from which grievous stenches came up"; the Cambridge Music Hall; the City of London Theatre, Shoreditch; and the Apollo Music Hall, Hare Street, which was so disreputable that it lost its licence but was bought up by the brewers Hanbury, Truman and Buxton, who for a time allowed the use of the hall free to the Salvation Army. Following a visit in April, 1867, the East London Observer described how there was an enormous crowd, the boxes and stalls being filled with "as idle and dissolute a set of characters as ever crossed a place of public resort." But the tattier the audience the greater the success, the Saturday Review summing up in July, 1879: "The fortresses of Beelzebub are music-halls, penny gaffs, dancing rooms and the like; of these in London and elsewhere the Salvation Army has stormed no less than 100 and turned the haunts of ribaldry into places of divine service."

Some Salvationists had their misgivings about paying rent to theatre owners whose activities during the rest of the week were not to their liking. The secretary George Scott Railton was not among these, pointing out in 1877 "Here is a theatre full of people, the vast majority of whom are sinners in danger of burning in hell for ever. We cannot possibly provide another building of such capacity for them even supposing that we should be sure of securing their attendance there. What more suitable building could we possibly have . . . every eye can see the preacher's face, every ear can catch his slightest whisper." After the Army dispensed with theatres William Booth, the Founder himself, had regrets at the change. Six years after the abandonment of the various London theatres he said: "The very same labour which is necessary to gather a few hundred working people into a building set apart for religious services and to set Christ before them would fill a large theatre or musichall and send home conviction to the hearts of thousands." Many unlikely characters who attended these "extra performances" (as they were sometimes billed) found themselves kneeling at the penitent stool erected on the stage; even a reporter sent by the Saturday Review remained to pray! Had they bought the Northampton theatre, the "Army" would have had to cross the road for their headquarters were on the opposite side of Guildhall Road, in the old County Gaol. However, East remained East and West stayed West.

At the end of Act One of *The Old Guard* on Wednesday, July 18, Tarry came before the footlights to announce the name of the new owner following the sale which he had that day conducted (how many theatre managers have had the task of wielding the hammer on their theatres?). First he felt he ought to say who was not the new owner. He thanked God that General Booth was not and was inclined to thank God that Thomas Phipps Dorman was.

The sale had been held at the George Hotel and before commencing Tarry had asked those present to drink a toast to Franklin. In his introductory remarks he said that a fair rent for the theatre would be £600 a year. Not only had the bars shown a profit, but existing drink licences were valuable in themselves as there was difficulty in obtaining new ones "in the face of the vexation of an insolent and aggressive tee-totalism now in fashion."

The theatre fetched £9,000. Other property sold at what was then the town's biggest auction sale to date included the 18-bedroom Franklins Hotel for which P. Phipps and Co. paid £8,500; the same firm gave £3,200 for the Swan Hotel, at the top of Cow Lane. Mr. Seckham, of Northampton Brewery Company, paid £5,600 for the Dolphin Hotel (later redeveloped as the Grand). Two licensed premises at Leamington, the Bath Hotel and the George Inn, fetched £7,900 and £2,500.

Regarding the impending changes at the theatre the Mercury recorded its views with candour: "If Mr. Franklin will pardon us a remark which appears gruff a new proprietor has been found who will not be a whit worse than the old one if he can help it. But this will be the last season under Mr. Tarry's management and that is a momentous matter. Though it may not be hard to find a good proprietor it is hard to find a good manager."

About this time the local tramway company arranged that attendants should be at the theatre to ascertain the exact moment when the curtain fell so that five minutes could elapse before the departure of the last tram on the various lines.

That August Miss Fortescue and Company appeared in *Sweethearts* by W. S. Gilbert, and *Nance Oldfield* by Charles Reade. From the wings a reporter watched as she took charge of the Monday morning rehearsal; squatting on a tub she gave instructions to the stage carpenter and scene painter for a tree to be built up here, a rustic porch there, a flower bed in this place, a garden chair over yonder. Miss Fortescue, who explained that a male member of the cast usually undertook this duty, evidently got on well with the journalist for he was invited to take breakfast with her at the George the following morning—"So long as you do not watch me eat my eggs" (Byron said that this was the worst possible thing for a woman's beauty).

September brought Miss Isabel Bateman "who was so long associated with

Mr. Henry Irving in his early triumphs at the Lyceum." On Friday she appeared in a benefit performance of *Mary Warner* by Tom Taylor and for the rest of the week in W. G. Wills' *Jane Shore.*

At this time the Opera House was said to be doing quite nicely and if this was the case (the evidence is somewhat contradictory!) it was a successful as well as a warmer theatre which Tarry was to hand over. The new owner presumably footed the bill of £300 for the "grateful warmth which not only pervades the theatre but also the approaches to it." From the first week of December, 1888, "every part is heated by coils of pipes fed by an independent boiler. Each coil can be worked separately." This was an advantage because it had often been warmer in the cheaper regions of the pit than it was in the circle so that those who paid the most had got the least warmth. This was probably because the pit was cosily down in the bowels of the earth whereas the circle was at street level and prey to icy draughts which even into modern times have been known to nip the hindquarters of top people in the circle, when the wind is in a certain direction. Following the 1888 heating installation by the local ironfounders, Rice and Co., the Opera House was advertised as "now thoroughly heated with hot water pipes and the most comfortable place of entertainment in the country."

It took nearly five years and a pantomime featuring Vesta Victoria to get some of the upper set into the theatre. The audiences for *Robinson Crusoe* in 1888-9 "included several distinguished members of the nobility and members of the old county families who have never previously visited the Opera House." Written by Isaac Tarry in collaboration with Sidney Cooper the parts had been printed and the "book of words" could be obtained for 6d. from local booksellers and music stores—at Marks, Drapery: Abels, The Parade; Warners, St. Giles Square; Huntings, The Mounts; and also in Wellingborough at Sanders and Bellamys and Dennes Brothers. During the latter part of the run Vesta Victoria changed from tights to skirt. Her numbers included You May Say You Don't and Saucy Cupid.

For one of the Saturday matinees every seat in the circle was occupied— "which has happened only once or twice in the history of the theatre" (which did not say a lot for the support it was receiving!) The occupants were, however, children from Northampton Workhouse and the Nazareth Homes, who were given packets of sweets, buns and oranges.

From Northampton Tarry had the pleasure of seeing his pantomime move on to the Grand Theatre, Nottingham, and then to the Opera House, Leicester.

Then came the end of the old management with a four-day run, from Monday to Thursday, of Arthur W. Pinero's *Sweet Lavender,* performed by the company of Mr. T. W. Robertson, son of the dramatist who wrote *Caste, Society, Ours, Home* etc. This allowed for a handover on the Friday and Saturday to the new regime, of Thomas Phipps Dorman as proprietor and Charles Rider Noble, a cousin of Mr. Kendal, as manager. They began the following Monday, February 4, 1889, with Wilson Barrett's *Golden Ladder* Company.

But first there was a farewell for Isaac Tarry whose efforts at the theatre had reduced him to a state of tension which demanded a rest. Pale and nervous, he appeared after the final curtain of *Sweet Lavender.* The Mercury caught the atmosphere of what was for him a momentous night: "He is suffering from nervous exhaustion and had in fact been in bed until nearly 10" (presumably 10 p.m.). "In that elegant and cultural diction with which he invariably clothes his spoken thoughts, with that grace of pose which comes to him naturally, and with a tinge of that exquisite dilettantism which is never absent from him, first he mentions his secretary Mr. Robert Perkins, whom he calls from the wings and presents a cheque for £200" (yes £200 and at today's value it would be ten times as much). "Next Mr. William George Arkell, formerly an assistant in his office, £50. A large red screen at the side of the speaker is withdrawn to reveal his portrait by Mr. Harris Brown, upside down on an easel (laughter), given by Mr. Franklin. To James Twist, orchestra leader, an ivory baton with silver ends; to scenic artist Sidney Thompson a volume by Paul Lacroix, Art In The Middle Ages and Renaissance. Also a silver watch to a carpenter, John Harris."

Perhaps the most significant element in Tarry's speech was that although by today's standards there was very little direct competition to the theatre, his view was that "The entertainments provided are so numerous as to be almost beyond the power of the public to keep pace with them. Indeed sometimes it seems to me that it is as if amusement were fast becoming the business of life with us." Of course the idea that the lower classes should not be encouraged to spend too much of their money on idle pleasures was not a new concept. The preamble to an Act of George II in 1752 ran as follows: "Whereas the multitude of places of entertainment for the lower sort of people is another great cause of theft and robberies as they are tempted to spend their small substance in riotous pleasures and in consequence are put to unlawful methods to supply their wants, be it enacted . . . " Precisely what it was that was being enacted I omitted to make a note of at the time.

Tarry had a word of commendation for his successor: "Mr. Noble will make the theatre a far greater success than I have done. He will devote the whole of his time and energies to it, whereas I have been able only to give a portion of mine. He is strong and active whereas my own health is broken, my eyes are beginning to cause me great anxiety and I begin to feel very old." His last lines were naturally from Shakespeare—

> Parting is such sweet sorrow
> That I shall say goodnight until tomorrow

which was scarcely appropriate.

Even this was not his big farewell scene. This was reserved for more splendid and honourable surroundings—the council chamber of the Town Hall. A fund for a farewell gift had raised £130, including guinea donations from the new owner, Dorman; S. S. Campion, newspaper owner; Edward Compton, a future joint owner of the theatre; and from Earl Spencer. A collection among the orchestra raised 10s. Surprisingly neither Dorman nor his manager, Noble, attended. Nor did Tarry's pantomime collaborator Sidney Cooper; it was the panto's last night at Nottingham and he felt he had to be there. Mr. C. C. Becke, Borough Coroner and chairman of the gift appeal, took the Mayor's seat. Henry Martin, who built the theatre, was present; so was the local music shop owner and composer C. J. Klitz, who had dedicated his Marche des Comediennes to Tarry; and Chief Constable Mardlin attended.

Agitated and near to tears, Tarry heard Mr. Becke say that he and Mr. Franklin had raised the level of drama in the town from the lowest depths. "Only three or four years ago our theatre was little better than a barn and I am afraid the companies who came here were fitted for the place they had to act in. It then seemed to strike some shrewd people in the town, amongst whom were my friends Mr. Tarry and Mr. Franklin, that not only would the town be benefited but also the individual who provided a better class of amusement."

Handing over silver tea and coffee services and a dressing bag he observed: "He has chosen things which will be useful to him in a state of life to which many of the young ladies of this town devoutly wish he may be called. Why gentlemen, four salt cellars are of no use to a bachelor nor are all these spoons. I trust this little help towards furnishing a house will be an encouragement to Mr. Tarry to get someone to employ the spoons."

Highly embarrassed, the bachelor began his reply with "Ladies and gentlemen" though there was not a single female present. Another gift, which probably meant more than the cutlery, was a watercolour of a scene from the last show of his management, *Sweet Lavender,* by W. B. Shoosmith, a local artist.

After the disposal of his theatre and other properties Mr. Franklin moved to Leamington with which town there appears to have been some sort of family connection as the Franklin business had once been in Leamington House, on the north side of the Market Square. Later he moved to Ealing where he died on the last day of June, 1908, at his home, Broughton Lodge, 65 Mount Park Road. Broughton is the name of a Northants village near Kettering where his father had lived, following his own retirement, and where he died in January, 1894.

Of all Franklin's properties the most ill-fated was the one which fetched the most money—and even then was said to have gone too cheap, he having accepted an offer of £17,000 before the auction. Within four years the company operating Franklins Gardens had gone into liquidation; the property was seized by the mortgagor after not a single bid had been made at an auction sale in 1892.

The chairman of the company formed to take over the Gardens in 1888 was Thomas Phipps Dorman, new owner of the theatre, who seems to have had a genius for losing the family fortunes. In October, 1888, no doubt because of Dorman's connection with the enterprise, Franklins Gardens had been loaned £10,000 on 4% mortgage by Phipps Brewery, of which Dorman was joint managing director. So presumably he lost some of the brewery's money too.

ACT TWO

A DORMAN NAMED PHIPPS

What's in a name? Thomas Dorman's middle name was Phipps and that meant a lot. It was borrowed from the powerful brewing family into which his father had married —that's how Thomas Phipps Dorman came to be joint managing director of Phipps Brewery, and to be able to buy the Opera House. To add variety he was a yachtsman while his manager was a former fireman and lifeboatman. On the stage the Play is not The Thing, the accent being on Effect and Spectacle. . . .

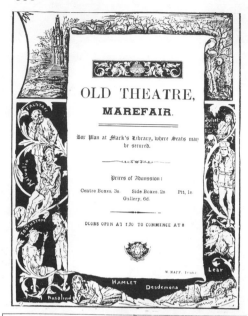

OLD THEATRE,
MAREFAIR.

For Plan at Mark's Library, where Seats may
be secured.

Prices of Admission:

Centre Boxes, 3s.   Side Boxes, 2s.   Pit, 1s.
Gallery, 6d.

DOORS OPEN AT 7.30 TO COMMENCE AT 8

W. NAFF. Printer

OPERA GLASSES may be had on Hire from the
Attendants, Sixpence per Evening.

PROGRAMME

Opera House,
Northampton.

Manager - MR. C RIDER-NOBLE.
Proprietor - MR. T. PHIPPS DORMAN

Monday, June 11th, 1894, for Six
Nights only,

Miss Minnie Palmer

AND

Specially Selected Company

IN

"MY SWEETHEART"

All Tickets are sold subject to the right of the
Manager to make any alterations in the Cast which
may be rendered necessary by illness or other
unavoidable causes.

Seats may now be secured at the
Theatre from 11 a.m. till 1 p.m. and
2 p.m. til 4 p.m., or by Telephone
No. 67

OPERA GLASSES may be had on Hire from the
Attendants, Sixpence per Evening.

Opera House   Northampton

Programme

Manager
Mr. C. RIDER-NOBLE.
Proprietor:
Mr. T. PHIPPS DORMAN.

Monday, May 9th, 1892,
and during the Week,
MISS ISABEL BATEMAN
AND COMPANY.

All Tickets are sold subject to the right of the Manager to make any alterations in
the Cast which may be rendered necessary by illness or other
unavoidable causes

Programme designs at the Opera
House—top left, the style in use in
1887, when the fire occurred, was by
Mr. Harris Brown and included Shakespearean characters; this actual programme was in fact the one for the
February week that year when the production was transferred to the "Old
Theatre, Marefair", the central type
being substituted: above, one of the
visits, this one in 1894, of the show
which was "top of the pops" in the early
years, *My Sweetheart*, on this occasion
with its creator, Minnie Palmer; on left
the design in use in 1892, during a visit
by the company of Isabel Bateman,
sister of Mrs. Edward Compton.

Scene One: 1889-99

BREWER PROPRIETOR, INVENTIVE MANAGER

The new owner of the Opera House was a man of propensities and temperament in complete contrast to the old and it is largely because he was much more of an extrovert that we know so much more about Thomas Phipps Dorman than we do about John Campbell Franklin. Their only common denominators seem to be that both were local and that both were businessmen.

Dorman was not only a Northamptonian but the son of a Mayor of Northampton, the Mark Dorman who had opened the new Town Hall in 1864. Thomas was the eldest son of Mark, who had come to Northampton from Ashford, Kent, ran a successful business, married well, become Mayor, and who was an enthusiastic amateur actor.

The business Mark ran was Dorman's Libraries in the Drapery which after his death was to become the booking office for the Opera House which his son was to own, though by then the Drapery premises had passed out of the family. The marriage was to Charlotte, only daughter of Alderman Thomas Phipps, a member of the Phipps brewing family. During his Mayoralty Mark opened the new Town Hall, or Guildhall, which gave its name to Guildhall Road, opposite the site of which it stood, and in which the Opera House was to be erected. It was an unusual Mayoralty in that a son was born to the Mayoress—first citizens and their spouses were usually too old for this to happen. That son Frederick was to act at the Opera House, both as an amateur and a professional, though he was a trained architect.

Isaac Tarry had unique acting connections with the Dorman family. In *The Merchant of Venice* he played Portia to Mark Dorman's Gratiano, Shylock to the Gratiano of Fred Dorman, and Shylock to the Judge of Thomas Phipps Dorman.

In 1877 Mark Dorman had felt ill and consulted a London surgeon who as his obituary recalled "curtly pronounced his disease incurable." He died a few months later, aged 48, leaving 10 children, the oldest of whom was the future proprietor of the Opera House.

Thomas Phipps Dorman—the middle name came from the brewing family into which father had married—was to own an ocean-going yacht, to build a splendid new hall for the Freemasons of Northampton, and to run the town's theatre for some 10 years. Perhaps the most eventful year in his busy life was 1881 for during it he married, was promoted, and joined the Masons. As his father had done he married the daughter of an Alderman—Alice, eldest daughter of Alderman and Mrs. James Wetherell, on June 23, 1881, at St. Giles Church, where she was a Sunday School teacher. As a wedding present he was made joint managing director of Phipps Brewery, his uncle Richard Phipps retiring to make room for him, leaving him in joint harness with Pickering Phipps M.P. The financial side of the change was that the brewery was valued at £160,000 and that of the £80,000 the retiring partner was to receive Pickering Phipps paid three-quarters and T. P. Dorman the remaining quarter.

The two events of marriage and promotion were celebrated at the brewery's annual outing which that year was to Easton Neston, stately home of the Hesketh family. From Northampton Market Square the parties set out in 30 conveyances with bunting flying. En route they were joined by a contingent from the Towcester brewery where the firm had begun. Pickering Phipps injected a note of political propaganda into his speech: "The firm owes a lot to the good servants whom we have gathered around us and though there are some who believe there is a screw loose in old England, good men make good masters and good masters make good men. Whatever may be said I am sure capital cannot do without labour and labour cannot do without capital. What is wanted is that each should be in its proper place." The old concept of the poor man at his gate and the rich man in his castle was very much the belief of the ruling classes, whether they ruled from the benches of the House of Commons or the boardrooms of the great commercial enterprises. Many did both and Pickering Phipps was one of them.

The third important thing that happened to Thomas Phipps Dorman that year was that he became Brother Dorman. He was initiated into the Freemasons as a member of Eleanor Cross Lodge and it was to be a life-long passion with him. Not for him mere ritual attendance at lodge and eating of the requisite banquets. He virtually married the movement and reached high rank including being Grand Deacon of the Grand Lodge of England and also wrote several books on "the craft." Taking into account all his other multifarious interests the amount of time he could spend with his wife Alice must have been limited. These other enterprises included making bicycles and sewing machines. Councillor John Bowes Corrin, who is a Patron of this book, told me that his grandfather had a genius for losing the family money. But, unlike some, his talent in this direction never landed him in serious trouble. Most apposite here, he also built a theatre in a London suburb.

Dorman briefly entered politics too but did not stay on. Perhaps the talking shop atmosphere did not suit him. Whatever the cause he did not fulfil the forecast sung by Mr. S. Norman at the brewery's annual dinner in January, 1883:

> *And Mr. Dorman who fills a councillor's chair*
> *We hope we shall soon see him our Mayor.*

But he did become a Freeman of the City of London and a member of the Worshipful Company of Skinners and the Worshipful Company of Distillers.

He was also interested in amateur drama. In January, 1885, he was stage manager at a performance at the Grammar School in aid of St. Edmund's East End Permanent Mission Room Fund and the following December he worked the limes at the charity performance of *The Merchant of Venice* previously referred to.

The month that he took over the Opera House he also occupied the chair at a meeting of the new board at Franklins Gardens and it was no doubt due to his influence that Phipps Brewery lent them money. The aim, he said, was to make the Gardens something Northampton could be proud of; 100 men were working on improvements including a mile-long pony racing track. Improvements in heating were by no means the only ways in which the new broom swept through the theatre. Although the house was scarcely in need of redecoration, having been done up two years before, following the fire, Dorman made many changes, as a Press account observed—"Mr. Dorman is determined to do big things and has commenced by redecorating the place entirely according to his own ideas of beauty. The visitor is first struck by the new and costly stage curtains. The old red baize and drop scene have been entirely abolished and in their place a pair of splendid ruby plush hanging curtains, fringed and tasselled with gold, have been fixed. These do not roll up as the drop scene did but fall gracefully from the sides like drawing room window curtains. They have been heavily weighted with lead so that they fall readily at the proper moment. Costing £100 they match the crimson hangings in the private boxes and correspond with the texture of the handsome gold-edged valance which has been fixed at the top of the proscenium arch. An important alteration has been made by the removal of the second proscenium arch. This was not part of the theatre but was put up by Mr. Tarry because it was thought that the charm of illusion was lost to the occupants of the first few rows of the pit by their seeing too far into the wings. Mr. Dorman and his manager have taken it down again and screened the view by new fixed wings. The advantage claimed is that it gives a greater stage width and facilitates the elaborate mounting of plays.

"A very important alteration has been made to the stage footlights. They are constructed on an entirely new principle just invented and patented by Mr. Noble. Like so many good ideas the scheme flashed across his mind by chance whilst he was in bed one morning. A long gas pipe runs along the front of the stage and the pipe is perforated with gas burners in the usual way. In the centre of the pipe is one gas jet which is under the control of quite another tap from that which governs the rest of the burners. The advantage is quite evident: when it is desired to make the stage quite dark instead of turning the footlights down low as hitherto, they can now be turned right out, the one small jet at the centre being left alight. The effect of darkness can be produced instantaneously and completely. When the line of lights is required to be ignited again the tap is turned and the jet in the centre lights all the rest of the burners immediately. This is good but Mr. Noble's invention comprises another valuable feature. On the stage just in front of the footlights two long slits have been cut. Beneath the stage, just under these slits, are two rods, worked by means of levers from the prompt side of the stage. Into the rods long panels of glass, coloured red in one case and pale blue in the other have been fixed. If the red lever is pulled the panels of red glass move up the long slit in front of the footlights. The effect is to flood the stage with a soft, even, rich beautiful sunset glow. Just in the same way if a moonlight effect is required the lever controlling the pale blue glass is pulled and the stage is immediately suffused with lovely lunar light. The general mode of producing these effects is by means of limelights worked from the wings. The rays are focussed in one spot in a most inartistic manner and the actor or actress is followed about the stage with a stream of light thrown on to him or her. Mr. Noble's patent will not, of course, obviate the use of the limes but it will produce the effects required in a more satisfactory manner than the old system. This is the first theatre in which the scheme has been tried. Mr. Noble hopes to see his patent adopted in many more theatres. It is clever in conception and economising for the gas it saves must be enormous.

"The proscenium arch has been elaborately decorated with gold and colour. A broad band of gilded lincrusta, an embossed material, runs round the arch and is prettily picked out with lines of blue, crimson, brown and grey. The corona—the circular ceiling over the pit has been painted blue. Formerly this was covered with decorative designs. The new cernian tint gives an appearance of loftiness and atmospheric area to the whole house. The whole of the decorations around the front of the dress circle have been regilded and cleaned.

"The form of the programmes has been changed. The Shakespearean design on the front page (by Mr. Harris Brown) has been superseded by a picture representing the ideal figures of comedy and tragedy drawing aside theatrical curtains. This design we venture to think is neither so artistic nor so appropriate as Mr. Harris Brown's drawing, defective as that was admittedly in one or two particulars." There were also staff changes. As his bill inspector and general assistant Mr. Noble had appointed Alfred Watson, "an experienced and active man in theatrical matters lately connected with the Roselle-Dacre Company and Mr. Wilson Barrett's companies. The stage machinist is now Mr. J. K. Young and the property master Mr. H. Young. Monday night saw new check-takers at most of the doors and there was a 'different' sort of feeling all round."

In a speech after the final curtain on the first night Dorman appeared to deny rumours that had been circulating that he proposed to take out three front rows of the pit and turn them into pit stalls. "I have been asked to do this for the sake of those who are suffering from deafness. (Cries of Oh! Oh!). Yes, it is a fact. But I don't intend to do it for the present (Loud cheers) as I consider the patrons of the Northampton pit cannot be put aside in that manner. I have also been requested to ask the ladies in the pit if they mind curtailing their headgear (Laughter and applause). There are some nice caps—in all colours—that can be bought for a shilling and it would be very nice if the ladies would wear some like that so that gentlemen who fetch refreshments for their friends shall be able to spot them immediately (Laughter). Ladies and gentlemen in the dress circle, I shall ask the editors of the papers to omit your names when you come to this house. That will be an improvement (Cheers)". Dorman then introduced the new manager who also made a few remarks.

The play that first week, *Golden Ladder* by Wilson Barrett's Company, was followed by another metallic title, *The Silver Fortune* which, said the Mercury, fell flat, being like *My Sweetheart* patched up to look like new. The last week of that month, February, 1889, brought a farewell visit of Genevieve Ward, in *Forget Me Not*.

All sorts of methods of prior publicity—we would term them stunts—were coming into use by advance managers. To publicise *Bootle's Baby* 2,000 piercing whistles were given away along with 20 watches engraved with the title of the piece. The advance manager, Mr. John Hawthorn, had bought 3,000 of the watches cheaply in Amsterdam, the Press explained. The play was by Hugh Moss, stage manager of the D'Oyly Carte, adapted from a story by John Strange

Winter, the alias of Mrs. Arthur Stannard.

The week that the show was being given in Northampton some background information about it emerged in a court case at Leamington in which Hawthorn was accused of threatening behaviour towards James O'Hara, father of the 18-month-old baby which had been taking the title role. It included an admission by the father, who had been paid £2.5s. a week, that he had been giving the child beer ("only a drop" he explained) and that it had gone to sleep, presumably in a drunken stupor, on stage at Blackburn. A counter-charge was that the father had stolen the child's stage clothes, which it was wearing for the court appearance. He was let off on promising to return these.

The question of all the Bootle's babies and other children employed on the stage was the subject of a campaign at this time and the Opera House's new manager, Charles Rider Noble, was among a deputation to the Home Office to put the side of theatre managements. Fellow members of the deputation, which was introduced by Dixon Hartland M.P., were Henry Irving, D'Oyly Carte, J. Pitt Hardacre and Augustus Harris. About this time F. A. Channing wrote to The Times demanding to know why the United Kingdom should lag behind the United States where an age limit of 15 was regarded as commonsense. "What becomes of the pantomime children?" he asked. "Is it not a fact that only a minute percentage of them ever are or can be educated for the lucrative branches of the profession. The rest earn a few premature shillings for a year or two and then have to look elsewhere. That means they have a worse start in life than other children" In fact it was not until October, 1904, that an Act affecting the employment of children on the stage came into effect.

Another stunt accompanied Mark Melford and Company in *Kleptomania* in March, 1889, bills being displayed cautioning tradesmen not to trust Lady Josephine. It was stated that in one town police had seized the bills from the shop windows in which they had been displayed. Melford, who was also the author of the play, had responded by sending round sandwich men with the boards chained to them. The police then admitted defeat . . . or was that story just another publicity stunt?

During Dorman's first year at the theatre there was a little incident which served to attract publicity even though it may not have been a stunt. The Harbury-Mathews Company were not doing the business the manager Mr. Russell-Rosse would have liked and one night he carried the statuette of Shakespeare from its place in the crush room to the doors of the dress circle and pointed to the scanty house. "Ah William," he said, "It would grieve you, could you feel emotion, to see how you are neglected nowadays. There is little money in you just now, William. People, I am afraid, prefer leg shows and common melodramas to your immortal works. Alas William, that you should come to this." Perhaps they also preferred the "underwater effects" for *The Diver,* which was the last show of that season.

In the summer of the year he took over the theatre Dorman went on a five week cruise round the South Coast aboard his steam schooner Eaglet. By the following year he had a 139-ton steam yacht, the Taxonia.

A Masonic enterprise in which theatre owner and theatre manager joined was the annual treat at the Corn Exchange for poor persons aged over 60. Dorman might give a slide show, including portraits of leading Freemasons, while Noble manipulated marionettes or did some conjuring tricks. Another cause they assisted jointly was Lifeboat Saturday which gave Dorman the chance to talk about his seagoing experiences and Noble the opportunity to yarn about the time at South Shields when he was a member of the lifeboat crew.

As regards corny plots the palm is by general consent awarded to *East Lynne*, a perennially popular tear-jerker based on a novel by Mrs. Henry Wood, its most notorious line being "Dead and never called me Mother!" Patrons had a very late night when this piece was staged by the J. Pitt Hardacre Company later that year. They had expected to leave the theatre at 10.45 but at that time the 4th Act was about to commence. The Press said this was due to "a mass of superfluous gags which lowers the tone of the drama, hinders the action and results in the piece running half-an-hour longer than it ought to." Among the cast, as Cornelia Carlyle, was Mrs. C. A. Clarke, wife or widow of a former lessee of the Marefair theatre. The four acts were entitled Temptation, Repentance, Through the Fire and Atonement. Two months later a Hardacre company presented *Current Cash,* which he had bought from C. A. Clarke, the author.

"Very much expurgated, of course," said the Mercury about Wycherley's old comedy *The Country Girl* in which Kate Vaughan, the former dancer and now the queen of comedy, appeared in September, 1889, supported by Frank Fenton.

The October, 1889, visit by the Compton Comedy Company was the first of half-a-dozen during the Dorman regime, others being in November, 1890; January, 1893; October, 1894, September, 1895; October, 1896, and November, 1900. The 1889 week introduced John Tobin's *The Honeymoon,* dating from 1805. It is the story of a Duke who marries a virago and tames her by pretending to be a peasant, taking her to a cottage and making her do all the lowly chores.

"She shares with Pears Soap and Beechams Pills the distinction of being one of the best advertised products in the commercial universe," said the Mercury of Minnie Palmer, the original *My Sweetheart,* who appeared in the show's fifth visit to the town in November, 1889. "How much of her success she owes to the unparalleled advertisement and how much to her discoverer and vendor John R. Rogers for ever remains like the problem of perpetual motion, an insoluble mystery. She is, however, a clever little baggage with many pretty airs and graces and a certain archness of manner that is peculiarly engaging. She is a saucy little mystery in short skirts." Besides being her publicist Rogers was her husband and the marriage was to end in a blaze of distasteful publicity. Certainly it would appear that Rogers was indulging his fancy in his claim that Minnie was wearing £30,000 of jewels in Act II. On the Friday night she appeared in the dual roles of brother and sister in *My Brother's Sister.* It was stated that she proposed gradually to drop roles of the *My Sweetheart* type but she seems to have failed to shrug off the image for she was back in the same show at Northampton in February, 1892, though with "new music, new songs, exquisite toilets."

Charity performances became a regular feature of the dull days of December and in 1889 Arthur Dacre returned for a matinee organised by Mrs. Lena Jameson for her fund for giving summer country holidays to sickly children from the East End of London. The play was *The Silver Shield* and Dacre took his original part of Tom Potter, as at the Strand Theatre, London, in May, 1885, when his wife Amy Roselle starred with him. At Northampton this role went to Miss Edith Herbert. Dacre supervised the rehearsals. Several of the front rows of the pit were replaced by pit stalls for the event. As a token of thanks Mrs. James presented the manager, Mr. Noble, with an inscribed tortoiseshell paper knife: "The Silver Shield, December 15, 1889. From L. J." In Dacre Noble was meeting an old friend for before settling at Northampton he was acting manager with the Dacres' company

Soon afterwards Noble had another presentation, this time of a gold Albert chain with a spade guinea pendant. It was given to him by Dorman as a reward for his work for the pantomime *Dick Whittington and His Cat,* during the rehearsals for which he had had a non-stop 42 hour session. Yet, said the Press, "He never loses his temper, never swears, a most remarkable thing for at pantomime time every manager swears." However hard working he may have been Noble seems to have miscalculated for on the opening night the show did not finish until 10 minutes past midnight and had subsequently to be trimmed by three-quarters of an hour. The Press praised Dorman's enterprise in funding such a show—"There has been more money spent on it than can ever be returned to the proprietor if the house is crammed every night."

During the early weeks of 1890 it was announced that Dorman's younger brother Fred, the architect, was going on to the stage. He had many times appeared as an amateur but now he was to "lay down the T square and angle arc to don the sock and buskin.". He first joined the tour of *London Day by Day* and in March Fred Doomar (that was his stage name) was seen in it at the Opera House in the double role of Lord Kempston and a detective. He "spoke his lines clearly but was inclined to hold down his head."

Another change of status which was regarded as sensational at this time was Amy Roselle's acceptance of George Edwardes' offer to play in musichall at the Empire Theatre, London. "She has overthrown completely the tradition that the gulf between theatre and musichall stage is impossible to bridge," said the Mercury.

At Northampton Fred Leslie and Nellie Farren, two of the leading performers of the day, appeared in a matinee.

At his benefit performance Mr. Noble spoke frankly about the completion of his first year. "I have travelled a good deal and had a lot to do with theatrical business. It is often said that London audiences are the most easy to please. That may be so but I know this, that Northampton audiences are most difficult to please. Please excuse me for being so severe upon you but I say that most sincerely."

In thanking the various performers and contributors to the pantomime Mr. Noble forgot the musicians, who are all too often taken for granted, though they work at least as hard as anyone on stage. And being in charge of the Victorian pit orchestra at panto time appears to have had its special problems. In filling the "thanks" gap left by the manager, the Mercury stated: "It is not like conducting an opera in which all of the people on the stage are trained musicians. In a pantomime most of the extras are altogether ignorant of music and have the most sublime contempt for time and tune. The conductor has to lead the band and those who can sing so as not to expose those who can't." The man who had performed the feat in this case was Mr. Twist.

A large crowd saw the panto company off to Coventry in two long railway carriages and four trucks for the scenery. After Coventry they were going on to

Longton.

Hubert O'Grady's Irish company appeared in March, 1890, in *Emigration*, which the Mercury described as "appealing to that class of playgoer which does not care two straws about probability or coherence of plot so long as virtue triumphs over vice." Most unusually the theatre was occupied on Good Friday that year, the J. W. Turner Opera Company giving two sacred concerts at 3 and 8.15. Soon after that the Robertson comedies, *Caste, Ours* and *School* returned, given this time by the H. Austin Company to whom Robertson the younger had sold the rights.

At Easter Franklins Gardens had been lit for the first time by electricity and in June they were visited by Ben Greet's Woodland Players, including Mrs. Patrick Campbell, in *A Midsummer Night's Dream*.

What's in a name? Cow Lane had been so called because cows used to be driven to pasture down it. The name was now altered to Swan Street, not because of any swans on the river which runs through that Cow Meadow but because the Swan Inn was at the top of the street. The Mercury did not approve—"The useful cow is to be discarded for a useless animal. It is a sad descent. If the inhabitants were anxious for a change they should have a more ambitious title. Avenue de L'Opera would have been the name for them." But the Highway Committee adopted Swan Street without comment. Later the name of Cow Meadow itself was changed—to Becket's Park.

On their third annual vacation tour the Lyceum Theatre (London) Company came to the Opera House that autumn. In the cast of *The Two Roses* was Gordon Craig, 18-year-old son of Ellen Terry, who played the blind Caleb Deecie. This brought his mother and sister Elsie to the theatre as members of the audience. On the Friday night they went backstage before being escorted to their box by the proprietor, Mr. Dorman. Mrs. Ratliffe, who was in the opposite box, sent over a bouquet and the management had provided a special programme printed in gold on white satin. The visit had been publicised in advance and the dress circle was full in consequence. The pair went again on the Saturday night.

One of the first Northampton buildings to be lit by electricity was the new Masonic Hall in Princes Street, which was opened in September, 1890, by the Earl of Euston who had just succeeded the late Duke of Manchester as Grand Master of the Province. Dorman, the theatre owner, was chairman of the Masonic Hall Company and it was he who had provided the new temple and premises. When he was installed as Worshipful Master of the Eleanor Cross Lodge a few weeks later, Canon Sanders, headmaster of Northampton Grammar School, said that the Masons could not measure their indebtedness to him for the erection of that magnificent building. As I write, this magnificent temple has disappeared in rubble to make way for a temple of consumerism—the Grosvenor shopping centre.

In January, 1892, the Opera House owner and manager walked in procession with their brother Masons from the Masonic Hall to All Saints Church for a memorial service to the Duke of Clarence, oldest son of the Prince and Princess of Wales and seemingly a future king. In London the Royal death was said to be the cause of a "time of depression such as is almost unknown in the history of matters theatrical." Despite this, said the Mercury, "There are more theatres in town than ever before and new theatres are still going up."

Princess Mary of Teck who had been betrothed to the Duke transferred her affections to his brother George, Duke of York, who later became George V. When the couple were married in 1893 some 1,250 people attended a celebration at Franklins Gardens while outside the Opera House a "pretty illuminated device" was exhibited.

October, 1890, brought to the Opera House the theatre's most celebrated visitor to date—Wilson Barrett appeared with Miss Eastlake and the Princess Theatre Company who were just back from a tour of the United States. On the first two nights it was *Hamlet;* Wednesday and Friday, *Clito;* and Thursday and Saturday, *Claudian.*

Sweet Nancy, by Horace Sedger's Company, was a provincial premiere, Horace Lingard brought *Falka* again, and then came the Compton Comedy Company in what, it was said, would be a last visit because Edward Compton was taking a London theatre—"In a very short time old English comedy will know Mr. Compton's face no more. After Christmas he will tempt fortune with a London season of modern plays."

Innovation was not always advance. Criticising *The New Mazeppa,* set in Tartary and written by Fred Cook and W. R. Waldron, the Mercury said that they had gone so far off the beaten track that they had lost their way, producing an entertainment which was neither burlesque, nor opera, nor even a circus, yet which trespassed upon the domain of all three.

Just before Christmas there was a visit by the London Juvenile Opera Company in *The Belle of The Village.* If they gave a good performance on the Monday it was surprising for they had spent the night in the train from Glasgow. It was certainly a shortened performance because the basket containing the costumes for the Harlequinade had disappeared en route. That awkward gap before Christmas was filled by three different entertainments on succeeding nights. On the Monday manager Noble appeared, with a beard for disguise, with a "specially selected company" which also included billposter Alfred Watson in *The Two Roses,* a benefit for Noble which was ruined by a dense fog; on Tuesday there was an amateur performance of *Trial By Jury* by members of Leicester Musical and Dramatic Club, with a chorus of Northampton folk, while on the Wednesday Mr. Dorman provided a magic lantern show for children from the Orphanage and Workhouse. Mr. W. F. Tipler, who now ran Franklins Hotel and Restaurant, gave a bun for each member of the young audience.

Franklins Gardens had now gone on the rocks. Pugh, a local solicitor, was involved in this as also in the subsequent crash of the Allchin engineering firm. Pugh did not appear at a bankruptcy hearing and was next heard of in Valparaiso in South America.

Instead of pantomime the Christmas attraction of 1890 was the Turner Opera Company and again they did the unusual by staging a sacred concert on Christmas Day.

Dorman clashed with church authorities in 1891 after promising £50 to the St. Edmund's Church Restoration Fund. The church had nevertheless organised opposition against public houses in general and the transfer of licences from old pubs to new ones in particular, even accepting in church signatures for a petition to the licensing bench. This, said Dorman in a letter to the Vicar, was "turning the House of God into a polling booth" and he diverted the £50 to a fund for erecting an armoury for the 1st Northamptonshire Rifle Volunteers. Among many letters to the Press, one said that "the Almighty must have been upset when he realised that henceforth he must work without the patronage of the great Thomas Phipps Dorman" but others praised his courage—"The brewers have been long suffering in this respect." The incident did not prevent the Phipps family paying for the erection of St. Matthew's Church as a memorial to Pickering Phipps.

C. W. Garthorne, brother of Mr. Kendal, appeared with his company as Talbot Champneys in *Our Boys* in February, 1891, and Fred Dorman was back as the villain Gilchrist in *Bootle's Baby,* to be greeted with "a storm of villainous applause—hisses."

The Phonograph was among the attractions of *The Dangers of London,* one of the many sensational works from the pen of F. A. Scudamore who regularly brought them to the Opera House. The first exhibition in Northampton of "Edison's wonderful phonograph" had been at the Corn Exchange in June 1885: it was also billed as his "talking and singing machine". Admission was 3d. On the stage it had been pioneered by Fred Karno in 1889. He bought a phonograph from an American sea captain in Bristol and pretended to be playing it by bicycle pump. Karno also talked some of the stars, including Dan Leno, into recording for him for nothing. As late as 1897 he was still operating the machine, the billing being "Fred Karno's Company of Speechless Comedians . . . also the most marvellous invention of the age . . . the Karnophone." Many people believed that he had invented it.

Scenery for *The Dangers of London* was stated to have been constructed by Noble and painted by Sidney Thompson. By now the theatre was also providing scenery for touring shows and for other theatres. Mr. Noble told 100 members of the theatre staff gathered for supper later that year that they had completely fitted up three other theatres during the past 12 months, besides equipping innumerable travelling companies. That very afternoon they had made a working model locomotive which would soon be seen at the theatre. In the chair at the supper was the boss, Dorman.

The under-the-road tunnel to the paint and workshop is believed to have been constructed about 1890, probably being another result of the change in ownership the previous year. It appears, surprisingly, that the artist's studio may have been on the opposite side of Cow Lane before the theatre was built. At all events the creation of the tunnel results in the unique situation that the theatre's stage door is on the opposite side of the street from the rear of the theatre!

April, 1891, brought to Northampton a number of Compton's players but this time in a "specially organised company" in support of his sister-in-law Isabel Bateman. It was managed by J. H. Savile, who had been with Compton since 1881. Miss Bateman was seen in *Leah, Jane Shore, Mary Warner* and *Clarissa Harlowe.* She was followed by Mrs. Bandman-Palmer in *Mary Stuart, The Lady of Lyons, Much Ado About Nothing* and *The School for Scandal.*

J. Pitt Hardacre brought *The Shaughraun* and then Kate Vaughan and J. H. Lethcourt were back in *The Country Girl,* which featured a new dance by Miss Vaughan. Having deserted his father's comedies T. W. Robertson returned with *Sweet Lavender* and *The Fair Equestrian. Lost By Drink* was given by Walter Raynham's Company and other shows that summer included *Randolph The Reck-*

less, the Juvenile Comic Opera Company, and Tom Craven and Company in *The Village Forge*, which began the new season.

The first time seat booking seems to have left Marks Library was in 1891 when John Hart's Company was staging *New Year Chimes* and patrons were invited to book by telephone or at the theatre between 10 and 4 o'clock.

When the French prima donna Madame Marie Roze came in a farewell tour with the Carl Rosa Opera Company the chorus and orchestra were conducted by Mr. (later Sir) Henry Wood. The eight tons of scenery required for *The Daughter of The Regiment, The Bohemian Girl* and *Fadette* was carried in a special train and a lady harpist was among the extra musicians travelling with the company.

Since her last appearance three years earlier Miss Fortescue had made a name for herself in the legal arena by successfully suing Viscount Garmoyle for £10,000 for breach of promise. The young actress who had been discovered by W. S. Gilbert was seen in *Moths, The Love Chase, The Hunchback* and *The Lady of Lyons*.

Familiar plays and familiar players were the usual routine. The autumn of 1891 brought *The Silver King, East Lynne, The Dancing Girl* (with Kate Vaughan), Little Tich was seen as Quasimodo in the Gaiety burlesque *Miss Esmeralda* produced by Rollo Balmain, lessee of the Theatre Royal, Plymouth, and in November Wilson Barrett was back, this time with Maude Jeffries, to be met at the railway station by hundreds of admirers. He performed in *Claudian, Hamlet, Othello, Belphegor, The Acrobat* and *Ben-My-Chree*.

In many productions, however, the play was not the thing but spectacle, sensation and incident were, with actors sharing the stage with trains, ships, horses, lighthouses, explosions, rabbits, earthquakes and pigeons. The Manchester Cup horse race was run on one occasion. Trains would not only run, complete with crew but would belch forth steam and sparks. Realism was all.

When Lincoln J. Carter's *The Fast Mail* was given by Hardie and Von Leer's Company in January, 1892, after successful production in New York, Brooklyn, Chicago, Cincinatti, St. Louis and New Orleans, the advertisement referred to "Niagara by moonlight, boiling foam and mist, genuine practical engine drawing 14 freight cars across the stage and having engineer and fireman mounted on it and throwing out real smoke and steam; river scene and steamboat explosion." A couple of months later posters showed a woman being run over by a steamroller—advance publicity for F. A. Scudamore's *Is Life Worth Living?*. Performed by the W. H. Hallatt Company it "found favour with the gods." You could measure spectacle and sensation either numerically or by avoirdupois. In May, 1892, *The Dark Continent,* presented by Morell and Mouillot, was stated to have "more real excitement than any five other plays." There were many boasts about the tonnage of the scenery.

Occasionally the Press cocked a snook at this sort of thing, sometimes obliquely when referring to something better. *Proof* was a play which had been staged at the Marefair theatre but which did not turn up at the Opera House until November, 1895, when it was given by the company of Louis Calvert and drew the comment: *"Proof* belongs to the school of drama which of late has been pushed into the background in order that modern taste may be satisfied with plays crammed with situations often badly strung together by the merest shreds of plot embellished with large amounts of mechanical scenery, some wonderfully startling introduction of the newest scientific instruments or the oldest racehorse that could be procured."

Among the plays of spectacle and sensation was one of which manager Noble was co-author. To stage it he got together a stock company in the summer of 1892. The play was *From Shore to Shore* and his co-author was Alfred England, the pen-name of Alfred Ewens, who was the local Official Receiver in Bankruptcy. The tone of the piece was quickly established in the prologue which was set in a rocky pass near Bombay with a party of Thugs (a cult dedicated to strangling and worship of the god Kali) trying to polish off a couple of passing Englishmen, an officer and a private. The Thugs came off worst on this occasion and their dying chief charged their sole survivor to see that vengeance was done. The curse of Kali was uttered against the Englishmen, lightning flashed and the curtain fell. The Englishmen were pursued to England where, happily from the spectacular point of view, the private is found working on a lighthouse.

The stock company, which had been supervised by Walter McEwen, also appeared in *Uncle Tom's Cabin, The Two Orphans* and *The Sensualist*. The last-named was an interesting choice, and not only because it was a first performance. After labelling it as "Ibsenesque" the newspaper went on to query whether the role of the drama was "to uncover the secret hideous vices which lay hidden beneath the polished exterior of social formalism" and to ask "Is the play the proper instrument of correction?" The Mercury thought not—"The theatre exists primarily as an agency for recreation and amusement." The play was by Michael Buenu and F. Allen Laidlaw with incidental music by Isidore de Solla.

The newspaper also commented on the subject of "stock" productions: "It is very many years since the days of the old stock companies at the old theatre in Marefair. The travelling show has almost entirely superseded them. But in various parts of the country theatre managers have made a temporary return to the old system at certain times of the year. The summer time is sparse in good bookings and playgoers may gain much by having a varied repertoire submitted to them by a sound stock company." As far as Northampton is concerned but for this stock season it seems unlikely that *From Shore to Shore* and *The Sensualist* would have been seen.

A few years later, in 1900, the Era stated: "The stock company is a dead horse. Let us by all means have a few useful training schools for the drama like that of the late Sarah Thorne at Margate. By all means let a practical manager in his dead season run a company for a week or two. But to dream we can turn the clock back and substitute for the polished repertoire of excellent travelling organisations the hurriedly rehearsed, poorly mounted and cheaply dressed productions of a resident company of necessarily second-rate artistes is absurd."

Red Indians entertained Northampton some years before the advent of the Western film. Buffalo Bill and his entourage did not appear on Northampton Racecourse until September, 1903, but at the Opera House in October, 1892, the Hardie and Von Leer Company included "a band of real Red Indians" to provide scenes of "blood-curdling massacres" and sounds of "wild war whoops" for *On the Frontier,* an adaptation of Fennimore Cooper's The Last Of The Mohicans. It returned in March, 1894, when the local critic remarked upon "an awful villain who for some inexplicable reason is constantly shaking his fist to heaven and hissing malediction at everything and everybody." Hissing and groaning at the villain was a vital part of the evening out for the lower orders on the top shelf and the quality of the villain's performance was judged by the amount of vocal reaction he managed to provoke.

Patronising references to the gallery were not infrequent. Regarding *The Plunger* in January, 1894, it was said in the Press: "From the glaring posters scattered broadcast throughout, the town was prepared for an ocean of startling surprises but the most ardent of the galleryites were more than surfeited with the gory galaxy served up." This was the piece in which "real rain descended in torrents." *The Plunger* was of American origin and in this respect the Mercury man was unimpressed: "It comes with the recommendation of seven years in America. The name of the author is not divulged but whoever he is he must have the most extraordinary idea of stage production for murders are committed and women are chloroformed to the accompaniment of comic songs and high kick dances and the Catherine wheels of pantomime." But spectacle abounded: "A real train rushes over a real railroad and the unconscious heroine stretched across the rails is saved by the skin of the teeth by the prompt application of the Westinghouse brakes. And so the story rushed enjoyably on amid the deafening applause of the denizens of the gallery who get almost wild with delight as the astonishing situations are revealed in bewildering array." The show had 16 specialities which were changed nightly! In September, 1897, the characters in *Two Little Vagabonds* "in three hours get through about as much trouble and worry as they could be expected to in that time."

The attraction of livestock on stage is well known. To compete with an attractive puppy is well nigh impossible for the actor, as also is the holding of an audience's attention in competition with the charm of a child. Besides eight sets of new mechanical scenery, statuary and armour *The World's Verdict* brought ducks, pigeons and rabbits in March, 1899.

A number of premieres took place at the Opera House. Not all of them were earth-shattering events. New plays, whether good, bad or indifferent, had to start somewhere and merely on the luck of the draw Northampton was bound to come in for a few "first performances on any stage." Of many of the plays premiered little more was heard. Among the exceptions was *The Lady Slavey* which was the very first theatrical venture of George Dance who left £157,272 when, as Sir George Dance, he died in October, 1932. *The Lady Slavey* was first given at St. Andrew's Hospital, the Northampton mental institution where the county poet John Clare was for many years a patient. George Dance was a journalist at Nottingham at the time and a fellow journalist who was present at the Northampton premiere on September 4, 1893, wrote: "I well remember his nervous anxiety about the show which was to bring him fame and fortune and lead to several great managements." Dance was so pleased with the success following the Northampton premiere that he repeated the procedure with *The Gay Parisienne* in September, 1894.

In 1894 a telephone demonstration meant that Northampton people could hear what was happening on the stage of the Leicester Opera House—a very early form of "outside broadcast." In June the following year the Mercury reported that the telephone was assuming an important place in the life of London, as new lines to the provinces had been opened that month.

That same month the two year sentence on the playwright Oscar Wilde was followed by a comment in the Mercury, as no doubt in many other provincial newspapers, that the case had led to protests about the unhealthy tendencies of much of the fiction and drama of the day.

In August, 1895, the old Plough Music Hall, which had been refurbished and renamed The Empire in September, 1894, was reopened with success by Frank Macnaghten and from this lowly beginning he went on to found a large chain of musichalls in the north of England.

"High class vaudeville" was the description of The New Barmaid by Frederick Bownes and W. E. Sprange, presented at the Opera House in February, 1896, and said to be in rehearsal for production at the Avenue Theatre, London. The month also brought Trilby, a Paul Potter adaptation of the novel by Gerald du Maurier, which was given by Mr. Abud's Company by arrangement with Mr. Tree. Almost immediately afterwards the play was back again among the repertoire of Otho Stuart's Company but in March the Mercury reported that in London the Trilby craze was beginning to pall and that the most marvellous craze supplanting it was for The Shop Girl, in which the star was Ellaline Terriss. Generally regarded as being the very first true musical comedy, it came to the Northampton theatre in November, 1896.

During an April week of 1896 three of the top stars of the day were seen at the Opera House. First for three days came J. L. Toole in Daisy's Escape, Paul Pry and The Birthplace of Podgers; for the second half of the week Mr. and Mrs. (later Dame Madge) Kendal were seen in The Ironmaster, A Scrap of Paper and The Greatest of These. There were special prices during the week, the dress circle being 5s. and the gallery 9d. (early doors 1s.)

August productions included The Telephone Girl, a new musical comedy with Ida Blanche and The Co-Respondent by Violet Melnotte's Company which was "shortly going to London" with the same company. Charles Hawtrey's Company brought An Ideal Husband in September.

Despite being a mere provincial manager, Mr. Noble was evidently a well-known and popular figure in the theatre world. Those who came to Northampton to appear in his benefit in June, 1893, included Lionel Brough, Osmond Tearle. the London musichall star Maude St. John (who gave a skirt dance), Ernest Montefiore, W. J. Robertson, Henry Arnecliffe, Hubert Druce, George Hazlehurst, G. Philip, J. J. Bartlett, the local amateur Mrs. Jameson, and J. Pitt Hardacre who had left Hamburg only that morning and therefore appeared in "travelling dress" to recite "The Villain of the Piece." It was as the villain of the piece that Hardacre, lessee of the Comedy Theatre, Manchester, as well as manager of several touring companies, emerged from a libel suit which he brought in 1902. He sued Mr. Holt, a member of the Manchester Watch Committee, for remarks about the way he conducted the theatre in the city. Defence witnesses included actresses who applied for work at the theatre and were offered champagne and seduction as a condition of employment. The most startling evidence came from P. C. Lynn who explained that he had not reported the goings-on at the theatre because the police department was corrupt and it would have been no use. Holt won the verdict but was left with a bill of £3,000 for costs. Whether it shows an affection for Holt, the opposite for Hardacre or merely a simple affection for justice I do not know but the Manchester public gave over £2,000 to a fund to help pay his costs.

Newspaper readers—remember that radio and television were far into the future—must have feasted upon the accounts of such scandalous goings-on. Nowadays when one in every four or five marriages ends up on the rocks and when the sexual athletics of leading film and television players are openly discussed it is difficult to imagine how enjoyable the reading public of Victorian times must have found the accounts of divorce cases of actors and actresses, whether stage heroines like Minnie Palmer or stage villains like William Abingdon.

The case concerning Miss Palmer in May, 1895, made particularly good reading. Her husband John Rogers was revealed to have been demanding money from a titled person with whom his wife had had connections. He was said to have asked for £5,000, as the price of silence regarding her adultery with Sir William Rose. These titillating facts emerged when Rogers sued his wife for adultery with Francis Jerrard, a member of her company, the pair having stayed together at Blisworth Hotel, on the main railway line four miles distant from Northampton. Mr. Noble gave evidence about the couple's visit to the Opera House at the time. The case was deferred and a decree was not granted until Minnie had gone into the witness box to testify that she had not spoken to her husband for years and to deny collusion with him or receiving any part of the £600 said to have been paid to him by Sir William Rose.

The following November William Abingdon, the Northamptonshire-born actor who was the leading stage villain of the day, was sued by his actress wife Rachel who gave evidence of finding a letter from another woman in his pocket and of his breaking her nose with a blow. She got her decree and Abingdon later married Bijou Vernandez, daughter of a wealthy New York merchant, and went to America in 1907 where he died 11 years later.

The tragic end of the Dacres was the talk of the world in November, 1895, but of especial interest to Northampton, where he had worked as a doctor, and later visited as an actor. After appearing at Northampton in the charity performance of *The Silver Shield* Dacre had been in *A Life of Pleasure* while his wife Amy Roselle had created the part of Mrs. Cortelyon in Pinero's *The Second Mrs. Tanqueray* at the St. James Theatre, London, in May, 1893. There had also been a disastrous tour of America and an even more disastrous production of *Man and Woman* at the Opera Comique, London. Then they went to Australia to recoup their fortunes but, embittered by further failure, made a suicide pact. In a hotel room in Sydney he shot her and then turned the gun upon himself. Despite his medical knowledge he missed a vital spot and had to cut his own throat, which he also did rather less than neatly. As servants of the hotel burst into the room he stood by the mantlepiece moaning "Oh the pain! The pain." and died soon afterwards.

Reams of analysis was written as to why they should have done this. Alongside a picture of them with their baby The Sketch said: "Mrs. Dacre was a brilliant actress. Her husband, with fewer histrionic gifts, was nonetheless a reliable actor and the pair would act together and 'star'. For some reason the public would not accept them in the only position they themselves cared about and thus trouble came . . . they chose rather to endure the hardships of prolonged travel rather than accept any but the leading positions in London." Arthur Dacre has been described as belonging to a group of actors known as stage beauties, remarkable only for their physical attractiveness, and including Handsome Harry Conway and Handsome Jack Barber. According to one writer Dacre was the victim of his own inordinate vanity.

There was a further theatre scandal with a local flavour in April, 1897, when Col. The Hon. Frederick Arthur Wellesley sued his actress wife Kate Vaughan for divorce, citing John Lethcourt. Mrs. Anetta Warner, a Northampton boarding house keeper, and her servant Annie Parker gave evidence that the pair had stayed together in the same room during their visit to the Opera House in August, 1895.

With such cases before them the public might have been sceptical when listening to Wilson Barrett from the stage of the Brixton Theatre on its first night in September, 1896. Barrett, who was appearing in *The Sign of the Cross,* declared that the theatre was one of the most powerful engines either for good or for evil in a community. A boy would probably forget his first essay, certainly his first sermon, but never his first play. Among his hearers were Messrs. Dorman and Noble—Dorman owned the new theatre and Noble was its manager. In a house lit by electricity generated by its own plant they heard Barrett say that though suburban theatres such as this were bad things for the West End, he must compliment Brixton on the lovely building it had acquired. This theatre had a spectacular end—it was blown up by a high explosive bomb on November 8, 1940, soon after being renamed the Melville Theatre.

Noble, who now controlled the Northampton theatre through a deputy, was himself not untouched by the breath of scandal for in January, 1894, he had been sued by his wife for judicial separation. Mr. H. Dorman appeared as a defence witness, contradicting Mrs. Phoebe Noble's claim that she was struck by her husband when she visited the theatre. It was merely an attempt to ward off her blow, testified Dorman. Her evidence provides one or two details of their life together. She had for 18 years been a member of a dancing act called the Sisters

Opened by Thomas **Phipps Dorman** in September, 1896, the **Brixton Theatre** stood at the foot of Brixton Hill, contiguous with the **Tate Library** and could from some angles be mistaken as being part of it. When the theatre was bombed in 1940 the library escaped major damage and remains almost unaltered externally. In the 1960s the theatre site was used for the erection of a small reading room and assembly hall and a car park (which is where the auditorium and stage were). *(Tate Library)*

Belton, so it was very much a theatrical marriage, with all the inherent dangers. In 1881, she said, she and her husband were in Dublin but she denied associating too closely with officers of the 48th Regiment, then quartered there. She and her husband had ceased living together in 1886. Other facets of Noble's past emerged from a talk he gave at a Lifeboat Saturday at Northampton Town Hall in 1889, when he recalled being a volunteer lifeboat crew member at South Shields in 1882 and rowing out to eight wrecks. He also had some experience in that line while manager of the Winter Gardens, Whitby. Noble was also an inventor and one reads from time to time of his brainchilds, such as patent footlights which were fitted at the London Globe and the Manchester Comedy, a "novel banjo rim", and an electric contrivance for chiming stage bells.

Dorman, who was also part proprietor of the Theatre Royal, Hull, does not appear to have made any more money out of his 1896 venture in suburban theatre than did Edward Compton and Milton Bode, as elsewhere related, at Dalston. Within three or four years he had parted with Brixton as well as Northampton.

Who then did make money out of theatrical enterprise? Was it the people who built theatres, the people who managed them, the people who owned them? Was it the actors and actresses? Or the people who wrote the plays, for which there was a steady demand during this period?

In January, 1891, the Mercury reported that the actor Hayden Coffin was receiving £47 a week for appearing in *Dorothy* in London and commented: "Not so long ago £5 would have been good. The artistic movement that has taken place of late has had a wonderful effect upon not only the salaries but also the social position of the artist. When the salaries rose it became worth the while of sons of professional men to take to the boards and there are many actors who have been officers in the Army, doctors, or sons of men of high position whose fortune is inadequate to their social status." Indeed a turn-round for what Macready termed the "pariah profession"!

Reporting the death of Arthur Cellier in January, 1892, the Mercury said that he had been paid £100 for the score of *Dorothy* and that this showed that composing music was "obviously a profitable profession."

One man of the theatre who made a vast fortune during this period was, like Isaac Tarry, a former auctioneer's clerk. It was at Paddington that W. S. Penley followed this vocation. He made his money through *Charley's Aunt* which came several times to Northampton and which, he said in a talk at the Savage Club, London, in April, 1895, then had 52 companies operating all over the world. On the other hand, one who had little enough to show for a long stage career of performing and management was August Van Biene. He made 6,000 performances in *The Broken Melody,* including a number at Northampton, but when he died on stage at the Brighton Hippodrome on January 24, 1913, he left a mere £288. (And this despite the showers of small change he used to receive after reciting *The Absent Minded Beggar,* as at Northampton in December, 1899, with a "super" coming on stage to collect the bombarded donations while the recitation was still going on.)

The often extravagant salaries commanded by some of the great actors and actresses and musichall comedians were by no means reflected in the wages of the scores of lesser minions both on stage, backstage and front of house. As late as

1913 a Northampton Socialist, Councillor Slinn, said that his party could not support the New Theatre in its application for a stage play licence because its management was paying people one shilling for five hours work.

In the 1890s the going rate for an assistant scenic artist at Northampton was £2 a week. We know this because it came up in evidence at Northampton Quarter Sessions when manager Noble sued assistant artist Cathermole Cathery for 10s., the balance of £1 borrowed while employed at the theatre from November, 1892, to January, 1893.

One theatrical manager confessed in court that he had paid a company of actresses the princely sum of 1s. 6d. each a week during the six weeks they were at Northampton. They appear to have been "resting" or stranded here. Robert Barton, of no fixed abode, was charged at Bow Street Police Court, London, in August, 1894, with obtaining money by false pretences. He had taken premiums from young women, promising them 52 weeks engagements as actresses. He took them on tour to Northampton and there abandoned them, first writing to the Actors' Benevolent Fund in London and obtaining money. Giving evidence, Noble said that he had asked the prisoner how he could bring himself to take money from the women when he knew it was impossible to carry out his promise. In his defence Barton said that he had been singing in public houses to raise money for the company. He took the money "for my wife's sake."

In 1902 the Daily Reporter said that it was "proof that the stage as a profession for women is overcrowded" when Henrietta Murton was charged in the Northamptonshire town of Wellingborough with stealing a piece of beef valued at 2s. 6d. She said that she was travelling with a company which had had a bad time and was going to share the meat with them.

In the closing years of the 19th century the Herald found it odd that the hybrid production of pantomime should continue to hold favour—"people may talk about the increasing seriousness of the nation with the ever increasing development of education; they may argue that the present day theatregoer likes his theatrical feast served up in the shape of a problem play, a psychological study; but it is still a fact that when the season of frivolity and gaiety comes round people young and old, gay and serious, delight in pantomime."

Noble and the Official Receiver Alfred England (alias Ewen) collaborated in the scripts of *Cinderella* (1897-8) and *Robinson Crusoe* (1898-9). The Mercury said that *Cinderella* was the most gorgeous pantomime Northampton had ever seen but noted that patriotic songs had displaced sentimental ditties (the Boer War was in progress). The cast of *Robinson Crusoe* took part in a light-hearted charity football match against the Thursday Football Club, with the scenic artist Ernest Howard joining in as a mock policeman.

Since 1876 the former Penny Readings which had provided a cheap form of amusement for the masses developed in Northampton into "Saturday Evening Talks" sponsored by the Museum and Free Library Committee of the Town Council and held in the Town Hall. Admission was still a penny, with an extra penny for "early doors" and "sixpence for the few seats available". Besides having a new name they also broadened in scope and at times became altogether too sophisticated in the opinion of some critics.

On at least two occasions Thomas Phipps Dorman provided competition for his own Opera House. On a Saturday night in March, 1892, the Town Hall was packed and hundreds were unable to gain admission to see his pictures of a trip to Niagara, shown on his powerful triple light limelight lantern. It was the same "house over-full" situation when he gave a repeat the following January; on that occasion Mrs. Mulliner, presumably a member of the famous coach-building firm founded in Northampton in 1760, was an added attraction, reciting "The Curfew Shall Not Ring Tonight." In February, 1897, Dorman was billed for a five night appearance at the Town Hall, in aid of five Northampton charities but after poor attendances on the first three nights he pleaded indisposition to call off the Thursday and Friday shows. And he took the opportunity to express the belief that the Saturday Evening Talks were "doing a great deal of mischief towards the success of other events for at the Talks people are often provided for a penny with entertainment worth half-a-crown."

The "Talk" had certainly gone a long way beyond its original aims when, as on a March Saturday in 1895, the bill included William Bonner, founder of the St. Cecilia Orchestral Society (later Northampton Symphony Orchestra) playing violin solos; items on the musical glasses, ocarina and Indian fiddle by Signor Talini; plus songs by Miss Ashford and Miss May James. Or a month later when the entire St. Cecilia ensemble, 60 strong, went along with Mr. Bonner. Sketches and playlets were also presented occasionally.

It was about this time that someone who had attended the talks since they began in 1876 wrote to the Press protesting at "unseemly shouting, yelling and whistling" at some of them, mentioning especially one by Dorman. Evidently it was a night for some working folk to let off their animal spirits after the long week in factory or shop. In March, 1898, the organising committee's attention was drawn to the overcrowding on some nights and the need for a police officer to be in attendance.

But broadly speaking the Opera House had it pretty well all its own way until the end of the 19th century. There was no other theatre in the town and any opposition provided by the Plough, later Empire variety hall, was fitful.

There were a number of attempts to set up musichall on a much grander scale but all foundered against the determined opposition of the Noncomformists and Teetotallers, who objected especially to the drink facilities for which the sponsors applied, and which were necessary to ensure a good return. There is no doubt that drink, which was the principal form of relaxation for the working man, was responsible for a good deal of neglect and squalor. But the housing conditions of some of the old courts and terraces were such as to make escape into the euphoria induced by booze seem all too attractive for the man who had worked hard for perhaps 10 hours a day only to return to a small and dingy dwelling with too many children crawling about the place—this was before the days of family planning and to have 10 or a dozen in the family was commonplace.

One of the proposed musichalls was to have been in Bridge Street, another in Abington Square and a third in Gold Street. Typifying the opposition attitude was the reply of Alfred Smith, representing the Sunday School Union at the 1894 hearing of an application for a drink licence for a 1,300 seater musichall which it was proposed to erect in Gold Street, adjacent to the Rose and Crown. Noncomformists had special cause for concern because the back entrance would have been opposite College Street Chapel. When Smith was asked by Mr. C. C. Becke, solicitor for the applicants, whether he had ever been in a musichall he admitted that he had not but: "I do not need to put my hand into the fire to know that it would burn me." When the ancient Peacock Hotel came on to the market in March, 1896, the Mercury suggested that its site, on the Market Square, would be splendid for "what is needed in the town—a first-class musichall." In fact it remained a hotel until the mid-20th century, when it was replaced by shops.

The fitful nature of the opposition provided by the Empire establishment is reflected in the proceedings one night in January, 1901, when the management failed to pay the artistes, including 40 youngsters who had been expecting 3s. each for their week's portrayal of Chinamen in a sketch called *China*. Word had got around that there were exchequer problems and the band at first refused to play until they were paid but subsequently relented. During the show one of the co-proprietors went round collecting all the takings and disappeared with them. His partner had to take to his heels, or rather a cab, and make for the Stags Head Hotel, Abington Street, pursued by the 40 pseudo Chinese and others. Getting no satisfaction they returned to the hall and smashed the place up. Even this episode was not the last. "Transformed from its old state" it reopened a few months later with new carpeting, new seating, new gas heating and with an orchestra pit rebuilt to accommodate 14, under the management of Humphrey E. Brammall, "of the Crystal Palace and Brighton Hippodrome." His timing was unfortunate for shortly afterwards the Palace of Varieties opened in Gold Street on a more palatial scale still and put paid to his efforts. By 1903 the old Empire had been turned into a two-storey workshop employing 200 and was the scene of the production of Mulliner coachwork for motor-cars. Among others they supplied the Duke of Bedford, Earl Cadogan and Lord Lilford.

In May, 1898, cars had been introduced as a great novelty at the Whitsun and August Bank Holiday fetes at Franklins Gardens. As an additional attraction to the bear pit, aviaries, peep shows, swings and lakes for a small fee visitors could ride round the cinder track in either of two cars.

The most significant opposition, in the long term anyway, was the arrival of the motion picture, or "animated pictures" as the innovation was at first known. There were a number of rival operators and systems, each claiming to be the best. In April, 1897, the Biograph was watched at the Palace Theatre, Cambridge Circus, London, "with breathless interest broken only by frequent applause." It seemed like black magic.

The following November the Velograph paid what was described as a return visit to Northampton Town Hall (I did not trace a previous call there) with "the latest perfected animated pictures including selections from 100 up-to-date photographs." There were pictures of Queen Victoria's Diamond Jubilee these being "the first living pictures of Her Majesty" who was seen at the State Garden Party. In between the films there was a humorous and musical entertainment. A month later came the first advertising films, with a programme presented by the makers of Nestle's Milk and Sunlight Soap.

Among other early shows were one at the Liberty Hall, Kingsthorpe, in January, 1898, when the projectionist was Mr. Wright, an Abington Street photographer. The following year Messrs. West and Sons, of Southsea, projected naval subjects at the Temperance Hall, including the fastest vessel in the world rushing through the waves at 41 m.p.h. This was arranged by Abel and Son who invited the Workhouse children to a matinee. Edison's Pictures paid a third visit in September, 1901, and included local scenes, one of which was a turn-out by Northampton Fire Brigade. It is difficult for the film-goer of today to conceive the fragmentary nature of these early film shows. The programme was very much a collection of shorts and snippets. At the Corn Exchange in December, 1901, Captain T. Payne's Electric Bioscope included "Burglary, murder and condemned cell", "Joan of Arc ascending to Heaven", hunting scenes with stags being killed, cod fishers in Newfoundland, the Lakes of Killarney, local views, scenes of South African War. In between there would be intervals while the machine was recharged with film and during these Captain Payne had arranged for songs and selections to be played on the "Concertophone" (presumably a gramophone) and for the Town Silver Band to play.

The "pictures" were also seen in the villages. In the National Schoolroom at Turvey in January, 1900, the Animatograph Co., of Bedford, exhibited their "wonderful living pictures", with proceeds for the church roof. In November the following year a show was given by Temple's Cinematograph Touring Co. at the Heygate School, West Haddon, on a Saturday night, a gramophone adding to the delights of the evening.

No-one then suspected the degree to which the new pictures were to be so powerful a rival to the live theatre. As the operators turned the projector handle, just as the cameramen had hand-cranked their cameras, it could certainly not be foreseen how the electronic successor to the medium, television, would 50 years later lead to the wholesale closure and demolition of theatres—including a Northampton theatre then yet to be built.

As the silent screen flickered into existence theatres were still going up and Mr. Noble was on the projected board of one to be erected at Bedford, 24 miles from Northampton. He figured along with Mr. A. C. Palmer, the well-known Northampton accountant, Dr. George Robinson, Mr. H. M. Burge, later headmaster of Winchester School and Bishop of Oxford, Dr. Archdale Sharpin and Mr. Carl Milberg St. Amory. Their rather high-flown project was abortive, however, a much more commercially minded plan by Mr. Edward Graham Falcon (or Graham-Falcon) coming to fruition. Falcon was lessee of the Theatre Royal, Canterbury, where he was living when the Bedford theatre opened on April 1, 1899. Soon afterwards he moved to Bedford and spent the rest of his life there, while continuing to tour companies. In November, 1901, the Compton Comedy Company appeared for three days at his theatre. One of the Patrons of this book has written a lengthy history of Bedford theatre, which sadly remains unpublished. He is the Rev. John Faulkner, who told me that Falcon also became lessee of the Grand Theatre, Luton, and of the Theatre Royal, Inverness—"I can remember the three day-bills hanging side by side in the Bedford box office."

A company which took the Northampton stage for the first time on June 23, 1898, is still in being today. Northampton Amateur Operatic Company commenced with *Yeomen of The Guard,* one of its main aims being to raise money for charities. The idea of forming the group originated with members of the choir of the Church of the Holy Sepulchre, the vicar, the Rev. Charles Brooke, giving considerable support. The initial officers included Mr. J. J. Hart, chairman, and Mr. Skevington, secretary. Shortly afterwards Dorman became chairman. Figures are available of the cash side. They show that £244 5s. 6d. total receipts included £217 17s. 3d. at the box office and £16 10s. in subscriptions. Fees of £29 8s. went to D'Oyly Carte. The £51 14s. 2d. paid to the Opera House covered rent, scenery, lighting, band etc. There was £23 16s. 1d. for the stage manager and £10 14s. for the orchestra (additional players perhaps?) so that the total expenses amounted to £181 5s. 1d. leaving a balance of £43 0s. 5d. of which sums of £20 each were given to the Northamptonshire Regimental Memorial Fund and the St. Sepulchre's Tower Fund.

The second performance 12 months later was of *The Mikado* in which the title role went to C. J. King, later conductor of Northampton Musical Society. Also in the cast were Harvey Reeves, later twice Mayor, as Pooh-Bah and Mrs. Helen Panther, later a director of Northampton Repertory Theatre.

That year, however, dissension occurred within the ranks and several members resigned to form a new society called the Guildhall Operatic Company, with Ernest Howe as secretary. The breach lasted until 1903 and in January, 1901, the breakaway group gained a niche in theatrical history by being about to take the stage on Tuesday, January 22, with *The Gondoliers*. The show did not go on that night, or indeed during the remainder of the week for shortly before the curtain was due to rise the manager, Mr. J. T. Hay Hill, went before the foot-lights to announce the death of Queen Victoria. The audience went home, after being given tickets for a future performance. The show was abandoned, or rather postponed, being held a fortnight later. This was the first time this work had been given in Northampton. At Wellingborough Corn Exchange on the night of the Royal death *A Dark Secret* was about to be given but was similarly abandoned, the orchestra playing the Dead March from Saul before the audience filed out.

This may be a convenient point to list all the company's shows up to 1922, when they began their 36-year link with the larger New Theatre. They were: 1898, *Yeomen of the Guard;* 1899, *The Mikado, H.M.S. Pinafore* (Guildhall Co., Town Hall); 1900, *Iolanthe, The Mountebanks* (Guildhall Co.); 1901, *The Gondoliers* (Guildhall Co), *The Pirates of Penzance, Trial by Jury, Box and Cox;* 1902, *Yeomen of the Guard* (Guildhall Co., Town Hall), *Dorothy;* 1903, *Falka* (Guildhall Co., Palace of Varieties), *Cigarette;* 1904, *The Mikado;* 1907, *The Silver Stick;* 1914, *Merrie England;* 1921, *The Duchess of Dantzic* and *Trial by Jury.*

The Opera House also played host to a number of performances by Nor-thampton Amateur Dramatic Company, notably with *The New Boy* in December, 1899.

Scene Two: 1899-1903

TWO PROFESSIONALS — & ELECTRICITY

Meantime there had been a further change in the ownership and operation of the theatre. Edmund Lockwood and James Dangerfield are first mentioned in October, 1899, when the Mercury said there had long been rumours and they could now confirm that Lockwood, "the famous theatrical entrepreneur whose companies include the one touring *La Poupee*" and Dangerfield, "a gentleman well-known in theatrical circles", were taking over.

First it had been two amateurs, Franklin and Tarry; then one amateur and one professional, Dorman and Noble; now it was two professionals.

Edmund Lockwood was not only an "outsider" as far as Northampton was concerned but was much more widely travelled than either of his predecessors as owners. Born in Kensington, London, in 1855, he had been educated mainly in France and then served briefly in the Army before sailing for New Zealand where he spent six years in the government's telegraph surveying and construction department, mostly roughing it in the bush. He returned to the United Kingdom in 1882 and after three years became wholly engaged in the theatre, both acting and as company manager, including touring the B Company of Charles Hawtrey's *The Private Secretary* and directing the tour of George Edwardes's *Gaiety Girl*. From Edwardes in 1896 he secured the rights of *A Night Out*. Subsequently he ran two *La Poupee* companies, his wife Midge Clark appearing in the title role with one of them. Lockwood also turned his attention to publications, assisting C. H. Fox in a dramatic and musical directory and himself bringing out Dangerfield's Entertainment Guide. He also compiled what the Era described as a "wonderfully ingenious railway fare map" for the use of travelling companies and made representations on their behalf to the railways for better consideration and comfort. An enthusiastic Freemason, belonging to the Yorick and Eccentric Lodges, Lockwood was co-founder with J. Bannister Howard and E. Graham Falcon of the Touring Managers' Association. He died in March, 1911, and was buried at Norwood Cemetery.

A delay in completing the change in ownership of the Opera House occurred and Dorman continued to be listed as proprietor until May, 1901. Before passing to the new management it may be appropriate to record that in 1904 Dorman was among a Masonic party led by the Earl of Euston, P.G.M., which attended the triennial enclave of the Knights Templar of San Francisco, he then being Grand Master of the Great Priory of England and Wales of the Knights Templar. His final Masonic honour came in 1921 when he was made Inspector General of the Northern Central District, embracing six counties. In 1910 he had presented a picture, Cupid Bound by the Nymphs, to the Eccentric Club, London, of which Sir Charles Wyndham, the actor manager, was president at the time. It was hung in the smoking room. When Dorman died in 1931, aged 73, his body was taken the 30 miles to Leicester for cremation—there was no crematorium in Northampton and district until 1939 when one was erected at the four miles distant village of Milton by a company of which George Bernard Shaw was a shareholder. Cremations had begun in Leicester in 1902. In May, 1964, Dorman's daughter, Mrs. M. E. Corrin, watched her son Councillor John Bowes Corrin, elected Mayor of Northampton in the council chamber in the extension of the Town Hall which had been opened in 1864 by his great-grandfather, Mark Dorman.

Mr. Noble, ex-manager of the Opera House, moved on from Brixton to a picturesque setting which ought to have inspired him to write another play. He went to Morocco, where he joined the staff of the progressive Sultan. His subsequent return to England on leave came at a fortuitous time for a revolution broke out almost as soon as he had left. A few years later he turned up again in Northampton showing films he had made himself in South America.

Premiered provincially in January, 1900, by a Morell and Mouillot company was Sydney Grundy's *The Degenerates.* presented by arrangement with Mrs. Langtry and simultaneously with her production in New York of the piece, which was described as "a daring indictment of the foibles and cynicisms of degenerate members of modern society." Miss Geraldine Oliffe took the role played by Mrs. Langtry at the Haymarket and Garrick Theatres, London, and in New York.

A June week that year brought what was to be Sir Arthur Sullivan's last comic opera to Northampton. For *Rose of Persia* he had collaborated with Captain Basil Hood. It was presented by a D'Oyly Carte company. Sullivan, who had been a fellow guest of the Prince of Wales at the Northamptonshire stately home of Easton Neston in May, 1897, died in November, 1900. A three-day premiere in August, 1900, was *In the Soup,* a farce by Ralph Lumley which was prior to a season at the Strand Theatre, London. The plot was not unfamiliar—that of an impecunious young man (a barrister in this case) who will inherit from his wealthy uncle if he remains a bachelor. When his uncle, a judge in India, comes on leave the barrister has therefore to conceal the existence of his wife. Ernest Howard designed and painted the scenery as he did for many London and touring productions. Miss Fortescue's Company had the house for the first half of the week, with *Moths* on the Monday and Wednesday and *The School for Scandal* on Tuesday. *In The Soup* was played again at Northampton a year later, by H. Richard and B. Yardley's Company. In September a Fred Karno company presented the celebrated *His Majesty's Guests* the "guests" being gaolbirds. Considered controversial at the time, Pinero's *The Gay Lord Quex* was given by a Morell and Mouillot company in March, 1901, and drew large audiences.

While Lockwood and Dangerfield briefly reigned at Northampton the Era looked back upon the last quarter of the 19th century. Marvellous progress and improvement had been made in provincial matters theatrical, it summed up.

Those speculators who had been alert and enterprising enough to come in on the wave of provincial theatrical prosperity had reaped the benefit of boldness. "In many a country town spirited local men have found the best investment to be in the bricks and mortar of a local playhouse. The bright new comfortable and up-to-date theatre is everywhere eclipsing the old fashioned dirty, odiferous den of the drama and the travelling company system, with its rich fund of variety and constant supply, has enabled the local playgoer to keep in touch with the more recent triumphs of the stage."

The most important events of the new regime at Northampton were in fact further improvements of the premises which were made during the summer break of 1901—the introduction of electric lighting in the pit and various parts of the theatre; replacement of several front rows of the pit by three rows of orchestra stalls seating 62 "in comfortable crimson plush with a capital view of the stage"; alteration of the pit seats into straight rows instead of curved ones; and improvement of the orchestra pit. A fundamental change in the theatre's architecture was concerned with the route by which the upper bracket patrons reached those 62 orchestra stalls. They could not, of course, be expected to rub shoulders with the pittites and stairway passages were therefore provided either side, running beneath the boxes and communicating with the dress circle corridors. Previously access to the lower level had been entirely from the pit entrance stairs at the rear of the auditorium. Another change at this time was the arrival of a new manager, Athol Blair.

A novel form of advance publicity was used by Mr. Kay Draco for *The Girl Up There* in September, 1901; he showed moving pictures of the Mouillot company, claiming that this was the first time this means had been employed.

Several Milton Bode companies visited Northampton during these years, including *Saved from the Sea, Lights of London* and *Tommy Atkins*. Bode was to be the next proprietor of the theatre along with Edward Compton.

At the end of December, 1901, came the first performance outside London of *Becky Sharp,* from the Prince of Wales Theatre. The pantomime came late, in February, following visits to Wolverhampton, Cambridge, Oxford and Swindon. *Robinson Crusoe* had no harlequinade and the Daily Reporter's view was that it would also have been better to leave out the transformation scene. At the Saturday matinee the house could have been filled twice over. The new management increased the number of matinees and the Press said that this was appreciated as it "provides an opportunity for country visitors and for the younger generation."

Sweet Nell of Old Drury, presented in March, 1902, came from the Globe Theatre, London, with Julia Neilson and Fred Terry, as Nell and Charles II; it had been the last show at the Globe before it was demolished.

Sherlock Holmes strolled up and down the Northampton stage on a number of occasions, on one of which Charlie Chaplin was among the cast but in so tiny a role as not to be mentioned in the Press report. In March, 1902, F. B. Woulffe appeared as the great detective in a play by Max Goldberg called *Bank of England.* That month saw the first performance in England of "the latest Parisian success from the Theatre de la Gaiete, the comic opera *Les Saltimbanquies* or *The Bohemians in England*" by Maurice Ordonneau and Arthur Sturgess, author of *La Poupee.* It was for three nights only, moving on to Edinburgh, Newcastle and Birmingham. The Daily Reporter doubted whether a piece burdened with such a stupendous name would succeed. Other shows of 1902 included J. M. Barrie's *The Little Minister, The Private Secretary, The Wrong Mr. Wright, The Toreador, The Country Girl, Les Cloches de Corneville, The Belle of New York, Floradora, The Silver King, The Two Little Heroes,* and *Zaza,* of which the Daily Reporter commented that "not even the Tanqueray-Ebbsmith-Quex series has caused so much controversy." This story of a woman musichall artist of low birth was said, however, to have been emasculated in its transfer from Paris.

On Saturday, August 9, 1902, the performance of *Two Little Heroes* began early, at 6.30, to enable Patrons to be in time for a Coronation Fireworks display in Calvesholme Meadow supervised by Thomas Phipps Dorman. The following week the Press published his letter of apology for the damp squib this had turned out to be. Because of the postponement of the Coronation following the illness of Edward VII the fireworks had deteriorated. "Everything was damp, the quick match would not run, the lances hung fire, the shells exploded low down (some at my feet) through the powder having caked and lost the power to propel them from the mortars and altogether nothing went satisfactorily. None could have been more disappointed than myself," wrote the former proprietor of the Opera House, who therefore arranged a repeat performance the following week, with fresh explodables.

Perhaps the largest ever attendance at the theatre came in October, 1902, though not for a theatrical performance. Some 200 chairs were placed on the stage to cope with the demand but still hundreds were turned away from talks in connection with the Congress of the National Waifs and Strays Association (Dr. Barnardo's Homes) which was then being held in Northampton. The audience was estimated at 2,000. Lady Knightley, of Fawsley Manor, was in the chair and speakers were Lady Frederick, whose husband had been a victim of the Phoenix Park murders in Ireland at the time when Earl Spencer was Viceroy, and Mrs. Benson, widow of the Archbishop of Canterbury and aunt of Frank Benson, the actor manager. The Opera House was also crowded for a talk that week by Dr. Barnardo himself, who said that 80 per cent of child neglect was caused by intemperance.

If you visit Northampton Repertory Theatre today you will find on the wall of what used to be called the crush room a glass case containing a walking stick. It is of double theatrical significance for it was made from wood from the mulberry tree which David Garrick planted at Abington Abbey, Northampton, in 1778 during one of his visits to the Thursbys and it was presented to Sir Henry Irving during his visit to Northampton in 1903. The man who had had the stick made— from a branch which had been blown off the tree during a storm he said—was that same Henry Martin who had built the Opera House. He had had the stick for many years following a visit to the Lyceum Theatre, London, during his Mayoralty of 1893. The play was *Becket,* which has scenes set in Northampton Castle and streets. Hearing that the Mayor of Northampton was in the house Irving asked him to an on-stage supper after the performance and later arranged for a carriage to take him and his party to Euston for the midnight train.

For years Martin had waited for Irving to visit Northampton again and it was ironic that when he did come Martin was in bed following a fall on one of his own building sites, and had therefore to depute his son John to make the presentation. The stick, with an inscribed silver mount, was added by Irving to a small collection of Garrickiana which he had formed including a ring given by the actor to his brother when he died, and a sword and scarf pin which he had worn on stage. This was Irving's only appearance at the Opera House though he had visited Northampton in 1878, for a benefit reading and reception by Northampton Shakespeare Society, of which Tarry was then a leading light.

It was announced that, owing to the smallness of the Opera House stage, *Becket* would not be possible and *The Merchant of Venice* was staged. Among the Patrons of this book is one who can remember seeing Irving's performance. He is 90-year-old Mr. Will Arnold, father of the composer Malcom Arnold, who told me "I remember him sitting at a table with his bags of gold "

It has been said that the pioneer actor of the 1870s had become the reactionary of the 1890s but several hundreds of Northamptonians turned out to greet him at the Castle railway station where he was welcomed by the Deputy Mayor. Many bowed as the legendary figure made his way to the brougham waiting in the station yard to convey him to the George Hotel. Prices were increased and some middle class folk sat in the gallery rather than miss the great man. When not at the theatre during the three day visit Irving spent most of his time in his hotel room learning his part for *Dante* which he was to stage in London after his short provincial tour. But he was a sick man and there were oxygen cylinders in his hotel room. Two years later he collapsed after playing *Becket* at the Theatre Royal, Bradford, and died in the lobby of his hotel.

Freemasons showed that they had a sense of humour by attending a performance of *RUA Mason* in February, 1903, the cast of which included Spencer Trevor, actor brother of J. T. Hay Hill, who was the Opera House manager at the time. The brethren had been assured by the Press that they might attend confident of no offence. The plot concerned a man who only pretended to be a Mason so that he could have an excuse to get away from his wife—to attend "Lodge Nights."

Edmund Tearle, cousin of the late Osmond Tearle, brought a week of four plays to the theatre in March, 1903— *The Three Musketeers, Richard III, Hamlet* and *Macbeth.*

April, 1903, found a long term Opera House favourite Horace Lingard, appearing at the Palace of Varieties which was turned into an opera house for one week only and a no smoking rule applied. This was for a production of *Falka* by the breakaway Guildhall Company. Another professional who joined in was Walter Wright. Perhaps because of the professional stiffening of the cast it was financially the most successful amateur show to date, taking some £450. Lingard, who was the manager of the Strand Comedy Theatre, London, had played his role in *Falka* some 1,400 times, including five in Northampton.

In April, 1902, the Guildhall Company had presented *Yeomen of the Guard* at the Opera House in aid of the Northamptonshire Orphanage. At the same time as their rivals were staging *Falka*, the original company were pressing on with preparations for *Cigarette,* which was to be much less successful. The Mercury stated baldly that it had had its day and "ceased to be" 12 years earlier. The only reason it was chosen was that C. J. King, the company's conductor, had been a close friend of the composer Haydn Parry, a young musician of promise who had died at the age of 29. The paper said the piece was "at times scrappy with rhythms lost in a maze of orchestrations." Before the performance came off there

was a joint meeting between the two amateur companies to patch up their differ-
ences. On the basis of forming a new company consisting of 12 members of each
of the two opposing ones, the 24 to be non-elective and self-perpetuating, a
marriage was declared and plans made for a joint production of *The Mikado*.

In May, 1903, while a George Dance company were presenting *Three Little
Maids,* a notice appeared in the Press stating that accounts of amounts owing by
the theatre must be sent in by May 26 as a new management was taking over.

The final show under the Lockwood and Dangerfield regime was *San Toy,* by a
George Edwardes Company—a capital and fitting finale to the present management, said the Mercury.

The Interlude on the Compton Comedy Company is self-contained. To continue the story of Northampton Opera House turn to Page 245.

Interlude

COMPTON COMEDY COMPANY

Edward Compton and Adelaide Neilson, the intended
bride who died in his arms a month before the wedding
date, and whose legacy made it possible for him to found
the Compton Comedy Company.

Pavilion Theatre
WINTER GARDENS, SOUTHPORT
LICENSEE · MR. J. LONG.

Special Engagement
FOR SIX NIGHTS ONLY
OF THE
COMPTON COMEDY COMPANY

MR. EDWARD COMPTON
Supported by Miss VIRGINIA BATEMAN & Full Company
COMPLETE CHANGE OF PROGRAMME EACH EVENING

TWELFTH NIGHT!
OR, WHAT YOU WILL.

SHE STOOPS TO CONQUER

FISH OUT OF WATER.

HEIR-AT-LAW!

PAUL PRY!

AS YOU LIKE IT

Friday, Feb. 10, BENEFIT OF Mr. EDWARD COMPTON.
SATURDAY, FEBRUARY 12,
LAST NIGHT!

ADMISSION, INCLUDING GATES:
Stalls, 4s.; First Seats, 3s.; Balcony and Second Seats, 2s.; Back Seats and Gallery, 1s.
Contractors Half-price.   Plan of Seats now ready.

On the first night of the Compton Comedy Company's life, at Southport on February 7, 1881, Edward Compton was Malvolio and Virginia Bateman was Viola *(Top picture, Nottingham Local History Library; lower, Theatre Museum)*

Interlude

THE LONGEST TOURING COMPANY

The propriety of including the story of the Comptons, who were a very significant theatrical family, as an Interlude in the history of a theatre as insignificant
as Northampton's Victorian Opera House does not rest only upon the facts that
the Compton Comedy Company were the first to perform in that theatre and
that Edward Compton, founder of the company, was for 15 years its joint owner.
The adopted name of Compton was itself derived from Northamptonshire. The
family's real name was Mackenzie. Hence "The Mackenzies Called Compton."

The profession of actor used to be as odiferous as many of the theatres in
which performances took place—it was doubly a case of Drama That Smelled. So
when Charles Mackenzie decided to defy the long Puritan tradition in his family
and go on the stage, in order keep the family name sweet, he chose an alias.
Instead of inventing a completely new name as many other actors and play-
wrights did—Brodribb became Irving, W. Jones became Silvanus Dauncey—he
chose one which did have family connections while ensuring that the link was not
so obvious as to cause embarrassment. He selected the name of a paternal grandmother, Susanna(h) Compton, of Northamptonshire. Charles Compton would
have had a fine alliterative sound but he decided to abandon his Christian name
too and made it Henry Compton.

Of Northamptonshire? The fact is baldly stated by Compton .Mackenzie,
author son of Edward, who reinstated the family name; he mentions it in Octave
One of his vast autobiography My Life and Times. I have not managed to
discover the county origins of Susanna(h) Compton but a family tree in Who's
Who in the Theatre shows that she was the first wife of John Alexander
Mackenzie, great-grandson of the Rev. Bernard Mackenzie, of Cromarty. Her
husband, who is described as a wharfinger, had Sara Vaughan as his second wife.
By Susanna(h) there was a son, the Rev. John Mackenzie (1782-1846), who wrote
a life of Calvin and who married Elizabeth Symonds. They were the parents of
Henry Compton, among a family of 11.

Charles Mackenzie, alias Henry Compton, was born at Huntingdon on March
22, 1805, and was later sent for training with his mother's brother, a Mr.
Symonds, who was a cloth dealer in London. The Symonds were very puritanical
and as Charles and Edward Compton recalled in their Memoirs of Henry
Compton, published in 1879, "had to battle with their consciences before
entering a theatre to see him perform."

By the age of 21 Charles Mackenzie had had enough of trade and applied to Mr. Simms, the dramatic agent of the period, who conducted his business at the Harp Tavern, Russell Street, Drury Lane. After engagements at Lewes, Leicester and Cromer he joined Henry Jackman's Company which covered a wide area ranging at various times from Bedford to Stratford-upon-Avon and as far south as Highgate. Next came three years with Mr. Robertson's Lincoln Circuit and then a spell with the York Circuit. It was during the latter that he and the rest of the company were ferried across the Humber. In those days the Yorkshire dialect term for strolling players was "lakers". Instead of the usual ferryboat they travelled in a flat-bottomed craft usually reserved for cattle. Half-way across they met another vessel whose skipper hailed to know what cargo was being carried. Came the reply: "Nobbut Lakers and Dung."

After many disappointments Henry Compton made the grade in London and became one of the most popular light comedians of the day. One of his roles was the First Gravedigger in *Hamlet* which up to that time had normally been buffooned by actors who peeled off up to a dozen waistcoats of various patterns and hues before getting down to the spadework of the part. Compton reformed this travesty, declining to stoop to conquer.

Appearing at Drury Lane in *Romeo and Juliet* he met Emmeline Montague, an actress whose father was a light comedian at Bath. They married in 1848, the wedding breakfast being held at the home of Mark Lemon, editor of Punch.

Mrs. Compton was asked to appear in a performance of *The Merchant of Venice* before Queen Victoria. The "command" came via Charles Kean who had been appointed to the revived post of Master of the Revels. Feeling that she was being asked to play second fiddle to Mrs. Kean Mrs. Compton tersely replied: "I thank you for your offer but beg to decline the part of Jessica." Royal Commands were not thus lightly to be brushed aside and a few days later she was compelled to reconsider: "I was not aware my letter was wanting in loyalty or respect. If so I beg to apologise. In regard to the part of Jessica, I refer you to Mr. Compton. If he approves of the selection you made for me I will with pleasure accept the part."

The humble submissiveness to her husband was in character. After their marriage he forbade her to appear on the stage, making an exception only for such amateur undertakings as Charles Dickens' company and for Royal Commands. She was with the company which travelled by special train, paid for by Queen Victoria, from London to Windsor on December 22, 1848, to perform in the Rubens Room at Windsor Castle, which had been converted into a theatre. In the cast list she was down not as Miss Montague, as she would normally have been, but as Mrs. Compton. The Queen thought it improper for a married woman to be announced under her maiden name.

In Stanford Road, Kensington, Compton built a house which he called Seaforth House after Lord Seaforth, once the head of the Mackenzie clan. The couple had seven children, six of whom Edward, Henry, Percy, Otway, Sydney and Kate went on the stage. The only daugher, Kate, was intended to be a musician and was trained as such but nevertheless took to acting, marrying the playwright R. C. Carton and appearing as leading lady in most of his plays. Her brother Sydney first appeared on the stage during the same February week of 1881 that saw the debut of Edward Compton's company at Southport and he later spent 18 months with his brother's company.

Born in London on January 14, 1854, Edward Compton made his stage debut at the New Theatre Royal (later Prince's Theatre), Bristol, on September 22, 1873, in the company of James Henry Chute, an old friend of his father. He played Long Ned, one of the Roughs of the Old Mint, in a revival of *Old London,* in which Henrietta Hodson, an old Bristol favourite, was guest star. He continued to play minor roles—little more than walk-ons—such as Francisco in *The Tempest,* Second Actor in *Hamlet,* both at the New and Old Theatre Royal right through the season, his last performance with the stock company being on February 28, 1874. Apart from Henrietta Hodson the stars he supported included Mr. and Mrs. Bandmann, Charles Mathews and Ada Cavendish. Miss (Kate) Bateman also appeared with the company but Compton does not appear on any of the bills with her. At Whitsuntide, 1874, "the eminent comedian Mr. Compton and his London Company" played a week at the New Theatre Royal, when Edward was a member, promoted then to higher things, Frank Hardy in *Paul Pry,* Captain Smith in *His First Champagne,* Henry Morland in *The Heir At Law* and Dr. Sasafras in *Friend Waggles;* then on Thursday, May 28, the company played for Chute's benefit with Madge Robertson as visiting star in *Twelfth Night.* Madge was Viola, Chute was Sir Toby, Compton was the Clown and Edward was Malvolio.

In a letter to Edward the following September his father wrote "By the bye I think it would be advisable for you to call yourself Mr. Edward Compton, in full, after this engagement; you will find it will prevent mistakes." In a letter to a third party in July, 1876, he commented that Ned (Edward) "has wonderfully improved, has a good light comedy voice and person, excellent delivery, and, if I am not mistaken, is destined to make a first rate light comedian."

After his 1874 Bristol engagement Edward toured with Francis Fairlie playing such parts as Richard Hare and Lord Mountsevern in *East Lynne,* Dr. Brown in *Robertson's Progress,* and Crabtree and Careless in *The School for Scandal.*

It is perhaps difficult for the well-mannered audiences of today to imagine the lively atmosphere of the Victorian provincial theatre and the degree of audience participation which sometimes occurred in it, in manner we associate more with musichalls. Edward Compton recalled how when he was a young actor at Portsmouth he was the hero in a melodrama. The heroine was Ada Blanche (who later entered the Salvation Army) and while she was in the villain's toils a sailor swarmed down a pillar on to the stage, via the pass door, and knocked the villain flat.

There followed a long engagement in Glasgow and Kilmarnock where he appeared with Edward Sothern and J. L. Toole and in 1876 he was in stock at the Prince of Wales, Liverpool, and the Theatre Royal, Birmingham.

Meantime Henry Compton had made his last London appearance in 1875, at the age of 70, at the Lyceum, as the First Gravedigger. In March, 1877, a benefit performance was given for him at Drury Lane, the playbill stating that "he has been suffering for a lengthened period from a severe and painful malady and is now compelled to relinquish all hopes of resuming his profession." In the first act of *Money* Edward appeared among a star cast including John Hare, Benjamin Webster, Mr. and Mrs. W. H. Kendal, Henry Neville, William Farren, Ellen Terry and Mr. and Mrs. (later Sir and Lady) Squire Bancroft. In fact Henry did

THEATRE ROYAL

DRURY LANE.

Sole Lessee and Manager - - Mr. F. B. CHATTERTON.

Under the immediate Patronage of
H.R.H. THE PRINCE OF WALES.

BENEFIT
IN AID OF A
TESTIMONIAL FUND
to the respected and popular Comedian,
MR. COMPTON,

Who has been suffering for a lengthened period from a severe and painful malady, and who is now compelled to relinquish all hopes of resuming his Profession.

THURSDAY MORNING, MARCH 1, 1877.
Doors open at 12.30 ; at 12.50 precisely, OVERTURE.

The Council Scene from SHAKESPEARE'S Tragedy of
OTHELLO.

Duke of Venice	- - -	Mr. T. Mead
Brabantio	- - -	Chippendale
Gratiano	- - -	Clifford Cooper
Ludovico	- - -	Horace Wigan
Othello	- - -	Creswick
Cassio	- - -	Henry Sinclair
Iago	- - -	Ryder
Roderigo	- - -	Charles Warner
Messenger from the Galleys		Charles Kelly
Senators—Messrs. W. Belford, F. Dewar, Flockton, F. Haywell, W. Holman, F. Huntley, H. Kemble, C. Sugden, R. Soutar, C. Wilmot.		
Desdemona	- - -	Miss Ada Cavendish

Recitation "The Charge of the Light Brigade" Miss Heath

The First Act of Lord LYTTON'S Play of
MONEY.

Lord Glossmore	- - -	Mr. Henry Neville
Sir John Vesey	- - -	Hare
Sir Frederick Blount	- - -	Kendal
Graves *(his original character)*		B. Webster
Stout	- - -	David James
Sharp	- - -	William Farren
Evelyn *(his first appearance in London)*		Edward Compton
Servants	- - -	{ Bancroft and { C. Collette
Lady Franklin	- - -	Miss Marie Wilton (Mrs. Bancroft)
Georgina Vesey	- - -	Ellen Terry
Clara Douglas	- - -	Madge Robertson (Mrs. Kendall)

Recitation "The Uncle" - Mr. Henry Irving.

Mr. MADDISON MORTON'S Farce of
LEND ME FIVE SHILLINGS.

Mr. Golightly	- - -	Mr. Jefferson
Captain Phobbs	- - -	Howe
Captain Spruce	- - -	Chas. Wyndham
Morland	- - -	John Billington
Sam	- - -	Thomas Thorne
Mrs. Major Phobbs	- - -	Miss M. Oliver
Mrs. Captain Phobbs	- - -	Amy Roselle
Guests at the County Ball—Misses Helen Barry, E. Bufton, Rose Coghlan, Harrison, Blanche Henri, Caroline Hill, Ellen Meyrick, Ada Swanborough, Kate Vaughan, F. Wright (Mrs. Osborne), Mrs. Billington, Mrs. Leigh Murray, and Mrs. John Wood.		
Messrs. J. H. Barnes, Walter Bentley, R. Carton, H. B. Conway, W. Gordon, Julian Girard, W. Herbert, Harold Kyrle, E. Leathes, Macklin, R. Markby, Lin Rayne, E. Villiers.		

Scene from MACKLIN'S Comedy of
THE MAN OF THE WORLD.

Sir Pertinax Macsychophant	- -	Mr. Phelps
Egerton	- - -	Herman V...

The Last Act of SHERIDAN'S
CRITIC;
Or, A TRAGEDY REHEARSED.

Dangle	- - -	Mr. H. J. Byron
Sneer	- - -	John Clayton
Under Prompter	- - -	Arthur Sketchley
Puff	- - -	Charles Mathews

Characters in the Tragedy.

Lord Burleigh	- - -	Mr. Buckstone
Governor of Tilbury Fort	- - -	G. W. Anson
Earl of Leicester	- - -	J. Clarke
Sir Walter Raleigh	- - -	E. Righton
Sir Christopher Hatton	- - -	E. Terry
Master of the Horse	- - -	W. H. Stephens
Beefeater	- - -	W. J. Hill
Don Ferolo Whiskerandos	- - -	J. L. Toole
First Niece	- - -	Mrs. Hermann Vezin
Second Niece	- - -	A. Mellon (Miss Woolgar)
Confidante	- - -	Chippendale
Tilburina	- - -	Miss E. Farren
Sentinels	- - -	{ Messrs. L. Brough and { W. Edouin

Selection or Overture.

The Dramatic Cantata, by A. SULLIVAN and W. S. GILBERT,
TRIAL BY JURY.

The Learned Judge	- - -	Mr. George Honey
Counsel for the Plaintiff	- - -	George Fox
The Defendant	- - -	W. H. Cummings
Usher	- - -	Arthur Cecil
The Jury, &c.—Messrs. Geo. Barrett, J. D. Beveridge, Edgar Bruce, A. Bishop, Furneaux Cook, H. Cox, F. G. Darrell, Everill, J. Fernandez, W. H. Fisher, G. Grossmith, jun., Hallam, F. W. Irish, H. Jackson, Kelleher, G. Loredan, J. Maclean, Marius, A. Matthison, A. Maltby, E. Murray, Howard Paul, H. Paulton, Penley, Harold Power, E. Rosenthal, Royce, J. D. Stoyle, J. G. Taylor, W. Terriss, W. H. Vernon.		
The Plaintiff	- - -	Mdme. Pauline Rita
Bridesmaids—Misses Carlotta Addison, Kate Bishop, Lucy Buckstone, Violet Cameron, Emily Cross, Ella Dietz, Camille Dubois, Kate Field, Emily Fowler, Maria Harris, Nelly Harris, Kathleen Irwin, Fanny Josephs, Jennie Lee, Fanny Leslie, Kate Phillips, Emma Ritta, Rachel Sanger, Florence Terry, Marion Terry, Lottie Venne.		

The Orchestra will be under the direction of Mr. Arthur Sullivan.

Instrumentalists—Messrs. Amor, Buziau, Betjemann, Earnshaw, Gibson, Morley, A. J. Levey, Ellis Roberts, W. H. Reed, Snewing, Scuderi, Wallace, Burnett, Brodelet, Colchester, Hann, Boutwright, Chipp, Shepherd, White, C. Harper, Jakeway, Radcliffe, Barrett, Lebou, Lazarus, Tyler, Hutchins, Mann, Garthwaite, Howard Reynolds, Neuzerling, Tull, Matt, and H. Pheasant.

Stage Manager	- -	Mr. James Johnstone
Acting Manager	- -	Mr. C. A. Jecks

The Benefit for his father at Drury Lane in March, 1877, marked the first appearance in London of Edward Compton. The amount raised remained a record for many years, so popular was the ailing comedian. *(Courtesy of Harry N. Greatorex).*

make further appearances, his last being as Mawworm in *The Hypocrite* at the Prince of Wales Theatre, Liverpool, in July, 1877. During this final 12-nights engagement it so happened that Edward was also appearing in Liverpool. "Personally speaking," Edward wrote in his memoirs of his father, "it will be one of my proudest thoughts, though necessarily a mournful one, to remember that I appeared in his support as Dick Dowlas and Col. Lambert on the Saturday, July 14, 1877." Henry Compton died of cancer exactly two months later in London, at the age of 72. When it became known that his widow was not well provided for a mammoth benefit was staged at Drury Lane for which Queen Victoria took two boxes, though she did not attend. The £4,000 raised remained a record until the one for Nellie Farren In the same house a quarter-of-a-century later raised £7,000.

It was in 1879 that Edward Compton and his brother Charles compiled a book of memoirs, in which tribute was paid to their father by many leading members of the profession. Charles, the oldest son, was a manager and novelist. He died in 1911.

One of Henry Compton's brothers was the famous surgeon Sir Morell Mackenzie who treated the 90-day Emperor of Germany, Frederick, for cancer of the throat. When the ailing monarch came to Britain for treatment and for the golden jubilee of his mother-in-law, Queen Victoria, in 1887 his wife "Vicky", the former Princess Royal, begged Queen Victoria to knight Morell on the spot, which she did at Balmoral Castle. But a good deal of controversy followed the emperor's death and the physician felt obliged to publish a book discussing the illness. Calling himself H. H. Morell, the surgeon's son became a theatrical entrepreneur and was operating in 1899, with his partner Frederick Mouillot, at the Theatres Royal, Dublin, Kilburn and Bournemouth; the New Grand Theatres at Southampton, Margate and Swansea; the Metropole at Glasgow; and the Queen's Theatres in London and Leeds.

Henry Compton's widow lived on for about 40 more years, dying at St. Leonard's around 1910.

Edward Compton's other early engagements included periods with H. J. Byron, Hermann Vezin, and Miss Wallis in Shakespeare, both at the Princes Theatre, Manchester, and touring. In 1878 he returned to Drury Lane playing Florizel in *A Winter's Tale* and the following year joined the Adelphi Company playing Sir Benjamin Backbite in *The School for Scandal* and Mons in *The Hunchback*.

Then came the engagement which was to change the entire course of his life, a tour of the United States with Adelaide Neilson, perhaps the best-known actress of her day. Lilian Adelaide Neilson was born Elizabeth Ann Brown in Leeds on March, 3, 1848. The name of her father is not known. In her early teens she learned of the circumstances of her birth and ran away to London, working at one time as a barmaid in a public house in the Haymarket, where she gained a reputation for reciting Shakespeare. She first appeared on the stage at Margate in 1865 and in London the same year. Subsequently she married Philip Henry Lee, son of the rector of Stoke Bruerne, a village near Northampton. Lee had been educated with the church in mind but as the Mercury put it, "inclination took him elsewhere." Just where I do not know but it was to do with the stage for he turns up in New York in the memoirs of J. L. Toole, by Joseph Hatton.

Many a time Mrs. Lee visited the rectory at Stoke Bruerne. As the Mercury recalled: "Most of the guests were county clergymen curious to see how the great London star would comport herself in their select society. Mr. Westland Moreton, a friend of the family, has left it on record how amusing it was to see the grave clerics at her father-in-law's dinner table brighten up as she amused them by her vivacity and how they would relapse almost to tears at the pathos of her tragic recitals. She was the very life and soul of the parties and repaid the profuse compliments paid by her priestly admirers with easy grace and frequently with arch repartee." There were more colourful reminiscences from the Evening Mail: "It was commonly believed at Stoke Bruerne that she was a Spanish lady and certainly her complexion and excitable moods favoured this idea, But in her intercourse with those who were thought to be far below her station she more resembled Elizabeth Ann Brown of Leeds than a haughty imperious Spaniard. Those who had seen her as Juliet would have scarcely believed their eyes had they seen her riding on the pole of a farmer's timber carriage down the village street, hat in hand, hair flying in the breeze. Neither would they if they had seen her holding her grey horse by a long rope as horse trainers are wont to do and with whip sending it running madly round in a circle while she stood laughing, happy and excited in the centre, like a wilful little fairy. On one occasion she is said to have run after one of the rectory servants holding a knife in a threatening attitude and this is sometimes spoken of as evidence of a passionate temper. I should rather think that it was done in a fit of playfulness or as a little dramatic rehearsal."

The rector arranged concerts and for a few pence villagers could see one of the greatest actresses of the day, in readings from Tennyson and others. A local dressmaker received the benefit of her custom: during one visit she was said to have bought dresses in the neighbouring village of Roade, one of which cost 100 guineas.

But the marriage to the rector's son was not happy and ended in divorce in 1877 with a decree obtained in the Supreme Court of New York. Two years earlier Adelaide Neilson's financial status had been safeguarded with an order made at Marlborough Street Police Court, London, asserting her rights as a femme sole and protecting her property from her husband and his creditors; at that time the property of a married woman normally belonged to her husband. Soon after the divorce Lee married again.

And in 1880 Miss Neilson planned to marry again. Her second husband was to be Edward Compton. As the reader becomes aware in the pages which follow of the regular-and-routine temperament of Edward Compton it will be seen what an odd life's partner he would have made for her. But it was not to be.

Since 1872 she had appeared in America and become extremely popular. Compton was among her company on the tour of 1879-80 and they fell in love, planning to marry soon after the return to Britain. The couple were to go to Paris to select her trousseau but the intended bride, a woman of property despite some ill-considered speculation on the New York market, had a premonition of death. Her existing will left £1,000 to Compton but Adelaide wanted to change it and leave everything to him. He, however, pooh-poohed her fears and the will was not changed. They went to Paris and while driving along the Bois de Boulogne on August 15, 1880, she felt unwell, stopped the carriage, collapsed and soon after died in Edward's arms. Aged only 32 she left some £25,000, the bulk of which went to the well-to-do Admiral Henry Carr Glyn, described in her existing testament as her "old and steadfast friend".

Henry Labouchere, millionaire Northampton Member of Parliament and former theatre owner, was among the thousands at the funeral at Brompton Cemetery where ropes were erected to keep the crowds back and there was a great jostling, with the chief mourners almost pushed into the grave. Whether Edward Compton was there I do not know. Perhaps not for he was distraught and as a result of the shock lost virtually all his hair. At 27 he was bald but the money he was left helped to set up the Compton Comedy Company—and the baldness determined its repertoire. Had Miss Neilson lived to become Mrs. Compton the company would never have come into being. Had he been left her entire fortune he would probably have been too rich to bother with such a provincial company. Had he been left nothing he would not have had the necessary capital.

By the following February, of 1881, Compton had assembled and launched the C.C.C. among the ranks of which was Virginia Bateman, who was to step into the role in Compton's life of which death had cheated Miss Neilson. I have not come across the precise circumstances of their first meeting: it may have been that they had encountered each other previously, on tour, or they may have first met when he recruited her for his company.

Virginia was the third of the four daughters of the American theatrical manager Hezekiah Linthicum Bateman and his wife Sidney Frances. The oldest girl was Kate, who married Dr. George Crowe, whose father was editor of the Daily News: they had one daughter, Sidney. For some years Mrs. Crowe ran an acting school in London and taught at the Beerbohm Tree School of Acting. Then came Ellen whose married name was Greppo and who lived in Paterson, New Jersey, and had five children.

H. L. Bateman was a Southern sympathiser and it was as a reaction against having his daughters educated at a Northern school that he decided to settle in England in 1863. He was without religion, having been overfed with Methodism by his mother, and never went into a church. As girls Kate and Ellen had scored an immense success in England both at Drury Lane and on tour, playing to packed houses when eight and six years old. Then came Virginia who was born in Walker Street, New York, on January 1, 1853, and finally Isabel Emilie, born on December 28, 1854, whose godmother was her sister Ellen, her senior by eight years. All four had strong religious inclinations and Virginia recalled how she and Isabel wondered whether they could achieve martyrdom and debated the most practicable form of self-torture, including the suggestion that they might eat a whole bar of yellow soap! Before they left for England the Bishop of New York held a special confirmation service for the pair. Except for short visits they spent the whole of the rest of their lives in Britain.

Virginia's first appearance in London was as *Little Daisy* in a play of the same name at Her Majesty's Theatre on December 22, 1865. When her father opened the Lyceum he had his youngest daughter Isabel as leading lady to Henry Irving and at 17 she scored perhaps her greatest success as Henrietta Maria in W. G. Wills' *Charles I*. Virginia also appeared there, as Glaucea in *Medea In Corinth* in 1872, Princess Elizabeth in *Queen Mary* in April, 1876, and Mrs. Racket in *The*

The Winter Gardens at Southport where the Compton Comedy Company began life on February 7, 1881. Today the Kingsway highway runs through the site. (*Sefton Libraries, Photo-copy by Christopher Oxford*)

Belle's Stratagem the following June.

When in her mid-80s Mrs. (Virginia) Compton was persuaded by her elder son Compton Mackenzie to write down some of her recollections of the Bateman family's connections with Irving. She described how his married life was unhappy and he was drinking heavily during the first years when he was engaged by her father. The great success of *The Bells,* that natural vehicle for Irving, saved the day and Irving's second son was given the second name of Sidney after Mrs. Bateman, who used to be in the theatre night after night dosing him up with strong beef tea. At the time when Isabel was 17 and Virginia nearly 19 Irving would come to their home and yarn until the early hours.

Mrs. Compton said that Isabel fell in love with Irving (I gain the distinct impression that she adored him too) but that after the death of her father the great actor grew further and further away from the widow and daughters. When Mrs. Bateman died in January, 1881, aged 58, Virginia took Irving to the room where she was laid out and told him: "You broke her heart." Oddly enough she also made the comment that while Irving adored acting "not one of us except Kate cared for it." Some years later while Irving was playing Shylock at Drury Lane Mrs. Compton took her daughters Nell and Fay to his dressing room and Irving became a prophet—"That's the one who will make a success," he said, pointing to Fay.

Mrs. Bateman had died penniless but Isabel and her sisters were determined to pay off the considerable debts resulting from rebuilding the Sadlers Wells Theatre with borrowed capital in October, 1879. Virginia played Lady Teazle there in *The School for Scandal* in December, 1879. Mrs. Compton recalled that her sisters decided to close the theatre and in the autumn of 1881 sailed for the United States to visit their sister Ellen, returning to England in 1882. But a few weeks after the death of her mother we find Virginia performing with her future husband on the first night of his newly-formed company.

It was in the middle of a blinding snowstorm that the Compton Comedy Company began its career at Southport on Monday, February 7, 1881. The Southport newspaper does not record the climatic condition in its account and in fact does not have much to say at all about this first week by a brand new company. It excused its scant coverage by explaining: "Mr. Compton and his dramatic company are providing excellent entertainment for playgoers at the Winter Gardens and it is to be regretted that the pressure upon our space, caused by the report of the town's affairs, prevents our doing full justice to the performances. We trust, however, to be able in Saturday's issue to make up for the neglect." This, however, it failed to do. The national mention given by the weekly stage newspaper Era was also cursory. More space was devoted to a "most enjoyable concert" given in the Winter Gardens the previous Saturday . . . "the artists being Madame Trebelli, Miss Anna Williams, Signor Vizzani and Vozoli, Mons Ovid Masin (solo violinist) and Signor Biscario (pianoforte). The several artists were frequently encored and good naturedly responded to each call. The audience was large and enthusiastic. During the week Mr. Edward Compton's Comedy Company have occupied the boards of the theatre and have had a warm reception. The programme comprises *As You Like It, The Heir at Law, The Poor Gentleman* etc." That was all, apart from the advertisements showing that the first week included: Monday, *Twelfth Night;* Tuesday, *She Stoops to Conquer* and *A*

156

THEATRE ROYAL,

DUMFRIES.

LESSEE, Mr A. D. M'NEILL.

MONDAY EVENING, February 21st, Special Engagement for Six Nights Only of the

COMPTON COMEDY COMPANY

Stage Manager,			Mr LEWIS BALL
Agent in Advance,	For Mr COMPTON		Mr JAS. F. CRAIG
Acting Manager,			Mr J. H. SAVILE

Mr EDWARD COMPTON, supported by Miss VIRGINIA BATEMAN and FULL COMPANY. Specially Selected for the portrayal of Characters in those Sterling Comedies which are so thoroughly associated with the name of the late Mr Compton, the Son making a Special Study of the Father's Dramatic Creations.

COMPLETE CHANGE OF PROGRAMME EACH EVENING.

MONDAY EVENING, February 21st, 1881, at 7.30, Shakespeare's Admired Comedy in Five Acts,

TWELFTH NIGHT,

Or, WHAT YOU WILL.

Orsino, Duke of Illyra,		Mr J. S. BLYTHE
Sir Toby Belch, Uncle to Olivia,		Mr LEWIS BALL
Sir Andrew Aquecheek, a Foolish Knight,		Mr WALTER VERNON
Sebastian, Brother to Viola,		Mr W. H. CALVERT
Antonia, a Sea Captain, his friend,		Mr HENRY KENNEDY
Fabian, (Servants to the)		Mr F. W. WYNDHAM
Clown, (Countess.)		Mr T. C. VALENTINE
Valentine, Mr WORRELL	Curtis,	Mr CLARKE
An Officer,		Mr BISHOP
A Sea Captain, friend to Viola,		Mr BERNARD ELLIS
Friar,		Mr WILMOT
Malvolio, Steward to the Countess Olivia,		Mr E. COMPTON
Countess Olivia, a Rich Heiress,		Miss CLARA COWPER
Maria, her attendant,		Miss MAY AUDLEY
Viola, Sister to Sebastian, in love with the Duke,		Miss V. BATEMAN

TUESDAY EVENING, 22d February, at 7.30, Colman's Sparkling Comedy, in Three Acts, THE

HEIR-AT-LAW

Daniel Dowlas, alias Baron Duberly,		Mr LEWIS BALL
Dick Dowlas, his son,		Mr F. W. WYNDHAM
Henry Morland, Mr W. H. CALVERT	Stedfast, his Friend, Mr H. KENNEDY
Zekiel Homespun, from Derbyshire,		Mr WALTER VERNON
Kenrick, an old Servant of Miss Dormer,		Mr T. C. VALENTINE
John,		Mr BERNARD ELLIS
Dr Pangloss, L.L.D. and A.S.S.		Mr EDWARD COMPTON
Deborah Dowlas, alias Lady Duberly,		Mrs BICKERSTAFF
Caroline Dormer,		Miss CLARA COWPER
Cicely Homespun, sister to Zekiel,		Miss VIRGINIA BATEMAN

The C.C.C. at Dumfries in the third week of its life, in February, 1881. *(Dumfries Public Libraries).*

Fish out of Water; Wednesday, *The Heir at Law* and *Paul Pry;* Thursday, *As You Like It;* Friday, *The Rivals* and *A Mutual Separation;* Saturday, *The Poor Gentleman* and *The Hypocrite.* Compton Mackenzie postulates that his father chose "old comedy" rather than the up-to-date variety because "the wigs of costume drama were preferable to the toupees that would be required for more modern drama." Founder members of the company were Virginia Bateman, Clara Cowper, Miss Audley, Lewis Ball, T. C. Valentine, J. S. Blythe, F. W. Wyndham, Walter Vernon W. H. Calvert and Miss Bickerstaff.

Southport laid claim to being an all-year-round resort because of the existence of the eight-acre Winter Gardens complex which had been opened in 1874, as a result of the enterprise of Walter Smith, four times Mayor of the town and also promoter of the Botanic Gardens, the Southport Tramways Company and the railways to Manchester and Preston. The main feature of the Gardens was the largest conservatory in England, 180 ft. long, 80 ft. wide and 80 ft. high, and housing oriental and tropical trees, hothouse plants and flowers, a cascade, and an aviary of exotic birds. From it ran a 170 ft. long and 44 ft. wide Promenade, at the other end of which was the Pavilion auditorium where the C.C.C. appeared. It seated 2,500 and had a promenade gallery and a stage on which a 30-piece orchestra normally gave twice-daily concerts, with special guest artists' concerts on Saturday nights. Gradually theatre companies and variety shows appeared. The full extent of the Winter Gardens was repeated underground, with two refreshment rooms under the Pavilion and an aquarium under the Promenade and Conservatory.

Frank Gosnay who was baggage man with the company at Southport, later became business manager of the Globe Theatre, London.

The "launching in a snowstorm" reference is from Compton's obituary in the Era in 1918, which commented that the blizzard must have seemed ominous. Judging by the cash surplus for the week, also mentioned there, it must indeed. The profit was 2s. 2d., a figure which seemed to bear out prophecies then freely being made that a company following such a policy as the C.C.C. was adopting would speedily find itself in the bankruptcy court.

When the company visited the Theatre Royal, Dumfries, a fortnight later the Era reported "We regret to chronicle very meagre audiences up to the time of writing." But however good or bad business turned out to be there was no shortage of bookings for the new company. Its date book was full right from the start. Here is a full list of the places visited, in sequence, during that opening season: Southport, Kilmarnock, Dumfries, Glasgow, Edinburgh, Manchester (two weeks), Rochdale, Dublin, Stratford-upon-Avon (three weeks), Liverpool, Leicester, Lichfield (four nights), Coventry (two nights), Brighton, Plymouth, and Exeter.

During the week at the Royal Theatre, Glasgow, the Era recalled that Compton had a few years earlier been a popular member of the stock company at the Royal Theatre. "It was, however, as a young juvenile that he was known hitherto and the power he displays as an actor of character parts must therefore be a genuine surprise to most of the visitors and is certainly sufficiently marked to justify Mr. Compton in assuming the roles in which his father was perhaps unrivalled." Of the fortnight at Manchester the paper's correspondent said that Compton "reminds us of his parent in face, voice, and demeanour. He avows the intention of reviving, or at all events, sustaining public interest in the old comedies and in this resolution he will have the best wishes of all lovers of English drama. At the same time he must not feel too disappointed if the public are not prepared to accord him the same amount of enthusiastic support as that which his father obtained after 50 years probation." From Dublin's Gaiety Theatre it was recalled that Miss Virginia Bateman was "long favourably known in this city as Virginia Frances." This was the name, her Christian names, under which she had previously appeared.

The three-week stay at Stratford-upon-Avon was the first of two Festival seasons there. Fewer than a third of the plays of 1881 and 1882 were Shakespearean, the balance including *She Stoops to Conquer, The Poor Gentleman, The Hypocrite, The Rivals, The Hunchback, London Assurance, All That Glitters, A Mutual Separation, Wild Oats, The Road to Ruin* and *The School for Scandal*. After the 1882 Festival all the company visits there were of three days only.

In June, 1881, Compton's "card" announcement on the front page of the Era stated that his company had concluded its first tour and "thus encouraged would commence a second in August." Letters were to be sent to 31 Ladbroke Road, Notting Hill Gate, London.

When the second season began at Bath, on August 22, 1881, there were three additions to the repertoire—*Wild Oats, The Road to Ruin* and a two-act drama written by Compton in collaboration with E. M. Robson, entitled *Faithful Unto Death*. The company was virtually the same, with the addition of Sylvia Hodson.

When the company played in the steel city of Sheffield a fortnight later the audience included Sir Henry Bessemer, inventor of the steel process named after him. Of that week H. T. Milner, writing in the publication The Theatre, said this about the revival of *Wild Oats:* "It is certainly a pity the piece is so seldom produced for it sparkles with wit and abounds with telling points. The revival was such a success that it should encourage Mr. Compton to include it in his regular repertoire." He described how T. C. Valentine brought the house down as Ephraim Smooth, the amorous Quaker.

Even allowing for the usual puffery it does appear that the company was improving the taste of its provincial audiences and presenting plays not often seen by them. For example, the first two months of 1882 found them at the Theatre Royal, Lincoln, where their visit was counted (in Era) as "a great treat" and Lord Monson patronised Compton's Friday benefit; Wrexham Public Hall where they encountered "very much better houses than, unfortunately, usually patronise the drama in this town" and the Friday benefit was attended by Col. Mostyn and the officers of the Royal Welsh Fusiliers; the Theatre Royal, York, where their visit was "an unusual treat with a large fashionable audience and the better seats filled"; and the Theatre Royal, Greenock, where the "playgoers seldom enjoyed such a dramatic treat."

The full itinerary of this second tour was as follows: Bath, Bristol, Sheffield, Oldham, Edinburgh (two weeks), Buxton (two nights), Lichfield (three nights), Scarborough, Middlesborough, Southport, Huddersfield, Glasgow, Dundee, Edinburgh (two weeks), Manchester, Hull, Liverpool, Coventry, Lincoln, Newark (three nights), Peterborough (three nights) Wolverhampton, Wrexham, York, Kilmarnock, Greenock, Belfast (two weeks), Cork, Dublin (two weeks) Oldham, Southport, Halifax (three nights) Burton on Trent (three nights), Stratford-upon-Avon (two weeks), Hanley, Birmingham, Leicester and Brighton, where the season concluded with a stay of a fortnight.

The Road to Ruin was played for the whole of the first week at Brighton, with a variety of plays during the second. As Miss Hardcastle in *The School for Scandal* Virginia Bateman was compared favourably by the Brighton Gazette with Mrs. Langtry who had recently appeared in the role in Brighton. The newspaper speculated on why the old comedies presented by the C.C.C. needed revival— why they had gone out of fashion. After comparing them favourably with more recent plays of shallow plot bolstered by bad puns and overdrawn and even fictitious characters it said that they had perhaps been confined to comparative oblivion because "the prudish refinement of the 19th century takes alarm at the slightest soupcon of what is after all but a faithful delineation of life and that society refuses to look upon, in public, that which is every day taking place in its midst and would rather rely upon what is after all to a great extent imaginary." It said that the gratitude of the public was due to Edward Compton who had fought prejudice. His example had been followed in London by Mr. Thorne at the Vaudeville Theatre with a stock company. It added that Compton had carried out his intentions "after much trouble and in spite of criticisms from many prudish and prejudiced individuals."

In a speech on his benefit night, on the Friday of the second week, Compton referred to the 42-week tour as being a gratifying success–"I have worked hard, played hard, travelled hard, and notwithstanding the hard times have netted sufficient hard cash to prevent my being hard up." He made no mention, it appears, of his impending marriage to his leading lady in Brighton the following Monday. It took place privately at St. Peter's Church, the only persons present being Mr. and Mrs. Crowe (bride's sister and brother-in-law), Mrs. Compton (bridegroom's mother), Isabel Batcman (bride's sister) and J. H. Savile (company business manager) and his wife. Henry C. Porter records the event in his History of the Theatres of Brighton from 1774 to 1885: "On June 12, 1882, Edward Compton Mackenzie, of 38 Kensington Gardens, son of Charles Mackenzie and Emmeline Montague, was married at St. Peter's Church, Brighton, by the Rev. Henry R. Beverley to Virginia Frances Bateman, of 81 Grand Parade, daughter of Hezekiah Linthicum Bateman, of New York, in the presence of George Crowe, Kate Crowe, L. Castel Hoey, Isabel Bateman and Emmeline Mackenzie (Miss Compton)". The Brighton Gazette report listed the guests as Mr. and Mrs. Crowe, Miss Isabel Bateman Mrs. Compton and Mr. and Mrs. Sainte, adding "The happy wedded started at noon for Eastbourne." The front page of the Era carried two cards, a separate one for Virginia Bateman besides the one for Edward Compton. The following week the two again appeared but this time the one for Virginia had an addition in brackets: (Mrs. Edward Compton). Just as Compton often quoted the opinion of the Sunday Referee that "As a genuine comedian Mr. Edward Compton has few equals and no superiors on the English stage" Miss Bateman quoted the view of Freeman's Journal that "There can scarcely ever have been a better Viola than Miss Virginia Bateman."

From the religious point of view it was an odd marriage for though Virginia was High Church and deeply religious, sharing some of the mysticism of her actress sister Isabel who was to become the Rev. Mother of a Convent, he was not at all interested in devotional matters. During Holy Week, when the company never performed, Edward's idea was to make it a busman's holiday, visiting theatres which remained open (except on Good Friday) while Virginia spent as much of the week as possible in church.

A departure from the company at this time was of founder member F. W. Wyndham who announced in an advertisement in the same issue that he had resigned and was now disengaged. The son of an actor-manager in Edinburgh he had started life adventurously by being rescued with his mother from their flat over the Adelphi Theatre, Edinburgh, when it was burned down in 1853; he was a week old at the time. After college studies he acted in London and the provinces but went on to do great things as an owner of theatres. In 1895 he teamed up with J. B. Howard to form the famous firm Howard and Wyndham Ltd. so that on subsequent visits Compton was playing at theatres owned by one of the founder members of his company. He died in April, 1930, aged 77. During that terminal week at Brighton Wyndham had appeared as Harry Dornton in *The Road to Ruin* and Young Marlow in *She Stoops to Conquer.*

The third C.C.C. tour, 1882-3, began at Harrogate where the venue was the Town Hall Theatre of which, one Era reference notes, the lessees were the Harrogate Amateur Minstrels. Then came West Hartlepool, Scarborough, Leeds, Huddersfield, Douglas (Isle of Man—at the Gaiety Theatre, not the new Grand Theatre opened in July, 1882, by Mr. Lightfoot on the site of the former Douglas Aquarium which, according to the Era, had been a "gigantic failure") where two weeks were spent, Wolverhampton, Cardiff, Bath, Exeter, Bristol, Brighton, Hull, York, Bradford, Southport, Newcastle, Middlesborough, Doncaster, Harrogate and Bishops Auckland.

When Edward and Virginia had found themselves expecting their first-born they had booked a small house at Keswick two months in advance of the expected date but the baby arrived early. After making the train journey from Bishops Auckland, where they had played the previous week, Mrs. Compton told her husband on the evening of Sunday, January 14, 1883, that things were moving. At York there had been a long wait while the carriage reserved for the onward journey to Darlington had been hitched on to the train. There again came a delay while the wagon was moved to the train for West Hartlepool. Thus it was after a trying journey—though they were accustomed to spend Sundays in this manner, in railway carriages, in railway waiting rooms, and on railway platforms —that they arrived at 23 Adelaide Street, West Hartlepool, where their bedroom was over an arch leading into a stableyard.

At the news of the impending early debut Edward set out on his 29th birthday to find a doctor but in fact the birth was delayed. On the evening of the Tuesday, before making his way to the theatre, Edward was told by Dr. Swanwick that if the birth had not occurred by the following morning it would be necessary to take the life of the child in order to save that of the mother. The doctor had wired to London for special instruments and if they came by the Wednesday morning it might yet be possible to save the life of the child. The child was safely born and christened Edward Montague Compton, with the surname entered, of course, as Mackenzie. The following weekend the company left for Carlisle but mother and child had to stay behind.

After Carlisle came Greenock, Glasgow, Belfast (two weeks), Dublin (two weeks), Cork (two weeks), Chester, Worcester, Cardiff, Swansea, Shrewsbury,

Southport, Birmingham, Glasgow, Dundee, Aberdeen, Edinburgh, Liverpool and Manchester after which the summer break was taken by the Comptons at Skiddaw View, Keswick, Cumberland, Mrs. Compton and the baby having at some stage rejoined the tour, he being taken to the theatre and breast-fed in a dressing room. Needless to say it was the ladies of the company who billed and cooed over young Compton Mackenzie, who was himself especially fond of Elinor Aickin, who took all the matronly parts and whom he called "Aicky", and Nellie Harper, whose roles included Maria in *The School for Scandal* and Julia Melville in *The Rivals*. "Aicky", who had been in stock with E. D. Lyons in Dundee in 1866 and appeared with Charles Kean on his farewell visit to that city had toured with Charles Dillon and Ellen Terry and visited the States with Mr. and Mrs. Bandmann. About this time she began a 10-year spell with the Compton company.

After opening for 10 nights at Scarborough the new season continued with two nights at Malton and four at Whitby and then they were back at West Hartlepool and at Harrogate, the latter being their third visit within 12 months. There followed Sheffield, Swansea, Cardiff, Bristol, Portsmouth, Brighton, Leeds, Hull, Newark (three nights), Doncaster (three nights), Huddersfield and Bradford.

Then, in December, 1883, came the company's first London season lasting six weeks at the Royal Strand Theatre. This was a new building, the previous one having been condemned by the Metropolitan Board of Works, who were beginning to get rather more particular about their approval of theatres. The old house had been closed on July 29, 1882, for rebuilding to the designs of C. J. Phipps—though his name was no guarantee of safety, as the Fire Interlude reveals.

Plays selected for the debut in the capital included *Wild Oats* and *The Road to Ruin,* both of which Compton had introduced into the repertoire after the first season. In the former he appeared as Jack Rover, the strolling player of the times when actors were glad to play in barns and outhouses with a carpet as a drop scene and an audience of yokels. The part is full of quotations from plays which the lowly actor uses as the staple of his conversation. In the latter he played Charles Goldfinch, patron of the turf and driver of anything from a curricle to a four-in-hand, the knowing tipster and Newmarket favourite, with his phrases cut up like those of Mr. Jingle in Pickwickian escapades.

It was with *Wild Oats* that Compton chose to open on Monday, December 3, and the national Press gave him almost as kindly a reception as he got in the provinces. The Manchester Guardian had said that Nature had fitted him for the part; the Birmingham Daily Gazette had declared that for ease, dash, humour and unflagging vitality a finer bit of comedy acting had never been seen; the Hull Eastern Morning News spoke of his "wonderful fidelity" to O'Keeffe's pages. In London The Times described him as "an actor of very versatile capacity, including the useful but rare quality of personal distinction and refinement"; the Daily Telegraph said that he "endowed the part with freshness, animation and refinement"; The Globe rated it as an excellent performance; while The Echo said that "an artist of so much genuine talent ought to find permanent engagements in the metropolis," a comment which was to prove ironic. In the play Virginia Bateman played Lady Amaranth, a role which had been taken by Henrietta Hodson in the most recent revival in London a few years earlier. Other plays of the season were *Twelfth Night* and *She Stoops To Conquer* (the title of which was probably suggested by a line of the Northampton-shire dramatist and Poet Laureate John Dryden . . . "But kneels to conquer and but stoops to rise.")

On their return to the provincial round the company visited York's Theatre Royal and the Central Hall, Darlington. Nearly all their engagements were in "proper" theatres; besides Darlington the few "fit-ups" included the St. James Hall, Litchfield, and the West Cliff Saloon at Whitby. From Darlington it was on to Carlisle, Greenock (two weeks), Dundee, Aberdeen and Glasgow where, at the Royalty Theatre, on March 5, 1884, Compton played for the first time the role with which he was to become most closely associated, *Davy Garrick*. Next came fortnights in Belfast and Dublin and weeks at Cork and Chester and then, on May 5, 1884, the company for the first time "christened" a new theatre—the Theatre Royal and Opera House, Guildhall Road, Northampton. The play chosen for the opening night was the one which had launched the company on its career in 1881—*Twelfth Night,* with Compton as Malvolio and his wife as Viola. The rest of the cast included John Burton, Lewis Ball, J. S. Blythe, William Calvert, W. H. Garboise, Percy F. Marshall, T. C. Valentine, G. H. Worrall, L. J. Clarke, Stanley Rogers, W. F. Gosnay, Nellie Harper, Sylvia Hodson, W. Gardiner, F. Bishop, Mr. Wheeton, Mr. Weatherby, Mrs. Bickerstaff, Rose Parker, and Virginia Bateman (Mrs. Compton). The plays that week were Tuesday, *She Stoops to Conquer;* Wednesday, *The School for Scandal;* Thursday, *The Rivals* and *Delicate Ground;* Friday, *The Comedy of Errors;* Saturday, *The Road to Ruin* and *Faithful Unto Death!* The theatre had been built for John Campbell Franklin, who owned a restaurant a few doors away up the street. The manager, Isaac Tarry, was doing the job on a part-time basis, he being an auctioneer. The L-shaped theatre had been built by Henry Martin's firm to the designs of C. J. Phipps.

It may be noted that the company did not now perform at the Stratford-upon-Avon Festival. Shakespeare now began to figure less in the repertoire, Compton having decided as a matter of policy that he would concentrate on the revival of the old comedies, no doubt believing them to be a better draw. It was probably for this reason that he rejected the entreaties of Mr. Charles Flower, the brewer who had been largely responsible for the opening in 1879 of the Shakespeare Memorial Theatre, that the company should return to Stratford for more Festivals. Flowers did not merely write to Compton but made the trip several times to appeal to him in person, wherever the company happened to be.

Instead of being at Stratford the company were in Ireland and could read in the Cork Examiner the depressing annual report of the Cork Theatre and Opera House Co. Ltd, for the 12 months ended March 31, 1884: "While the present commercial depression, absence of county families, and scarcity of money among all classes continue the utmost that can be expected from a provincial theatre is that it should escape serious loss." The report was signed by the managing director and secretary Mr. James Scanlan whose own annual salary was revealed in the accounts to be £60.

It was during a visit to Cork that baby Mackenzie was much distressed while sitting in his perambulator by the sight of the local children without shoes or stockings and offered them his own shoes and stockings, as well as the penny he had been given to buy some sweets. A friend of the Comptons, Jack Cronin, who was a wine merchant, had had a large crate made to transport the perambulator and cot from place to place. The latter was called the Shakespeare Travelling Cot and the youngster used to enjoy supervising its weekly packing, along with his other infantile impedimenta. The cot had several wooden rods, fitted with brass sockets which had to be put together as a framework for the canvas of the bed. When dismantled it was stowed in a canvas bag. There were curtains at the head which gave Compton a sense of security and may have been a reason why he always liked to sleep in a four poster.

In traversing the country the company were making a sort of domestic grand tour. Though they could not have had a great deal of time to savour the delights of any particular town or city, it must have been quite an education for them to be among Southerners one week, Lancastrians the next, followed closely by spells with the Scots and Irish. Compton Mackenzie, whose remarkable (but not entirely reliable) memory stretched right back to baby days, could call to mind the various parts of the United Kingdom which he saw from his cot, though these recollections do not include Northampton, where he was 15 months old and was asleep in his cot in a dressing room while his father was playing Malvolio on the opening night of the new theatre in May, 1884. Indeed, he gives the impression that the company moved directly from Ireland to Scotland. He also commented that in later years this direction would be reversed but that at this time his father was not able to dictate his tours. In fact the company moved from Northampton to Birmingham before travelling north to Scotland, for dates at Glasgow and Edinburgh, then concluding the season at Southport, Sheffield and Manchester.

Consider what immense distances were covered in the course of a year by these touring companies and what fine services the Victorian railways must have provided to enable them to do so! Apart from the five week summer vacation, taken that year at Lowestoft, the company spent Sunday in the train and from 1884 Compton Mackenzie recalled the metallic sound of the footwarmers being pushed into the compartment, and of looking up to the roof where the oil swung to and fro in the lamp which was the feeble means of illumination. During the life of the company an attempt was made to stop this large scale sabbatical migration. With a Mr. Hornbeck as their spokesman 900 shareholders of the London and North Western Railway Company petitioned the Board in August, 1898, to stop providing Sunday trains for theatricals. They urged that "if actors could not transport their persons and property from one town to another on Sunday they would soon find another day, which would lessen the labour of railway servants." This request was turned down by the Board who said the demand for the service was irresistible and "to refuse facilities to the players would be a severe blow to a hard-working and popular class who have frequently to play in one town on a Saturday night and another perhaps 200 miles away on Monday, transporting their scenery and property from one place to the other and re-erecting them in the interval."

As regards scenery, however, this was one chore the C.C.C. did not have to face. As Compton Mackenzie recalled, touring repertory companies did not carry scenery, every provincial theatre being expected to carry a drawing room set, a library set, a parlour set, an inn set, two open-air backcloths with wooden wings and four or five front cloths of interiors and exteriors.

The resumption in September, 1884, was at Bournemouth and then, within six months of opening the Northampton theatre the company were back there.

About this time baby Mackenzie was parted for the first time from his mother when his nanny fell ill. Father took him to London to stay with his aunt and god-mother Isabel Bateman who was at the Adelphi in *In The Ranks,* one of the long-running successes of Geo. R. Sims and Henry Pettitt. Mrs. Compton carried on performing but then fell ill herself and had to be left behind. When next she saw the baby, on rejoining the company in Huddersfield, she was appalled to see that his father had had the baby's curls cut off, under the impression (according to the victim) that it would in due course save him going bald as Edward had done!

Edward Compton was a great believer in giving the local touch to his curtain speeches and at Coventry that Christmas he added the extra touch of learning Tennyson's Lady Godiva to recite at his benefit night.

Quite apart from the fact that times were depressed it was an uphill struggle at many places they visited for the first time. In February, 1885, for instance, they paid their first call at the Theatre Royal, Old Wells, Cheltenham (not to be con-fused with the earlier Theatre Royal controlled by the Watsons, father and son). The Cheltenham Examiner reported that they "received but scant encourage-ment" and bemoaned the fact that "the Cheltenham public can scarcely be cognisant of the excellent company now occupying the boards at the theatre or we feel sure their patronage would have been more liberally bestowed than it was on Monday and again last evening. For four years Mr. Edward Compton's talented company have been before the public and have performed with marvel-lous success." In an adjacent column "A Visitor" wrote a letter to the editor also regretting the lack of custom and adding: "On inquiry I learned that it is Mr. Compton's first visit here and he is therefore comparatively unknown, which may in a measure account for the apathy of the Cheltenham public." As Comp-ton was to say many times in speeches, it was a case rather similar to that which the new theatre faced in Northampton—of creating a public where one had not existed before.

Compton rarely missed an opportunity to mark anniversaries, whether of the first performance of a play or of the company itself. At Cork Opera House that February the company apparently celebrated its "birthday" for the first time with a supper and smoking concert for all the members. This fourth anniversary was the first of many such annual parties.

At Cork the audience had been asked to vote in advance to decide which plays should be performed and the polls were declared in the newspaper. In this "Grand Ballot Programme" the scores included: Tuesday, *The Rivals,* 432 votes; Wednesday, *The Road to Ruin,* 388; Thursday, *The School for Scandal,* 457; Friday, *Davy Garrick,* 549; Saturday morning (i.e. matinee), *The Comedy of Errors,* 497; Saturday night (Compton's benefit), *Money,* 633. Regarding *The Comedy of Errors,* this explanation was offered: "This play is rarely acted in consequence of the difficulty in procuring a likeness to the Twin Dromios; but the wonderful resemblance between Mr. Edward Compton and Mr. William Calvert so realises the author's intentions that it now presents one of the greatest novelties and dramatic curiosities that has for many years been offered to the public." In *Money,* the advertisement also pointed out, the Club Scene was frequently omitted in provincial theatres but on this occasion several prominent gentlemen had promised to appear. This novelty of including local personalities as "extras" was often employed, including Northampton where in January, 1887, they included Messrs. Isaac Tarry and T. P. Dorman, manager and future owner respectively.

During a subsequent visit to Cork Compton had what he imagined to be the inspiration of asking the colonel of troops quartered in the district to allow the regimental band to take over in the pit. The audience loudly applauded the military musicians until the final curtain when they played the National Anthem and uproar broke out. The Irish patriots objected to it. At first it appeared that the guest band's appearance would be for one night only as on the morrow it seemed certain that an audience forewarned would take along suitable objects to throw at the musicians, as a mark of displeasure at the Royal salute. Compton Mackenzie recalls that a compromise was reached. On Compton's suggestion they played half the anthem and then beat a hasty retreat under the stage. Such nationalist tendencies never affected the warm place which the C.C.C. had in Irish hearts and the affection was a two-way affair. From Limerick Compton wrote to a friend that the place had a splendid audience in a theatre that was a "thorough old barn" and that they deserved something better.

That summer the young Compton Mackenzie had another spell away from the company, rejoining them at Hastings. It was at the next play date, at Brighton, that he first attended a performance; his critical faculties appear to have been well developed already for he says that his father put on a "very bad play."

Edward Compton was as systematic in his conduct of the business of touring theatre as any desk-bound bank manager running his financial domain. For many years he put himself down in the company accounts for a salary of £10, with £5 for his wife. He had two portable desks which stood on a table in the window of whatever theatrical digs he happened to be staying in. One would contain his own personal correspondence, the other the company papers.

It would invariably be "digs". Compton detested hotels and would never stay in one if he could find suitable lodgings. He would make only a·few exceptions, two notable ones being at Llandudno and on the Isle of Man, the latter depending on his friendship with the theatre manager, Alfred Hemmings. His son said that he would normally strike a town off his list if digs were not available. This, one may feel, is an extension of writer's licence but does not alter the fact that Compton did prefer lodgings and nearly always stayed in them. He must have been one of the most welcome of the theatrical landladies' regular callers for he was most regular in his habits and did not live the life of Riley as did some touring managers. None of his landladies found themselves giving evidence about him in the Divorce Courts. And just as he looked forward to the familiar face of the landlady she would look forward to the visit of the C.C.C. In many towns it must have been her most regular and longest-lasting piece of business. Apart from the odd hours it was more like having a civil servant stay with her than an actor-manager, a type of person whose way of life was normally regarded as being extravagant and unpredictable. In the early years, of course, his wife was with him.

Compton told a story against one of his landladies at a place beginning with G (Glasgow or Greenock?) and relating to the days before the formation of his company, in the autumn of 1876. He told the yarn to a reporter in his dressing room at Leamington, during his second visit there in 1885: "My landlady—I suppose with an order—went to see the play. The night's programme consisted of the comedy *All That Glitters* and the old nautical drama *The Anchor Of Hope,* in which I appeared as Stephen Plum and Tom Topreef respectively. The house was not exactly crowded so I was able to distinguish my good landlady sitting rigidly attentive during the performance and occasionally, as I fondly imagined, pointed out special points in my acting to her somewhat imbecile-looking friend. But I was wrong. On arriving home I had occasion to pass the kitchen door when the following specimen of wilful stupidity forced itself upon my ear. 'Don't you see my dear, that that there young man, that Sugar Plum, he married Martha. Then he leaves to go and be a sailor; comes 'ome and marries another wife and in consequence of such wicked goings-on we had all that clashing of swords and firing of pistols, which was brought about by that old man with the pole (Abraham Moses, the Jew in *The Anchor Of Hope!*) who was the father of the first wife come to revenge her.' I retired sadly to my apartment; the dear old soul, in spite of her programme, had ingeniously woven the modern comedy and the ancient drama into one piece!"

Compton's usual daily routine was to take dinner at 3 p.m., never smoking before that time. With the meal he would take two glasses of claret (later champagne) and smoke one cigar before making the journey to the theatre. Returning afterwards to the lodgings he would have a light supper and smoke two cigars and a pipe before going to bed precisely at 1 a.m.

During the summer break of 1885 there was a family get-together attended by three of the four Bateman sisters—Kate and her husband Dr. Crowe, Virginia and Edward and their two sons (Frank was the new baby) and Isabel and her two dogs.

At Greenwich that August Sydney Paxton became a recruit to the Compton Comedy Company—or the "Ompton 'Omedy 'Ompany" as it was sometimes known by the young, from the poster motif of a single C, embracing the three terminals. In his memoirs entitled Stage See-Saw, published in 1917, he throws considerable light on life with the company . . . "a very fine company it was at that time and for many years until Mr. Compton fell into the bad habit of accepting paying guests as actors and taking premiums from the inexperienced and the unitiated. The year that I joined him, although we were mostly young people, we had gone through a useful apprenticeship, knew at least the rudiments of our business and were ready for plenty of work, and did it. Mr. Compton and his wife were indefatigable workers; then there was that incomparable old actor Lewis Ball and sterling actress Elinor Aickin. The other members of the company on that tour were that admirable actor Sydney Valentine, at that time not 21, but a well experienced actor whom I had met previously in Wales and Inverness; Charles Dodsworth, who was to make his mark as a fine character actor with most of our great stars including Sir Henry Irving; Percy Marshall, an excellent light comedian; Clarence Blakiston, Hawley Franks, Stanley Rogers, Alice Burton and Nellie Harper."

The tour of 1885-6 went well, Paxton recalled. "The C.C.C. was already thoroughly established and business was everywhere splendid. If there was no outstanding talent apart from that great old man Lewis Ball there was at any rate care, correctness and earnestness that made the performances good value for money; and the company was thoroughly appreciated in every town and city in the United Kingdom." Life with the C.C.C. was "a very steady, respectable business. Mr. Compton, although not exactly a philanthropist with regard to salaries, was a very just, level-headed, manager who certainly appreciated his artistes and their work. He might have been a little more generous without in any way risking the fortune I understand he has made; still it was a most comfortable engagement. True we did not get much money; but we were most of us young and unmarried. We played 46 weeks in the year; visited all the best towns and cities; and became favourites with our audiences, getting our individual receptions on Monday nights; and we were a recognised first-class company! We added frequently to our repertoire; and in my time it numbered 25 pieces, any of which could be played with but little rehearsal; they were all kept so well in order."

When the repertoire was added to it was not without long and patient rehearsals "which made first nights as smooth as natural anxiety and nervousness can ever make them. *True Love,* a modern piece, and *London Assurance* were among the new pieces: I think Mr. Compton liked himself in trousers though they never became him like knee breeches. Belphegor was also produced. Compton was very lady-like and his performance didn't convince anybody. He wisely dropped this piece. In *Twelfth Night,* as Malvolio, he was really fine and Ball's Sir Toby Belch inimitable. As Sir Andrew Aguecheek I used to have the honour of taking a call with him and his charm and encouragement are an abiding and pleasant memory to me."

One play on that tour was a failure because of the success of one of its episodes. This was Edgar Pemberton's *The Actor,* written originally for E. A. Sothern. It was "absolutely damned" by a mock mad scene, an opposite number to the mock drunk scene in *Davy Garrick.* "I have heard the applause last for three minutes after it, but it was an anti-climax. There was no interest in the play after it was over. We rehearsed it many weeks and it was altered and re-altered, written and re-written; but it was no good; so it was never seen in London and had to be given up in despair. It was a great disappointment to Mr. and Mrs. Compton and to most of us who had good parts." Paxton himself was among those who had good parts and "Mr. Compton very generously allowed me to introduce some specialities that he had seen me do in my entertainments at a smoking concert."

Paxton summed up: "We enjoyed ourselves and we enjoyed our work. What could be better? Of course we had our individual weaknesses; we shouldn't have been actors or human if we hadn't; but we weren't prigs, which so many actors seem to be today" (the Memoirs were published 30 years later.)

Among recruits to the company during the period covered by Paxton were Henry Vibert, A. E. W. Mason (who distinguished himself as a novelist but not as an actor), Harrison Hunter, Harcourt Beatty, Fred Permain, Eille Norwood, Clyde Meyness and H. H. Morell. Recruits after he left included Norman McKinnel and Arthur Wontner.

For the second anniversary of the Northampton Opera House in May, 1886, the manager Isaac Tarry had booked the C.C.C. to appear on the stage they had inaugurated. Despite the timeliness of the booking their *London Assurance* was greeted by a thin Monday night audience. But on the Tuesday, the actual anniversary of the first night of 1884, the house was overflowing for *Davy Garrick* and in the scene in which Compton (Garrick) is ordered to leave the house of Alderman Gresham the play came to a standstill—"The enthusiasm of the audience could not be restrained and though it left the rest of the characters in a ridiculous status quo it insisted on recalling him again and again, a breach of etiquette very pardonable under the circumstances," according to the Northampton Mercury.

Compton had written a special epilogue for the occasion, beginning:

Kind friends! The actor Garrick drops his mask
For now the actor Compton fain would ask
Your leave his gratulation warm to pay
On this your second anniversary day!
When this day two years dawned upon this earth
'Twas mine to celebrate this house's birth
This house, which like a flower bed in a waste
You owe to Franklin's pluck and Tarry's taste
This term of waste consider no offence
I do but speak in a theatric sense
Long you've been noted—for fame could not choose
But follow wheresoever went—your shoes!
Shoes made by sterling hands of honest leather
And 'Warranted to stand the roughest weather'
But while your manufacturers owned no peer
The drama's lot was dark indeed and drear!
The art I serve, wherein my soul delights
Had no fit place to celebrate its rites
Till wizard Franklin waved his magic wand
And lo! This temple rose at his command
Let him and Tarry share the laurel crown
They filled a void in their native town!

Into the rest of the piece Compton had worked the names of the plays performed by his company, a favourite device of his.

Shakespeare stood sponsor to the Babe so fair
And Twelfth Night revels filled the ambient air.
Since then I've wandered, north, south, east and west
To please my friends, allowing nought of rest
To all the towns I've sped—sad theme for boast—
Scattering my Wild Oats upon every coast!
Success—strange paradox—my steps pursuing
E'en though my steps have traced The Road To Ruin
Old English comedies, so bright, so sunny
Still spell—and I am proud to own it—Money.
Be that day far distant when her fame departs,
And other Rivals occupy your hearts.

Edward Compton in his favourite role of Davy Garrick, for which he used the Muskerry version. In all he played the part 1870 times his first appearance being at the Royalty Theatre, Glasgow, on March 5, 1884; the last was at the Theatre Royal, Rochdale, on March 27, 1915, which was also the last appearance of his career. I believe this picture to be taken from the oil painting presented to Compton on the occasion of the company's 25th anniversary in 1906. Sir Squire Bancroft, president of the Actors' Association, and Beerbohm Tree were among the contributors. *(Courtesy of Arthur Howard)*

Three pictures of Francis (Frank) Compton who was the least-known member of the family this side of the Atlantic but who made quite a niche for himself in the United States. On left he is seen in costume, probably for *The School for Scandal,* in which he appeared with the Compton Comedy Company before breaking away to join the Army (centre picture) and to go to Australia and America. He again served in the British Army in the 1914-18 War. On right he is seen in later life.

Hezekiah Linthicum Bateman, father of the four Bateman sisters including the one who was to become Mrs. Edward Compton, was an American. A Southerner he decided to settle in Britain rather than let his girls be educated in a Northern school.

Compton Mackenzie, a snapshot taken by Arthur Howard on honeymoon on Barra—"He greeted us in his kilt, like a laird." To Arthur Howard, who never met his own father-in-law, Frank Compton, until after his wife's death, Monty was "like a father-in-law".

Charles Mackenzie who changed his name to Henry Compton when he went on the stage, to avoid embarrassing his family with connections with "the pariah profession."

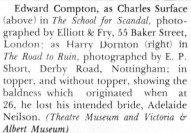

Edward Compton, as Charles Surface (above) in *The School for Scandal,* photographed by Elliott & Fry, 55 Baker Street, London; as Harry Dornton (right) in *The Road to Ruin,* photographed by E. P. Short, Derby Road, Nottingham; in topper, and without topper, showing the baldness which originated when at 26, he lost his intended bride, Adelaide Neilson. *(Theatre Museum and Victoria & Albert Museum)*

Virginia (alias "Fay-ginger", as she was then called by sister Ellen, leading to the name Fay) Compton as a baby.

Anthony Pelissier, son of Fay Compton and H. G. Pelissier, as a boy.

Fay Compton with son Anthony on a birthday postcard.

Fay Compton in the title role of *Mary Rose,* from which she took the name of her autobiography, Rosemary, in 1926 *(Four pictures, Theatre Museum, London)*

Virginia Bateman (Mrs. Edward Compton)—three pictures from the Compton Collection at the Theatre Museum, London, show her in stage costume for a role unidentified, a portrait in middle age, and in old age at her desk at the Theatre Girls Club, London, of which she was the founder and moving spirit until her death in 1940, at 87. American born, she was one of the four daughters of Hezekiah Linthicum Bateman.

Nell (Ellen) Compton—a publicity postcard for the first visit of the C.C.C. to Northampton after the death of Edward Compton.
It was in November, 1918. *(Theatre Museum,
Victoria & Albert Museum)*

Ellen Compton—a splendid portrait of
almost ethereal quality of an actress who was
under-rated. *(Theatre Museum, Victoria &
Albert Museum)*

Two snapshots with grandmothers of Tony **Pelissier** and Jean Compton, with Mrs.
Edward Compton (left) and with Isabel Bateman, actress turned nun, and another lady.
(Courtesy of Arthur Howard)

Mr. EDWARD COMPTON and Miss ADRIENNE DAIROLLES
in "The American."
"I thought I was'nt what he wanted to see!"
ELLIOTT & FRY   Copyright.   55, BAKER STREET
AND AT 7, GLOUCESTER TERR.

Two publicity postcards used by the Compton Comedy Company, featuring *The American* and *The Actor,* the latter by Moffat, Edinburgh, showing Compton in the role of Geoffrey Dare. Below Compton and car, taken by J. Garratt, North Street, Leeds.

Sidney Crowe, daughter of **Kate Bateman**, took the place of her aunt, Virginia Bateman (Mrs. Edward Compton) in the C.C.C. when she was pregnant and at other times. Miss Crowe also played in the company of another of her aunts, Isabel Bateman. *(Courtesy of Valerie Skardon)*

This picture by Studio Hugo shows the Cheltenham Winter Gardens, scene of Ellen Compton's repertory venture in the 1930s. Viewed here through the railings of the bandstand, this local "Crystal Palace" was built in the 1870s to attract the sort of people who went abroad to Carlsbad and Baden. It was pulled down at the start of the 1939-45 War, partly because it was a landmark for enemy planes, and the railings also went during the war, the bandstand following later. The site is now occupied by the Imperial Gardens. *(Cheltenham Libraries)*

For who would be by foreign gee-gaws led,
While British worth and talent pine for bread
By French farceurs, unfit to tie the sandal
Of him who wrote th' immortal School for Scandal
For them to trace old England's acting creed
A Comedy of Errors were indeed!
But lately something's cleared the public sight,
Again old Comedy shines fair and bright;
Well dressed, well mounted, above all well played
Goldsmith and Sheridan need never fade;
London Assurance don't to me impute
E'en though I claim some portion of the fruit;
The seed of which I was the first to sow,
In this your temple of the Guildhall-row.
Long may the drama flourish here; may fame
Crown it, and those who gave it, with high aim
A local habitation and a name.
Ere this week close and I my way pursue
To Stoop to Conquer fields and pastures new
I trust to've earned your praises true and frank
For though Belphegor, I'm no mounte-bank
And, before we let the curtain fall
From my heart's core, a kind goodnight to all
'Parting is such sweet sorrow' that I fear
'I shall say goodnight till it be' NEXT YEAR

As he retired the band played Old Lang Syne. The company that week included Lewis Ball, Sydney Paxton, Sydney Valentine, Stanley Rogers, Percy F. Marshall, Charles Dodsworth, Clarence Blakiston, F. Francks, Lewis J. Clarke, W. F. Gosnay, Elinor Aickin, Alice Burton, Nellie Harper and Virginia Bateman.

After playdates at Birmingham and Manchester the season ended at the Royalty Theatre, Chester, where there was some perceptive comment in the Chester Chronicle. First the critic outlined the plot of the Monday choice, William Muskerry's *Davy Garrick*: "The daughter of a city merchant has fallen in love with the great tragedian and Garrick is invited to dine by her father on the understanding that he will undertake to disgust the young lady with her stage hero. The scene in which Garrick feigns drunkenness and insults the company all round with gibes and buffoonery, brings down upon himself the dismissal of his loved one, and takes his farewell with a burst of pathetic declamations drawn from the works of the greatest dramatists, was magnificent." The writer observed that Miss Bateman "played the part of the daughter with the delicacy and refinement of style which is her distinctive characteristic but we must confess she appeared to have become slightly conventional, not quite so careful in her following of nature and sadder in tone than on former occasions." The play the following night, *The Rivals,* was "an even greater treat" but on Wednesday there was little enthusiasm for Lord Lytton's comedy *Money*: "It must be confessed that this company was hardly at home. What a contrast it was with the previous night! What a change from the beauty of colour and grace of the old English costume of knee breeches and skirted coats to the wretched, miserable concatenation of all the modern gentleman—black trousers and a frock coat. The crook-kneed attitude of the horsey Bob Acres hardly looked well when transferred to the black-leg-cylinders yclept trousers of the scholarly Alfred Evelyn. Excellently as Mr. Compton played the part, the gestures and movements, graceful as they are, which were more than appropriate to the old English comedy, here seemed stagey and unreal." As the widower Graves, Lewis Ball was also "like a fish out of water". Evidently quite a follower of the C.C.C. fortunes, the critic added that he would much have preferred to see Mr. Compton in *Wild Oats* "in which both he and Mrs. Compton are seen to the greatest advantage". Completing that end-of-season June week were *The School for Scandal, The Actor,* and *Belphegor the Mountebank.*

That same month Edward Compton took possession of a house at 54 Avon-more Road, London, having taken a 99-year-lease terminating in 1985. Ever a traditionalist he called it Seaforth House, the name his father had given to his home. Now that the family had a fixed home the children were normally left behind there and Compton Mackenzie recalls the great joy of seeing his parents arrive, in a four-wheel conveyance. For four years this was an annual Palm Sun-day event, before the week "out" for Holy Week.

Sydney Paxton mentions that he spent that summer break of six weeks at Stratford while the Comptons went to Southsea. Then there was a week's rehearsal and a week at Scarborough before the company's second London season at the Strand Theatre, this time of six months. Paxton recalls the excite-ment of the company at this prospect but none was more excited than Compton himself, who longed for the acknowledgment of the West End. In his memoirs of his father Compton recalls his father's chagrin at failing to get a job in London: "My father found it absolutely impossible to get employment in London. Deep and bitter was the disappointment. The impression made by the blow was never effaced and he always mourned the precariousness of the profession. 'I never feel safe' he would say in after life. So uncertain did he consider the profession that he would never advise anyone to enter it."

The first play at the Strand, on August 9, 1886, was to be *Davy Garrick* and this Charles Wyndham (later Sir Charles) tried to prevent by injunction. Wyndham had not yet appeared as David but had bought the rights of Sothern's version (by T. W. Robertson) and tried unsuccessfully to prevent Compton from staging the Muskerry one. Perhaps it would have been better for Compton's self-esteem had Wyndham succeeded for, as Paxton records: "We were not a success. Mr. Compton, who had always attracted crowds in the provinces to see his Davy, did not do so in London. The Press were very unkind to us and openly sneered at us as provincial." The tone changed, however, when *The Rivals* was staged on September 10. The Fourth Estate became more respectful—"principally no doubt," observes Paxton, "owing to Lewis Ball's superb Sir Anthony, Elinor Aickin's excellent Mrs. Malaprop and Sydney Valentine's Captain Absolute." After six weeks *The School for Scandal* was put on and was equally successful. *She Stoops to Conquer* followed—"Sneering at the provincial company ceased altogether; we were an unequivocal success". In this play Compton at first took his usual role of Young Marlow but when Sydney Valentine, as Tony Lumpkin, fell sick (he was to be seriously ill for two years) Compton found it easier to get a

Young Marlow than a Lumpkin and took over that role himself—and continued to play it always. Valentine was replaced by Young Stewart, who also replaced Dodsworth when he left to appear in H. A. Jones' *Hard Hit* at the Haymarket— "and became a real London actor." Finally there were two special performances of *Wild Oats* and *The Road to Ruin* (in which Compton "spoilt a really fine performance of Goldfinch by attempting to double Harry Dornton with it") and the London season closed on February 5, 1887, with cries of "Come Back Soon."

"On the Sunday we travelled to Oxford where, having been London actors for six months, we became provincial mummers once more and on tour again," recorded Paxton, who died on October 13, 1930, aged 70.

On this visit to the university city a comparative provincial guide to the quality of the efforts of the C.C.C. was provided by the Oxford Magazine critic who in two succeeding weeks wrote about the *Jim the Penman* Company, which was then about to make the last pre-fire performance at Northampton Opera House, and the Compton company. Whereas the Balsir Chatterton Company's approach to the former play led the writer to the most vituperative comments on performances that were "persistently ridiculous" and "completely farcical" he complimented the Compton company on "the truthful and conscientious spirit in which *She Stoops to Conquer* was given", adding that it "should wake us up to demand more of such treats."

One day soon after this Mrs. Compton went to the stage door of the Manchester theatre where the company were appearing, to collect her letters. Among them was one from her sister Isabel who was "resting" at the time. Mrs. Compton had an inspiration—why should not Edward form a separate company for Isabel to tour with? He readily agreed and parted with his own business manager, J. H. Savile, so that he could run the new company. The main play chosen for this venture was *Jane Shore* by W. G. Wills and with it the new company opened at Nottingham on August 15, 1887. Along with her husband Mrs. Compton travelled to the city for the occasion and it is typical of the sisters that they attended Communion together to dedicate the new venture. With them knelt Sidney Crowe, only child of their eldest sister Kate. Aged 16, Sidney had just left school and was to tour with her Aunt Isabel for three happy years— which she described as "the happiest time of my life." Isabel's plays usually called for a child or two and she acted as a mother to them, teaching them and looking after their welfare—as befitted the future Mother General of the convent which had been founded at Wantage by William John Butler, Vicar of Wantage, in 1848.

Wills had written this version of *Jane Shore* about 10 years earlier, for Miss Heath (Mrs. Wilson Barrett) who had since died. The original tragedy, by Nicholas Rowe, was first produced in 1713. The Nottingham cast included William Morrison (as the hunchback Duke), G. R. Peach, Edward Price and Ada Mellon. At the final curtain Compton, who had not, of course, been in the cast, took a bow and said: "I find myself in a very humiliating position. It is so seldom I appear before the public in propria persona that I must ask leave to introduce myself, for I feel like a parish beadle without his laced coat and cocked hat, a peacock minus its tail or a policeman in plain clothes. In short, I am utterly unrecognisable and you are entitled to an explanation. Edward Compton is my name. Wherever I may happen to be the Compton Comedy Company is my

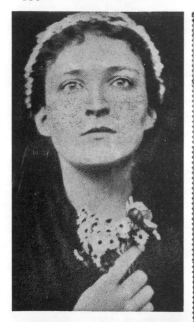

Monday, May 9th, 1892, at 7-45, for Six Nights only,

Engagement of the Distinguished Actress, Miss

ISABEL BATEMAN

SUPPORTED BY

Mr Edward Compton's Specially Organised Company.

Monday and Thursday, May 9th and 12th,

The Great Princess's Play, in Five Acts, by Special arrangement with
Mr. WILSON BARRETT—

JANE SHORE

Richard, Duke of Gloucester, afterwards Richard III.	..	Mr. HENRY VIBART
Prince Edward / The Duke of York } Sons of King Edward IV.	..	LITTLE CISSIE / LITTLE BERTIE
Henry Shore, a Goldsmith ..		Mr. G. R. PEACH
Lord Cootes / Catesby } Courtiers		Mr. HAWLEY FRANCKS / Mr. ROBERT GREVILLE
John Grist, a Baker		Mr. EDWARD PRICE
Walter Ludlow / Humphrey Dynecourt } Tradesmen		Mr. E. L. FORD / Mr. W. H. WILLIAMS
Hardingley, Head Servant at the Palace		Mr. H. LANGFORD
Old Peter, a Pensioner of Jane Shore		Mr. THOS. HARDY
First Ruffian / Second Ruffian } Creatures of the Duke of Gloucester		Mr. F. W. FREEMAN / Mr. A. S. HOMEWOOD
Elizabeth Woodville, Queen of England		Miss ADA MELLON
Lady Cootes / Lady Melles } Ladies of the Court		Miss ETHEL HOLMES / Miss Amy CROWE
Dame Ford, Housekeeper to Henry Shore		Mrs. F. R. VERE
Mrs. Grist, John Grist's Wife		Miss FRANCES RAYMOND
Dame Margery, a Pensioner of Jane Shore		Miss J. WATSON
AND		
Jane Shore		Miss ISABEL BATEMAN

Ladies, Lords, Soldiers, Citizens, &c.

Act 1—Scene - -	The Palace of Westminster
Act 2—Scene - -	The Home of Henry Shore
Act 3—Scene 1 -	The Old Cross, Whytefryars
Scene 2 Jane Shore's former Apartments in the Palace.	
Scene 3 - -	Westminster Abbey
Act 4—Scene -	Old Cheapside on a Winter's Night
Act 5—Scene -	The Home of Henry Shore

Acting Manager .. .. .. Mr. WILMOT HARRISON
Stage Manager .. .. Mr. HAWLEY FRANCKS
For Miss ISABEL BATEMAN

ISABEL BATEMAN, the leading actress who became Mother General of a community of nuns. The sister of Mrs. Edward Compton, she is pictured at eighteen, in 1873; and at seventy-five in 1930. The cast list is from her appearance at Northampton Opera House in 1892, six years before she became a postulant of the Community of St. Mary the Virgin, Wantage.

dwelling place." He did not miss the opportunity to mention that he would be back in a few weeks, at the head of his company. For the C.C.C. this was the last week of the summer break. They resumed the following Monday at Scarborough's Spa Theatre.

T. C. Valentine had evidently left the C.C.C. by this time for he appears in the company, and as stage manager, of Edward Terry at the opening of Terry's new theatre on the Strand site of the old Cole Hole, a new theatre being built "with special precautions against fire, all concrete and iron including the roof, no wood except for the doors and windows and all the wood before and behind the curtain coated with Sir Seymour Blane's fireproof paint." Valentine's fellow artists included Clara Cowper and William Calvert, both founder members of the C.C.C.

In 1888 the Comptons' usual Holy Week pattern was reversed: instead of father and mother travelling to London the family travelled to be with them at Blackpool. It now included Viola, born in 1886.

In May, 1888, the Northampton Mercury chronicled the experiences of the C.C.C. in two "small Scottish towns". At Dunfermline in the scene in *The Road to Ruin* in which the stage has to be darkened and suddenly re-lighted the "man of all work" put out the footlights altogether. Admonished by the prompter to light them again instead of using the long pole as intended he calmly strolled on to the stage in his shirtsleeves, struck a match and threw a new light on the subject in full view of the audience. At Ayr a family of temperate inclination found the drunkenness of Mr. Compton in his role as Garrick too good to be mere acting and walked out, declaring that this was carrying things too far!

At the end of the season the Mercury reported that after another "best on record" with their company Mr. and Mrs. Compton were "taking in a stock of health at Cromer to prepare for the nine month tour starting in August."

December found them back at Southport, which according to Compton Mackenzie was an unrivalled place to be at Christmas time, with its Lord Street festooned with strings of fairy lights, each with a nightlight inside it which had to be lit individually. This was, of course, long before days of such electric wonders as the Regent Street lights of London or the Blackpool Illuminations. The company were again in Southport the following Yuletide.

The Northampton programme of the C.C.C. in November, 1890, included *The Wonder! A Woman Keeps A Secret* by Mrs. Centlivre which may have had sentimental associations for Compton—it was in this play, in the role of Don Felix, that David Garrick took his farewell to the stage on June 10, 1776. The week had been heralded as Compton's own adieu—"In a very short time old English Comedy will know Mr. Compton's face no more. After Christmas he will tempt fortune with a London season of modern plays." In fact this visit was to be the first of half-a-dozen to Northampton during the ownership of Thomas Phipps Dorman, who had bought the theatre from J. C. Franklin (wielding the hammer at the sale was Isaac Tarry the theatre's auctioneer-manager) the previous year and begun his reign in February, 1889. Succeeding calls at Northampton during the rest of the century were in January, 1893; October, 1894; September, 1895; October, 1896; and November, 1900. The 1889 week introduced John Tobin's *The Honeymoon,* dating from 1805, the story of a duke who marries a virago and tames the shrew by pretending to be a peasant, taking her to his cottage and making her do all the lowly chores.

There appears to have been a survival of Puritanism in some aspects of Compton's habits. He would never travel first-class on the railway, never take a hansom cab if public transport was available. Indeed when he was in London for a season at the Opera Comique in September, 1891, he did not even travel second-class but endured the discomfort of the third-class compartments of the District Railway, more like a galleryite than the star of the show. After taking the train from West Kensington to the Temple he walked the rest of the way to the theatre.

This London season was to prove a turning point. Its main offering was a new play by Henry James, *The American*. The previous autumn James had visited the company on tour at Sheffield, sitting on the stage with his back to the auditorium and reading the new piece to the members, ranged in a semi-circle. Compton's verdict was that of a sub-editor—"Too long"—and he suggested that Mrs. Compton, who was good at that sort of thing, should have the job of pruning it. The result was that for two months telegrams passed between her and the author, each usually resulting in the surrender of a few lines. James attended the provincial premiere at Southport on January 3, 1891. The play was further improved in performances at the various towns then visited throughout the country but was a flop in the capital. Londoners who had read Clement Scott's denunciation of Ibsen thought James was trying to copy him. For his part, as Christopher Newman, the American, Compton had to wear a toupee—and toupees in those days were by no means the advanced examples we see widely advertised today but "a sadly obvious make-believe", to quote Compton Mackenzie. Nor was Compton himself any more convincing than his headpiece. There was praise, however, for the performances of Kate Bateman as the Marquise and Adrienne Dairolles as Noemie Nioche. Mrs. Compton was to have been in the cast but the birth of her second daughter Nell (Ellen) ruled her out: she had left the company at Holy Week, 1891, her place being taken by Sidney Crowe, her niece. Compton obstinately kept the play on for 60 nights, losing heavily, and followed it with *The Mayflower*, based on Longfellow's Miles Standish, which was even more of a failure and had to come off after a week.

Compton Mackenzie saw this as the point at which his father faced the fact that it was not his destiny to be a London actor-manager and that he must return to the provinces where he was so much respected and where, in a white wig instead of a toupee, he would make money and reputation instead of losing them and would be doing more for the cause of British drama than by competing in the capital. Mrs. Compton rejoined the company as it went back on to the road.

In 1893 another new play saw the stage debut of Viola Compton, at the age of six. During the Christmas break from St. Catherine's Holland Park, London, where she was being educated, she appeared as the little St. Evremond in Edgar Pemberton's *Sydney Carton,* a dramatisation of A Tale of Two Cities, at the Theatre Royal, Norwich, on January 2, 1893. Her brothers Monty and Frank were in the audience along with the author and they collapsed with merriment when they heard their sister declaim her single line, "Yes, I will mother" and had to be escorted out by Mr. Pemberton. Three weeks later the new play was given at Northampton Opera House with J. H. Savile as the swaggering Mr. Stryver. The bill that week included *The American* and a one act play *Oliver Goldsmith* which had been written for Compton and given at the tercentenary celebration of Goldsmith's old college, Trinity College, Dublin. Its author was a Mr. Moore, a journalist and Trinity man. The piece was set in Goldsmith's lodgings at Islington. Other plays by Edgar Pemberton in the C.C.C. repertoire at various times were *The Actor* and *Edmund Kean.*

Mrs. Compton, whose appearances that week included Violet Gresham in *Davy Garrick* and Lucie Manette in *Sydney Carton* was near the end of her acting career. According to Compton Mackenzie his mother was not at all keen on acting and it seems that she gave it up altogether after the birth of Fay on September 18, 1894. The decision as to whether a wife should accompany her actor-manager husband on tour is, of course, a difficult one, because actors are not monks. Compton Mackenzie refers to the tricky choice between staying with the children or remaining leading lady. With so many theatrical marriages coming to grief Mrs. Compton had initially stayed with the company so as not to submit her husband's great attraction for women to too strong a temptation; he did, apparently, have a roving eye. Among those who took Mrs. Compton's parts were her daughters Viola and Nell and her niece Sidney Crowe.

Sidney Crowe, who had joined the C.C.C. at the same time as Harrison Hunter, son of an Edinburgh doctor, subsequently married him. The union was not a success and Compton Mackenzie said that if ever he wrote a book on great liars, Hunter would be included. By Hunter Sidney Crowe had a daughter, who appeared on stage as Leah Bateman, notably with the Macdona Players in Shaw plays, and a son but both died in the mid-30s. While going through the then lengthy process of divorcing Harrison Hunter, Sidney Crowe met a handsome young actor named Herbert Skardon, the only son of a Dorset country doctor, who had been disowned by his family when he decided to go on the stage. Skardon, who had a flair for writing melodrama, took over several theatres in the north-east including Stockton, Darlington and Jarrow, where his wife presented him with a daughter Valerie. After the first World War they decided reluctantly to give up the theatre and he joined the firm of Nestles where he was a well-respected figure, although he loathed the commercial world which the needs of security had forced him to enter

When the C.C.C. visited Cheltenham Opera House in September, 1894, the Cheltenham Looker-On commented that "To Mr. Compton perhaps in an even greater degree than to Mr. Benson thanks are due for the opportunity to witness many of the old standard plays." The newspaper noted that it had been 10 years since the company's previous visit to Cheltenham, which had been to the Theatre Royal, Old Wells, closed in 1890, the year before the opening of the Opera House.

In her mid-way memoirs of 1926, under the title of Rosemary, Fay Compton described the rapture of welcoming father back to West Kensington: "Father's homecomings from his very long tours were times of great excitement, looked forward to for weeks ahead. On the day itself we could scarcely contain ourselves when commanded to stay quietly on the library landing; had we not been listening to the cab for hours before the train was even due? At last the slow trot of the horse was heard and the scrunching wheels of a vehicle bowed down with luggage. I can remember turning vaguely over in my mind why one of his hat boxes was such a funny shape and what he could have put in it to make it so;

this mystery has never been solved for me. Once the front door was shut we poured down the stairs and surrounded father with a welcoming mass of arms and legs, simultaneous conversations and offers of assistance. The dinners which celebrated these events were almost as grand as Christmas ones and included health drinking for Kay and myself in a liqueur glass of champagne and soda.''

Kay, incidentally, was one of the aliases of Ellen, who was christened Katherine Isabel Ellen. She was Nell on stage, Kay at home, but also Kaytrude to her sister Fay. Fay also mentions visits to the company on tour, along with Kay, and of their endeavouring to copy their father in his drunk scene in *Davy Garrick*. Fay's real name was that of her mother, Virginia; she was called Fay because her sister Ellen, as a little girl, could not pronounce the name of her baby sister and called her "Fay-ginger". While on the subject of names, it was in May, 1894, that Compton Mackenzie first became a Mackenzie. At Colet Court School he had been entered as Compton and he kept pressing his father to know why he did not call himself by his correct surname of Mackenzie, having realised from the time he was two that the family were flying false colours.

When Fay had been at school some time her mother had a serious illness and Fay was chosen to accompany her to Palermo for convalesence.

One of the most remarkable stories of the C.C.C. concerns not a member of the family but Marie Hassell, an Irish Catholic actress who was left with a three-year-old baby daughter when her husband Charles Boote was killed by a star trap when playing Harlequin. She asked Charles's brother to look after the little girl but he refused to take a Catholic child into his Nottingham home. In the train back to London, Marie met a nun who said she felt sure that the child would be taken care of by her convent. A couple of days later Marie had two offers in the post, one from a manager offering her a part if she could take her child with her and the other from the Mother Superior confirming the offer to take in little Rosie. Marie made her choice, took the child to the convent and lost the chance of the job. She got work later and saved enough to send her daughter to a Paris finishing school. At 19 Rosie was in the chorus at the Gaiety Theatre from which she was selected by George Edwardes to sing Maisie Is A Daisy, in which she made a great hit. She then figured in one of those celebrated Gaiety girl weddings into the nobility, marrying Lord Alfred Taylour and later becoming Marchioness of Headfort. All this intrigued Compton Mackenzie and he used the story line for his novel Rogues And Vagabonds.

In 1897 Edward Compton took the decision to close down his touring company. Approached by Milton Bode to become his partner in building a new theatre at Dalston, Hackney, London, and in other theatrical enterprises he decided after due contemplation that at the age of 43 he had done his fair share of touring.

What was intended to be the C.C.C.'s final tour began at the Grand Theatre, Boscombe, on August 30, 1897, running through to a "final" week at the Theatre Royal, Manchester, on June 4, 1898. Towns and cities in between, in order, were Great Yarmouth, Southend, Fulham, Scarborough, Portsmouth, Brighton, Croydon, Folkestone, Holloway, Kilburn, North London (Queen's Opera House), Richmond, Norwich, Brixton, Hastings, Dover, Salford, Grimsby, Wolverhampton, Paisley, Aberdeen, Dundee, Edinburgh, Glasgow, West Hartlepool, Huddersfield, Leeds, Southport, Oldham, Belfast, Dublin,

Birmingham, Sheffield, Bradford, and Newcastle.

In the town where the company had been launched in 1881 Compton must have glowed as he read the Southport Visitor's comparison of him with his idol of the 18th century, David Garrick, the actor who had stepped up almost immediately into the heights of London theatre and who mixed with the nobility of the day. The critic wrote: "The actor seems to be speaking for himself in Garrick's splendid defence of his profession . . . Davy Garrick in the flesh could not have sustained the painful role with more exemplary fidelity." This was not at the natal theatre but at the Winter Gardens Opera House which had been opened on September 7, 1891. Restricted space in the Pavilion Theatre had led to the erection of the new one on the site of a skating rink in Lord Street. It had a flamboyant facade, with arched windows, curved gables, with scroll work, pinnacles and Islamic cupolas. Seating 2,000 and with a 50 ft. deep stage it was to be reconstructed in 1906 as a variety theatre and twice renamed, first the Albert Hall and after that the Empire. In an address Compton said: "This is our 18th visit to Southport and allowing for four fortnightly Christmas engagements it is our 22nd week here, practically six months of old comedy in one place. This says much, very much, for you, and I hope a little for my brother and sister artistes and for me when I mention that the Compton Comedy Company originally started in Southport; that its birthplace was in fact the old Pavilion Theatre. You will readily understand with what affection I always regard your beautiful town and how pleasant it is for me to reflect on the many happy engagements here in the past 17 years."

And so the tour went on, each town and city being made to feel that it had lost one who was a townsman, if only an honorary one, qualified as such by annual or regular visits over such a long period. Everywhere audiences went into nostalgic raptures of regret that they were seeing Edward Compton and the Compton Comedy Company for the very last time. Theatrical farewells are notoriously lacking in finality but in this case there can be no doubt that Edward Compton genuinely believed that he was quitting the provincial paths, well trodden over a period of 17 years of almost continuous touring and would not pass that way again. Not trodden literally, of course, but covered by tens of thousands of miles of railway journeys. As Compton himself put it in those carefully prepared and rehearsed farewell speeches: "For 17 years and more I have been constantly travelling, constantly rehearsing, changing the bill every night, doing the stage some service I hope in the cause of old comedy and of legitimate plays generally but a Strolling Player always and everywhere, here today, gone next week, happy but homeless. And so I feel that the time has fairly come when I should seriously make for myself in the great city from which I come a 'local habitation' and even perhaps a home."

But apart from the local references and figures the speech was the same everywhere. Compton Mackenzie said that his father had a wonderful way of making any audience in Great Britain and Ireland feel that the particular town or city in which he was playing that week was the one place to which they had been wanting to return since last playing there. Each speech also included the stringing together of the various play titles in the company's repertoire. Predictably he borrowed his final lines from Davy Garrick: "Whatever may be the changes of my future life, the deepest impression of your kindness will always remain here—

here in my heart, fixed and unalterable."

At the Gaiety Theatre, Dublin, in May, 1898, Compton recalled that it was in 1876 that he first appeared in the city, with the late H. J. Byron. Afterwards he had paid visits in support of Miss Wallis playing such parts as Romeo, Orlando, Claude Melnotte, Wildrake and Benedick—"with all the fervour, the enthusiasm, and I fear, a good deal of the incompetency of youth." On one of these occasions he appeared for the first and only time with Dublin's grand old actor Granby, a former colleague of his late father. Then the usual statistics. He said that this was his 18th visit and 32nd week with the company in Dublin—practically eight months of old comedy in one place.   On the last night in the Irish capital Lewis Ball also came before the curtain showing a deep and probably unsimulated emotion. He said that as far back as the time of the late Henry Webb he had received offers to go to Dublin and had declined, though he wanted to go. The reason? Apparently Dublin was almost as severe a test of theatrical acceptability as Glasgow's proverbial graveyard of Thespian confidence: "In Dublin if they do not like an actor they never fail to make the fact apparent beyond doubt or question." On the other hand if an actor was in their favour no people in the world made their kindness so marked and unmistakable. He ended: "May God Bless the Irish people."

The next call was at Birmingham where, in his dressing room at the Prince of Wales Theatre, Compton talked to a reporter from the Birmingham Daily Gazette about the changes he had witnessed in the provincial theatre: "The stock company, Sir, is dead and I don't see how it is to be revived. The touring system has come; the public is satisfied and I can't see how any reversion to the old order is to be effected. In the old days the visiting company was an unknown quantity; indeed Buckstone was the first to take an entire London company into the provinces, touring the country with the old Haymarket. It has been stated that Craven Robertson was the leader in the movement, but it is a mistake. The honour is due to Buckstone and to no-one else. That tour was the beginning of a new system which, as time went on, ousted the stock companies and transformed the provincial theatre proprietor from the director of a company of artists into a man who let his theatre to travelling companies." He recalled his early days as a member of the stock company at the Birmingham theatre when it was run by Mercer Hampson. "We had to depend largely for public favour on staging the latest London successes. Of course we had visits from the stars of the day, who came down with one or two colleagues and were supported by the local company. Sothern came, and Charles Mathews, Miss Neilson, Miss Ada Cavendish and the other lights of the London stage. But do you think their successors would enter into such an arrangement? Would they sacrifice all the carefully worked-up business; the finesse of detail, carried into the smallest episodes; the general harmony that comes from the working together of a company under one overseeing eye? Would they give all this up for one or two rehearsals with a different stock company each week? I assure you they would never do so. Such a system might be good for the members of the stock companies, especially the younger and more impressionable but fancy the feelings of one of our modern stars who found the greater part of his carefully preconcerted business spoiled through the lack of knowledge of some of the stock company.

"You see the stock company took part in everything. They seconded the star in

Shakespeare and in Sheridan; they produced many of the classics and the London successes unaided. Within the limits of his physical capacity there was no part that an actor might not be called upon to undertake. This was excellent, if severe, training, you will admit."

Where then were young artists to receive their training? Frankly, said Compton, he did not know. "When Repertoire companies, which have done much in the training of the present generation, have had their day I cannot see where the budding artiste is to learn the rudiments of his art." All this of course was before the days of the Royal Academy of Dramatic Art which was not founded until 1904. Did he think a "conservatoire" would meet the case? Compton forecast correctly; "They will probably make an experiment in that direction in the Metropolis before long. Depend upon it that when the seriousness of the situation is thoroughly realised some earnest effort will be made to provide proper training for the growing generation of artistes. But I do hope that if a conservatoire is established its professors will teach those things which make for acting—deportment, dancing, fencing, reading—rather than try to give definite form to the artistic individuality itself. You want to avoid making an elocutionist of your actor. I can tell an elocutionist—or an elocutionist-trained actor for that matter—in a moment. Instead of obeying the dictates of his heart, he is forever thinking how he is to do what comes next. It is all mechanical, machine-made, unnatural and consequently ineffective. Granted the essential of a graceful natural carriage—one of the things that can generally be taught—acting is a matter for the voice and features. What I object to is the parrot-teaching of acting. At the very best a teacher can only impose his own view of a passion or a character on the student in this way. But intelligent reading—reading that shall convey the emotion of the text to the hearer—is a matter of personal interpretation and depends on the sensibility of the reader. You can't make a man interpret a shade of feeling who has not the wit to understand it or the depth of character to sympathise with it."

Finally he explained why he was giving up the company. After 17 years unremitting hard work on tour—"rehearsing every scene in every play myself, taking cognisance of every detail, artistic or commercial, in the whole enterprise —I think I am entitled to a little repose. After all those years I feel that a blending of work with the quiet of domestic life is my due. Not that I contemplate giving up the stage. Far from it. I am taking a suburban theatre in the North of London and there, with the usual run of touring companies, I shall hope to continue a limited repertoire of the plays that I especially care for. I also hope to take an occasional engagement in the West End of London."

After Birmingham came Sheffield, Bradford and Newcastle (where the Weekly Chronicle said that ill-health was the reason for Edward's retirement) and finally Manchester. Thus Manchester appeared to be the terminus for the Compton theatrical train which had travelled so far and for so long. The Friday night audience for *Henry Osmond* included the Lord Mayor and Lady Mayoress (Alderman and Mrs. Gibson), Sir Richard and Lady Mottram, Sir William and Lady Bailey and members of the Arts Club. Needless to say *Davy Garrick* had been chosen for the Saturday farewell and at the end of Act II Compton made a speech thanking one and all especially A. D. Corry, the manager, who had sent up a laurel wreath "To my friend Edward Compton. Not goodbye but au revoir.

From his admirer A. D. Corry." The band then played Auld Lang Syne.

A valedictory article in the Manchester Guardian said that the company had visited 134 towns, while in London it had appeared at the Opera Comique, Strand Theatre, Pavilion Theatre and theatres at Camberwell, Brixton, Crouch End, Elephant and Castle, Fulham and Kilburn. Among 40 plays it had presented were five by Shakespeare, three by Sheridan, two by Bulwer Lytton, and others by Goldsmith, Sheridan Knowles, Tobin, Colman, O'Keeffe and more modern dramatists. It recalled that Compton's mother had not only been the leading lady at the old Manchester Theatre Royal in Fountain Street and at the subsequent theatre in Peter Street but that it was there that she made her final appearance, as Mistress Ford in a performance of *The Merry Wives of Windsor* given by Charles Dickens and others in memory of Douglas Jerrold.

For one member of the C.C.C. it was truly farewell. The Irish actor Lewis Ball, the only original member remaining apart from Mr. and Mrs. Compton, now stepped down. He died on February 14, 1905, aged 80.

When he had been told in advance by Compton that the C.C.C. was to be wound up J. H. Savile, business manager since the foundation, decided to follow the example of his employer and himself go into theatre management. First he took the Paisley Theatre and then, in April, 1898, he announced that he was also to be lessee of the new 1,300-seater theatre then being built at Perth. The scenery was to be interchangeable between the two theatres.

Now our Compton scene changes to another new theatre, the one erected at Dalston by Bode and Compton. A previous house on the site, opened in 1886, had been called in turn the Dalston Circus, Dalston Colosseum and Dalston Theatre of Varieties. The new one seated 3,516 and was lit entirely by electricity, duplicated throughout by gas. The main innovation was that the theatre, said to be the first to be constructed on the "safety" lines advocated by Sir Henry Irving, had only two levels instead of the usual three or four. On the ground floor were orchestra stalls and pit and on the balcony the dress circle, upper circle and gallery. A steep rake in the pit ensured a good view while the galleryites benefited from not being in an eyrie-like position, being in fact behind the upper circle, a continuation of it.

Almost inevitably it was as *Davy Garrick* that Edward Compton appeared on the opening night, July 25, 1898. The evening began with Frank Clive singing the National Anthem accompanied by the orchestra, conducted for that night only by Walter Slaughter. The regular conductor, who had been displaced for the grand opening, was E. T. de Banzie. The acting manager was H. Emmerson. Then came a comedietta, *Hook And Eye,* by Eille Norwood who also appeared in it, along with Clifford Bown, Mona Harrison, and A. W. Munroe. Next Mrs. Edward Compton appeared to recite one of those rather stilted doggerel monologues including:

> All hail! good friends—a welcome of the greatest
> We hope you're satisfied with "London's latest"
> Our species is a fast increasing brood
> But still—there's room—"We hope we don't intrude"

She was presented with a bouquet and then the curtain went up on *Davy Gar-*

rick in which her husband was supported by Reginald Dartrey (Alderman Gresham), Eille Norwood (the Hon. Tommy Tallyhaut), Gertrude Scott (Violet) Clifford Bown (Rumbelow), Edward Fitzgerald (Lowesberry), A. Keith Williams (Simkins), Jessie Cross (Mrs. Rumbelow) and Bessie Thomson (Silvia). After the second act came a speech by Compton in which he urged that first night audience not to go to the extra expense and inconvenience of a journey to the West End when they wanted a night's amusement—"Just walk right in here and then go home early to bed, a richer and happier people." He himself did not need any introduction to an audience in London, he said, but his partner did, and he therefore called Milton Bode forward and did the honours.

What Compton asked the audience to do was precisely what did NOT happen. The theatre did not prosper even though trams passed regularly by the door (perhaps they took custom away rather than bringing it!) What an anxious and trying time it must have been for Compton after giving up the mobile security afforded by his popular touring company to find himself in immobile insecurity waiting in vain for customers to turn up at Dalston.

Compton Mackenzie always wondered what it was in his father that attracted Bode. Edward Compton had no taste whatsoever for gambling whereas Bode was a shrewd speculator. Perhaps Bode felt that the revered name of Compton would ensure respectability for his enterprises. It may have been for the same reason that Robert Arthur made Compton a director of the Court Theatre, Liverpool; the Princes Theatre, Manchester; and Her Majesty's Theatres at Aberdeen and Dundee. In the case of the link-up with Bode it was to be several years before the actor-manager was to reap a harvest of anything but anxiety. In the case of Arthur it cost Compton a lot of money to extricate himself from the financial problems Arthur brought upon himself by building the Princess Theatre, Kennington, opened in December, 1899. Eventually, in September, 1912, Bode and Compton took over this theatre. In 1899 Bode also secured a long lease, from April, 1900, of the Theatre Royal, Huddersfield, which was then being reseated, lit by electricity, and having some new dressing rooms built. It faced competition from a new theatre then being erected by the Northern Theatre Company.

The disastrous start at Dalston meant that Compton Mackenzie's chances of going to university rested solely on his ability to gain a scholarship. He recalls that gloom had descended upon 54 Avonmore Road because the new theatre lost money heavily in the first year and his father had also been hard hit by having to meet heavy bills which he had backed for his friends. Compton Mackenzie relates how Bode came round to reassure Mrs. Compton that a new policy of lower prices and providing the audiences with nothing but strong melodrama and musical comedy would soon turn the tables. Moreover they were going to send out Dan Leno in *Orlando Dando,* a musical comedy written specially for him which was to have its premiere at Dalston. Unhappily this was another gamble which did not pay off. Leno could not adapt his stage genius to the disciplines required by musical comedy and the piece was not a success.

The outcome of the Dalston failure was that Compton decided to reform his company and set out on the road once more. With many of the former members, he started up again at Eastbourne in mid July, 1899. It was very much a case of business as before, the old comedies with an occasional new piece such as *The*

Scarlet Coat, a romantic comedy which was premiered at Oxford in November, 1899, when the author Walter Grogan took his bow. The Oxford Magazine commented that when some unnecessary padding had been removed Mr. Compton should have no fault to find with the fit of his new investment. This was a three-day visit only the other pieces being the inevitable *Davy Garrick* and *The School for Scandal.*

As regards theatre management Bode and Compton did not allow themselves to be put off by the Dalston disaster. Gradually their empire began to extend and in 1903 it took in the Northampton Theatre Royal and Opera House, which they bought from Edmund Lockwood and James Dangerfield.

Frank Compton, who was to be the least well-known of the Compton family this side of the Atlantic, joined the company about 1903 playing Trip, the foppish footman in *The School for Scandal* a role which set a pattern—in later years he was to make a speciality of suave butlers. But meantime he decided to join the Army and by about 1908 was Second-Lieutenant Francis Sidney Mackenzie, of the Enniskillen Fusiliers. Then he changed his mind again and left the service to return to acting, but not to his father's company. He went to Australia where he married Peggy Dundas. Evidently of a roving nature he took her to America where in 1912 he made his U.S. debut in *The Whip* at the Manhattan Opera House.

In 1904 there was another family recruit to the company. Viola Compton made her adult debut on Boxing Day at Leamington Opera House as Selina Sowerberry in *Davy Garrick,* after which she appeared as second lead for nine months and then, at 18, became her father's leading lady for 15 months. Billed at first as Miss Mackenzie, she later reverted to the adopted name. Compton Mackenzie thought it idiotic of his mother to persuade his father to cast her as Lady Teazle, Lydia Languish, Kate Hardcastle and similar roles when still 18 and particularly ludicrous to give her love scenes with her father in some of the new plays, such as *Tomorrow.* In 1907 she appeared in this play during a C.C.C. London season at the St. James Theatre when it was renamed *The Eighteenth Century.* Under its original title, *Tomorrow,* which was by an anonymous author, was first produced at Paisley in 1904 but though having a useful idea—of a peer about to marry waking up to find himself translated back two centuries—it proved unsatisfactory and Compton Mackenzie rewrote it and presented it to his father as a birthday present. It opened at the St. James Theatre on July 29, 1907. *The School for Scandal* was also given with Lilian Braithwaite as Lady Teazle and Viola Compton as Lady Sneerwell. It appears that for this season Compton abandoned the idea that the players with whom he was successful in the provinces were suitable for immediate translation to the London stage. With a few exceptions his regulars of the C.C.C. were not in the St. James company which included Henry Ainley, Eric Lewis, Charles Groves, E. M. Robson, Grace Lane and Suzanne Sheldon. The season ended on October 23, 1907.

At the conclusion of the last performance Compton said in a speech: "I have played *The 18th Century* for seven weeks and *The School for Scandal* for five. I could have squeezed in one or two more revivals but I was very far from well when I opened in London and unfortunately I have gone from bad to worse in these 12 weeks so much so that the doctors have ordered me to take a week or two's rest before going on the road again." The first call "on the road" was at Hastings where Compton said that he would produce many more modern plays if he could get them—"I look through a great many manuscripts of new plays but very few come up to my ideal—I suppose I have become hard to please through having so much to do with the old comedies."

When Kaiser Wilhelm of Germany visited England in November that year and attended a gala performance in his honour at Drury Lane Edward Compton managed to smuggle Fay backstage.

As the company matured in years there were other special anniversaries to celebrate, as well as the annual birthdays on or near February 7. The company's silver jubilee was marked at Aberdeen in 1906 when Compton was to receive a gift of a portrait of himself in oils in the character of Davy Garrick. A guinea had been fixed as the maximum subscription and it was in fact a cheque which was handed over by J. H. Savile. Many past and present members of his company had contributed as well as leading figures of the profession including Sir Squire Bancroft, president of the Actors' Association, and Beerbohm Tree. Savile expressed the hope that Compton would be spared to celebrate the company's golden jubilee, a wish which was not to be granted for not only was it to be precluded by Compton's demise but that of the company too. From Compton came a typical speech of acknowledgment: "Twenty-five years devotion to legitimate and old English comedy must be allowed to count for something and when I think of the plays old and new that I have rehearsed and produced and re-rehearsed and produced during that quarter of a century I must confess that it does represent a huge amount of patience and perseverance, as well as a large measure of the inevitable worry, and wear and tear, and disappointment inseparable from such undertakings. For you must remember we are not like the London manager on tour who visits in two or three months the principal towns and cities, who travels en prince, and finds it 'roses, roses, all the way'. We are on tour, as a rule, from August Bank Holiday to Whitweek. We take all kinds of journeys; we sample all sorts of theatres from the best to the worst; we have to put up with inconvenience and discomfort as well as to enjoy good equipment and everything as it should be; and we have often had to play to audiences who could not understand or appreciate our plays at all at first but whom we have usually, if gradually, conquered in the end. Add to that that we are invariably rehearsing all the time, and that I, at any rate, have been doing all this for 25 years, and I think I have made out my case for work and worry and anxious times . . . but as a set-off against that I have the satisfaction of feeling that the stage is none the worse for my 25 years traffic in it, that I have given honest, healthy and beneficial employment to hundreds during that time, and that I have placed before my audience nothing but pure, wholesome and worthy entertainment." After paying tribute to his wife, " the only partner I have ever had in the Compton Comedy Company," he said that when the race was run for him and his wife, he was sure the picture would be the cherished possession of their children and their children's children. Whether this wish was fulfilled I do not know, having found no further mention of the picture. Arrangements for the presentation were made by a committee of which the secretary-treasurer was H. G. Fitzgibbon, who was the company's business manager at the time. Later that year a new theatre was opened at Aberdeen, His Majesty's.

On a February Monday that year Bode and Compton took over two theatres at Leicester—the Theatre Royal and the Opera House, both of which had been run by Col. Winstanley. The Theatre Royal had been opened in 1836 and the Opera House in 1877. Edward Compton had appeared at least once at the Theatre Royal in the pre-C.C.C. days; this was in March, 1879, when Elliott Galer was the lessee and he was seen as Orlando in *As You Like It*. The company's earliest appearance at Leicester was in May, 1881. We have Compton Mackenzie's word for it that the Leicester Opera House was one of the finest theatres in the provinces. He had particular cause to take note of it for it was there that the first reading took place of his play *The Gentleman in Grey*. It happened in what was then the Green Room but which later became the manager's office. This was in 1907 and Compton Mackenzie notes that his father's digs were at 169a London Road. He anticipated that his father would object to the play because the first scene was set in a maze at Curtain Wells and would involve carrying scenery, to which his father had a strong objection.

Henry Crocker, who was stage manager with the company at this time and who was to marry Nell Compton, went off briefly to stage manage with a company got together by an Australian actor, Cyril Keightley, and consisting of old Bensonians and members of the C.C.C. There he was able to give a friendly welcome to a newcomer to the profession, Basil Dean. As he recalls in his autobiography, Seven Ages, An Autobiography, 1888-1927, Dean got a guinea a week for eight performances. Any time that he was late by more than ten minutes for rehearsal he was fined half-a-crown. Crocker invited him to share rooms with him and his assistant. Dean's first appearance on any stage was at the Opera House, Cheltenham, on September 3, 1906, in what he described as "an extremely silly costume drama entitled *Miles Carew, Highwayman*". He recalls that the Bensonians suffered his presence as the youngest member "with their tradition of good fellowship" while the Compton ladies "gave me fleeting smiles of encouragement." But goodwill did not prevent a traditional practical joke. When Dean volunteered to help with the stage management he was sent from one to another hunting for the key to the Act Drop, an entirely imaginary object.

In 1907, the C.C.C. played for the first time at the new Kings Theatre, Glasgow, and Compton Mackenzie says that his father found it difficult to desert the old Royalty, adding: "I do not believe he ever brought himself to desert the old Royalty Theatre at Edinburgh for the new Kings Theatre opened that year."

As he came down from Oxford, Compton Mackenzie was offered stage work by Arthur Bourchier who was astonished to hear that he preferred to seek his living with the pen. He told the budding author that on the stage he could earn £2,000 a year, a figure he surely could not match by writing. It was equally incomprehensible to Edward Compton. Indeed he could not understand how he had sired the young upstart. He could not credit that a son of Edward Compton and grandson of Henry Compton would not want to follow in the family footsteps. Compton Mackenzie, whose re-adoption of the old family name may have been symbolic of his dislike of the stage as a way of earning a living, did in fact act at various times. He appeared with the C.C.C. on a number of occasions and played Sir Toby Belch with the Oxford Union Dramatic Society. He was a fast learner and when he wrote *The Gentleman in Grey* for the company and Edward lost his voice during rehearsals he stepped into the gap left in the cast of other plays, sitting up all night to master the scripts. But overfamiliarity had bred contempt: whereas most people at that time regarded the acting profession as being the height of glamour and variety in life he saw it only as repetitive boredom. After the first night of his own play at Edinburgh in February, 1907, he pondered on whether he was not too good an actor to be a good playwright. He said that right from the age of two he had not had the slightest desire to go on to the stage. Perhaps it was the result of being carted round the country as a baby. Anyway father looked upon son as a "mysterious creature of inexplicable origin" and they never understood one another. The son saw the situation as one of the heir apparent running away from the old fashioned family business. His view of Fay's work on the stage, expressed in his preface to her autobiography, was that it was "essentially a job"; while her work on the film screen was "a detestable labour".

Though Compton Mackenzie did not fancy the stage he did at one time have a hankering for what has sometimes been regarded as its sister profession—the Church. When in 1907 he told his mother that he was considering being ordained, she "of course" was very pleased at the prospect. But one October evening that year the die was cast in another direction—he wrote the first lines of his novel The Passionate Elopement. By the summer of 1910 he had spent two years sending the completed manuscript to various publishers and receiving it back accompanied by regret slips. With characteristic cocksureness he resolved not to begin another novel until the first was on his bookshelf, printed and bound. Meantime he did find it necessary to earn a living and took an acting job with the London presentation of Hall Caine's play The Bishop's Son at the Garrick Theatre, sharing a dressing room with Shiel Barry Junior. He confessed to relief when it flopped after only a week. It was Barry who introduced him to Harry Gabriel Pelissier from whom he received a commission to write material for a revue to be produced at the Alhambra. At about this time the publisher Martin Secker accepted that first novel. It came out in 1911 and was still in print over 50 years later.

In the preface to the 1949 edition of his novel, Sinister Street, Compton Mackenzie recalled that it was begun in July, 1912, but that the writing of it was interrupted by the dramatisation of his novel Carnival and "then more seriously by my going to America in September to take part in the production of the play". In 1920 the play was to pop up again under the new name of Columbine. The author's last play was to be The Lost Cause, in 1931.

Another member of the family who had quit acting was Isabel Bateman. Her last appearance had been in Pinero's Trelawney of the Wells in 1898, after which she had, to use Shakespeare's phrase, got herself to a nunnery. A few years later came a final public message from Isabel Bateman, now Sister Isabel Mary, a member of the community of Wantage Convent. In an appeal for the Diocesan Home of St. James, Fulham, she recalled her life before taking the veil: "Dear Worldlings all, I want £5,000. Will you give it to me? Listen. Tonight I saw a little row of lights flickering at intervals on the wall of my convent cell, only the street lamp shining across the room and I, a nun, looking absently at them thought: they are just like a row of footlights. Footlights. What a world of memories came dancing into my mind in the wake of that one word. Twenty eight years, 18 in London and ten on tour, spent in happy blameless camaraderie behind the footlights makes me quite sure of the true ring of hearts that beat there. Have I not wrung tears from you, night after night, year after year, for Charles I on his way to execution, parting from his wife; for Ophelia's broken heart; or Nelly Temple's lost child, or any of my mimic woes and can I believe you will harden your hearts when I speak of the great world sorrow I am asking aid for tonight. Give me but one shilling for all the tears we have shed together for Hecuba and I should have the £5,000 and what's Hecuba to this? . . . God keep you, Worldlings all. Goodnight." Who could resist? In 1912 she became Assistant Superior and from 1920 to 1931 was Mother General.

Back to the materialistic world outside. When Edward Compton finally bought a car in 1909, at the age of 55, it was a Mercedes costing £2,000. At that particular moment the success of *The Arcadians* had brought prosperity to him and to the other two partners in the enterprise, Milton Bode and Robert Courtneidge. But in 1911, according to Compton Mackenzie, the five £1,000 policies which he had taken out for his children were all pledged as security against bank loans to purchase theatres. He also noted that his mother's marriage settlement was becoming exhausted and that she was beginning to put a brake on her generosity "owing to the theatre buying in which my father was engaged."

When Edward Compton, actor-manager, visited the Northampton Opera House in January, 1909, it seemed to be on the cards that there would be a demonstration against Edward Compton, joint owner of the theatre. The reason was that the poorly paid musicians of the pit were on strike for more money. But the rumour that there was to be a protest was not borne out in fact. I draw the conclusion that while Compton was no spendthrift where actors' salaries were concerned it was Bode who was the real skinflint—he refused to undertake any of what we would now term "meaningful negotiations" with the strikers. The dispute went on until the following August by which time most of the players had found employment elsewhere and in fact only one was re-employed as part of the settlement. Many of the bandsmen went to the Castle Rink, St. James, this being during the time of the craze for roller skating.

At 18 Nell Compton made her stage debut on Monday, December 27, 1909, at Northampton. By a coincidence that visit by the Compton Comedy Company is the only week of which an Opera House poster survives at Northampton Public Library. She was seen in the curtain-raiser *Tom Noddy's Secret* which preceded *Davy Garrick*. The Northampton Independent explained that her appearance on the stage was entirely her own choice, following her older sister Viola who had appeared at Northampton and was then at the Coronet Theatre, London. "Edward Compton has two sons and three daughters. He intended only the sons to take to the stage profession but as so often happens they show no inclination for it while all the daughters showed exceptional histrionic ability." Nell had studied under Madamoiselle Favotte Faylis at the Theatre Francaise. "Off stage she is of a shy retiring disposition with a penchant for the violin but when acting-evinces such self-possession, flexibility of movement and absence of nervousness as to render unnecessary any allowance for lack of experience. As Sophia Free-love she threw into the character a perfect delineation of the artless girl with a most lovable disposition and one could scarcely realise it was a novice playing the part." As Maria in *The School for Scandal* she acted "with a dignified restraint befitting the young lady who detests the scandal mongers."

OPERA HOUSE
NORTHAMPTON.

Sole Proprietors and Managers........MILTON BODE & EDWARD COMPTON.   Resident Manager........W. E. BARNETT.
Telephone No. 67.

FREE LIST ENTIRELY SUSPENDED.

Early Doors 7.0 | **Monday, December 27th, 1909,** | Commence 7.45

FOR SIX NIGHTS AND

SPECIAL MONDAY MATINEE 'DAVY GARRICK' at **2.30**

Early Doors at 2.0.   The Gallery will be opened for the Matinee at usual Prices.

MR.

EDWARD COMPTON

And the CELEBRATED COMPTON COMEDY COMPANY.

MONDAY & SATURDAY
December 27th 1909,
and January 1st 1910
at 7.45., and
SPECIAL MONDAY MATINEE
Doors open at 2; Commence 2.30.
The Universal Favourite.

The Brilliantly Successful Comedy, in Three Acts, by WILLIAM MUSKERRY—

DAVY GARRICK

David Garrick, of Drury Lane Theatre (1584-5-6th Performances) ... Mr. EDWARD COMPTON
Alderman Gresham, of the East India Co. ... Mr. H. CROCKER
The Hon. Tom Tallyhard, of the Clubs ... Mr. FRANK ROYDE
Rumblelow Wholesale, Retail, Mr. PHILIP GORDON
Sowerberry and for Mr. J. W. AUSTIN
Simkins Exportation Mr. C. MARQUAND
John, Gresham's Servant ... Mr. LAURENCE MEADE
Davis, Garrick's Servant ... Mr. FRANK SNELL
Mrs. Rumblelow, Rumblelow's Better half Miss MARIE HASSELL
Selina Sowerberry's Maiden Sister ... Miss LORRAINE STEVENS
Violet, Gresham's Daughter ... Miss KATHLEEN LEIGH
"The Performance throughout is well, consistently, and cleverly executed."—*Morning Post.*
Acts 1 and 2, Alderman Gresham's House. Act 3, Garrick's Study.

Preceded by a Comedietta, in One Act, by T. HAYNES BAYLY, entitled—

TOM NODDY'S SECRET.

TUESDAY,
and **THURSDAY,**
December 28th & 30th,
at 7.45.
Special Revival of Mr.
Compton's Great Success.

THE FINE OLD COMEDY, IN FOUR ACTS, BY THOMAS HOLCROFT.

THE ROAD TO RUIN

Charles Goldfinch, a Sporting Character, "Thats your sort" (571st-2nd Performances) Mr. EDWARD COMPTON
Mr. Dornton, Head of the Great Banking House of Dornton & Co. Mr. HENRY CROCKER
Harry Dornton, his Spendthrift and Prodigal Son Mr. FRANK ROYDE
Jack Milford, Harry's Friend Mr. CLIFFORD MARQUAND
Mr. Sulky, Partner in the House of Dornton & Co. Mr. J. W. AUSTIN
Mr. Smith, Chief Cashier ... Mr. LAURENCE MEADE
Mr. Silky, a Jew Money Lender ... Mr. PHILIP GORDON
Jacob, his Clerk ... Mr. FRANK SNELL
A Hosier ... Mr. H. WETTON
Sheriff's Officer ... Mr. H. WETTON
The Widow Warren ... Miss MARIE HASSELL
Jenny, her Maid ... Miss LORRAINE STEVENS
Sophia Freelove, her Daughter, by her First Husband Miss NELL COMPTON
"As a genuine Comedian, Mr. Compton has few equals and no superiors on the English Stage."—*Referee.*

Preceded by the Charming Comedietta, in One Act, by ELLIE NORWOOD—

HOOK AND EYE.

WEDNESDAY,
December 30th, at 7.45.
BY SPECIAL REQUEST.

Only Performance of SHERIDAN'S Immortal Comedy, in Five Acts—

THE SCHOOL FOR SCANDAL

Charles Surface, Younger Nephew of Sir Oliver (with son, "Here's to the Maiden") (1570th Performance) Mr. EDWARD COMPTON
Sir Peter Teazle ... Mr. HENRY CROCKER
Sir Oliver Surface ... Mr. PHILIP GORDON
Joseph Surface, his Elder Nephew ... Mr. FRANK ROYDE
Crabtree ... Mr. J. W. AUSTIN
Sir Benjamin Backbite ... Mr. CLIFFORD MARQUAND
Careless ... Mr. LAURENCE MEADE
Rowley ... Mr. FRANK SNELL
Toby Friends to Mr. BISHOP
Sir Harry Bumper Charles Mr. WETTON
Moses, a Money Lender ... Mr. J. W. AUSTIN
Trip, Servant to Charles ... Mr. EDWARD BOILE
Snake ... Mr. MEYNALL
Servant to Lady Sneerwell ... Mr. WINTON
Servant to Joseph ... Mr. RICHARD FASS
Lady Sneerwell ... Miss LORRAINE STEVENS
Maria, Peter's Ward ... Miss NELL COMPTON
Mrs. Candour ... Miss MARIE HASSELL
Maid to Lady Teazle ... Miss AGNES WILLIAMS
Lady Teazle ... Miss KATHLEEN LEIGH
A Minuet will be danced by the Characters at the end of Act One.
"The fine old play went with such roars of laughter that it seemed as if half the spectators had become acquainted with Sheridan for the first time."—*Daily Telegraph.*

FRIDAY,
December 31st, at 7.45.
BENEFIT OF MR. EDWARD COMPTON.
Mr. Compton's Brilliant Success.

The New and Highly Successful Comedy, in Three Acts, by PELHAM and WALTER E. GROGAN, entitled—

A REFORMED RAKE

Harry Jasper, B.A.' a Reformed Rake (157th Performance) Mr. EDWARD COMPTON
Mr. Thornton, a City Merchant Mr. HENRY CROCKER
Adolphus Thornton, a Green Young Enthusiast Mr. CLIFFORD MARQUAND
Frederick Adderley, an Unreformed Rake Mr. FRANK ROYDE
Andrew Wylie, a Money Lender ... Mr. PHILIP GORDON
Matthew, a Butler ... Mr. J. W. AUSTIN
Binks Servants Mr. FRANK SNELL
Markham Mr. EDWARD HOILE
Mrs. Thornton, Mr. Thornton's Second Wife Miss NELL COMPTON
Joyce Thornton, his Daughter by his First Wife Miss KATHLEEN LEIGH
Miss Arabella Mountstuart ... Miss LORRAINE STEVENS
"In the part of Harry Jasper, Mr. Compton touches the height which he has attained in Davy Garrick."—*Independent.*

Business Manager and Treasurer ... Mr. HENRY CROCKER | Advance Manager ... Mr. CHARLES GRATTAN
Stage Manager ... Mr. A. E. SALTER

MONDAY, JANUARY 3rd, 1910, FOR SIX NIGHTS ONLY.

THE ENTIRELY NEW AND ORIGINAL DRAMA

THE IDOL OF PARIS

W. Mark, Printer, The Drapery, Northampton.

By a remarkable coincidence the only Opera House poster surviving at the Public Library in Abington Street, Northampton, is one of the Compton Comedy Company—and of the week in 1909 during which Nell Compton made her stage debut—in *The Road to Ruin,* by Thomas Holcroft. *(Northamptonshire Public Libraries).*

In June, 1910, eight months after appearing at the Coronet Theatre, London, as Nell Gwynne in *An Impudent Comedian* Viola Compton turned up at Northampton, not with the C.C.C., but in a playlet heading a twice-nightly variety bill. Called an "episode" the piece was *The Multitude of Two* by Walter MacNamara. Also in the bill were Alfredo Marchall who "catches a cannon on his neck", a conjuror, a male soprano, a comedian, a juggler and "The Pictures."

The Compton Company's 30th birthday on February 7, 1911, found them at Aberdeen, as the 25th had done. In a speech Compton declared that the event was not only a record but a world record—"No other company in any part of the globe has toured the same country, with the same plays, and if I may say so the same star or principal boy for a similar number of years and though it is unseemly to be puffed up I hope you will not blame me if I freely confess that I do feel an honest pride in that achievement. I am not going to dilate on my early struggles, on the difficulties I encountered and overcame, on the anxieties I have undergone, or on the years of hard labour to which I sentenced myself and which sentence I think I may venture to say I have honourably and successfully worked out. Tonight I would rather pay tribute to the great plays I have been privileged to produce, to the loyal and talented companies I have always been associated with, to the steadfast support of the entire press, and above all to the kindness and sympathy and constancy of the great British public. To all I offer up the warm acknowledgment of a grateful heart, and encouraged and gratified by your enthusiasm tonight I shall commence my thirty-first year tomorrow with pride and delight and go on my way rejoicing". That night *Davy Garrick* had been preceded by *Tom Noddy's Secret* with Nell Compton. The following night, which saw in the Compton new year, it was *Tomorrow*. In the company that week was Henry Crocker upon whom had devolved the old man parts played in the early days by Lewis Ball, such as Sir Peter Teazle, old Hardcastle and Sir Anthony Absolute. Also among the players were J. W. Austin, Charles Stone, Marie Hassell, Clifford Marquand and Agnes Williams.

The completion of 30 years by the company was also marked by a dinner given by professional colleagues at the Princes Restaurant, Piccadilly, with the novelist A. E. W. Mason in the chair. Mason, who had been a member of both the C.C.C. and the Isabel Bateman companies, said that they were celebrating an achievement without parallel in the history of the modern stage. Not only had actors been given an opportunity of varied experience, while taking their first tottering steps, but they had long engagements and "certainty of salary." Compton had, he said, played 52 parts with the company. When he began, theatrical taste in the provinces was not very high; he had raised it and kindled enthusiasm for old comedy—"Not only did he revive old plays, but also old playgoers." Replying, Compton favourably contrasted the comedies of the 18th century with the modern drama—"My experience shows that the former is still able to attract a more representative audience than the latter. Why? The object of a comedy is to give you a large slice of life in tabloid form, crisply humorous, but the apparent object of modern comedy is to combine a pulpit service with a circulating library."

The hand of Compton rarely appears as regards the management control of the theatres he owned or leased jointly with Bode, to whom he seems to have left all the administration. But he did take part in the battle to survive at Northampton where a menacing cloud appeared on the Opera House horizon in June, 1910, when the Highway Committee passed plans for a rival and much larger theatre to be built in Abington Street. This New Theatre, as it was to be called, was referred to in the Press as "the new variety palace" but the ambitions of its sponsors went beyond variety. They wanted a stage play licence which would not only enable them to stage legitimate drama but also to sell intoxicants. Alarmed at the possibility Bode and Compton announced that they would build a further theatre in St. Giles Street, to be used for variety while the Opera House carried on with plays. When the New Theatre's application for a stage play licence was heard by a meeting of the full Town Council in December, 1912, just after the new house had opened, Compton himself attended to put the case for the Guild hall Road theatre and to promise that if the New Theatre did not seek to present plays the Opera House would drop the summer variety seasons which it was then operating. By the casting vote of the Mayor (Alderman Harvey Reeves) the application was refused.

The following year a letter appeared in the Era suggesting that theatre was old hat. E. Rye of Lewisham, wrote: "The theatre is getting out of date. It suited our fathers and mothers. They didn't mind waiting for the long intervals between the acts. They were used to taking life slowly and easily. We get impatient of anything slow. I suggest theatres should be run more on the lines of picture palaces. Do away with waiting outside. Let all seats be booked. Reduce prices and do away with long waits between the acts."

At Crewe on Monday, September 4, 1911, at the start of his new season and with a play entirely new to his repertoire, Compton launched his second new theatre (the first being Northampton in 1884). The original theatre on the Heath Street site had been in an adapted Roman Catholic church which was reconstructed as the Lyceum in 1887 at a cost of £7,000, to the design of Alfred Darbyshire, a leading protagonist for safer theatres. The safety-mindedness of its architect did not prevent the house being burned down in March, 1910, leaving a company stranded and minus most of its gear. The replacement theatre opened by Compton was designed by Albert Winstanley, of Manchester, and was leased by H. G. Dudley Bennett, who was also the proprietor of the

Twenty-seven years after "christening" the Northampton Opera House the Compton Comedy Company inaugurated its second new theatre—at Crewe, in September, 1911.

PUBLIC NOTICES.

THE NEW THEATRE, CREWE.

GRAND OPENING WEEK,

MONDAY. SEPTEMBER 4th, 1911, for Six Nights, and

MATINEE. WEDNESDAY, at 2.30.

The Eminent Comedian,

MR. EDWARD COMPTON,

And a carefully-chosen Company including
MISS MARY FORBES,

MISS EMMELIE POLINI,   MR. VICTOR R. G. MOORS,
MR. LAWRENCE ROBBINS,   MR. NORMAN CLIFTON,

In the Famous Play in Three Acts, written by Palgrave
Simpson and Herman Merivale,

"ALL FOR HER"

Shakespeare Theatre, Clapham; the Opera House, Coventry; and the Opera House, Burton-on-Trent, among other enterprises. In a curtain speech Compton recalled that he was for many years a friend of the late Mr. Taylor at the old theatre. First produced at the Mirror Theatre in 1875 and based on Dickens' A Tale of Two Cities, the play was *All for Her,* by Palgrave Simpson and Herman Merivale. The company was not billed as the Compton Comedy Company but as "the eminent comedian Mr. Edward Compton and a carefully chosen company". Compton's speech was typically punny, likening the lessee to the "captain of the good ship New Theatre starting on a series of weekly voyages with a differently attractive port in each view each trip, weighing anchor from your good town he is bound to sail away with a good Crew(e)" . . . . He enjoined them to" fill up his boat week after week, crowd his cabin and swarm his decks and so enable him, at the end of each year, to sail smoothly into the harbour of success."

Towns visited immediately afterwards were Eastbourne, Hanley, Leamington, Stratford, Nottingham, Hastings, Windsor, Reading, Doncaster, Wakefield and several Scottish towns. The company included Mary Forbes, Emelie Polini, Victor R. C. Moors, Norman Clifton, Laurence Robins, Leslie Kyle, Edmund Sulley, Helme Grasswell, Austin Dene and Charles Grattan (business manager).

Surprising as it may seem Nell Compton managed to keep quiet her marriage to the actor John Austin, son of an Edinburgh bank manager, even from her sister Viola, so that when Viola was herself married six months later at St. Cuthbert's, London, in June, 1911, Nell was a bridesmaid but should have been a matron-of-honour! Viola was piqued when she heard the truth soon afterwards. She had been determined to marry her father's stage manager Henry Crocker from the time when Compton Mackenzie's play was first produced in 1907. Crocker had been equally determined to remain a bachelor. In the outcome Viola's marriage survived while Nell's ended in divorce and she subsequently married Ernest H. G. Cox. Viola, whose marriage Compton Mackenzie described as being "as happy as could be wished for", had two sons, Nicholas and John. Fay now followed her sisters on to the stage and this led to her following them also into matrimony. Her first appearance had been at the Royal Albert Hall, London, on January 10, 1906, in a Christmas fantasy called *Sir Philomir* or *Love's Victory.* In July, 1911, her brother Compton Mackenzie secured for her a voice test with Harry Gabriel Pelissier, inventor of the Follies, for whom "Monty" was working at the time. Fay became a Follies girl at £3 10s. a week and almost immediately Pelissier, who was 38, fell in love with the 16-year-old. Compton Mackenzie regretted making the introduction, especially as Pelissier was drinking a bottle of brandy a day at the time, and he tried to persuade Mrs. Compton to veto the match. She, however, considered that a girl could not get married too early and the wedding took place on Fay's 17th birthday, September 18, 1911. A son Anthony was born but just over two years after the marriage Fay became a widow. Pelissier died on September 26, 1913, at his father-in-law's house in Nevern Square, leaving Fay some £13,000. At the funeral at Golders Green Crematorium there was a huge wreath of white roses from the young widow and a little bunch of violets, lilies of the valley and maidenhair fern with the inscription "Baby's Bunch." The ashes were buried in the grave of Pelissier's mother at Marylebone Cemetery.

Until May that year Fay had remained with the Follies. In the November, a few weeks after the death of her husband, Louis Meyer offered her the part of Anise in *Who's The Lady* at the Garrick Theatre, London. He asked whether she spoke German and was told she did, though she did not in fact know a word. When she was handed the part she found it was all in German but by next morning she had mastered it.

During this run Robert Courtneidge offered Fay her first musical comedy role in *The Pearl Girl* which had by then clocked up 200 performances at his Shaftesbury Theatre. Thus, in March, 1914, Fay began a lifelong friendship with Robert's daughter, Cicely Courtneidge, and in the company she also met Lauri de Frece, to whom she speedily became engaged. They were married quietly the following October. Born in 1881 de Frece was the son of a musichall proprietor, Henry de Frece (1835-1931). His brother was Sir Walter de Frece, musichall proprietor and one-time Member of Parliament (1871-1935). The pair appeared together again, along with Dorothy Ward, Harry Welchman, Cicely Courtneidge and Jack Hulbert in *The Cinema Star* which Hulbert had written from the German musical play *Kino Konigen*. As Robert Courtneidge recalled in his memoirs the play promised to be his most successful but when war broke out the German origin proved to be fatal and he was reduced to selling the lease of his house, his car, his furniture and, "hardest blow of all", his books.

After the piece had proved to be too Teutonic Fay went to America to appear in a Gaiety Company production of *Tonight's The Night,* her husband accompanying her. Her two sisters were already in the United States—things had been moving for all three, and in each case away from the family company. Fay, who was now emerging as the star of the trio, recalled in her 1926 memoirs, Rosemary, that at the Hotel Astor Viola came down to meet her on arrival and that the next day Kay (i.e. Nell) showed her the sights of the city. With Viola was her "twin"—her son Nicholas really, but in those days so like her as to earn this designation. Nell who had, according to the Era, of July 1914 "made such a pronounced success on tour in India and the Far East," had been engaged by William A. Brady for his production of *The Elder Son* in New York, sailing on August 8, just four days after the outbreak of the Great War. Viola was appearing at the Boston Opera House in January, 1915, in a stock season at the Castle Square Theatre, Boston, the following December; and at the Selwyn Theatre, Boston, in October, 1918, in *Information Please.*

Meantime, what of the sons? Compton Mackenzie had joined up and was serving on the staff of General Sir Ian Hamilton in the Dardanelles. As soon as war was declared Frank, who was in America, sent his name and address to the War Office in London, offering his services and subsequently received instructions to report for duty. As the Era said on March 10, 1915: "He is therefore hastening home to proceed, he hopes, to the front, to his own delight and the expressed satisfaction of his parents." Frank and his wife had a daughter Jean, whom we shall encounter later in the story but the marriage broke up and he later re-married and had a second family.

How, meantime, was the Compton Comedy Company faring? Before answering that question the death of a "member of the family" must be noted. It was as such that Mr. and Mrs. Compton regarded long-term members of their company and this certainly applied to Elinor Aickin who had spent the decade from 1884-94 with them, one fifth of the acting life of half a century which she completed before retiring in 1912. After leaving the Comptons she had toured with Frank Benson. At the funeral in May, 1914, Mrs. Benson and Mrs. Compton stood side by side at the graveside at West Mitcham, along with another C.C.C. stalwart, Nellie Harper. Compton himself could not be present but sent his regrets.

For the first time in 30 years Edward Compton went on tour without the Compton Comedy Company in the autumn of 1913. It was with "Milton Bode's and Edward Compton's Company" that he appeared as Nobody in *Everywoman,* "the latest Drury Lane triumph and modern morality play, of Everywoman and Her Pilgrimage in Quest of Love", by Walter Brown, revised by Steven Phillips. The title role went to May Congdon. The entire Drury Lane production and effects were said to have been transferred to the company which visited Dalston, Leicester, Liverpool and Glasgow during the tour.

During the following spring there was a C.C.C. tour with Henry Oscar in the ranks, starting in February at Kennington where Compton played *Richelieu* for the first time. Then, on the very day that the Great War broke out, Monday, August 4, 1914, Compton began what was to be his last tour with his company. This was the non-stop itinerary, with only one week "out", caused by the closure of a theatre: Bristol, Leeds, Bradford, Sheffield, Manchester, Huddersfield, Chester, Scarborough, Leicester, Burton, Northampton, Blackpool, Bedford (three days), Norwich, Grimsby, Darlington, Aberdeen, Glasgow, Edinburgh, Perth (two weeks), Kilmarnock, Greenock, Paisley, Ayr (three nights), Dumfries (three nights), Carlisle, Middlesborough, Sunderland, West Hartlepool, Liverpool, Newcastle, Halifax, Bury (three nights) and Rochdale (three nights).

Initially the outbreak of war had the effect of decreasing attendances. There was a "small audience because of the declaration of war" for *Money* at the Princes Theatre, Bristol, and later that August Compton made a farewell speech at Leeds thanking those who had "come to lend us a helping hand—believe me, I shall look forward with the greatest pleasure to meeting you again in the prosperous days of a glorious peace."

This final tour with Compton at the head of his 33-year-old company was typical in many respects. There were tatty theatres in less noted centres as well as splendid theatres in great cities. The plays remained basically the same. The Era commented that during the tour Compton would clock up 2,000 performances as Davy Garrick (actually it was rather fewer) and 1,200 as Charles Surface. For actors long runs are good news financially as they provide that stability of income which so often eludes stage folk. But with the regular income they have to accept repetition. Compton must often have been asked as he passed his various milestones, e.g. his 1,500th performance as Davy Garrick: "Don't you ever get bored?" One who put the question was the editor of the Northampton Independent. Compton replied "No, because I am so much attached to it and the tendency to monotony is relieved because I do not play a role on consecutive nights and hardly ever more than twice a week." Also there was something new coming along at intervals. On this last tour a brand new play was to be given its world premiere.

He was also asked about his nationality. In March, 1914, he told a St. Patrick's night audience at the Theatre Royal, Dublin: " I am a Scotsman by descent, an

Englishman by birth, and after your invariable kindness to me for so many years I thank heaven I am able to say I am an Irishman by adoption."

Pasted up on the wall of a corridor of Northampton Repertory Theatre, along with other souvenirs of its past as a Theatre Royal and Opera House, is a page from the managerial accounts of the theatre for the week of October, 1914, when Compton made his last appearance at the theatre. It shows the plays and the takings. They are as follows: Monday, *Davy Garrick,* £24 8s. 6d.; Tuesday, *The Lady of Lyons,* £19 11s. 9d.; Wednesday, *Money,* £24 5s. 3d.; Thursday, *Richelieu,* £51; Friday, *Hamlet,* £29 15s. 6d.; Saturday matinee, *Richelieu,* £13 19s. 9d.; and Saturday evening, *Davy Garrick,* £50 0s. 6d. Of the total takings for the week of £213 1s. 3d. the management took 33 per cent leaving Compton with £95 17s. 7d. As joint proprietor he would of course, in the long run, receive his cut of the rest as well.

The last birthday of the company which Compton was to act-ively celebrate (if you will excuse that rather atrocious example of word-coining) was at Middles-borough on February 7, 1915. That week a new play by Cunningham Bridgeman, *Memories,* was introduced on the Friday.

In the various places where it might be said that he played times out of number (but it would not be true, because he was a great statistician) Compton was greeted like an old friend. At Liverpool in March, 1915, he received a letter from a theatre-goer: "It is more than 25 years since I first had the pleasure of seeing you upon the stage and you must have seen more changes and more of the trials through which the drama has passed than most of your colleagues of to-day. Of one thing I feel certain and that is that no-one has done more by constant endeavour to keep the drama alive amongst us." The writer went on to thank him for "the great treat of witnessing that grace of action displayed by your talented daughter who should win the highest laurels in the future." This latter tribute was inaccurate, of course, for Compton's three daughters were all at that time covering themselves with varying degrees of glory in the United States. The leading lady was in fact Constance Pelissier, niece of Fay's late husband.

At the Theatre Royal, Newcastle, the following week Compton observed the 31st birthday of his *Davy Garrick* role by presenting one of his Compton Comedy Company birthday books to each lady in the audience. In a speech from the stage he observed: "Thirty one years ago tonight—I know I don't look it!—David Garrick came into being at the Royalty Theatre, Glasgow, and he has now made his bow to the public, his friends and his sponsors, 1,867 times. This is a unique record. And the best of it is that the play and the players are not in the least exhausted but if I may be allowed to say so, they are going better and stronger than ever before."

Then came a week at Halifax, three days at Bury and three days at Rochdale where Saturday, March 27, 1915, saw the last public performance by Edward Compton. The Theatre Royal, Rochdale, which had changed its name from the Prince of Wales in 1883, was scarcely the place where Compton might have chosen to say his last lines. The final three productions were: Thursday, *Richelieu;* Friday, *Money;* and Saturday, *Davy Garrick.*

The Rochdale newspaper coverage is cursory but if there is any impression of a triumphant farewell the Bury Times of March 24, 1915, provides a deflationary corrective: "Mr. Compton opened a three nights engagement at the Theatre Royal, Bury, on Monday with the presentation of *Davy Garrick*. Its frequent representation in Bury of recent years may probably have been responsible for the poor audiences that assembled to welcome this accomplished and versatile actor, the lineal descendant and the last distinguished interpreter of old English comedy. His 1800 portrayals of Garrick have resulted in the establishment of a remarkable facial resemblance between the illustrious 18th century actor and Mr. Compton himself. Versatility is the distinguishing characteristic of his presentment. Although in each of the three acts an apparently distinct characterisation is observable, there is nevertheless a perfect unity of conception. The debonairness of a Charles Surface, the emotionalism of a Belphegor, and the idealism of a Claude Melnotte are presented with a delicacy of treatment, facility of expression and artistry of purpose dramatically effective by an actor possessed of high intellectual and emotional endowments. In a tactful speech before the curtain on Monday evening, Mr. Compton, while referring to the pleasure he experienced at renewing his acquaintance with Bury audiences, expressed regret at the paucity of the attendance." But it was not only Compton who drew small support—"Almost every distinguished actor visiting the Theatre Royal, Bury, has been discouraged from paying a return visit through the lack of patronage extended."

The main new play of his terminal season, which had been introduced at His Majesty's Theatre, Aberdeen, was the five act *Sir Roger de Coverley*, by Justin Huntly McCarthy. It was typical Compton material, the Aberdeen Daily Journal finding it "eminently agreeable that the doyen of comedy actors should have returned to this medium after flirting with heavy and tragical drama. It is a pleasant romantic play, redolent of the leisurely atmosphere of the early 18th century, wonderfully rich in character drawing and not without arresting situations or pointed dialogue." Along with the famous Sir Roger, it depicted other members of the Spectator Club, gathered at his Worcestershire home. Constance Pelissier played Lady de Coverley and others in the cast were Henry Oscar, William Daunt, Ernest E. Imeson and J. C. Stewart.

This was the play with which Compton finally planned to conquer the capital. The London season was to begin on August 23, 1915, at the Shaftesbury Theatre, run by his friend and colleague Robert Courtneidge but in its issue of July 28 the Era announced: "Mr. Edward Compton's projected season in the West End will not materialise at present. Unhappily he is suffering from an affection of the throat and, under doctor's advice, has abandoned his intention." Instead the Shaftesbury would present a series of operatic performances in English, under the direction of Courtneidge and Thomas Beecham. In the newspaper Compton's name was no longer listed "On The Road" but still appeared among the business cards, the address being 1 Nevern Square, London, S.W.

Although Edward was not the man to feel envious of the success of his daughter and son-in-law it must have been with some frustration that he saw Fay and her second husband return from the United States in August, 1915, to take the leads in two shows opening in London. Lauri de Frece was in *The Dummy* at the Prince of Wales while Fay was at the Apollo in *The Only Girl*, a musical comedy which she had "discovered" in America.

That summer Edward had a personal "first appearance" in another sphere when he turned up to support his wife at an "At Home" at the Theatre Girls Club at 5 Little Portland Street, Oxford Circus. The previous January Mrs. Compton had been a moving spirit in founding the club as a residential home for theatre girls who were in need through unemployment. The outbreak of war had put some of the stage girls in such desperate straits that they were obliged to sing and dance in the streets. If there were not enough out-of-work girls to fill the club's 25 cubicles girls working for low salaries could be admitted at from 7s. to 12s. 6d. a week. Leading actresses who had paid £6 each to endow a cubicle included Mrs. Crowe (Kate Bateman), Madge Kendal, Gertie Millar and Marie Lohr. The club, which received a weekly grant from the Actors War Emergency Fund, had been opened by Adeline, Duchess of Bedford. Mrs. Compton was chairman of the committee which became one of her principal interests.

At Huddersfield the twice-nightly system was introduced by Bode and Compton in August, 1915, whenever the length of the play permitted. This, said the Era, was "falling into line with Birmingham, Liverpool and other big cities." It was the "wish of patrons and the desire of London producers." At the same time it was reported that following the success of a repertory season at Paisley J. H. Savile was extending it to his Perth theatre.

The final company celebration which Edward Compton was able to attend came at a time when the company was no longer active—in January, 1916, when Lilian Braithwaite presided at a dinner at the Cafe Monico, London, given by the O. P. Club as a 35th birthday tribute. Compton was by then deteriorating. Compton Mackenzie wrote in his memoirs that it was during that year that his father had an operation for cancer of the throat which reduced his voice to a whisper.

However he was not too sick apparently for a last burst of energy, which he displayed in taking over sole control of the Kennington Theatre. In February, 1918, the editor of the Northampton Independent wished his "old friend" well in his new venture. "After being a sleeping partner with Milton Bode in the Kennington Theatre he has suddenly become wide awake. He has begun management of that theatre on his own with *Peg Of My Heart*." According to the Independent the theatre had been renamed the Compton Theatre. The editor quoted from a copy of the Compton Birthday Book which Edward had given to him. Compton's birthday was on January 14 and the entries for that day were from *Davy Garrick*: "Only an actor", and *Romeo and Juliet*: "He that hath the steerage of my course direct my sail."

In her memoirs Fay describes her father's brave effort to conceal the fact that he was dying. She and Nell were shown in by their mother with "Here are both your little girls to see you dear." Compton could not speak but smiled and waved his hand "with that grace and courtliness of an old time gesture, trying to indicate that he was better and going to get well." Compton, who was not spared the last miseries then inevitable for a sufferer from throat cancer died on July 16, aged 64, and was buried at Brookwood Cemetery.

Compton Mackenzie had his own ideas on the cause of cancer, believing that his father's illness had been caused by long-term frustration. He recalled how Adelaide Neilson, his intended bride, had died in his arms a month before the intended marriage, how he had then lost all his hair and been thus restricted in his field of acting, how in spite of his financial success he always regarded

204

The C.C.C. at Scarborough in 1910.

A Bournemouth visit the year after
Edward Compton's death.

The Gaiety Theatre, Hastings. On right
an advertisement of the re-formed C.C.C.
visit of November, 1918. Note the proud
reference to "Theatre War Tax", i.e.
Amusement or Entertainment Tax.

himself as an unlucky man, how he yearned for a big London triumph.

Within a little over two months of his death the C.C.C. was back on the road. It was indeed a modest re-opening. Instead of a nostalgic night of triumph in one of the great theatres in a large city where they had performed many times the re-birth was in the small Lincolnshire town of Gainsborough, where the company had not previously appeared at all. Instead of being hailed with fervour in say the Manchester Guardian the event was noticed in a few lines in the Retford, Worksop, Isle of Axholme and Gainsborough News which stated "It was one of Compton's last wishes that the company should be carried on after his death." The Kings Theatre, where they appeared was in alternate use as a cinema and the attraction the previous week had been a celluloid one—The War Mother. The newspaper also mentioned that Nell Compton, who was with the company, was the sister of Fay Compton who was "attracting such appreciative audiences to the Prince of Wales Theatre, London." The account added that the same company would, however, shortly visit the Prince's Theatre, Manchester, and also "Mrs. Compton's own theatre in London." The reference here is to the Kennington Theatre, of which Mrs. Virginia Frances Compton Mackenzie appears as licensee from July 16, 1918, to May 5, 1919. In addition to their normal fare the new C.C.C. brought back Shakespeare and introduced Shaw's You Never Can Tell. The 1,200-seater Kings Theatre, Gainsborough, was reported to be crowded nightly for this dramatic event of the year. Originally built as an Albert Hall it was burnt down in 1884 and reopened the following year by James Marshal. In 1904 it was renamed as the Kings Theatre and subsequently modernised prior to becoming Kings Theatre and Picture Palace.

The next visit was to the Princes Theatre, Bristol, where the Bristol Evening News was of the opinion that "the company, deprived of its famous founder, can never be quite the same again." Then came Kennington, Worthing, Canterbury, Northampton, Reading, Torquay, Brighton, Hastings, Huddersfield, Manchester and Southport, most of which were on the track beaten out since 1881. Calls during 1919, which began at the Cork Opera House, included Bournemouth and Newport in May; Swansea in July; Bradford and Salisbury in August; Barmouth and Farnsworth in September; Cambridge, Ramsgate and Hastings in October; Northampton (where the publicity postcard of Nell Compton appearing on page 174 was issued); Cheltenham, Brighton and Leamington in November; and Merthyr and Limerick in December.

Roles previously taken by Edward Compton, including Davy Garrick, now went to H. Worrall-Thompson who also acted as producer. Among the cast lists of this period I was intrigued to note one George Sanders, who did not, however, prove to be the film actor: he appeared in such minor roles as Gregory in Romeo and Juliet, Joseph's servant in The School for Scandal, Balthazar in The Merchant of Venice and Tom Tickle in She Stoops to Conquer. Viola's husband, Henry Crocker was stage manager, Robert Gilbert manager, H. E. Bellamy business manager and H. Wallace Hill advance manager..

After the new year of 1920 had again begun in Cork, this time for a stay of a fortnight, the company remained in Ireland for visits to Waterford, Londonderry and Belfast. A February visit was to Reading; March and April took them to Scotland for appearances at Perth, Berwick-on-Tweed, Greenock, Falkirk and Aberdeen (by this time Viola had joined her sister in the company), Inverness,

Paisley, Dumfries, Carlisle and Glasgow, where they stayed three weeks at the Theatre Royal, from May 17 to June 5, and included Hubert Henry Davies's *Outcast*. Dates for the seven final weeks of this period of mobility were Newcastle, Sheffield, Edinburgh, West Hartlepool, Rhyl (three days), Llandudno (three days) and Dublin, where they finished up in July.

In addition to the two visits actually made to Northampton after the death of the founder the company was booked for a third, in October, 1920. But a few weeks before that date Milton Bode put an advertisement in the Era seeking a substitute company for that week "to suit Mrs. Edward Compton". The reason for the C.C.C. not keeping that appointment was that it had left the open road. Possibly because of poor business, perhaps with other reasons contributing, one of which will be considered presently, Mrs. Compton had decided to turn the C.C.C. into a repertory company, based at the Grand Theatre, Hyson Green, Nottingham. At considerable expense she first had the theatre redecorated and refurnished and a new electric system installed. Every seat became tip-up and every seat was bookable. In the programmes the theatre was stated to be under the lesseeship of Mrs. Edward Compton, the management of Viola and Ellen Compton, and the direction of Eade Montefiore. In 1899 Montefiore had run a summer stock season at the Dalston Theatre experiencing, according to the Era, "great loss through unparalleled fine weather" leading him to "abandon the full term of the season and close up most of his ventures as speedily as possible." Listed as producers at Nottingham were H. Worrall-Thompson and Viola Compton while Henry Crocker was stage director, Arthur J. Statham stage manager, Leonard Wright acting manager, Hugh Fleming publicity manager and Frank Gomez musical director.

The theatre had been built by R. J. Morrison, who was, indeed, closely involved with development of the entire Hyson Green area. "Radford Road, in which it stood, was known to local inhabitants as 'The Green' when I lived there in the 1950s." said Mr. Stephen Best, of the city's Local History Library. Its first lessee, a Captain Kennion, was also concerned with the Theatre Royal, Leicester; his actress wife, Emily, appeared several times at the Nottingham theatre. From 1888 until the late 1890s, when he went to London and later built the Kings Theatre, Hammersmith, the lessee was Mr. J. B. Mulholland who ran it as a typical touring theatre. The best surviving pictures of the theatre are in his programmes, which were quite a work of art.

A new play by Compton Mackenzie was a special attraction of the first season, which began on September 20, 1920, with *The School for Scandal*. This was his *Columbine,* based on his novel Carnival—the name had to be altered because Matheson Lang had already given the new name of *Carnival* to an Italian play he had bought, originally called *Scirocco*. A prior announcement by Mrs. Compton in the Era stated: "Can negotiate prior to London production for October 18, November 1 and 8." At first it seemed likely that the author would be asked to bolster the company's prospects in Nottingham by himself appearing in his play, supporting his sister Ellen in the leading role, and he expressed relief when this was thought not to be necessary. Opening on October 4, the play had a "West End cast" including Vernon Sylvaine, later the author of farces. One actress in the Nottingham cast was the original of the part she was playing—Christine Maude, who had been in Pelissier's revue *All Change Here,* was the original of

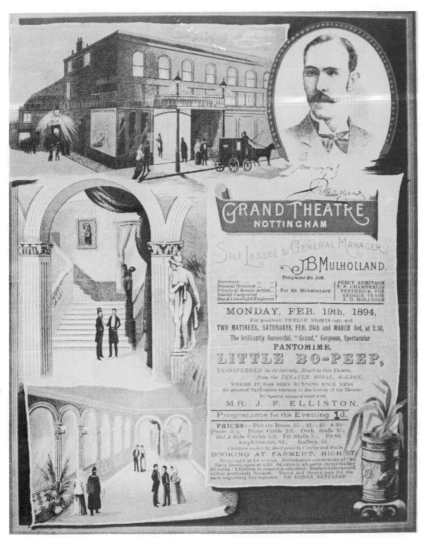

Oddly enough the best surviving pictures of the Grand Theatre, Hyson Green, Nottingham, scene of the Compton Comedy Company's "adventure in repertory" of the 1920s are these of the 1890s, appearing on a programme during the time when J. B. Mulholland was lessee. Didn't they have some splendidly attractive programmes in those days? (*Nottingham Local History Library*)

NOTTINGHAM REPERTORY THEATRE.

MISS VIOLA COMPTON.   MISS ELLEN COMPTON.

AUTUMN SEASON, 1922.

OUR Autumn Season for 1922, will open on Monday, September 25th.
During the Season we will give initial productions of five new plays,
and four productions of established successes; we have also been able to
arrange for three London Successes to visit our Theatre. We wish to
convey our gratitude to the Nottingham Public who have supported us so
faithfully during our previous Seasons, and to assure them that the
programme we are now announcing will even exceed in interest anything
we have hitherto had the privilege of presenting.

We are,

Very faithfully yours,

Viola & Ellen Compton

Jenny Pearl, featured in a dressing room scene. Now Mrs. John Mavrogordato and the mother of a small son she did not continue in the play when it went from Nottingham for a fortnight at Kennington and a month at the Princess's Theatre, London.

Compton Mackenzie also tried to help by suggesting that his mother should stage two plays by D. H. Lawrence, whose own reaction to the idea was summed up in a letter: "About the theatre, thrilling, but terrifying. You know my horror of the public. Well it's a phobia of phobias in Nottingham. Nottingham! Cursed, cursed, Nottingham, gutless, spineless, brainless Nottingham, how I hate thee. But if my two plays could be thrown so hard into thy teeth so as to knock thy teeth out, why then good enough." The plays under consideration, *The Widowing of Mrs. Holroyd* and *Touch and Go,* were not in fact produced.

At Christmas the pantomime was *Aladdin* presented by Macdonald and Young with lyrics written and music selected by George M. Slater and "powerful cast of specially selected London artistes, magnificent scenery and full beauty chorus" which ran for a fortnight from December 27, Mrs. Compon simultaneously staging the nativity play *The Hope of The World,* by Father Andrews, at the Circus Street Hall.

Surveying the first 13 weeks at Nottingham in a programme note at the beginning of the new year, Montefiore took the unusual step of giving precise attendance figures, no doubt because he thought they were encouraging. The opening week of *The School for Scandal* and *Davy Garrick* attracted total attendances of 5,231. Then came more of the traditional C.C.C. fare, with a week of *The Rivals* and *She Stoops to Conquer.* The new play by Compton Mackenzie proved a considerable success, 13,055 paying to see *Columbine* during its two-week run. Three weeks of Shakespeare, with just two plays, *As You Like It* and *The Merchant of Venice,* accounted an even higher attendance of 13,943. Then came the nativity play, *The Hope of the World,* Oscar Wilde's *Lady Windermere's Fan,* Sydney Grundy's *A Pair of Spectacles,* Pinero's *The Second Mrs. Tanqueray* and Shaw's *You Never Can Tell,* surely an excellent selection for a repertory company to present at that time. The aggregate attendance for the quarter was 65,435. Montefiore could justly be proud of the achievement: "To convert a frankly cheap melodramatic theatre with somewhat primitive comfort into a high-class repertory theatre with admittedly every comfort was an adventure looked at askance by many but applauded by all." He looked to the future with confidence.

The programme for the 40th anniversary on Monday, February 7, 1921, included facsimiles of the opening playbill and programme at Southport on February 7, 1881. The choice of play that week at Nottingham was the same as the week of launching at Southport, *Twelfth Night.* Following the birthday week came *Outcast,* with Miles Malleson's one act play *Michael,* Harry Wall's *Renovating Eve, Mrs. Dane's Defence* by Henry Arthur Jones, Robert Buchanan's *A Man's Shadow,* F. F. Montrésor's new historical drama *Katharine the Queen,* the morality play *Everyman* dating from 1500, J. M. Barrie's *Quality Street* and John Galsworthy's *Justice.* In the late spring the company even attempted a six-week Shakespeare Festival consisting of one-week runs of *Romeo and Juliet, The Merry Wives of Windsor, Measure for Measure, Much Ado about Nothing,* and *Othello,* followed by a week of one night performances of these plays plus *Twelfth Night.*

At the time of the 41st anniversary the following year a newly-formed Play-

Nottingham Repertory Theatre

"The Rep."

Trams 3 and 4 pass the door.   Phone 5578-9.

Commencing Monday, February 5th,

FOR ONE WEEK ONLY.

MATINEE, THURSDAY at 2-0.

Viola & Ellen Compton

PRESENT

The brilliant drama of Society Life

'The Walls of Jericho'

BY

THE EMINENT DRAMATIST,

ALFRED SUTRO.

SIXTH REPERTORY SEASON.

EVENINGS—Curtain rises every evening at 7-30.

PRICES—(Please note REDUCED SCALE OF PRICES)

RESERVED ORCHESTRA STALLS   3   9
STALLS   -   -   2   8
PARTERRE STALLS   -   1   10
CIRCLE   -   -   2   4
BALCONY (1st 3 rows)   1   6
"   (2nd 3 rows)   1   0

All reserved seats in this Theatre may be booked in advance.

UNRESERVED CIRCLE   -   -   1   6
BALCONY   -   -   9

MATINEES—Every Thursday, Curtain rises at 2-0.

At the same POPULAR PRICES as last season, 6d. to 2/4.

ALL seats for the matinees may be booked in advance.

SUNDAY "POP" at the "REP." Feb. 4.

Artistes—FRED MOUNTNEY, Violin
ENID TAYLOR, Piano
HAROLD GLOVER, Songs
DOREEN BURTON, Recitation

POPULAR PRICES, 6d. to 2/4.

to seats reserved and unreserved.   Admission Free.

The last celebration of the "birthday" of the C.C.C. was almost certainly the one at Nottingham on February 7, 1923—when the company reached 42 years of age. The play was Alfred Sutro's *The Walls of Jericho*, a choice with ironic overtones for as far as the company was concerned the trumpets were about to sound and the walls fall down. (*Nottingham Local History Library*).

goers' Club had collected almost 200 members, with Alderman E. Huntsman as president, and after *Common Clay,* then in its third week, the club "showered innumerable gifts upon all the members of the company not forgetting the call boy and later entertained them to supper on the stage", as the Nottingham Trader and Citizen reported. Members of the club then retired to the auditorium leaving on stage their officers and members of the company led by the Compton sisters. After praising Viola and Ellen, Alderman Huntsman said that he was not sure which of them was the better actress: one week he was convinced it was Ellen, the next Viola. He commented on the various ways in which they spent their leisure (do rep. players have any?): "If one takes up the programme of the Sunday Morning Institute one finds the name of Miss Viola Compton down for an important part of the proceedings whilst at a football match we discover that Miss Ellen Compton can not only play but that she can also kick off." Both sisters replied acknowledging these and other compliments to their missionary work in publicising the activities of the company. Other speeches were by Viola's husband Henry Crocker and W. G. Fay, who received the gift of a two-volume History of the Harlequinade. He said that without the help of societies like the playgoers' club it was practically impossible at that time for repertory or any drama at all to be done in this country because the theatre must be in possession of a more or less fixed audience. [There is no doubt in my mind that he had a fundamental point here: if a theatre has a regular audience with fixed habits of theatre-going the management interferes with those habits at its peril.] Mr. Fay also fired off an indignant broadside at a Manchester parson who had been attacking the stage while advising his flock to cut out theatre-going during Lent. "If this affects the livelihood of the artists," the cleric had said, "I am sure some more serious form of occupation can be found for them during the Lenten season." Fay declared that it was time that the average person learned that work on the stage was just as serious and demanding as any other art.

The number of towns and cities running repertory companies at this time could be counted on the fingers and the Nottingham venture came in for a good deal of praise in the Press, including the national newspapers. In the Observer on December 3, 1922, St. John Ervine wrote: "The list of plays done by the Nottingham Repertory Company is remarkable . . . it is clear to me from my correspondence that there is a hunger for drama all over the country, and that the hungry will not be content with monotonous food which was prepared for the palate of an earlier generation." In The Illustrated London News J. T. Grein commented that in one season at Nottingham more plays had been presented than in the ten theatres of the Metropolis . . . even the Old Vic could not show such a record of variety. "It is truly wonderful what the Repertory Company has done for Nottingham . . . it has become a new dramatic centre . . . running through its splendid record I am tempted to add 'Wake Up London!' ". "Theatrical pioneering of whose importance in the future they are as yet unaware" was how the Daily Mail referred to repertory efforts at Nottingham, Birmingham, Liverpool, Plymouth, Hampstead, and Southend. The Morning Post said that the Nottingham company had a fine record and had also set up a dramatic training school. This was the Nottingham Dramatic Repertory Training School, "a school for the theatre that is in a theatre" offering "complete stage training", supervised by Viola Compton.

New plays introduced by the company included *Cautious Campbell, The Portrait, Angela Brown, Robin Hood, A Tale of Young Lovers, Bloggs, Ordeal,* and *The Hill of Vision.* Star guests during the period included Sybil Thorndike, Henry Ainley, Tom Walls, Ralph Lynn, Robertson Hare, Isobel Elsom, Leslie Faber, Dawson Milward, Viola Tree and Julia Neilson-Terry who appeared in *The Wheel* and who was booked for *A Roof and Four Walls* for a late 1923 season that never was.

One touring date I have come across for the C.C.C. was at Bedford in June, 1922, when Viola and Ellen, Henry Crocker and H. Worrall-Thompson were among the cast. In April, 1923, while the C.C.C. was still at Nottingham, Ellen Compton appeared at the Northampton Opera House in two plays. The Gerard A. Neville and Ellen Compton Company performed *The Portrait* from Monday to Wednesday and *Too Much Money* the rest of the week. The latter title was inappropriate as the surviving accounts of the theatre reveal. A mere £68 was taken at the box office, of which the company share was £34. The identity of Gerard A. Neville is something of a puzzle, for the 1930 edition of Who's Who in the Theatre lists him as Ellen's second husband—it could have been a stage pseudonym for Ernest Cox.

What may have been the last observance of the company's birthday was the 42nd, in February, 1923, which occurred while they were presenting Alfred Sutro's *The Walls of Jericho,* described in the programme as "the brilliant drama of society life." In the original production at the Garrick Theatre, London, on Monday, October 30, 1904, the leading parts had gone to Arthur Bourchier and Violet Vanbrugh; at Nottingham in 1923 they were played by Alfred Goddard and Viola Compton. This was the play in which Sutro set out to draw a modern parallel with the Biblical situation "when the priests blew with the trumpets, the walls of Jericho fell down." He "relentlessly holds up to scorn the wretched sexless women who do nothing but flirt and gamble . . . lose hundreds at cards . . spend a fortune on dress . . . and the fop, the smirking dandy . . . the men who make love to their neighbours' wives . . . who whisper and ogle and tell bits of scandal." A modern School for Scandal?

After the birthday performance of the play on February 7, 1923, Viola was handed bouquets from the Playgoers Club, the front-of-house staff and the manager, Leonard Wright. The event was noted in the programme but by then the company was losing its traditional shape and stability in more ways than one: a Press comment was that in this piece, with the exception of Viola, Henry Crocker and Frank Follows, practically every member of the cast was a stranger. In times which were extremely difficult for theatres everywhere, the support of the public was falling away and as the rot set in Viola set out to retrieve the deteriorating situation. Quietly and privately at first she appealed for funds to keep the repertory venture going, interviewing some 170 people and writing to a further 3,600 as a result of which there were 231 subscriptions of from 5s. to £250 and totalling over £3,000. Then she "went public" with a letter to the Press: "GIVE NOW. Nottingham is one of the few cities in England to have a repertory company. Remember that with Liverpool, Birmingham, Plymouth, Hampstead and Southend, Nottingham has a public which is supporting a repertory company. And don't forget the many towns that have not got and never have had a repertory company and, alas, have not got one now." Appealing for another £2,000 to bring the fund up to £5,000 she urged: "Is it not worth while for Nottingham, which is so justly proud of its clean and beautiful city, its parks, its libraries, its school of art, its university, to help towards a Repertory Company it can be proud of too?" Donations were to be sent to her or to Alderman Huntsman at 1 Bridlesmith Gate.

It was, alas!, all in vain. When the end came it was sudden. On May 4, 1923, the club had given a reception for the players "at the close of their present season", the Press report expressing the hope that the club "would accord increased support when the repertory season is resumed in the autumn." At this stage there was no suggestion of finality as *The School for Scandal* was performed the following night. The company then went on tour handing the Nottingham stage over to a melodrama company booked by Mrs. Compton.

When their season ended on June 9 it was planned to re-open on August Bank Holiday but Mrs. Compton decided on an earlier start which took place in a heatwave on July 21. Performing at the theatre at the time when the chopper fell the following Saturday was Andrew Melville's Company with "the well-known cowboy actor Young Buffalo" in *The Savage and the Woman,* previously seen at the Lyceum, London. Although bookings had been made for the rest of the year, including a pantomime for Christmas, Mrs. Compton suddenly decided on Saturday, July 26, that she could not afford to lose any more money, gave orders

The 40th anniversary programme, at Nottingham, during the Repertory era.	The end of the adventure in repertory—July, 1923.

for the shutters to be put up and left for London. The Press treated it as a bomb-shell: "Nottingham Theatrical Sensation, Sudden Closing of the Repertory. Compton Era Ended" ran the headline in the Nottingham Guardian while a comment in a leaderette was: "Many people will deeply regret the announce-ment that the connection of the Comptons with this city is ended. We sincerely trust that Mrs. Compton is not a heavy pecuniary loser by her splendid enter-prise and can assure her that she and her daughters will take away the sympathy and good wishes of many citizens. Unfortunately it is not an easy matter to carry on a high-class theatre remuneratively and few people can afford to carry on a theatre at a loss. The people who patronise theatres expect a good deal and they are prepared to give as little as possible. It is a pity that this is the case because the theatres play a valuable part in the life of this nation and they might easily be made to play a much more valuable part if only they were better supported." There was no suggestion, it may be noted, of the possibility of saving the situation by civic or governmental support, which would have been unthinkable then to the same degree as it is today taken for granted.

The sudden closure left not only the Wild West high and dry—the Melville Company were to have remained for several weeks, the next two shows planned being *A Mystery Man* and *Young Buffalo in New York*—but also the musicians in the pit and this had a sequel in Nottingham County Court the following December when the musical director, Henry Harrington, and the seven members of his orchestra sued Mrs. Compton for two weeks wages of the three weeks contract for which they had been signed. They had the backing of the Amalgamated Musicians' Union. Why Mrs. Compton, who was described as "the former proprietor of the Compton Comedy Company" allowed the case to proceed, besmirching somewhat the good name she had in the city, is a mystery. She was not represented and inevitably lost the case. The court hearing was useful, how-ever, as court hearings so often are, in revealing a few facts and figures. The wages for the eight music-makers totalled £36 a week of which the conductor got £6 10s.

Mrs. Compton had, in fact, lost quite a lot of money, just how much it is impossible to say but sufficient to annoy Compton Mackenzie. He, the oldest of the family, and his sister Fay, the youngest, had proved well able to look after themselves and he to a degree resented their mother's dissipation of the family fortunes. The fact that Mrs. Compton felt that Viola and Nell needed a chance to shine was a powerful motive in carrying on the company and trying to set it up permanently at Nottingham. Another reason was that she could not get on at all with her late husband's former partner, Milton Bode, and had sold her shares in the various theatres. When she was ill in 1925 the 72-year-old Mrs. Compton spoke ruefully of the losses: "I'm afraid I wasted a good deal of money at Nottingham but I couldn't possibly have continued as Bode's partner." She added: "I think it's time I left this world." But there remained for her an important job on the edge of the world of theatre, an interest which was to continue right up to her death—which was not in fact to occur for 15 years after the expression of the death-wish. This was her beloved club in London, of which J. T. Grein wrote in the Christian Science Monitor that she "now devotes her life to the Theatre Girls Club in Soho where she guards and cozies those who work hard for little pay." For it she had secured new leased premises at 59 Greek Street which were blessed by the Bishop of London.

Under the banner of the Nottingham Grand Theatre and Estates Co. the theatre carried on until the following summer when the last show was *Trilby* on June 21, 1924. In October, 1925, it became a Gaumont British Cinema, going over to talkies in April, 1930.

A second "adventure in repertory" in Nottingham was not to be launched until the wartime year of 1942 when Tod Slaughter and his Lyric Players opened with Edward Percy's *If Four Walls Told* on January 22 at the Repertory Theatre, a former picture house in Goldsmith Street, under the proprietorship of Tom Wright* who had previously run it as a cinema. In November, 1943, the house became known as the Little Theatre and five years later as the Nottingham Playhouse, forerunner of the celebrated new Playhouse opened in 1963.

From Nottingham the C.C.C. carried on touring. At the Lesser Free Trade Hall, Manchester, in December, 1923, it put on a single play for three weeks, *Cautious Campbell,* one of the new pieces staged at Nottingham. One newspaper referred to it as the Compton Company, another to the Nottingham Repertory Company. Still it played in some of the other great cities including York, Birmingham and Glasgow though it did not venture across the Irish seas to Belfast, Dublin and Cork. At Cheltenham in September, 1924, an old friend was encountered in the person of Harry Bellamy, former manager of the company who was then manager of the Theatre Royal and Opera House in the spa town. Here is the final list of playdates, starting on February 11, so that there was, as far as I know, no celebration of what was in effect the company's final, 43rd, birthday: Blackpool, Bolton, Ayr, Greenock, Perth, Dunfermline, Falkirk, York, Liverpool, Scarborough, Sheffield, Glasgow, Newcastle, Birmingham, and then starting on August 11, after the summer break, Blackburn, Hull, Huddersfield, Walsall, Cheltenham, Weston Super Mare, Newport, Torquay, Bath, Guildford, Folkestone, Eastbourne, Hastings and Westcliff-on-Sea.

And there, at Westcliff's Palace Theatre, it all ended. Just as no bell sounds when the Stock Markets are peaking or at the lowest point of a depression, so there is often no inaugural peal or parting knell when a theatre company starts or ends a long career. Initially its longevity cannot be foreseen; terminally it often just fades away, the point of death not being realised at the time. This can happen also to theatres, one instance being the New Theatre, Northampton, which closed only "temporarily" in August, 1958, with *Strip Strip Hooray!* but was in fact to stage no more shows before the demolition men moved in 17 months later. No fanfare had sounded at Southport in 1881 and there was to be no elegy at Westcliff-on-Sea in 1924, to indicate that at the age of 43 the company had passed on. So far as I know no programme of the week survives (my informant being one of the Patrons of this book, Peter Wilcox who in 1975 moved from the Northampton theatre for a six month spell at the Palace, Westcliff) but the Southend Standard did carry a criticism of the first night, November 10, of *She Stoops to Conquer.* More than half the lengthy write-up was not about the company but concerned itself with Oliver Goldsmith, the author of the play. Members of the cast who were mentioned were Nell Compton and her second

---

* Tom Wright was the father of the late Eric Wright who ran the Coliseum Cinema, Northampton, from 1948 until its closure in 1958.

husband Ernest Cox, Oswald Lingard, Ethel Arden, Clement Hamelin, Marjorie Raeburn, Fred Piper, Buchanan Wake, Leslie Kyle, Elinor Blomfield, Carleton-Crowe, and Adam Brown. On the Tuesday it was *The Passionate Elopement;* Wednesday matinee *The School for Scandal;* Wednesday evening *Davy Garrick;* Friday *The Rivals;* while on the last night there was a repeat of *The Passionate Elopement.* This final choice of a play based on Compton Mackenzie's novel seems to have been the only recognition of finality: there appears to be no record of any speeches, such as Edward would surely have made had he been present.

Thus, with gaps in 1898-9 and 1915-8, the Compton Comedy Company had endured for 43 years, playing much the same sort of plays for most of the entire period. To the public of the provinces it had presented the standard classics of old English comedies which they would otherwise almost certainly not have seen. The C.C.C's place in English theatre history should not, of course, be exaggerated but neither should it be underestimated. Whether the David Garricks or the Edward Comptons play a greater part in the story of developing theatre is debatable. But there is something that is dogged and devoted, stable and solid, reliable and reassuring about people like Edward Compton. Nothing fly-by-night about the son of Charles Mackenzie.

There was no-one to fill the gap left by the company. Indeed within a couple of months of its termination the Era was noting that "The abnormal distress which at present exists in the ranks of the theatrical profession is seriously pressing on the resources of the Actors' Benevolent Fund." At this time of distress in many spheres of life besides that of the stage some writers adopted an anti-amusement attitude. A writer in a national newspaper said that 50 per cent of the dole (unemployment pay) was going to benefit places of amusement. He did not mean, of course, that actors were receiving all the money but that the unemployed were spending their State hand-out money on visits to picture houses and theatres. He included the world of amusements among the "more or less parasitic trades." The war-time burden of entertainment tax continued despite the fact that the war was long over. The month the C.C.C. came to an end, the Shaftesbury Theatre, London, threatened to sell boxes of chocolates as admission passes instead of tickets, so as to avoid the tax.

And there the story proper ends, with the demise of the Compton Comedy Company. But, of course, some members of the family had gone their separate ways and the rest were now to do so. Of them all I have picked up a few lines here and there.

While the fortunes of the company led by the two sisters had been on the decline those of the third sister were in the ascendant. May, 1921, found Fay Compton among the remarkable cast of a remarkable play—J. M. Barrie's *Shall We Join The Ladies?,* a who-dunnit to which we shall never know the solution, performed at the opening of the theatre of the Royal Academy of Dramatic Art on May 27. When Barrie failed to carry out his promise to write a one-act play for the occasion he offered instead the first act of a murder mystery he was then working on. It proved to be the most splendid tantaliser of all time, for he never completed it! It was a story of Sam Smith entertaining 12 dinner guests (making 13 in all) with the aim of finding out which of them had murdered his brother in Monte Carlo. The cast included Dion Boucicault Junior, Charles H. Hawtrey, Sybil Thorndike, Cyril Maude, Lady Tree, Leon Quartermaine (Fay's third husband), Lillah McCarthy, Nelson Keys, Madge Titheradge, Sir Johnston Forbes-Robertson, Irene Vanbrugh, Marie Lohr, Norman Forbes, Hilda Trevelyn and Gerald du Maurier. Following the death by drowning of his adopted son Llewelyn Davies, a few days before the production, Barrie lost interest in the theatre and as a result the second and third acts were never written. They were planned but the few close associates who knew the answer were sworn to secrecy and the identity of the criminal never emerged. So nobody knows who killed Smith's brother. It is a mystery as fascinating as that of Edwin Drood.

Fay's second husband, Lauri de Frece, died in 1921 and she married Leon Quartermaine the following year. He had divorced Aimee de Burgh who then married Gilbert Frankau. Fay took Leon to Nottingham to meet the family and in Rutland, en route, they had an accident, meeting a car on the wrong side of the road. On recovering consciousness Fay showed the correct sense of priorities. She asked Leon whether her face had been damaged in the collision and on being assured that it was all right instructed him: "Well pull down my skirt!" After which she felt free to faint again. Both were bruised, however, and Leon arrived at Nottingham with his arm in a sling.

Besides her eminence on the stage Fay made many silent films so that in Northampton, as elsewhere, she was competing with the live stage from the (silent) screen. Her films at this period included *A Woman of no Importance, A Bill of Divorcement, The Loves of Mary Queen of Scots, Settled out of Court, This Freedom, Diana of the Crossways, Old Wives' Tale* and *London Love.*

She maintained a correspondence with the editor of the Northampton and County Independent who recalled in 1926: "When she was a little girl I recall her coming to the Opera House with her father, the late Edward Compton, who was then part proprietor. She was full of fun and agile as a squirrel. Although she comes of a long line of distinguished artists it was little thought that she would win such resounding fame on the stage and in films. Moreover she possesses literary gifts like her famous novellist brother. Her poetic powers of composition are reflected in the following letter which she has sent me from the Haymarket Theatre: 'Those mysterious people who decree fashion's whim and steer her capricious course, the designers of the dresses we wear on and off the stage, have been, I am glad to see, unusually happy in their choice of colours. The war which naturally brought England and France very close together equally naturally provided a good natured rivalry between the two nations in almost everything. The stage, the tennis court, the river and the racecourse are now recognised meeting places for spirited exchanges between French and English skill, enterprise and friendly competition. That is quite as it should be. Competition begets elegance.''

The story of the first half of Fay's long life is told in her book Rosemary published in 1926, the title being taken from one of her most famous roles, Mary Rose, in a Barrie play of that name. First produced in 1920 it had three major productions within 10 years. The 1939 edition of Who's Who In The Theatre stated that she was first seen on the London music hall stage at the Coliseum in 1939 but she had appeared in variety long before that, as, for example, at the Bristol Hippodrome in November, 1924, along with her then husband Leon Quartermaine, in a playlet entitled *A Unique Opportunity.*

Picking up the threads of the post-C.C.C. career of Ellen (Nell) Compton is complicated by the fact that, unlike her sister Viola, she was entirely ignored by Who's Who in the Theatre. It was by chance that I discovered that she and her second husband Ernest G. H. Cox appeared with the Kingsley Players in *The Mollusc* at the Pavilion in the Montpellier Gardens, Cheltenham, situated behind the Queens Hotel, in September, 1929. In front of the hotel were the Winter Gardens and it was there that Ellen and her husband began a repertory company in 1935. This followed the tour of a play called *Worse Things Happen at Sea,* in which a fellow member of the cast had been Arthur Howard, Nell taking the Yvonne Arnaud part, in which her fluent French came in useful, with Arthur in the role taken in London by Frank Lawson.

Arthur Howard (real name Stainer) was the youngest of a family of five, the oldest being the film star Leslie Howard, 16 years his senior. One of their uncles, also Arthur Howard, died in his 30s while on tour with the C.C.C., from pneumonia caught from damp sheets in his "digs", it is said. Recalling that pre-Cheltenham tour in an interview in 1976 Arthur Howard told me:" Nell and I got on extremely well together and this resulted in an engagement for me with a company which she and her husband ran at Cheltenham. Nell was an under-estimated actress and could have been a great one. I never played with Viola but saw her from time to time—a dear woman." But if Arthur got on well with Ellen (as she now called herself, as opposed to Nell) he got on even more famously with her niece Jean, who was also in the Cheltenham company, and married her.

The Cheltenham theatre was a make-shift, fit-up affair, in one of the wings of the Winter Gardens, Cheltenham's "Crystal Palace", begun in 1876. Ellen and her husband, who had been shell-shocked in the 1914-18 War, opened the "Cheltenham Repertory Company" in partnership with Barbara Kent, paying £5 a week rent for the theatre, according to local records. A resolution passed by Cheltenham Town Council on December 2, 1935, approved the letting of the north transept of the Winter Gardens as a repertory theatre, up to the Saturday preceding Whit Saturday, 1936, with an option for the following season, provided the building was not required for the Town Hall extension scheme, when two months notice would be given. Thus the wing which had formerly been a cinema became a theatre.

The opening play on December 9, 1935, was *Viceroy Sarah,* by Norman Gins-bury, who attended the first night. It was warmly greeted by the local Press: "With one performance they have established themselves as a very decided asset to Cheltenham and the large audience was not slow to show appreciation." With the premises the company had "done wonders": though "simple and unembel-lished to the point of austerity it was a very pleasing theatre." The interior was uniformly painted grey, the stage was spacious and was set in a wall "which has apparently been constructed between the main body of the Winter Gardens and the wing and which gives an impression of wholesome solidity." The seating was comfortable and the December audience found the place admirably heated."

In this drama of court intrigue the title role of Sarah, Duchess of Marl-borough, was played by Ellen Compton who "has the beauty and presence which one expects of the woman and she strikes with accuracy the character of the tempestuous, egotistical, domineering but by no means unlovable and entirely womanly woman." The plot turned upon the usurpation of Sarah's dominating position with Queen Anne (Margaret MacGill) by her cousin, Abigail Hall (Barbara Kent) for whom she had secured the position of lady-in-waiting. Barbara Kent also assisted H. Worrall-Thompson in producing the play. James Hoyle played the Duke, Arthur Howard Captain Vanbrugh, and Arthur's sister Irene Howard was another lady-in-waiting, Mrs. Danvers; later she became a casting director with the Metro Goldwyn Mayer film company. Frank Follows was Queen Anne's husband, the Prince of Denmark, Henry Douglas the Lord Treasurer while Sarah's four daughters were Jean Compton, Alicia Travers, Phyllis Olsen and Beryl Johnstone. Others in the cast were Keith Beer, Anthony Rousse, Bush Bailey and William Nutton. Afterwards there were speeches by Ellen Compton and the Mayor (Councillor D. L. Lipson) who offered a civic welcome.

Jean Compton was the daughter of Frank Compton by his first wife Peggy Dundas whom he had met in Australia; she had been born after they went to America. As a child she visited England, making a playmate for Fay's son Tony Pelissier, who was about the same age, and staying for a time with Compton Mackenzie in the Channel Islands. In 1920 Monty had become the tenant of Jethou and Herm, the latter having formerly been for many years in the posses- sion of Prince Blucher von Wahlstatt, who was deported from the island when war was declared. Returning to America Jean had gone round with her father on his theatrical tours, attending convent schools whenever possible, but some time before the break-up of the marriage in 1931 he sent the 19-year-old to England to stay with her grandmother, Mrs. Compton, at the Theatre Girls Club, from where she attended the Fay Compton Dramatic School. At first Frank's wife was reluctant to give him a divorce but was persuaded to do so by Mrs. Compton. Jean was devoted to the father she was never to see again. Frank's second wife was Mary Wetmore Wells, who ran a dancing school.

At Cheltenham Jean and Arthur Howard fell in love and it was quite a Compton family occasion when they were married in July, 1936. Owing to being unwell Mrs. Compton was unable to attend but it was at the matriarch's insist- ence that the ceremony was held at Brompton Oratory. The bridegroom re- called: "Most of the Comptons were there and my brother Leslie was best man, though he was so vague about keeping appointments that I felt sure he wouldn't turn up. His daughter Leslie was a bridesmaid and so were Nell's daughter Jane and my sister Irene. Viola's son, John Crocker, was page boy and Tony Pelissier, her childhood playmate, gave the bride away on behalf of her father who was, of course, in America. Our honeymoon was spent partly in Kent at Fay's home, which was provided complete with servants and a white Packard, and partly on the Scottish island of Barra where Monty greeted us in his kilt, like a laird. To me Monty was like a father-in-law. My wife was known on the stage as Jean Comp- ton or Jean Compton Mackenzie. During our second season at Cheltenham she carried on acting while pregnant—after playing my daughter, she played my mother. When our son was born on August 5, 1937, he was christened Alan Mackenzie, with Monty as godfather."

The Cox-Kent Company operated at Cheltenham for three seasons, the first carrying on until at least June, 1936 and the others running from September, 1936, to at least May, 1937, and September, 1937, to May, 1938, the final per- formance on May 21 being of Noel Coward's *Tonight at Eight*. A month later

Barbara Kent applied to renew the lease but the matter was adjourned until tenders for the Winter Gardens scheme had been considered by the Town Council—there were plans to modernise the buildings, the glass roof of which had become unsafe. The following autumn Mr. J. D. Carran applied for a tenancy of the Repertory Theatre but was refused because of the condition of the roof and soon all ideas of improvements were obliterated by rumours of war. The building which had become an expensive and little-used luxury, was dismantled early in the 1939-45 War, another consideration being that it was a very considerable landmark for enemy aeroplanes.

What had intrigued me about the period at Cheltenham was a reference by Compton Mackenzie: "The Repertory Theatre lasted for over two years at Nottingham by the end of which my mother had lost too much money to carry on. Nevertheless later on she started a Repertory Theatre at Cheltenham and managed to lose a great deal more." At Cheltenham there were no clues to Mrs. Compton's participation. The answer was to be found in the minute books of the Theatre Girls Club which were deposited with the British Theatre Museum in 1974, along with a collection of Compton and Bateman family portraits and several of the Compton Comedy Company's prompt scripts. It was there, too, that it became clear why nothing was to be found at Cheltenham—the club share in the venture, which resulted in Mrs. Compton's losses, was on a confidential basis.

The records of the Theatre Girls Club ought to be compulsory reading for girls wanting to go on the stage, showing an entirely unglamorous side of the picture. But for anyone interested in theatre they make compulsive reading, these accounts of the proceedings at what was perhaps a unique institution, with an atmosphere rather like that of a school, with Virginia Compton presiding as a God-fearing, no-nonsense, moralistic yet always loving perpetual incumbent of the headmistressship.

One of the principal aims of the establishment was to provide accommodation and as homely an atmosphere as possible for stage girls, whether in work or out. A reference elsewhere to the early years stated "By arrangement with the Hand-in-Hand Society meals were obtainable at incredibly low prices. A meat, vegetable and pudding tea was priced at 5d." Initially girls out of work were admitted free; if they did not fill the 25 cubicles on the two upper floors of the premises in Little Portland Street working girls on low salaries could be put up, at from 7s. to 12s. 6d. a week. Later, in the Greek Street premises, the financial arrangement was that girls in work paid £1 10s. a week while the unemployed paid a guinea, these figures including four meals a day. There was also an annual subscription of 2s. 6d., presumably aimed at giving them a feeling of "belonging". A second principal objective was to find them work, primarily in the theatre or musichall, if that could be achieved. Many a time Mrs. Compton would herself go along with a girl seeking an interview with an agent or manager, especially if she knew them personally, sharing a waiting vigil outside their doors, sometimes sitting on the cold stairs. If stage work was not available the regulations at the time of founding the club said that the girls were expected to attend County Council continuation classes in such subjects as cooking, dressmaking and bookkeeping. In times which were often difficult for the stage the object was to train them for other work, perhaps as a stop-gap, and get them employment so as to avoid their simply "resting" between engagements or being given a free ride. The other work done by the girls covers a wide range; the minutes contain references to girls being cakemakers, waitresses, nursemaids, barmaids and cinema attendants. One girl was trained as a typist under the Margaret Bondfield Scheme (Maggie Bondfield was M.P. for Northampton and the first woman Cabinet Minister).

In 1936 one girl was reported to be a florist, another was working as a lift attendant in Selfridges, while two were at a reformatory school. Every school has its delinquents and in an establishment full of girls with the temperament suitable for actresses there were certain to be some who would step out of line. In April, 1930, one girl was "defiant and disobedient to the Matron" and had to be asked to leave. The same year they were "always having thefts." When 10s. was stolen from a girl's drawer in 1938 a notice was put up appealing to the conscience of the thief and the money found its way back into the drawer. The mother of a girl who "seemed to be stage-struck and who was seen talking to strangers and asking for film work" was asked to take her away as the club could not accept responsibility. In 1938 a girl who stayed out all night without permission was sent away. When an old girl was in a French prison the same year, charged with shooting at her husband, the club sent a letter testifying to her general good character, hoping that this would aid the defence. The minute book accounts of meetings used regularly to be under three principal headings, Health, Spiritual and Work but in 1935 under the additional heading, Morality, there appeared a brief reference to two girls being found one night in each other's beds (the girls were all in cubicles—no separate bedrooms) and being sent away, Mrs. Compton calling the rest together in the club room for a sermon against such deviationism. Religious devotions played a part, passion plays being produced and masses held regularly in the club's own chapel. Expense items include buying figures (Mrs. Compton was very High Church) and candlesticks for the chapel. Students from the Fay Compton School were invited to Communion.

Probably because the girls were so high-spirited filling the post of matron proved a great problem. Matrons normally came and went in quick succession: one broke down, another left after a fortnight because she could not stand the noise, a third excused herself after a similar period because the sewing was too much for her eyesight. Undoubtedly the best, to date anyway, was Miss Bourne who arrived in September, 1939, and was not only described as efficient but "a good Churchwoman, which it is a real necessity for the Matron to be". She stayed only six months, however, leaving the following March to return to a boarding house at Newquay in which she had an interest.

The Greek Street premises held about 40 girls when full, which they usually were, of whom the majority were not usually in stage jobs at the time of residence. In April, 1930, for instance, one was with the Carl Rosa and 19 were rehearsing. The usual story was that there was some work for dancers but little for actresses. "Straight work is very difficult to get," said a 1930 entry. In 1936 Mrs. Compton is recorded as wondering what was going to happen to acting as a calling—whether the Thespian profession would survive—"Except for the repertory companies it is difficult to think what will happen to the art of acting." This was the year, coincidentally when the first British television service began but the old lady could not be expected at that early stage to envisage how much work it would one day provide. Sometimes the minute books recorded pay and conditions. In July, 1934, Gladys Holmes and Pearl Dadswell "open tonight at the Aldwych Theatre as supers, getting 30s. a week and have to wear their own frocks." The club could expect to fill up when several shows came off the road in the provinces at once, as in 1934 when *Words and Music, Bitter Sweet,* and *Wild Violets* came to the end of tours at the same time. Conversely, numbers would go down when several tours began at once, as in July the following year when "14 girls left on Sunday for various tours, *White Horse Inn, Waltzes from Vienna* and *The Gay Divorce.*" From the club girls also went abroad, no doubt with Mrs. Compton praying in the chapel for their moral well-being. There are mentions of girls in Chile, Morocco, Barcelona etc. Four went to France for Francis Mackenzie in 1933 "but two have already returned". In 1934 one was in Marseilles with *Rose Marie,* another with *White Horse Inn* in South Africa.

Wherever they went at home or abroad the fortunes of the girls or ex-inmates were followed as far as possible. In March, 1934, Odette Vinton "had a very quiet wedding at Wellingborough (Northants) where she had been producing *Rose Marie* for an amateur company. She is going to live at Lowestoft." Another joined a circus but was "stranded and very disappointed." A letter from Peggy Davannah who was in *Conversation Piece* in New York reported that the show was not a success there. The special atmosphere of the club was largely due to the personality of Mrs. Compton, who regarded the girls as her family, and cherished and admonished them accordingly. In 1934 the club bought a portrait of its unique "head of the family" painted by Grace Rosher, for exhibition on the premises. Each year there was a Christmas party and in 1938 Mrs. Compton sent off 21 dozen Christmas cards and presents to old girls. At the Christmas party of 1938 Mrs. Compton's grandson 13-year-old John Valentine Crocker recited and her 18-month-old grandson Alan Howard "led and finished the applause, contributing to the singing in his own fashion". There was also an annual birthday party for Mrs. Compton in January. At the one in 1935 she was helped to blow out the 82 candles on her cake by the youngest guest, a boy aged three. Her health was varying and in 1938 she could not get downstairs and the party had to be on a restricted scale. At the annual meeting of 1939 Mrs. Compton apologised for not replying to some of the speeches, explaining that she had been unable to hear them.

The school set up its own troupe called the Merry Maids and got engagements for it. This carried on even after all the original members had got married. Finding theatrical work for the girls was, of course, the main intention and it was in one of her endeavours in this direction that Mrs. Compton came to lose money, as referred to by her son. It happened in late 1935 and 1936, shortly after the club had passed its own 21st birthday and become incorporated. At the first annual meeting of the incorporated society Mrs. Compton opened the proceedings as follows: "I am sorry for you all but I am afraid I have to propose myself as the perpetual chairman and president of this society and unfortunately you won't be able to get rid of me because I am here for life."

This was the meeting at which that great character Lilian Baylis, of the Old Vic and Sadlers Wells, who had supported the club since it was formed, moved the adoption of the balance sheet. Praising the club for its financial stability she commented: "I wish I could say I was as sure of my future expenses!" Her fellow vice-presidents included Cyril Maude, Dame Sybil Thorndike and Compton Mackenzie. The 21-strong council included Fay's son, Tony Pelissier. Another prominent supporter was Dame Madge Kendal, that grand old lady of the stage, who gave a talk to the girls in 1933.

If it was all right to spend money on setting up a tea shop and rest home at Clacton, where girls could be trained in catering and domestic duties, which represented a secondary objective of the club, why should not the club put money into launching a repertory theatre where the girls might be employed? It sounded very reasonable and plausible to Mrs. Compton, who, however, had a secondary motive, albeit quite likely an unconscious one. At a meeting she called in October, 1935, especially to consider the project, she told the committee: "I was lamenting to my daughter Mrs. Cox that we had no place where we could give girls work on the stage . . . well, she said, we are trying to get a repertory theatre and start it ourselves. We have found a partner and she will put in £500 and we want another £500."

The theatre was, of course, the one at Cheltenham. To Mrs. Compton's support rushed Mrs. Arnold Glover, the treasurer, who had first come in contact with the club when it was founded in 1915 in Portland Street, when the girls used to eat at a nearby dining centre for business girls, run by Mrs. Glover. She now said: "As well a repertory theatre Mrs. Cox means to open out in other directions with tea rooms and winter gardens, and she promises to give first chance of work to our members—waitress jobs and minor parts and so on." Evidently very quick on the uptake, another member, Mrs. Russell, wanted to know what security they would have for the money, and was told by Mrs. Glover that it was simply the security of the theatre; it was a risk, she admitted. Mrs. Compton came back: "Repertory is the thing in the country now. There are no tours, no companies that go about any more. That is all finished. The only chance for the theatre part of it now is the repertory theatres which are all doing really well. I have a grand-niece up in York in repertory and they are doing remarkably well." Another member, Miss Bull, said that she had just heard of a repertory theatre in the Midlands which had failed badly.

Mrs. Compton plunged unheedingly into the administrative details. The initial £500 was being put in by the lawyer father of Barbara Kent, a Cheltenham woman who acted and who "knows all the people." She and Mr. and Mrs. Cox were each to receive £5 a week salary. The theatre was to be rent-free in exchange for certain alterations and improvements they were to carry out, such as fitting dressing rooms under the stage. The work was not to be done by builder's contract—"My son-in-law understands and can do that sort of thing. He has a stage carpenter who was with them in Bristol who they know is an admirable workman." She estimated the weekly outgoings at £130 a week—£17 a performance. The total possible takings were £385. Custom could be expected from Gloucester, nine miles away, which was without a theatre. It was mentioned, however, that there was a twice-nightly variety theatre in Cheltenham, so there was some competition. This was the Opera House which existed mainly on touring companies until it too became a cinema. It is now the Everyman Theatre. The reference to Bristol is to a five-week repertory season by Alfred Brodis at the Little Theatre from July 23, 1934, the company including Ellen and Jean

Compton and Ernest Cox.

The minutes capture the atmosphere of near-dissension among a committee which normally took its decisions on the nod, without the necessity of a vote.

Miss Bull: Mrs. Compton, do you think it is all right to spend the money that has been given to benefit the club—to give it away to other people?

Mrs. Compton: We are investing the money.

Mrs. Glover: We are trying a venture—a venture that will benefit the girls.

Mrs. Russell: My feeling is that we have no security. Can I think it over and let you know?

Miss Bull: I must do the same . . . things are terribly precarious in the provinces.

Mrs. Duckworth: With touring companies, yes. But the repertory company is here to stay. There are more repertory companies starting and the theatre of the future in the country will be repertory. Of course there is a risk, but not a big risk.

Despite the misgivings of Mrs. Russell and Miss Bull, which were all too justified by events, a vote was taken. The pair did not in fact fall out with Mrs. Compton so far as to vote against but they did abstain. Mrs. Compton did not vote either but there were four "ayes" and the "investment" was made with the Cheltenham Company—£500 at 2%.

The following June, after making a visit to the theatre, Mrs. Compton painted a rather different picture. She was delighted with the production of *Macbeth* which she had seen but not so delighted with the business being done. Also the Corporation ran open air brass band concerts at the Winter Gardens in the summer and the musicians blasted forth outside the theatre—which proved to have "very thin" walls. "The noise would be formidable . . . they will have to shut down as they couldn't get themselves heard." Mrs. Glover said that Cheltenham was a difficult place with all those retired colonels and admirals but both the schools had taken up with the company as they had a name for being refined and safe. "It is a very conservative old town. I have heard that the week the King died and was buried nobody in Cheltenham went to the theatre—and they had to pay the staff just the same. It was a dead slump."

In spite of the uncertainties of the situation and, no doubt, with the best intentions Mrs. Compton asked the committee to follow up the £500 "investment" with a £500 loan, making £1,000 in all. And they did so, this time with scarcely any objections.

At this meeting copies of the Daily Sketch of May 14 were passed round, containing a description of the new spa which was to be built at Cheltenham and members probably felt reassured as they heard that the new theatre which it would include would be offered to the Coxes and their partner. In fact the scheme was abortive.

Mrs. Glover said that "our girls" were running the box office as well as being waitresses; whether any were acting is not mentioned. Mrs. Watson observed that when they offered the first £500 "one of our objects was to do what we could for Mrs. Compton, some sort of appreciation for all her splendid work." After all, it may be said, Mrs. Compton, who rated herself a good beggar, had been largely instrumental in raising £10,000 for the club, by appeal. After the loan had been approved Mrs. Compton fairly tempted fate with a few final remarks: "I just want to say that I feel that it is safe. Of course you know I am a very bad business woman . . . I do feel that I have a wonderful committee."

When the accountant of the club came across these items he said they were a very bad investment but passed them "with reluctance": the auditor, on his quarterly check-up, proved to be less accommodating. This also applied to the club solicitor to whom the matter was then referred. He said that the club could not make such an "investment" and the money should be paid back. Needless to say, the £1,000 was not available at Cheltenham, so Mrs. Compton faced up to the music. At the committee meeting of November 20, 1936, she said that to meet this situation Mrs. Glover, like a female knight-errant, had immediately provided £500. But, of course, Mrs. Compton could not allow her to be the loser so she sold the lease of her house to raise the £1,000. She told the meeting that she still felt that the original actions were quite in order and quoted parts of the articles which she felt served to prove the point, being "in furtherance of finding work for our girls." But in any case "I am very happy to have been able to start my daughter. Ordinarily I should not have been allowed to sell the house to do so and whether my daughter succeeds or not she has had her chance so I am very happy about the whole thing." In putting forward the scheme Mrs. Compton had described Ellen as "a remarkably good actress" and this view is supported by Arthur Howard. But of course, in matters of theatrical actor-management you need luck as well as talent.

On at least one occasion cash aid was given to an old girl—in the autumn of 1938 when a £20 loan was granted to a former girl to enable her to keep her school open during times when it was being affected by the crisis. This was later converted into a gift.

Recently arrived from Germany that Christmas was Ruth Sandler, who was of Jewish descent. After an engagement fell through she stayed at the club, meanwhile endeavouring to get her parents over from Berlin.

"The Crisis. We have all got our gas masks," said the club minutes. "Mrs. Compton has had a notice put up suggesting that those who have homes and parents to go to should go there if war is declared." Following the actual declaration a further notice was posted asking every girl who had a home to go to to go at once. The club decided to keep open. The top floors were evacuated as the staircase was all wood. The little office was boarded up and sand-bagged and wire netting was put over the windows of dining room and kitchen.

On February 29, 1940, Virginia Compton signed the club minutes for the last time. She died on May 4, 1940, at the club. Despite her various illnesses she had been very active in club affairs and it is surprising to read in her son's memoirs that after her sister Isabel died in June, 1934 "She longed to join her." Aged 87 Mrs. Compton had been ill for a fortnight but retained her pungent wit and sense of humour. When a nurse used a bit of hospital conversational shorthand, "P.D.Q." Mrs. Compton heard it and interpreted it aloud as "Patient Decidedly Queerer." In fact it stood for "Pretty Damn Quick" and those were her last words. The incident was related by Faith, wife of Compton Mackenzie and daughter of Christopher Stone, the first gramophone record compere, in Always Afternoon, the third volume of her memoirs. Monty himself had been summoned from Barra but arrived too late to say farewell. After solemn requiem mass at All Saints, Margaret Square, Mrs. Compton was buried beside her husband in the huge cemetery at Brookwood on May 8, the day before the Germans invaded the Low Countries.

It was Mrs. Compton's report for the year, up to March 28, which was read at the annual meeting on May 31 at which she was succeeded as president by her son Compton Mackenzie, the election of whom, in his absence, led to the immediate resignation of Mrs. Glover as treasurer. She asked for her protest to be registered, against the election of a MAN—the club was run solely for girls and Mrs. Compton, as a woman herself, was able to appreciate their points of view and understand what was best for them. A defence of the selection was offered by Tony Pelissier, who later became president himself. At the same time as Compton Mackenzie became president his wife Faith, joined the council.

The club's air raid shelter soon came in for use, first in the blitz of 1940-1, early in 1944 when a bomb fell very near the premises, and later that year with flying bombs and rockets. During the early part of that year the theatres kept going as usual, but the flying bombs did affect them adversely. Most of the club girls were sent to the provinces and the place closed down for a month to give everyone a rest. Many girls were then abroad, with E.N.S.A. The club continued for a few more years.

Memories of visits to the Theatre Girls Club to see "Aunt Ginnie" are recalled by Valerie Skardon, of Harrogate, Yorkshire, whose mother, Sidney Crowe, only daughter of Kate Bateman, acted as Edward Compton's leading lady and was a member of the company he formed for Isabel Bateman. "As a young girl I used to visit Aunt Ginnie at the club. With great reverence and awe I used to be taken to her office, to find a very small lady dressed in black with immaculate white trimmings. I used to have a photo of her as a young woman taken seated on a lawn leaning rather romantically against Henry Irving." She describes the part played by her mother in the C.C.C. thus: "The exhausting travels used to upset Virginia and my mother used to take over her roles during her several pregnancies. Mother always spoke of Edward with respect and affection. He was a strict disciplinarian in the theatre but a most attractive man. The four Bateman sisters varied much in appearance. Both Virginia and Isabel were beautiful but Virginia was very fair and Isabel very dark."

Valerie, who was herself an actress with the British Broadcasting Company's drama department in Leeds, told me that she was very proud to belong to such a wonderful family but with one or two exceptions the theatrical streak seemed to have faded out.

Besides her appearances with the C.C.C. Sidney Crowe also acted with Beerbohm Tree and Forbes Robertson. When she married for the second time it was to a theatrical manager, Herbert Skardon, and she toured with his company in north-eastern England. When he went into business she settled in Leeds where she died on February 14, 1962, at the age of 91.

Ellen's acting career was to last only another five years. Her nephew Nicholas Crocker told me: "After Cheltenham she was with the Wilson Barrett Company for a bit and later with the Old Vic under Tyrone Guthrie. She was also, I think, with E.N.S.A. during the war. She retired from the stage in 1943."

Further information came from an actress who was her companion in railway compartments and ship's cabins during a 1939 tour of European and Mediterranean countries—Freda Jackson, film actress and former member of Northampton Repertory Company, who lives at Hardingtone, Northampton. "In my childhood I had seen the Compton Comedy Company at Nottingham. In 1938 Nell and I had been together at the Old Vic—in *The Rivals* she was Mrs. Malaprop and I was Lucy. I liked Nell enormously, she was great fun, very gay indeed for her age. We got on extremely well. After the Old Vic we went on tour together in Europe and around the Mediterranean. The war was about to break out as the tour ended but I heard that she had gone back to Malta within a week of our arriving home."

Ellen had a daughter and son by her second husband, Ernest Cox. The daughter Jane is married and living in Dublin but the son Ewan died in a boating accident in East Africa in about 1936. Ellen's own last years were tragic as after some matrimonial problems she became unhinged and was the first patient, I understand, to have the pre-frontal leucotomy operation to relieve mental tensions. It pacified her but reduced her largely to a cabbage. She died at the Actors' Home, Denville Hall, Northwood, Middlesex, on May 30, 1970, at the age of 78.

Now I turn back the calendar 40 years to follow the career of Ellen's sister Viola, her senior by five years. It will be recalled that she was with the C.C.C. at Nottingham. Just as she was overshadowed in the world of acting by her sister Fay, she outshone Ellen, at least as far as recognition was concerned. Who's Who in the Theatre, which ignored Ellen altogether, did list Viola. It located her at the Drury Lane Theatre in May, 1928, in *The Show Boat;* at the Dominion Theatre in October, 1929; at the St. James in 1930 (Mrs. Welland in *Odd Numbers*) and His Majesty's Theatre in May, 1931 (Mrs. Joe in *The Good Companions*). Next she took part in three tours, from September, 1933, as Petrova in *The Gay Hussar,* and as Lady Mary Crabbe in *Fresh Fields.* Back in London she was at the Gaiety in February, 1935, as Mrs. Featherstone in *Jack O' Diamonds;* at Drury Lane in May, 1936, as Miss Sibthorpe in *Rise and Shine;* and at the London Hippodrome the following September as Lavinia Skindle in *Certainly Sir.* For the Charta Theatre she was Mary Clifton in *Lot's Wife* in October, 1936. Two years later she was touring again as Diana Ebury in *Wise Tomorrow* and as Mrs. Conway in *Time and The Conways.* That Christmas she played The White Queen in *Alice in Wonderland* and *Through the Looking Glass* at the Q Theatre.

During the 30s she also took a leading part in setting up the Fay Compton Studio of Dramatic Art, with the financial help of her sister, at first in premises in Red Lion Square, London, and later in Baker Street. She also took part in the activities of the Theatre Girls Club though most references to her in the minutes are of apologies sent while on tour. Who's Who in the Theatre of 1939 gave her recreations as riding, swimming and rowing. After 1939 she devoted most of her time to teaching drama and voice production in various schools. Among her tutorships was one at the Webber Douglas School from which I have a picturesque recollection of her from one of the Patrons of this book, Mrs. Julia Nutt (formerly Gordon-Lennox): "During my last year at drama school my class was fortunate enough to encounter a truly splendid dragon in the person of Miss Viola Compton, in whose features, alas!, was to be detected an infinitely more marked resemblance to the masculine attributes of her brother than to her lovely sister Fay. A quite unforgettable character and a first-rate teacher."

Viola and her husband, Henry Crocker, had two sons, Nicholas and John. A student at University College, London, from 1933-6, Nicholas then worked as a freelance script writer in the radio department of G. Walter Thompson, the advertising agency handling programmes for commercial radio transmitted from Radio Normandy and Radio Luxemburg. After war service from 1939-45 he joined the Western Region of the British Broadcasting Corporation where he was at first producer in charge of outside radio broadcasts, handling among many other programmes the first three years of the long-running Any Questions series. Following a spell in television he became head of the B.B.C. Natural History Unit in Bristol, from 1952 until his retirement in January, 1973. His home is at Portishead, Bristol.

John Crocker is one of the best known authors of pantomimes and wrote several for Northampton Repertory Company, which has now completed 50 years in the former Northampton Opera House. With Fay and his mother Viola, John Crocker attended the 75th anniversary celebrations of the theatre in 1959. Fay, who made a short speech from the stage, brought a message from her brother, Compton Mackenzie, apologising for his absence but saying that he was proud to think that he was in some small way in at the beginning—asleep in his cot in a dressing room. Also present were Sir Emrys Williams, Secretary General of the Arts Council, among a circle that was "dressed" to see *Twelfth Night*. Lionel Hamilton took the part of Malvolio which had been played by Edward Compton 75 years earlier. In 1884 Mrs. Compton had portrayed Viola; in 1959 it went to Jennie Goossens, daughter of the oboist Leon Goossens. After that anniversary show Fay and Viola stayed the night at Lamport Hall, home of Sir Gyles Isham. The sisters had evidently not met for some time because they sat up long into the small hours exchanging reminiscences, so much so that Sir Gyles, though most interested in the theatre, went to bed and left them to it!

Mrs. Crocker (Viola Compton) died on April 7, 1971. Her husband had pre-deceased her in November, 1956. After his stage career had ended in 1943, following a period as business manager at the Old Vic under Tyrone Guthrie, he lived in Wales.

Thus two of the sisters are accounted. The third, Fay, now the sole survivor of the five Compton children, has attained the great age of 82 and is in a nursing home at Hove, Sussex. Greatly to my regret she has not been well enough to grant me an interview, so that I could hear first-hand what it was like to be a child of Edward and Virginia Compton. From the two pages she merits in Who's Who in the Theatre I will mention just one or two entries to show how varied her talents have been. In December, 1930, she played Dick in *Dick Whittington* at the Palace, Manchester; in 1933 she toured variety theatres in *This That and the Other;* she played Ophelia to the Hamlet of John Barrymore in February, 1925, at the Haymarket, and to that of John Gielgud at the final performance at the Lyceum in June, 1939, and in Elsinore, Denmark; for 15 months from June, 1941, she played Ruth in *Blithe Spirit* at the Piccadilly; she toured in Shakespeare for the British Council in Belgium, Holland, France and Switzerland from September, 1946; and in May-June, 1965, she was seen as Anna in *A Month in the Country* at the opening of the Yvonne Arnaud Theatre, Guildford, Surrey. As well as a long career in both silent and sound films she has been on television, notably as Aunt Ann in *The Forsyte Saga*. All in all a quite fantastic career, completely eclipsing that of her father but now that career is closed, her final bow having been taken on radio in Roy Plomley's "Desert Island Discs" in February, 1974.

What, then of the two Compton sons, the internationally famous Compton Mackenzie and the almost unknown, in this country, Frank Compton? As Compton Mackenzie chose to turn way from the family occupation of acting as a means of livelihood, he does not really fall within the scope of this book. He was not a Mackenzie called Compton, but a Mackenzie called Mackenzie. In any case the famous novelist has more than adequately covered his own life story in his multi-volumed autobiography, which is so valuable a source of information about the life of the C.C.C. It is there that we read how three days after his mother was buried he was broadcasting, on Sunday, May 12, in *The School for Scandal*, delighted when Val Gielgud allowed him to double the roles of Charles Surface and Moses, moving from one microphone to another in the dialogue between them. When Sir Compton Mackenzie—he had been knighted in 1952—died in November, 1972, aged 89, even the Daily Telegraph made the common mistake about his name. The newspaper's 1,250-word obituary stated that he was born Edward Montague Compton and for the purpose of writing "assumed an old family name, Mackenzie." Sir Compton, who became a Companion of Literature in 1968, fought many battles for authors including one for the right to sell copyright to make a capital gain, which he himself wished to do. He lost this particular fight but the law was later amended. For the last years of his life he was almost blind and found it difficult to dictate the words he had found it so easy to write.

It was only by procuring his obituary in the New York Times that I found that Frank (Francis Sidney) Compton was born at Malvern. Following service in the 1914-18 War, to which I have already referred, he took up fruit-growing in Canada but within two years was back on the stage and over the years performed with many stars, though stardom eluded him, perhaps because he made a speciality of suave butlers. In summer stock in the mid-50s he played Caesar to Paulette Goddard's Cleopatra and other notable appearances included *Cyrano de Bergerac* with Jose Ferrer, *Othello* with Paul Robeson, playing Achille Weber, international financier in Robert E. Sherwood's first Pulitzer Prize play, *The Idiot's Delight,* and Mr. Justice Wainwright in *Witness for the Prosecution.* He also appeared in films and on television.

After the war his daughter Jean was with the Midlands Theatre Company at Coventry. In the 50s she contracted cancer and died towards the end of the decade while in her mid-40s. One of her last consolations, shortly before her death, was a farewell letter from the father she had not seen for nearly 30 years but to whom she was still greatly attached. For a long time she had not heard from him and it was Fay who was instrumental in persuading him to send a last message to his dying daughter. Arthur Howard never met his father-in-law until the year after his wife died, and even then it was a chance encounter, at a New York audition. "I went along as a spectator—everyone goes to auditions over there. I saw a man the other side of the room, walked up to him and said 'You must be Frank Compton'." Frank Compton died on September, 17, 1964, at St. Joseph's Hospital, Stamford, Connecticut, at the age of 79, after having been on the stage, with intervals, for nearly 60 years. His home was at Noroton Avenue, Noroton, Connecticut. The profession of acting has figured in the life of one of the four children of his second marriage. Mary Fay (named, of course, after her illustrious aunt) has returned to her earlier vocation as an actress in New York after a career in publishing and business; both Ian Compton Mackenzie and Edward M. C. Mackenzie, two of her brothers, are school teachers, the former in the U.S.A., the latter in a London primary school; while the fourth, Francis Colton Compton (he prefers the adopted surname) is also in teaching, being an English master in a large suburban school system in Chicago.

Most of this I heard in Arthur Howard's dressing room at the Strand Theatre, London, where he was playing in the "fifth hysterical year" of *No Sex Please, We're British,* which I had gone to see because its co-author, with Anthony Marriott, was my old friend and colleague, the late Alistair Foot, who died at the age of 40 during final rehearsals of the show which was to prove the smash hit he had longed for during his years as a journalist in Northampton. I dropped in unannounced at the stage door but in that friendly way which is a commonplace with theatre folk Arthur asked me in and not only proved most helpful then but later invited me to his flat at Finchley and gave me introductions which proved invaluable in completing this part of the book. Not only that, he actually subscribed to the book—while confessing to being virtually a non-reader! Arthur's own best-known role was as the bumbling Mr. Pettigrew in Jimmy Edward's television Whacko academy but his most interesting experience in the entertainment world was coaching Maurice Chevalier in English for the film The Blessing. His spell in the Strand success spanned three-and-a-half years, with a break, and ended in January, 1977.

Now I must invite readers to hark back to Cheltenham in 1936, to the child with Compton blood in his veins, the son born to Arthur and his wife Jean following their meeting in Ellen Compton's repertory company. For as I talked to his father in the Strand Theatre that "baby" was performing at the neighbouring Aldwych Theatre—as *Henry V* with the Royal Shakespeare Company. Apart from this surely being a unique father-and-son situation, to be playing in theatres only a few yards apart, it is ironic that Edward Compton's great-grandson has achieved the success in London, and indeed internationally, for which Edward yearned. Alan, who is today one of our best-known Shakespearian actors, played with his illustrious aunt, Fay, in Sir Laurence Olivier's first season at Chichester. After being in *Henry V* at the Aldwych, he went on tour to New York and Western Europe before returning to the Aldwych (his father was still in the farce next-door at the time) to forge an even more notable family link. When the Royal Shakespeare Company revived John O'Keeffe's *Wild Oats* on December 14, 1976, Alan was cast in the role played so many times on tour by his great-grandfather, Edward Compton. This play by the 18th century Irish dramatist concerns Rover, a wandering player who adopts a feigned identity to win the heart of a Quaker lady. First performed at Covent Garden in 1791 it was frequently revived in the 19th century with Charles Mathews, Charles Kean, Samuel Phelps and Charles Wyndham. This role of the wandering player was surely the most appropriate played by Edward Compton, for he was ever a Rover. But however well he played the part in the 1880s he was surely outshone in 1976 by his great grandson whose portrayal was thus praised by John Barber, critic of the Daily Telegraph: ". . . a central performance of dazzling virtuosity as the hero, a strolling player . . . capricious, ardent, with a swagger which never conceals his basic insecurity . . . a definitive portrait of the genus actor." To crown the achievement of Alan Mackenzie Howard there was the award about the same time of an "Actor of the Year" award by the Theatre Managers' Association for his Henry V. It was thus with an "Actor of the Year" that I drank champagne from a mug in the No. 1 dressing room of the Aldwych after the rapturous applause greeting the first night of *Wild Oats*.

It is nice to know that the Compton flag is still flying, although the name on it is now Howard. It is also nice to know that these family links are not forgotten: when Alan Howard and his journalist wife Sally had a son, born in November, 1974, they named him James Carlos Alexis Mackenzie. He is thus a Howard called Mackenzie.

What now survives of the Compton Comedy Company? What mark has it left? Precious little, it must be admitted. It made no great impact on artistic trends, set up no milestones on dramatic highways. But what it did over a period of 43 years may be counted equally as meritorious as the efforts of those who did do these things. It attracted as many people as possible to the scores of theatres which it visited and entertained them with worthwhile plays. To get the people into the theatre and actually entertain them is an objective so obvious yet often forgotten in the subsidised theatre of today.

Dramatic performances in the theatre are by their nature evanescent and it is difficult, if not impossible, to know just how good or bad the actors and actresses of the past were, by modern standards. In the future there will be films, both of the cinema and television, for reference, not to mention recordings of radio plays, to assist in evaluation but of the Compton Era nothing of this nature survives, apart from the early silent films of Fay Compton. All that we have are the reports in the Press and there are also a few prompt scripts in the possession of the London Theatre Museum, at present in the Victoria and Albert Museum and in the Library of London University. The plays covered at the Victoria and Albert are *The Poor Gentleman, Paul Pry, Fish Out Of Water, The Road to Ruin* and *The Way to get Married.* The copy of *The Poor Gentleman* is inscribed "Edward Compton's Comedy Company, arranged for representation in three acts by Edward Compton," but the date, May, 1877, pre-dates the company. Parts of the script are hand-written, the rest consisting of cuttings from the printed version. *The Road to Ruin* is dated April, 1881, and was evidently purchased when it was decided to introduce the play into the repertoire. Written in it is "Note for Bills—An Original Epilogue written by Mr. Edward Compton will be spoken by the characters."

The prompt script of Compton Mackenzie's *The Gentleman in Grey* is among a set of seven in the library of London University, which also includes *The Ninth Lancers* by Leicester Vernon and Edward Compton, Sheridan's *The Critic,* Planche's *The Loan of a Lover, The Desperate Lover* by Henry Alexander, C. Z. Barnett's adaptation of *A Christmas Carol,* and John O'Keeffe's *Wild Oats.*

For all but a tiny few, the C.C.C. is beyond the reach of memory. I was, for instance, six months old when its last performances were being given at Westcliff-on-Sea. One of my Patrons encountered the company and family at various stages of his life—the late Sir Gyles Isham, Bart, of Lamport Hall, who was among the faithful band of patrons who have supported me through all four books of the Northampton Theatre History series and who died shortly after subscribing to the present volume. He acted with the first company at the present Royal Shakespeare Theatre, Stratford-upon-Avon, when it was built after the fire at the old one; later he became a member of the Board of Governors and shortly before his death he told me: "The Compton Comedy Company visited Hastings when I was at school (so I didn't see them) and I remember my father telling me all about it. It must have been during the first War. Alderman Blackman, the Mayor, took the whole of the dress circle and invited prominent citizens to see *School for Scandal*." While still a schoolboy Sir Gyles saw Fay Compton three times in *Mary Rose* and also in *The Circle*—"She and Allan Quartermaine played the best love scene I have ever seen and they never even kissed!" Later Sir Gyles himself acted with Fay, at the Open Air Theatre, Regents Park, in *A Midsummer Night's Dream*. She played Titania while he was Theseus. "In 1935, armed with a letter from Fay I went to see her aunt, one of the famous Bateman sisters, who was living in Los Angeles. She had a wonderful collection of theatrical photographs. I wonder what happened to them." Sir Gyles also recalled the 75th anniversary night at the Northampton theatre in 1959: "Earl Spencer sat in a box that night and told me he remembered seeing Fay with her first husband, H. G. Pelissier, at the Follies. This was between August, 1911, and May, 1913, mainly at the Apollo, London. Pelissier died in 1913 and by all accounts was something of a genius."

Another Isham link with the story is that Miss Virginia Isham, Sir Gyles' sister, now of Mill Lane, Kingsthorpe, Northampton, was the very last person to speak lines on the stage of one of the theatres where the Compton Company played— the Gaiety Theatre, Hastings, built on the site of the stables of the Castle Hotel in 1882. This was just before its conversion to a cinema in 1932. It is now the Classic Cinema, part of the premises being let as a shop. She recalled: "It was a farewell programme made up by local amateur groups and societies some of whose members were ex-professionals. The proceeds went to a fund to benefit the manager, Mr. Charles E. Scute, whose wife Jessica Thorne also appeared in one of the short plays. She was an old 'pro' and was related to Sarah Thorne who in her day was a well-known actress-manageress. The little epilogue I spoke was written by a local lady."

So that is what happened to one of the theatres where Compton called. As there were about 150 of them it is clearly impracticable to describe here the fates of them all and I have therefore selected a few interesting ones, which may be typical.

First, what happened to the theatre where the C.C.C. itself began? The fate of the Pavilion Theatre, Southport, has been the same as that of Northampton's 19th century Theatre Royal in Marefair—a roadway runs straight through the site. Largely supplanted in 1891 by the Winter Gardens Opera House the Pavilion was converted in 1906 into a variety theatre called in turn the Albert Hall and the Empire. Under this title it became a cinema, later changing its name to the Scala. In 1933 the Winter Gardens were demolished including the Scala, and the Kingsway road now runs through the site. Meanwhile the Opera House to which the C.C.C. had moved burned down in 1929 but three years later the Garrick Theatre arose on the site, later to become a cinema and now the Lucky Seven Bingo Club. From 1953 to 1962 it was the home of Southport Repertory Company. The Winter Gardens is remembered today only in the names of the Winter Garden Terrace, off Duke Street, and of the Pavilion Buildings, an office block on Coronation Walk.

From the coastal town of Southport to a spa town far inland—Leamington, which had several theatres including one built by Mr. Simms in 1814 and an old chapel in Clemens Street but was then theatreless for some years until a company of which Lord Brooke, heir of the Earl of Warwick, was a director, opened a new one in October, 1882. Within six months its lessee Patrick Tempany was bankrupt and when the Company took over they followed him into liquidation in 1886, when the theatre was bought by its builder, Mr. John Fell, for £4,900 less than he had been paid for erecting it. Later lessees were Mr. William Bennett, of Coventry; Milton Bode and Edward Compton (about 1903-10); Messrs. Dottridge and Longden; Mr. Charles Watson Mill, who introduced repertory and who was behind the company which built the St. John's Theatre, Warwick. Following Mr. Mill's sudden death in a London Tube train in July, 1933, it became a cinema. In the early 1960s it turned briefly to bingo and is today used by a garage firm.

The theatre visited by Compton at Chester survives but in a different guise. The city has an exceptionally interesting theatre history dating from the 13th century when monks performed plays in the monastery of St. Werburgh and in front of the Abbey gateway. A restriction on theatre performances in Chester in 1616 was that plays should not be acted within the liberties of the city after six o'clock in the evening—which must have been a most effective dampener. A Royal Patent was granted in 1777. The Royalty Theatre, Chester, was originally a wooden building constructed in 1869 on the site of a former tannery. A new Royalty built by B. E. Entwistle, of Southport, was opened on April 3, 1882. Five years after Bode and Compton secured control in 1904 Bode purchased an adjoining site, formerly a carriage factory and stableyard, with the idea of erecting a 4,000-seat Hippodrome but was frustrated by opposition from publicans and clergy. Instead he opened a skating rink on the site, called the Grosvenor, which later became a garage. Bode parted with the theatre in 1932 and five years later plans were under consideration for reconstructing it. In fact this operation did not take place until 1957 when a lot of money was spent on virtually rebuilding the interior. In gutting it the old pillars were got rid of in favour of cantilevered circle and upper circle (former gallery). It was re-opened on July 8, 1957, but the brave speculation proved ill-timed and the metamorphosis lasted only until 1962 when plans were announced for turning it into a theatre club. This involved a false ceiling sealing off the so expensively reconstructed former gallery. The stage remained but the front rows of the stalls were removed and a dance floor constructed. The theatre licence was surrendered and after alterations costing £10,000 the premises reopened as a theatre club with meals and drinks served while cabaret took place on the stage and dancing on the small dance floor. It has since become the Celebrity Club featuring cabaret and discotecques. Nowadays Chester has a Repertory theatre, The Gateway, opened as a new building in Hamilton Place in November, 1968.

Some of the Scottish cities and towns provide absorbing examples of the various transformations and fates which awaited theatres on the Compton itinerary. The cases of Edinburgh and Glasgow are especially interesting. Retention as a civic theatre has been the destiny of the Royal Lyceum Theatre,

Edinburgh, which had been opened in September, 1883, by Mr. J. B. Howard, after he had that spring severed his connection with the city's Royal Theatre. In 1895 he joined with F. W. Wyndham, a founder member of the C.C.C., to form the company of Howard and Wyndham Ltd, which owned the theatre until it was taken over by Edinburgh Corporation in 1964. Meantime the theatre had been renovated and partly reconstructed in 1935 but in 1975 there were plans to redevelop (that means knock down) the theatre; on the site, together with adjacent land in Castle Terrace, a new house would have arisen, but in April, 1976, the District Recreation and Leisure Committee decided to dispose of the Castle Terrace plot and use the proceeds to "upgrade" the Lyceum and the Kings Theatre, also in civic ownership. At the same time the committee decided to express no interest in acquiring the former Playhouse Cinema as a third theatre. In these decisions current economies no doubt played a leading part. During 1977 the Royal Lyceum is to be closed for six months for the necessary "upgrading" to take place.

Edinburgh had also cherished hopes of possessing an Opera House costing £20 million. Government promises of support for Scottish Opera to carry out the scheme were withdrawn but help was subsequently given to the organisation's project to convert a Glasgow theatre—the Theatre Royal, Hope Street, another theatre where Compton played. Built in 1867 this theatre was burned down in 1879 and again in 1895, having been bought in July, 1888, by Howard and Wyndham. In October, 1956, they sold it to Scottish Television who, having built themselves new premises in 1974, sold the place to Scottish Opera for £300,000, so that this organisation is now the only opera company in the country outside London to have its own building. The idea was to recreate a Victorian theatre with coffee and gold decor and mahogany and brass rather than plastic and chrome. To foot the bill for the project the sum of £2m was required, a task which was set about not by professional fund-raisers but by a committee under the chairmanship of Mr. Gavin Boyd, who called on the expertise of business friends and the generosity of their firms, whose duty it was, he pointed out, to support the arts! This 38-strong committee included Sir Hugh Fraser, Lord Clydesmuir, Sir Robert Maclean, Sir John Muir and Lord Strathalmond. After they had raised £835,000 within 12 months the Government offered £1m and Glasgow Corporation provided a bridging loan of £500,000. Some gave in kind, the antique chandeliers being provided, for instance, by Rank Hovis Macdonald. Some are gambling as their way of helping—a pilot lottery scheme began in November, 1976, with monthly prize money of £1,490 and an anticipated monthly profit of £2,500. Announcing this the general administrator, Mr. Peter Hemmings, pointed out that Sydney Opera House was partly financed by a State-run lottery which had raised £62m. On the marketing side there was a cut-price offer of 10 seats for the price of seven. The house reopened in October, 1975.

A second Glasgow theatre in which the C.C.C. appeared represents another exciting survival—the former Royal Princess's Theatre is now the home of the Citizens Theatre, a company whose style and policy are claimed to be unique in Britain. Begun in October, 1943, in the city's Athenaeum Theatre, with James Bridie as its leading light, the company moved to the Princess's in September, 1945, the owner, Harry McKelvie having given a 10 year lease on generous terms.

At the end of that period the house was purchased by Glasgow Corporation and let to the company. There is not space here to elaborate on the theatre but indications of its unusual approach are the facts that all seats are the same price (50p) and all actors and actresses get the same salary. The audience is predominantly a young one. The building, which reaches its centenary in 1978, has deteriorated, however, and is due for demolition at a date yet to be fixed

Another former C.C.C. call in Glasgow was in Sauchiehall Street, at the Royalty Theatre, where they played early in the company life. Later known as the Lyric it was acquired by Howard and Wyndham in December, 1884, and continued as a theatre until 1914, latterly as the home of the Scottish Repertory Theatre Company. During the 1914-18 War it became a Y.M.C.A. Soldiers' and Sailors' Home and afterwards remained the property of the Y.M.C.A. Later it again came into dramatic use under the name of the Lyric. Destroyed by fire in 1953 it was, somewhat surprisingly rebuilt in 1956, to survive only three more years before being bought by Gula Kulumpong Rubber Estates Ltd who demolished it and built shops and offices on the site.

The stage of Scotland's oldest surviving theatre, which the C.C.C. visited in the third week of its life, in February, 1881, is now occupied by amateurs—the Theatre Royal, Shakespeare Street, Dumfries, now the home of the Guild of Players, founded in 1913. Dating from 1792 and renovated in 1876 to the designs of C. J. Phipps, the theatre closed in 1909 to re-emerge two years later as a film and variety house. Nine years after that it became a roller skating rink, the former pit serving as a basement. Subsequently it reverted to a picture house, the Electric Cinema, until 1954, when it stood empty for five years until being bought by the Guild whose reconstruction included a new stage. The organisation moved there from its Little Theatre in the same street, which it had acquired in 1943 but which had fallen under the shadow of redevelopment. Earlier the Guild had performed and met in a variety of premises, including a church hall, assembly rooms and the Y.M.C.A. and had also considered purchasing a church, the upper storey of an old mill, a synagogue, and a disused washhouse; it was indeed on the point of signing a contract for the last-named when members got wind of the chance of buying the old Theatre Royal.

Another of the former C.C.C. ports of call is now a cinema club. Opened in December, 1882, the Theatre Royal, Bournemouth, was "converted" into a Town Hall, according to Mr. Percy Newlyn, a former manager of the Bournemouth Winter Gardens, speaking in 1943: "The theatre was built by Mr. Harry Nash, a stationer, but the straight-laced town would not allow him to call it a theatre and it became the 'New Town Hall'. There was then much local prejudice against there being a theatre in the town." During part of the 1939-45 War the premises were used as a club for the Forces but were seriously damaged by fire in October, 1943. In 1949 William Hammer turned them into a theatre again but after his death in 1957 this was closed for two years and then reopened as an opera house by the Pearson Brothers. Three years later it was converted to a cinema, was then used for bingo and in July, 1971, opened as the Tatler Cinema Club. Along with the Grand Theatre, Boscombe, known from February, 1905, onwards as the Boscombe Hippodrome and run as a musichall, the theatre was among those operated by Frederick Mouillot who presented many shows at Northampton and who died in 1911, at the age of 47, after which his widow took charge.

Another "Compton" theatre has stood derelict for the past seven years, although its interior is "listed" as being of historical or architectural interest. This is the Sheffield Lyceum which opened as the City Theatre in 1893 and assumed its new name in 1898, when it was visited by the C.C.C. on its "pre-disbandment" tour. In June, 1920, the company paid its last visit to the city, just prior to the Nottingham repertory venture. The house closed in 1969. The other Sheffield theatre where the Comptons appeared, initially in their first year, was the Theatre Royal, Tudor Street, which was burned down in 1935.

A great many of the theatres visited by the company have been demolished, including the Theatre Royal, Huddersfield which Bode leased from 1900-18, being partnered by Compton from 1903 (1961), and the Kennington Theatre (1949, replaced by flats). After a loss-making period of municipal control, His Majesty's, Carlisle, is now in bingo occupation. Among those which survive in municipal control is the Spa Theatre, Scarborough, formerly owned by the Cliff Bridge Company and the Spa (Scarborough) Co. Ltd. The annual *Dazzle* summer show is now staged there.

Precisely how many of the theatres have survived as theatres I have not had the energy to discover. One is at Wolverhampton where in December, 1969, the Borough Council took over the Grand Theatre which Milton Bode operated for some years in partnership with E.H. Bull, former touring actor and manager of the D'Oyly Carte Opera Company. The council leased it to a non-profit making company and as well as plays, musicals, ballet, grand opera and pantomime, the theatre is used by the South Staffs Operatic Company and the Bilston Operatic Company. With theatres being pulled down (as at Northampton) and cinemas turning to bingo (as at Kettering and Wellingborough) amateur groups have often had problems resulting from the loss of their stages and difficulty of finding suitable alternatives.

At Yarmouth the C.C.C. played at both the Royal Aquarium and the Theatre Royal. The former survives, though as a twin cinema; the latter was demolished after a final performance in January, 1929, and replaced by a cinema. Still open is the Theatre Royal, Norwich, where there has been a theatre on the site since 1758, with rebuildings in 1862 and 1934, the latter following a fire, and further modifications in 1970.

The theatre in which Edward Compton made his personal debut in 1873 had a spectacular finale—the Princes Theatre, Bristol, was destroyed in the first blitz on the city on November 24, 1940. So did the Theatre Royal, Rochdale, where he made his last appearance—it went up in flames in November, 1954.

Before describing the tragedy I cannot forbear from injecting a note of irrelevant comedy, a funny page from the history of theatre in Rochdale. It happened in the former theatre in Toad Lane, which was on the site of a Methodist Chapel where John Wesley had preached and the well-known local evangelist had been one Dr. Banks, who was interred in the adjacent burial ground. Playing the gravedigger in *Hamlet* was a local low comedian called Dick Hoskins who took exception to the haughty attitude adopted by a visiting tragedian and resolved to take him down a peg. In the famous scene in which there is speculation upon the identity of a skull the low comedian inserted his own solution: "The skull, sir? This is Dr. Banks's skull." The house went into peals of laughter as the graveyard scene continued with the tragedian protesting that the skull was "Yorick's sir, Yorick's." Dick coolly picked up another skull: "This is Yorick's sir, but t'other's Dr. Banks's as I told you." The infuriated actor leaped into the grave and an unseemly fight took place from which Dick emerged the victor, one hand holding down the tragedian while the other held the skull aloft, as he triumphantly proclaimed: "Dr. Banks's skull!" As Vandenhoff recounts in his memoirs: "The curtain dropped, amidst roars and shrieks of laughter, in which king, queen, monk and courtiers, who had been sent on with Ophelia's empty coffin, were compelled to join, forming a tableau, which finished the play for that night." This theatre was pulled down in 1865 and replaced by a co operative store.

It was as the Prince of Wales that the Theatre Royal was built in Manchester Road in 1867 but it was destroyed by an earlier fire, in January, 1894. After the rebuilding and re-naming its staple diet was at first provided by touring companies but during the inter-war years it developed a policy of repertory in summer and variety in winter, with a month of pantomime at Christmas. With the outbreak of war in 1939 variety took precedence and continued until the 1950s when, in face of decreasing attendances, an effort was made to revive interest. In April, 1954, there began a flag-waving variety festival with such stars as Issy Bonn, Gladys Morgan, Jimmy Young, Beryl Ord and, during the week of disaster, Tessie O'Shea, Semprini and Arthur Haynes. At six o'clock on the morning of Wednesday, November 24, Fred Hargreaves, who kept the Theatre Hotel next door, was awakened by the sound of falling timber, looked out of the window of his bedroom and saw flames shooting out of the upper windows of the theatre. He gave the alarm and evacuated the hotel. By the time firemen broke down the doors most of the interior was an inferno and fire engines summoned from Oldham, Bury, Royton, Ashton and Middleton faced a hopeless task. A lot of the property owned by the artists was lost but not so a ukelele which had been given by Cliff Edwards (Ukelele Ike) to the second comedian, Billy Shakespeare; Billy dashed into the rear of the theatre to save the valued instrument and had to jump 15 feet from a window to escape. He told a reporter that the week's booking had been his first in three months. Northern Theatres Co. Ltd, who owned the theatre, had recently installed new electrical equipment costing £4,000 and new drapes costing £1,000. The total damage was estimated at £50,000. John Hindle, the manager, told the Press: "We were showing definite signs of a return to prosperity after struggling through a lean period and now all our hopes for the future have gone up in smoke. Thank God it didn't happen during a performance. It was so dry and warm inside that there would certainly have been a disaster." What had caused the fire remained a puzzle.

Within a few hours of the flames being damped down Gracie Fields, the celebrated popular singer and comedienne, was standing in what remained of the circle of the theatre where a month earlier she had introduced her husband, Boris Alperovici, to the people of Rochdale, at the time of the Mayor's Charity Ball. Boris came with her to see the ruins and as they stood there she told a reporter: "When I think of the lovely sight this beautiful intimate theatre presented a month ago it breaks my heart to see the shambles it is now." Gracie had driven over specially from an engagement at the Lily Mill, Shaw, then operated by the ill-fated Cyril Lord carpet concern. The bills for that final week, advertising Tessie O'Shea and Semprini, fluttered on the shell of the building until it was demolished to make way for new police headquarters.

Rochdale also had the Hippodrome built in 1908, replacing on the same Newgate site the largely wooden Circus and Hippodrome, known locally as "Th'owd Circus", erected by an acrobat named Ohmy in 1882, and the place where Gracie Fields, a native of Rochdale, first appeared on the stage in 1905, at the age of seven, when she won 10s in a singing contest. She also appeared at the new Hippodrome where her mother was a stage cleaner and washed clothes for the artists. Another "local" who appeared there was G. H. Elliott, later famous as the Chocolate Coloured Coon. Subsequently the Hippodrome also showed silent films and I cannot resist the story concerning a musician in the orchestra which accompanied them. He was a trombonist named Greenwood who was on hand when a man with a horse-drawn van delivered items for the film Ben Hur, including the music parts. "You'll never play this—it's too difficult," he jokingly told Mr. Greenwood, who replied "We can play owt that thy horse can pull."

In 1930 came the "talkies" and in January, 1931, the first of the Gracie Fields Variety Weeks in aid of local charities, for which the comedienne gave her services. After closing as a cinema in 1957 the Hippodrome was acquired by Rochdale Corporation for a new but short lease of life during which it became the home for many of Rochdale's amateur actors and societies, the last stage show being given at the end of 1969—*Patience* by Kirholt Gilbert and Sullivan Society. There was also bingo, which was played on the very last night, February 28, 1970. A week after the last "House" the demolition men moved in and today the Crown Offices occupy the site.   This leaves Rochdale with the Curtain Theatre, an amateur establishment begun in 1925 which operates for six months of the year.

Unlike Rochdale, the other two of the last three theatres where Compton appeared still survive though not as theatres. The Theatre Royal, Halifax, where he appeared in the penultimate week of March, 1915, was one of the oldest legitimate theatres in Yorkshire, having been opened in 1790, but had been completely rebuilt in 1905. It was converted to a cinema in 1933 and became a bingo hall in 1966. Of 1889 vintage, the Theatre Royal, Bury, where Compton played from Monday to Wednesday of the final week, was also converted to a cinema in 1933, as the Royal, and remains as such though under other names, the Essoldo (1971) and Classic (1972).

If the shades of Viola and Ellen Compton hie themselves to Nottingham to have a final look at the theatre where their repertory venture came to a sticky end in 1923 they will find an empty site. Nothing has been built there since the Grand Cinema, which it had become, was demolished in 1964, eight years after the last films were shown, following 30 years as a cinema.

At the Palace, Westcliff-on-Sea, where the company took its very last bow in November, 1924, on the other hand the theatre is still a going concern. It is unusual, if not unique, among houses visited by Compton in being purpose-built as a cinema and theatre. It was opened in Leigh Road in October, 1912, by the Raymond Animated Picture Company, whose proprietor, Mr. Matt Raymond, owned several halls in London. According to the Southend and Westcliff Graphic, the object at his 1500-seater three-tier New Palace Theatre was to "include the best bioscopic pictures, coupled with a high class variety entertainment, in sumptuous and luxurious surroundings." The name of the street in which it is situated was changed to London Road in 1914.

And what happened to the modest theatre at Gainsborough where the C.C.C. was re-born in 1918? Its fate seems a little uncertain. My correspondent there reports: "By 1925 it was being used almost exclusively as a cinema but was gutted by fire in January, 1927. When it reopened the following September it was used mainly as a cinema but visiting companies and a number of repertory companies provided occasional live entertainment until after the second World War. I have been unable to verify the date of the theatre's closing and demolition; I do not believe the building still stands."

At Crewe the new theatre inaugurated by the C.C.C. in 1911 kept going through the first war and into the second but then faded away. In 1946 it revived, weakly, with touring repertory which did not pay. Later came the familiar recipe of striptease, wrestling and the universal bingo, with the occasional amateur show, the Crewe Corporation meantime, in 1955, buying the premises for £15,000 and spending £10,000 on re-equipping them. Some touring shows were booked but generally the local attitude was that it was a municipal white elephant. That jaundiced outlook continued at first when, in 1964, the Crewe Theatre Trust was formed with Arts Council and Corporation support and with the then Mayor Councillor James Golding as chairman and with leading parts being played by the Town Clerk, Borough Surveyor and the Old Students Operatic Society. Julian Oldfield, the first artistic director, recalled: "It was not just passive disinterest we had to contend with. People were actively hostile. I had no staff, no actors and hardly any stage equipment . . . the whole thing had to be built up from scratch." I cannot applaud too highly the sentiment then expressed by Mr. Oldfield, defining his policy: "To offer worthwhile entertainment to as large a proportion of local people as possible." In April, 1968, he left to face new challenges as the first director of Chester's new Gateway Theatre, being succeeded at Crewe by his associate director Ted Craig, who was followed in 1973 by Charles Savage and in 1976 by David Sumner. The present assistant manager, Chrissie Borrett Sykes, reports: "The theatre is open from September to May with a season of repertory plays and during the summer months various other events take place within the building, including beauty contests, dancing school productions, and amateur shows. There are also Sunday night concerts varying from orchestral to country and western music, from TV stars in variety shows to international singing stars. The theatre is certainly managing to keep its head above water, in spite of the economic situation.' Thus, with very varied fare, the second theatre launched by the C.C.C. is also alive today.

Finally, to the theatre which is the subject of the rest of this book, the Northampton Theatre Royal and Opera House, known since 1927 as Northampton Repertory Theatre. Not only does it still stand but, despite the fire of 1887 the building is today very much the same as it was on May 5, 1884, when Edward Compton stood on its stage as Malvolio, on the very first night. At the time of writing it has just passed (though through somewhat troubled waters) a golden jubilee (of repertory) in January, 1977, and can now look forward to a centenary (of the building) in May, 1984.

Though he would be surprised to encounter a 15-strong Board of Management in the manager's office, would be quite unfamiliar with such bodies as Arts Councils and Associations, and entirely puzzled by the subsidised theatre world of today, Edward Compton would be pleased to know that the theatre which he inaugurated and later partly owned was still struggling to keep flying the flag of English comedy, old and new, as well as tragedies, romances, farces, documentaries, musicals etc. etc., although he might not approve of one or two of the modern plays with words in their prompt scripts which Edward would not, I feel sure, have uttered to his wife in private, let alone before the world and his wife, on the public stage. Moving with the times was not Edward's way of life.

With a final salute to him and his Compton Comedy Company it is now time to drop the curtain on the Interlude and get on with Act III of the main production.

The very last play performed by the Compton Comedy Company, in November, 1924, was Compton Mackenzie's *The Passionate Elopement,* at the Palace Theatre, Westcliff-on-Sea. The company that final week included Nell Compton, Ernest Cox, Oswald Lingard, Ethel Arden, Clement Hamelin, Marjorie Raeburn, Fred Piper, Buchanan Wake, Leslie Kyle, Elinor Blomfield, Carleton-Crowe and Adam Brown.

Edward Compton.

April /81.

—in his prompt script of *The Road to Ruin.*

Virginia Compton

—in the Minute Book of the Theatre Girls Club, London, in 1936.

ACT THREE

UNLIKELY PARTNERS?

Milton Bode and Edward Compton. Unlikely partners, per-haps. Compton Mackenzie could never understand what his father could see in the hard-headed man of theatre business. For his part Bode probably hoped to gain lustre from the association with the "eminent comedian." In any case, they ran the Northampton and other theatres together for 15 years. After Compton's death in 1918, and wartime prosperity, came the Trying Twenties and eventually a sell-out to the opposition. . . .

244

The 1920's Account Book which was
used as a prop in the 1940's. Right and
below the advertisement and accounts
of one show it covered.

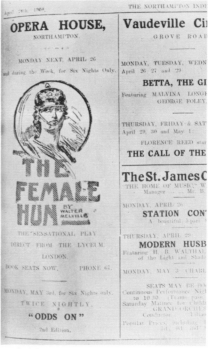

23 Mr Walter Melville's "The Female Hun" Co								
1920		Tax		Bt forward		8976	3	1
apl 26		5 8 10			23 3 6			
27		7 7 5			33 9 7			
28		8 11 1.			39 2 4			
29		9 0 7			42 19 3			
30		6 5 11			28 6 11			
May 1		14 11 11			75 6 2			
	Tax £ 51 5 9	Gross receipts	242 7 9					
apl 30 per cheque £ 70-0-0		5% of over 300	Coy share @ 50%	121 3 10				
may 1st -	£ 51-3-10		Theatre share	121 3 11	121 3 11			

Scene One: 1903-26

MELODRAMA, VARIETY, WAR-TIME PROSPERITY, THEN BLEAK TWENTIES

The new management taking over Northampton Opera House in 1903 was another partnership, consisting of Milton Bode and Edward Compton, the actor-manager whose company had opened the theatre 19 years earlier.

Compared with what had gone before Bode represented big business in the world of provincial theatre. He was not an auctioneer, a hotel owner nor yet a brewer, but was a man of the theatre; yet he was probably more of the hard-headed man of business than his predecessors who were in those categories. Nor was he the type of man to be content with a single theatre, nor yet a couple of them. He was ambitious, systematic, calculating and perhaps even ruthless.

Bode was clearly disliked by Compton Mackenzie, son of his partner Edward Compton, despite the fact that Bode gave the youngster an occasional guinea. The Mackenzie who was destined to be a world-famous novelist and who simply detested acting as a means of livelihood could not understand what his father could see in Bode.

At Northampton Bode made his money-conscious, no-nonsense, approach felt very quickly. Perhaps pinch-beck or short-sighted might be more appropriate terms for his attitude on the subject of those bills which people in public houses and shops display free in return for free admission to the theatre. With an announcement that the Free List was permanently suspended he got the backs up of members of Northamptonshire Licensed Trades Association. Debating the matter at a meeting at the King William IV public house in Augustine Street, they heard that Bode had replied to their protests by declining to enter into a correspondence, observing that if they accepted his ruling of one ticket a month everything would be all right.

At the same time the association had asked the manager of the Palace of Varieties, Gold Street, what his position was. Mr. Kemble told them that he had no changes in mind. The L.T.A. recommended members not to exhibit Opera House bills unless Bode changed his tune. The incident can scarcely have brightened the image of the new regime.

Another change was the introduction for the first time of half-price admission. Half-price tickets at 9 o'clock or 9.15 may have made some sort of sense half-a-century earlier when the evening might consist of at least two major plays or farces and sometimes three, with songs and dances in between. Someone arriving at 9 would then be in time to see at least one complete piece and perhaps hear a song or two, but it appeared to be nonsensical when people were admitted half or two-thirds of the way through a single play. Furthermore it was no compliment to the entertainment or the entertainers, nor yet to the audience who had been there from the start. The tendency would be for a noisy drunken rabble to spoil the pleasure of those who were already there and immersed in the thread of whatever plot the piece may have had. But it meant picking up a few extra coppers and that suited Milton Bode.

Born in Birmingham on January 7, 1860, and christened William Ernest he was educated at Birmingham Grammar School. His early appearances as an actor included at least one in London, at the Adelphi Theatre, and his first effort at organising a tour was of *Monte Cristo* or *Dantes the Magnificent* and *The Masher's Holiday* which opened at Taunton, Somerset, in July, 1886. Other shows which he toured, most of which came to Northampton either before or during his regime here, included *A Chinese Honeymoon, Liberty Hall, Tommy Atkins, The Belle of Mayfair, Woman and Wine, The French Maid, The English Daisy, The Best of Friends, The French Mistress,* and *Gentleman Joe.* Some of these were written especially for him, the last two being commissioned from Basil Hood and Walter Slaughter.

Every theatrical producer putting out so many shows must make the occasional error of judgment and one of Bode's was in believing that the great musichall comedian Dan Leno could be disciplined into star material for comedy drama. This was not the case and *Orlando Dando,* the chosen vehicle, was not a success. Leno, who had also appeared for Bode in *In Gay Piccadilly* and *Mr. Wix of Wickham,* suffered from mental trouble and died a few years after these experiments.

Bode's most successful speculation, as it was also for his partners in it, Robert Courtneidge (father of Cecily Courtneidge) and Edward Compton, was *The Arcadians.* It was one of the most profitable musical comedies of all time and toured many countries.

Pantomime, a fairly sure money-spinner whatever theatrical fortunes had been the rest of the year, was a Bode speciality and he produced over 100. In 1899, for instance, he had five of them out at once, at Salford, Glasgow, Cardiff, Exeter and Clapham. Nor were these restricted to a strictly seasonal production in one town or city, starting on Boxing Day. After a run of a week or two they would move on elsewhere to a town which had either had one pantomime already or where a musical comedy, play or even grand opera had been the post-Christmas fare. A town might thus get two or even three pantomimes, or if only a single one, it might turn up in mid-February.

The Royal County Theatre, at Reading, which was to become the centre of his operations was among his early theatre acquisitions. He became lessee and manager in 1897, taking over from Ormsby Trench who had converted it from a chapel and assembly room. The conversion had been timely because the Princes Theatre in the town had been struck by lightning and destroyed in September, 1894. Bode's successful policies at the Royal County Theatre meant that it could operate on a year-round basis.

It appears to have been in 1897 that Bode persuaded Compton to become his partner but it cannot have been long after the Compton Comedy Company's "final and farewell season" ending in Manchester in 1898 before Compton regretted taking the step: things did not go well at first and after a year he was back on the road with a reformed company.

Bode had first made his headquarters at the Dalston Theatre, which the pair had built and it was the lack of success there which forced Compton to return to touring. Bode then moved to Reading, appointing Mr. William Ritchie King to be his manager at Dalston. Compton did not become co-proprietor of the Reading theatre until 1911.

At the time that he took on Northampton, Bode ended a partnership with Stewart McKim at Her Majesty's Theatre, Carlisle, which the two had run since 1895. The following year McKim died and the theatre was burned down. When it was rebuilt it was run by McKim's widow and Thomas Courtice, who had managed it for Bode and McKim from 1900-2. After television had delivered its body blow to the live stage it was taken over by Carlisle Corporation in August, 1960, and lost £30,000 before closing in January, 1963.

At various times Bode controlled the Kennington Theatre; the Grand at Wolverhampton; both the Theatre Royal and Opera House at Leicester; the Theatre Royal, Birmingham; the Royalty, Chester; the Theatre Royal, Leamington; the Theatre Royal, Huddersfield; and he had an interest in the Savoy Theatre, London.

Milton Bode moved his managers around like chessmen. Gone were the days of long term stability. There were some colourful characters among his pawns, perhaps the most interesting being his inaugural manager at Northampton, Mr. W. J. Andrews. In turn he had been actor, sculptor, magician, journalist and theatre manager. His first stage appearance was as one of the schoolboys in Wilson Barrett's original production of *The Silver King*. Then after being apprenticed for some years to a French sculptor he became assistant to various men of magic, including Victor Andre, The Great Hermann, The Great Keller and The White Mahatma. Following a tour of the United States he settled into management at the Grand Opera House, Nashville, Tennessee, and the Eden Musee, where vaudeville shows were presented at the New York Madame Tussaud's.

The first production of the new era, which began on July 20, 1903, was the seventh visit to the theatre of the W. W. Kelly Company in *A Royal Divorce*. The Daily Chronicle described it as "opening a new chapter in its more or less chequered career," and noted two other changes in the theatre's procedure— "the patron who had not booked his seat before the theatre opened had to be content with any seat that was not reserved" while the dress circle patrons now had to submit to having pass-out checks.

Pantomime did not occupy the boards that Christmas; instead it was the 70-strong Moody-Manners Opera Company who invited the audience to fill in ballot papers to select the pieces to be performed. Later, however, there were two pantomimes, *Cinderella*, which had been at Hull and Huddersfield, and *Aladdin*.

The first year of the Bode regime at Northampton was summed up in a criticism of *A Path of Thorns* in September, 1904: "An exceptionally strong gathering of drama lovers spent an evening very much after its own heart; showing not the faintest trace of satiation by an almost record season of melodrama, pit and gallery were soon in the alluring net which Messrs. Arthur Shirley and Sutton Vane have once again cast." Bode was applying the maxim he had learned at some cost in his joint venture with Compton at Dalston—give 'em melodrama: it cannot fail. Other pot-boilers that year were *Home Sweet Home, Called Back, City of Sin, The Altar of Friendship, Because I Love You, A Woman of Pleasure, Why Woman Sins, Bound to Win, That Woman From France, Alone in London, Second Time on Earth, The Terror of Paris, A Life's Revenge, The Power of Gold.*

There was some relief. J. M. Barrie's *Quality Street* was presented the Press commenting that it was a long time since a work of this character had been given at the Opera House. Pinero's *The Second Mrs. Tanqueray* was produced on the Friday night of the week of *The Altar of Friendship* (and was repeated on the Saturday "by special request"). Charles Frohman's Company brought back *Sherlock Holmes,* with H. A. Saintsbury in the title role. Edmund Lockwood again presented *La Poupée* and George Dance showed off *The Girl From Kays.* Tolstoy's *Resurrection* was given by a Mouillot Company, by arrangement with Beerbohm Tree, while Tree's own company, including Miss Essex Dane, staged Hall Caine's *The Eternal City,* which cast Pope Pius XII as the reputed father of a lost child.

In March, 1904, *The Blue Moon* was given its first production prior to being staged in London, Robert Courtneidge saying a few words on the first night. He was presenting the show jointly with Arthur Hart and J. A. E. Malone.

In October, 1904, there was some gimmickry for *Sunday,* a musical play so called because one of the characters was born on Sunday. Samples of a perfume called Sunday were given to ladies purchasing programmes, along with copies of a piece of music of the same name.

At the close of the year a newspaper comment was that the theatre had perhaps been the worst sufferer from the trade depression which had held the town in its unrestrained grip for most of the year.

Miss Mackenzie (Viola Compton) appeared with the Compton Comedy Company in January, 1905—the first month of the year became a regular port of call at Northampton for them. On this visit they included two new pieces, *A Reformed Rake* and *Tomorrow.*

During the following months there is an absence of consistent advertising and editorial coverage and it seems that Bode or his manager had fallen out with the Press or else he had had an economy drive to meet "the times". Regular advertising recommenced in August, 1906.

Fred Karno's Company made several visits, the one in May, 1905, being of *Saturday to Monday* which was in three parts, *The Wedding, The Departure* and *The Honeymoon.* Fred Kitchen was the bridegroom.

Pastoral competition appeared in June with the Hannan-Clark and Philip Sanders Company performing in the open air at St. Andrew's Hospital. Sanders was the son of Canon Sanders, former headmaster of Northampton Grammar School.

In August, 1905, the Northampton Independent, which had just begun publication as an illustrated weekly paper, announced that Mr. J. Hutchinson "who for several years twirled the baton at the Opera House" had been appointed musical director at the Alexander Theatre, Stoke Newington.

At the Palace of Varieties Fred H. Anderson, the proprietor, was at least putting up an appearance of prosperity. There are reports of his being prosecuted for furious driving in his large motor car and of going off for holidays in his boat. In October, 1905, he opened another musichall, the Empire Palace of

Varieties at Dudley.

There was some unusual competition for the Opera House in April, 1906, when the former public hangman, James Berry, conducted a week's mission at St. Michael's Road Baptist Union Church. He was also an ex-publican and confessed to having been his own best customer.

The following autumn Mr. Harry Esden took over the management of the Opera House, on the 10th anniversary of appearing there in *The World,* and at Christmas he invited the children of Northampton Workhouse to a pantomime performance: some 120 crippled children were also there as the guests of Mrs. Ratliffe. Esden left the Opera House in July, 1906, and a year later became the first manager of the new Empire Theatre of Varieties, Sunderland, said to be the largest musichall in the country. At Northampton a new manager was not appointed immediately, the duties being taken over temporarily by Mr. Reginald Taylor, Milton Bode's general manager, who was described in the Press as "one of the smartest young men in the business." When the new manager was appointed a few weeks later he turned out to be another of Bode's right-hand men, Mr. Frank Seddon, who had at one time managed touring companies for Henry Dundas and Haldane Crichton but who had for the past 12 years been with Bode, with special responsibility for music. Among Bode's empire of 10 theatres Mr. Seddon had in his charge eight musical comedies and six pantomimes—they also toured in other theatres, of course. The following December Mr. Seddon went to Cardiff for 10 weeks to be producer and musical conductor of *Red Riding Hood* for which he had written the music—as indeed he did for all the Bode pantomimes. The Northampton management was meantime in the hands of Mr. Charles Herrman.

As I have mentioned before, Northampton had for many years an Official Receiver who was also a writer for the stage as well as being "a masterly Shylock". His official name was Alfred Ewens but for the stage he had the alias of Alfred England. He had provided the book for *The Swineherd and The Princess* which had been staged at the Royalty Theatre, London, in 1901, for which the music was by Carl St. Amory, of Jesus College, Oxford, former president and stage manager of the Oxford University Dramatic Society. Now the pair collaborated again for *The Silver Stick,* the piece which Northampton Amateur Operatic Company selected for their comeback in December, 1906. The comparative financial failure of *The Mikado,* staged by the two reconciled companies in 1903 had led to a gap in productions and the company's future now rested, it was stated, upon the response to *The Silver Stick.* The script had received the approval of the Lord Chamberlain (Viscount Althorp, of Althorp, Northamptonshire) shortly before the production. The title was the name of a decayed Elizabethan mansion in Cornwall, now used as an inn. A witch among the cast was played by Mrs. Compton James (nee Darnell). Dresses for the show were made in a local pinafore factory in Talbot Road. First there was a copyright performance, for which the proprietors gave the free use of the theatre. Such performances were then necessary to safeguard the authors' rights and tickets were priced at a guinea. Compton James himself appeared as a thieving lawyer who became a Mayor. Harvey Reeves, who was in real life to be Mayor of Northampton on two occasions, played a broken down tragedian. The Independent reported that the show "did not flourish as had been hoped" but nevertheless it did make £70 which was divided between the Good Samaritans and Police charities and the show was repeated the following Easter, "smartened up with new songs and dances."

Edward Terry visited the Opera House in October, 1906, in *Liberty Hall, The Magistrate* and *Sweet Lavender*.

At this time the Independent commented that "some ancient memories are revived by the news that Minnie Palmer is still touring in *My Sweetheart*. It will be the farewell week at Camden next week. She has played the part 4,000 times."

Pinero's *His House in Order* was brought to Northampton by the company of George Alexander, of the St. James Theatre, London, with Dorothy Grimston, daughter of Mr. and Mrs. Kendal, among the cast. Another February attraction was George Warren's adaptation of Edgar Wallace's *The Four Just Men,* given by the J. Bannister Howard Company.

Madame Jane Hading's flying visit for one matinee on June 4, 1907, was announced as a great attraction. She appeared in *Frou Frou* with her own company "direct from the Gaiety Theatre, Paris," seat prices being increased. What announcements failed to inform the public was that the show was in French. It was indeed and the gods did not take to it at all well, venting their displeasure at the constant flow of the alien tongue. They were relieved only when she sat down at the piano but the titters re-started with the French. When she began the death scene Madame Hading looked appealingly at the upper echelons as if to ask "Please let me die in peace!" but they did not. One wag commented: "She's gone right enough this time." Her costumes, said the Independent, must have been a source of admiration to the ladies in the audience, who were left in no doubt as to her dressmaker and milliner. Indeed the programme was more like a trade catalogue, said the jaundiced critic. One suspects that he wrote about her dresses because he could not comment seriously on the play. In those days entrants to journalism were not obliged to have scholastic qualification, such as French. He restricted himself to saying that the play was old-fashioned. In May, 1909, Madame Hading again met scant support when she returned with *Avenuriere*.

More comprehensible stars followed in 1907. Seymour Hicks and Zena Dare were among them, a fortnight later, with a one-night only performance of *Scrooge, Papa's Wife* and *You And I*.

Another show of local manufacture was *The Lady's Maid* by Ernest Sykes, of Northampton. Besides appearing in his home town it was produced at Bury and at the Grand Pavilion, Ventnor, Isle of Wight.

August, 1907, brought Hall Caine's *The Manxman,* dramatised by the late Wilson Barrett and that month the architect-actor Fred Dorman was seen with Poole's Myriorama at the Temperance Hall. By then he appeared to have quit the stage as a full time profession and instead of building castles in the air on the stage was to design more permanent buildings to be added to the Northampton scene, including the Pearl Assurance offices in The Drapery, Creaton Hospital, and extensions to Northampton General Hospital. At the time of his death in 1926, at the age of 61, he was preparing plans for a new operating theatre at the latter, together with a nurses' home.

The Gentleman in Grey by Montague Compton (Compton Mackenzie) was included in the Compton Comedy Company's week in January, 1908, and at the close Edward Compton said that it was usual to say something in eulogy of a new piece but as he was the father of the author he was in a delicate position.

Later in 1908 came return visits by *The Blue Moon, The Hypocrites* and *The Dairy-maids. The Merry Widow,* which had at last brought a change in the fortunes of George Edwardes, came for the first time in March with Louie Pounds in the title role.

Ellaline Terriss and Ellen Terry were two of the year's notable visitors, Miss Terriss being in a matinee of *Sweet and Twenty* in May and Ellen Terry appearing with her husband, J. L. Carew in *Captain Brassbound's Conversion* and *The Private Secretary,* for three days each in October. The Independent could make little of the Shaw play and commented that without Ellen Terry's fascinating personality it would have been a weary night. Now ageing, despite her continuing vivacity, she was paying her first acting visit to Northampton. The "picturesque attire" she wore in *Captain Brassbound's Conversion* had been designed by her daughter. Nearly four years later, in January, 1912, she gave a recital at the Town Hall which had been designed by Godwin, father of her children. She told a reporter: "He was in advance of his time, just as I am three generations back." Her final words concerned the Town Hall: "Don't ever allow your beautiful Town Hall to be altered." She also visited Oundle School to give a Shakespearean recital to pupils.

After serving the theatre for nearly a quarter-of-a-century Ernest Howard left the paintshop in Swan Street during 1908, moving to London. A statement in the Northampton Independent that he was born at Chesham, Bucks, a "nephew of the famous Dr. Benjamin Howard," naturally led me to inquire at Chesham after the famous man but I found no knowledge of his existence— Such is the transience of fame! From Northampton Howard had painted the scenery for many touring shows including three which had been premiered here, *The Lady Slavey, The Gay Parisienne,* and *In the Soup,* as well as *A Night Out, The New Clown, The J.P., Two Little Vagabonds, Alone in London* and *A Chinese Honeymoon.* He had painted the scenery for the London Hippodrome and the Act Drop for Sir Edward Moss's New Palace at Edinburgh.

In July, 1908, the death occurred of the founder of the Opera House. John Campbell Franklin had failed to survive an operation. The obituary stated that he had interests at Leamington and in the Channel Islands.

Three months earlier there had been a change of which he surely did not approve, assuming that it came to his notice. This was the introduction at the Opera House of twice-nightly variety. Such a move was usually a sure sign that the theatre was not prospering. The season began at Easter, with prices of seats reduced to 3d. to 2s. Smoking was allowed during the variety period. In 1913 Pinero, the playwright, expressed the belief that if smoking was allowed in theatres the failure of many would be turned to success! The same year a correspondent in the Northampton Daily Chronicle suggested "smoking only" compartments in cinemas!: "I must confess that I am surprised that smoking is allowed in the picture house when so many young people are present. If smoking is allowed why not permit it only in a separate compartment?"

Variety seasons were operated from 1908 to 1912. Writing in a Repertory Theatre programme in 1935 George M. Weldren recalled the episode: "Poor presentments of vaudeville were given week after week. Variety always seemed out of place and what novelty existed soon faded away and so did the box office receipts. County patrons abruptly ceased their visits and many of them never returned."

Ernie Leno, son of Dan Leno, was in a typical variety bill in April, 1911, appearing alongside the Lukushimas, Japanese entertainers; Colbert, with clubs and hoops; Harry Kirk, comedian; the Sisters Draycott, with harmony gems; Walter Barrett, vocalist; Les Narsumas, comedians on wheels; Carl and Carr, comedians; and "Premier Imperial Pictures as usual." Yes, the Opera House did borrow from the film competition at this time.

Just before the variety season of 1912 the experiment of twice-nightly plays was tried for the first time. Under the direction of the author the first twice-nightly choice was Herbert Darnley's *What Should A Woman Do,* presented at 7 and 9 at "popular prices"—the same as for variety. The Mercury noted that the play was truncated into the time available by greatly curtailing the usual intervals. This was the very point against which some actors rebelled. Taking the chair at an anti-twice-nightly meeting at the Chandos Hall, London, in 1914, Clarence Derwent described the innovation as an abomination—destructive to health and productive of nothing else but irritation, friction and discord between artists and manager. Referring to the musichall dictum of No Play, No Pay, he suggested a new one, Double Play, Double Pay. Henry Bedford said that in twice-nightly what was curtailed was the actor's rest between the Acts. It was decided to form an Actors Pay-for-Play League.

In September, 1912, actors in London had revolted against a surprising suggestion that theatres should open on Sundays (surely it would have been illegal?). It had been pointed out that in London the previous year picture houses had taken £120,000 on Sunday nights. The protest meeting was arranged by the Actors' Union and took place at Her Majesty's Theatre.

The actual 1912 variety season at the Northampton Opera House was also interrupted by a number of twice-nightly plays, Mark Blow's Company appearing in *At Cripple Creek, Under Two Flags, The Luck of Roaring Camp, From Slave to Princess* and *A Sailor's Sweetheart.* The Daily Chronicle said that although *At Cripple Creek* lasted only one-and-three-quarter hours it was crowded with as many thrilling incidents as one usually got in three hours. Later in the year a once-nightly *The Bad Girl of the Family* was said to have "piled sensation upon sensation in four acts and 18 scenes—as much excitement as would serve for three plays in the ordinary course of things."

This vaudeville season of 1912 was to be the last. What put a stop to variety down Guildhall Road was the opening in Abington Street of the New Theatre. What a whirlwind this must have seemed on the Guildhall Road horizon when the plans first came to light!

Soon after the announcement of the rival project Milton Bode and Edward Compton proclaimed their intention to build a musichall of their own in Northampton. The Opera House would confine itself to opera and drama while the new theatre, for which they were said to have acquired a site in St. Giles Street, would accommodate variety. In fact the scheme came to nothing and whether it represented a serious intention or merely an alarmed reaction one can only guess. But Edward Compton felt that the matter was sufficiently important for him to go along personally to the meeting at which Northampton Town Council discussed whether it should grant a stage play licence to the Abington Street theatre; and he offered to drop the variety seasons at the Opera House if the "New" did not receive its licence to compete in the field of drama. He said that while the Opera House did not "seek an immemorial monopoly" it would be impossible to run two theatres with success. From his point of view the offer was a sensible compromise because, owing to its limited seating capacity compared with the New Theatre, the Opera House could scarcely hope to compete in booking first-rate variety artists.

Local temperance interests also fought the New Theatre's application for a stage play licence, not primarily because they were against plays but because such a licence was normally accompanied by drinking facilities. In fact the New Theatre did not receive a stage play licence for some years but after 1912 there was no more variety at the Opera House.

Changing attitudes towards the world of musichall and variety were reflected a few months before the opening of the New Theatre by the attendance of the King and Queen at the Palace Theatre, London, on June 10, 1912, for a special performance to which leading artists of the vaudeville stage had been asked to contribute. It was in fact the first Royal Command performance of this character. The King had intended to honour the Empire Palace at Edinburgh but it had been burned down.

The week that the New Theatre opened, from Monday, December 9, 1912, the play at the Opera House was Pinero's *His House in Order* which was described as "the play of the year" and seemed fated to mark turning points in the theatre history of Northampton—it was the first play to be presented by the newly-formed Repertory Players in 1927. The New Theatre's musical director, Albert Heyes, had transferred from the Opera House.

The New Theatre was in fact one of the last musichalls to be erected. The month before it opened there died the great pioneer of the commercial music-hall, Sir Edward Moss, who had revolutionised the scene by organising the cir-cuit system and building theatres in many towns.

When the New Theatre opened the rival Palace of Varieties immediately succumbed and became The Picture House, opening on Boxing Day, 1912. Its manager was Graham Morrison, a former business manager of the Compton Comedy Company. It was a short-lived venture and when it was wound up six months later it was revealed that its operators, the European Cinema Co. Ltd., had agreed to buy the premises for £12,500. Gross profits had been £109 but the net loss was £285. Failure was attributed to trying to run it in too high-class a manner. This referred to attempts to attract custom by offering books of 25 one-shilling tickets for £1; offering the use of the cinema as a collecting point for letters; storing prams and cycles without charge; and offering free local tele-phone calls for patrons.

But The Picture House was an exception in its failure. The competition with the Opera House had really been hotting up. By 1910 the Country Electric Pavilion picture house was open in Gold Street, at the top and on the opposite side to the Palace of Varieties (Picture House). In 1909 Grapho and Jackson had begun their pierrot entertainments by Abington Park Gate.

The gramophone was another competitor and not only in the domestic sphere. In July, 1908, 3,000 people went to an open air gramophone concert in

Abington Park, Northampton, and many sat in a heavy downpour to listen to music from gramophones "specially adapted for open air concerts", provided by Abels, the old-established music shop on the Market Square. The artists included Caruso, Harry Lauder, Peter Dawson, and the Coldstream Guards Band, whose music was no doubt among that reported as being heard by all; on the other hand Madame Melba's rendering of Lo Hear The Gentle Lark did not penetrate beyond the 300-seat enclosure.

In appearing on disc Madame Melba took a different attitude from Dame Clara Butt, who several times appeared in person at Northampton but who the previous October had stated her reasons for not submitting to being recorded. She refused to "sing into the gramophone" despite the offer of large fees because she would have no control of the records. It appears that she had once been into an oyster saloon where the customers were informed "So-and-so sings while you eat" and she objected to the idea of people eating while she sang, even though she might be disembodied.

Again in January, 1910, Abels lent three gramophones for a public concert, this time in the Town Hall on a Saturday night. Three years after that the Northants Talking Machine Society was in existence and holding a New Year function at the St. James Restaurant.

Two cinemas had opened in 1912, in October the Kingsthorpe Electric Cinema in the Liberty Hall, Washington Street, and in November the East Park Picturedrome, on the site of Robinson's former stonemason's yard. There were also the East End Picture Palace, known at one stage as Bentley's, in Wellingborough Road; and the Castle Cinema in a former skating rink at St. James End, whose proprietors, F. W. Giddings and J. de Chastelain, pointed out in their advertisements that it was "built and decorated by Northampton men for Northampton patrons—stick to your guns, patronise local people."

In this respect the Temperance Hall, which had been in regular operation for some years following its occasional use for picture shows, represented the opposite extreme. It had become part of a big chain—a tendency which was to accelerate over the years until the majority of cinemas were in one group or another. "Northampton's new entertainment" was how Messrs. Andrews announced their opening of the Temperance Hall as a permanent cinema, in September, 1908. It was to endure until 1963 when it could claim to be the longest continuous cinema in Britain.* The Andrews Brothers had opened their first cinema in 1902. When they went public in July, 1910, their advertisement in the Northampton Press showed that they had eight other cinemas and were about to open seven more. Besides the 900-seat Northampton house they had 1,200-seat picture palaces at Southsea, Burnley and Dewsbury; 1,000-seaters at Rochdale and Plymouth; and others at Stalybridge (800), Colne (700) and Edmonton (300). The ones being added with the floating of a new £50,000 public company were at Gateshead (2,000), Wembley (650), Westcliff-on-Sea (600), Putney (500) and 450-seat houses at Romford, Stockwell and Tottenham. From all these a profit of £250 a week, or £13,285 a year, was likely, based on how the existing houses were faring—and this represented a return of 27 per cent on

---

*A claim since overtaken by that of the Haven Cinema, Stourport-on-Severn, Worcestershire, which closed in 1976 after continuous performances since 1904.

capital. The two brothers, A. H. and E. H. Andrews, were to be managing directors of the company for a minimum of four years at the modest salaries of £10 a week, inclusive of directors' fees.

When Kings Picture Palace, the former East End Picture Palace, changed hands in February, 1913, its new owners controlled 30 cinemas. One of their local efforts to pull in the crowds against the growing opposition was the provision of "dainty teas" free at the Thursday matinees (seats 2d. to 9d.). Another attraction was "private boxes seating up to five."

Leon Vint, who took over the former Palace of Varieties and Picture House, Northampton, in September, 1913, already ran at least 14 other places of entertainment—the Theatre and Palace, Rugby; the Theatre and Picturedrome at Nuneaton; the Hippodrome, Loughborough; the Picturedrome, Long Eaton; the Picturedrome, Ilkeston; the Palace, Barry Dock; the Palace, Aberavon; the Theatre, Port Talbot; the Palace and Hippodrome, Neath; the Palace, Llanelly; and the Palace, Carmarthen. He seemed to make a speciality of having two houses in the same town. After renaming his Northampton acquisition as Vint's Palace he introduced cine-variety, the Daily Chronicle explaining: "Many people find a continuous exhibition of cinematograph pictures rather trying to the eyes. In order to give a pleasing relief and variety Mr. Vint's policy is to alternately show films and give performances by high class artistes."

The Independent did not believe there was enough money about to pay for all the competing entertainment houses. "But we have to consider," it pontificated," that the present generation is consumed by a passion for pleasure in leisure moments and after all considering how hard they have to work under the modern speeding-up conditions of manufacture it is scarcely to be wondered at if they prefer to have their senses tickled rather than spend laborious nights in self-improvement."

Certainly it may not be surprising that people preferred an evening of escapism at theatre or pictures to listening to political sermons. When a mere handful attended a Socialist meeting at the Town Hall on the question of adult suffrage in January, 1913, Councillor Slinn said he was grievously disappointed, pointing out that long queues of young people waited for admission to the entertainment houses. Furthermore the Town Hall was crowded into the corridor when a meeting was held to discuss whether to sell a football player. This was the same Councillor Slinn who said his party could not support the New Theatre application for a stage play licence because it employed people at the miserable rate of 1s. for five hours work.

Certainly there seems to have been entertainment for all, even those in prison. In January, 1913, Wellingborough Adult School Prize Male Voice Choir were described as "pioneers of prison music" by Captain Rich, governor of Northampton Prison, when they sang there for the third year running.

Meantime, while the competition was increasing, there had come in February, 1910, a return visit to the Opera House of the Frank Benson Company which was stated to carry 20 tons of scenery to mount its selection of Shakespearean plays. That same month Miss Marie Studholme paid a first visit to the town in *Miss Hook of Holland* which was publicised as "the most successful musical of the last 10 years". In September, 1923, Miss Studholme married Claud Borrett, son of General Borrett, of West Haddon, Northants; Claude, who had a good voice, had obtained an engagement in *Lady Madcap* to be with her (there's a plot for you!) Other famous musicals of the pre-war period were *The Dairymaids, Our Miss Gibbs, The Merry Widow, The Gay Gordons, The Arcadians, The Dollar Princess, The Quaker Girl, The Girl in the Train, Floradora, The Chocolate Soldier, The Mousmé* (for which Robert Courtneidge had gone to Japan to get the local colour right), the performance in December, 1911, being the first out of London.

A Royal Divorce, the story of Napoleon and Josephine, which came to Northampton for the umpteenth time in February, 1910, was still presented by W. W. Kelly, who operated theatres at Liverpool, which probably explained why the show was then paying its 53rd visit to that city. Another old favourite at Northampton in August, 1910, was *Les Cloches de Corneville,* by Milton Bode and John Hart's Company. *The Whip,* which came with 40 tons of scenery in both 1911 and 1912, continued to draw the public. On the latter occasion George Dance's Company were stated to be carrying duplicated machinery so that they "may arrive some days before the opening night to undergo rehearsal." In October, 1911, came a play by A. E. W. Mason, former member of the Compton Comedy Company, entitled *Witness for the Defence.* Following this were two three-day runs of *The Degenerates* and *Trilby,* staged by Alban B. Limpus's Company, with Mrs. Langtry. Her former Royal lover had died in May the previous year, being the second monarch to have his funeral screened in Northampton cinemas. Cinematograph shows on the Racecourse were a feature of the Coronation celebrations of his successor, George V. When he and his Queen visited the town in September, 1913, Andrews Pictures promised to screen a film of the event the same night.

The year 1912 saw the deaths of the man who had built the Opera House, the man who might have had it built, and the man who first conducted the orchestra there—Henry Martin, Henry Labouchere and William Oates. Henry Martin, who left £129,000, had had a spectacular building career since first coming to Northampton as a carpenter in 1849. He had tackled pretty well every sort of job. Almost every main street in Northampton had its quota of Martin-built shops. Martins had built breweries at Watford and Reigate as well as the Dorman and Pope one at Abington, Northampton. They had restored or added to the churches of St. Peter's and St. Edmund's in Northampton and others at Kingsthorpe, Weston Favell, Boughton, Brixworth, Creaton, Hanslope, Haversham, Holcot, Shuckburgh and Wicken. In the field of industry they had put up the factories of G. T. Hawkins, Dawson and Son, John Branch, H. E. Randall, Arnold Brothers, and Bassett-Lowke. Where stately homes were concerned they had installed new sanitation at Althorp, added to Mr. Agnew's manor at Farthingstone (since demolished), and worked on many others. Housing estates on the edge of growing Northampton had been given the firm's attention and with Alfred Cockerill as a partner Martin had bought the land on which they put up Lutterworth, Loyd and Wycliffe Roads, the first name being after the native town they shared. The pair also laid out the Southampton and Euston Road districts. Perhaps his most notable commission in many eyes was the construction of the Masonic Boys School at Bushey, Herts. The "might-have-been" was that of Henry Labouchere, the millionaire former M.P. for the town, who had retired to Florence where his wife, the former actress Henrietta Hodson, had pre-deceased him. Now he died, aged 80, leaving over £2m. An occasional patron of the

August 7th, 1909. THE NORTHAMPTON INDEPEND

OPERA HOUSE BAND STRIKE OVER.

A strike for better pay by the Northampton Opera House Band lasted 23 weeks in 1909 but achieved little. It was part of a country-wide agitation for improved wages for the musicians of the pit. In October, 1913, the Amalgamated Society of Musicians, a forerunner of today's Musicians' Union, demanded increased salaries of 42s. a week for twice-nightly performances and 36s. "for those in theatre orchestras". *(Northampton Independent)*.

The first municipal repertory theatre in the United States was set up in Northampton, Massachusetts, in 1912-13. It was housed in the Academy of Music, given to the city by Mr. Frank Lyman in the late 19th century, which is seen in the right half of this picture, opposite the Edwards Church. After being in use as a cinema for some years the theatre was restored in 1976 as part of the Bicentennial celebrations. *(Daily Hampshire Gazette)*.

Two pictures of Milton Bode, Birmingham-born actor who became the owner of several theatres, including Northampton Opera House, some jointly with Edward Compton.

Captain James Dardie, formerly of the Worcestershire Regiment, a pre-Rep. manager.

Mrs. Irene Osgood, of Guilsborough Hall, several of whose plays were given copyright performances at the Opera House.

Henry Labouchere, an M.P. for Northampton for many years, at one time owned the Queens Theatre, Long Acre.

Henry Martin whose firm built the Opera House. Lutterworth-born, he was Mayor of Northampton in 1892.

A picture, in the Northampton Independent of an outing of Opera House staff to Aspley Guise in January, 1919 —note how many there were of them!

Picture postcards were used for theatre publicity, pre-printed with the local theatre's name added either on the reverse or in a space left on the front. This one is for George Dance's musical comedy *A Chinese Honeymoon*, presented by Milton Bode's Company, for four nights from Boxing Day, 1906.

Temptation is the name given to this scene from Nita Rae's *The Sins of a City*, one of the many melodramas presented during the early years of the regime of Milton Bode and Edward Compton. This presentation by Winifred Maude's Company was in December, 1905.

One of the most popular shows both in the early years and after the turn of the century was *Les Cloches de Corneville*, presented on this occasion as an "enormous attraction for the Race Week" by E. S. Alban's Comic Opera Company Note the vast number depicted in the chorus. *(all three postcards from the Osborne Robinson Collection, by courtesy Colin Robinson)*

"LES CLOCHES DE CORNEVILLE." Act II.

Jean Compton (right), granddaughter of Edward Compton, met her husband Arthur Howard (centre) while acting at Cheltenham in 1935 in a company headed by her aunt Ellen Compton (left). The play title has been forgotten by Arthur Howard except that "It was a Marie Tempest play."

Mr. and Mrs. Arthur Howard (Jean Compton) before a picture of his brother, film star Leslie Howard in his role as Peter Standish in the play *Berkeley Square* at the now demolished St. James Theatre, London. The picture was a prop.

Fay Compton with Mr. and Mrs. Howard's baby son Alan—now a member of the Royal Shakespeare Company and winner of a 1976 "Actor of the Year" award.

"This is Your Life"—in December, 1956, Sir Compton Mackenzie was the subject of this popular television programme, then on B.B.C. Television. With him in this picture are Jean Compton ("his favourite niece"), Eamonn Andrews (who presented the show) and Lady Mackenzie. *(B.B.C.)*.

Part of the "crush room" at the Northampton theatre as it is today. Glimpsed through the doors is Osborne Robinson's mural of the interior of the theatre while on the wall on right is the glass case containing the walking stick formerly owned by Henry Irving, made from wood from the mulberry tree planted at Abington Abbey by David Garrick in 1778. *(Bryan J. Douglas)*

Members of the Compton and Bateman families who have carried on the acting tradition—Alan Howard, great-grandson of Edward Compton, and Valerie Skardon, daughter of Sidney Crowe and granddaughter of Kate Bateman. *(Picture of Alan Howard by United Newspapers Ltd.; of Miss Skardon by H. Atkinson, Huddersfield)*

Betty Reynolds, who was for 42 years on the staff of Northampton Repertory Theatre, 1928-70, pictured at a Repertory garden fete at Boughton Hall which was opened by Errol Flynn, a former member of the company. *(W. J. Bassett-Lowke)*

The late Sir Gyles Isham, Bart., (right) who played in open air theatre with Fay Compton, is pictured at his home, Lamport Hall, Northants, with Emlyn Williams, who was appearing in a one-man show at Northampton Repertory Theatre. *(Chronicle and Echo)*

The "Good Old Days"—a happy picture of members of the staff in Edwardian costume for an old-time musichall performance in December, 1965. In rear, Dennis Richards, James Fisher; middle row, Jill Farmer, Barbara Higgins, Jean Wallis, Pamela White, Audrey Douglas, Joyce Isham; front row, Marjorie Hart, Betty Lilley and Nancy Farmer. *(Bryan J. Douglas).*

Christopher Denys, most recent Director of Productions at Northampton Repertory Theatre, began in August, 1975, with a splendid production of *The Lion in Winter* and ended with his own play *Lilian,* based on the life of Lilian Baylis, in October, 1976, when he resigned. His was a controversial regime but included some memorable productions and saw the formation of a thriving Playgoers' Club. *(Bryan J. Douglas)*

Mr. A. Dyas Perkins, chairman of the Board of Northampton "Rep" from 1961-75, receives a farewell presentation from his successor, Mr. John Bennett, in January, 1976. Mr. Perkins joined the Board in 1954. *(Chronicle & Echo)*

Scene from John O'Keeffe's *Wild Oats,* presented by the Royal Shakespeare Company at the Aldwych Theatre, London, from December, 1976 to March, 1977. In this scene are Joe Dunlop (Trap), Richard Simpson (Lamp), Alan Howard (Jack Rover) and Lisa Harrow (Lady Amaranth). The drawing below left is of Edward Compton as Jack Rover at Stratford-upon-Avon in 1882. On the right is another picture of his great-grandson, Alan Howard, in the role in 1976. *(Photographs by Reg Wilson. Drawing by courtesy Shakespeare Birthplace Trust)*

Opera House he said that it was a model of what a provincial playhouse should be. The third death was of William Oates who had been musical director from the opening of 1884 until the fire of 1887—why he left at that time is not clear. Later he conducted the orchestra at Whitworth Road Conservative Working Men's Club and was first flute with Northampton Musical Society. Thirty seven years of his working life was spent in the offices of Phipps Brewery from which he retired through ill-health the year before his death, at the time of which, in August, 1912, the Opera House orchestra was conducted by Albert Heyes who was later that year to be seduced away to the larger New Theatre.

In 1912 there were two double copyright performances at the Opera House of plays by Mrs. Irene Osgood, of Gullsborough Hall, a rich authoress of novels with sensational names which ran into many editions. American-born she had caused her own sensations when her third husband was Mr. Robert Harborough Sherard, a picturesque hard-drinking character and fellow author. There were some colourful incidents at the hall, including one when she fired a pistol to attract attention when he was trying to batter down her bedroom door after having had one too many. She divorced him in 1914 there being meantime some unusual litigation over the ownership of a cat.

However, back to the drama on the stage. In April, 1912, members of variety acts performing at the Opera House joined in the reading of Mrs. Osgood's two act musical comedy *The Maid of Beb-Azour* and three act society comedy *The Southern Widow;* and in December there was another "morning performance" of an Osgood double bill, this time *The Demon Lover* and *An Intense Interview.* The public had to be admitted, so as to qualify the occasions as public performances, but in order to restrict their numbers, if not wholly to exclude them, the price was one guinea.

J. W. Turner who had been bringing his opera company to Northampton since 1888 came personally for the last time in the autumn of 1912. The ageing owner, a tenor, had not latterly taken any roles but on the last night he went on stage in the interval of the opera to sing some ballads. This unconventional "natural break" delighted the audience and served as his farewell for he died the following January. Two months later came a visit by F. Castellano's Italian Grand Opera Company and the Moody-Manners Opera Company also paid a number of visits. The Turner Company came back, too, minus their founder.

At this time and indeed for many decades afterwards any suggestion that the theatre in particular and the arts in general should be encouraged by state or municipal subsidy would have caused an uproar in the United Kingdom. It is surprising, therefore, that in our daughter city of Northampton, Massachusetts, a theatre owned by the municipality was given such assistance in 1912-13. The Academy of Music had been given to the town by Mr. Frank Lyman late in the 19th century. In 1912 the Northampton Daily Chronicle reported: "Last Spring the trustees of the theatre decided to provide a Citizen's Company of competent actors and actresses so that the people of Northampton should no longer depend upon what New York managers may send them." This was the first instance of municipally supported theatre in the U.S.A. Our Northampton was not so avant garde restricting itself at this time to considering the first scheme for municipal housing, which it termed "Workmen's Dwellings". The Town Council discussed whether to put baths in them and leave out cellars but resolved not to do so as it would lead to an annual deficit of £4 5s. 8d. It is interesting to note that at the time of writing, in 1976, Northampton, Mass., has received a 15,000 dollar grant from the State's Bicentennial Commission to restore the theatre, which had latterly been used solely as a movie house.

When *The Glad Eye,* which had been very popular in London, first ventured into the provinces in January, 1913, Northampton Opera House was selected for the provincial premiere. The London cast included Daisy Markham who about this time secured the record award of £50,000 as breach of promise damages against the Marquess of Northampton. At Northampton it was given by the Louis Meyer Company, while the original company, minus Daisy Markham, was still packing audiences in at the Strand Theatre. Within months the show returned to Northampton.

In 1913 the Mark Blow and Ida Molesworth Company returned to provide a five week season of twice-nightly repertory beginning in May.

In September that year the Castle Cinema showed a film of the unveiling of the local memorial to Edward VII, designed by Sir George Frampton and placed outside Northampton General Hospital.

After a gap of five years since the production of *The Silver Stick,* Northampton Amateur Operatic Company came out of limbo in 1913 with an announcement by the chairman, Mr. Tom James, that the company had been inactive only because they could not get a suitable building in which to perform. It was through the good offices of the Mayor that they were now able to return to the Opera House. The Mayor who thus used his powers of persuasion was Alderman Harvey Reeves who had appeared in previous shows and who was now president. *Merrie England* was to be staged in 1914. Mr. James said that although the society had always been charitably minded the main object would now be to afford the people assisting in the production as much pleasure as possible.

Musicals in January, 1914, included George Dance's *The Girl On The Film* and *Waltz Dream* and in February came *The Dancing Mistress.*

Fire gutted the Abington Skating Rink, a wood and corrugated iron structure, second in size among Northampton buildings only to the Corn Exchange. Pierrots used it in inclement weather. The 1914 season was to have opened on a Saturday in May but two days before that the place was burned down. Wardrobe and properties were lost in the blaze. The Corn Exchange itself was in a state of dereliction: the roof was in such disrepair that it had been impossible for some time to hold public gatherings there. The Corn Exchange function had been transferred to a skating rink at the rear of the George Hotel. The Exchange was sold for £5,000 to Major W. Hughes, the old Corn Exchange company being wound up.

During August, 1914, the month that the Great War started, the Opera House had a twice-nightly season the resumption of once-nightly being on September 7 when Robert Courtneidge presented *The Arcadians,* from his Shaftesbury Theatre in London. There followed *Brewster's Millions* (Emma and Percy Hutchison's Company), the final visit by the Compton Comedy Company with the founder in charge, the Castellano Grand Opera Company, *Napoleon and Josephine* by Arthur Jefferson's Company including M. Joan Buonapart, said to be a direct descendant of Napoleon, and *The Marriage Market* by a George Edwardes Company, in which Miss Gladys Guy sang the recruiting song Your King and Country Need

You.

The day the Great War broke out Philip B. Ridgeway was in Northampton as manager of *The Silver King* company. He went straight to the recruiting office of Northamptonshire Yeomanry to join up as a trooper in the Duke of Lancaster's Own Yeomanry and later received a Commission in the Lancashire Fusiliers. On this basis he laid claim to being the first actor to join up after the outbreak of war. A year later, on August 4, 1915, he had to leave the forces having strained his heart while rough riding. While in the Army he had made recruiting speeches from various stages, often using recitations supplied by Lilian Braithwaite and had thus convinced several hundred men that "Your Country Needs You."

Whether it applied at the Northampton theatres I have been unable to find out but many safety curtains at this time also carried recruiting propaganda: "This is the safety curtain of this theatre. The men of England are the safety curtain that shield our country from ruin and our women and children from death and worse than death. Are you part of the khaki safety curtain? If not, why not?" No doubt this had a powerful effect on the audiences but it does not appear to have been as effective with some of the theatre folk who appeared on stage. Some appealed against being called up on the grounds that they were indispensable. In February, 1916, a Tribunal at Holborn rejected an application by a theatrical employer, the Mayor demanding to know what it was that made it impossible to replace the actor. He was told that the man was the life and soul of the piece— "He plays the part of a dude and is a very good singer and dancer. His deputy has already been called up." Deferment was not granted. In some parts of the country, on the other hand, tribunals with hunting men on them did give deferment to hunt servants who were deemed to be indispensable.

At Northampton Borough Court the question of calling up actors cropped up three times in one day during June, 1917. Rupert Chauncey Morris had been arrested the previous week at Leicester where he was managing F. G. Kimberly's *Just a Little Pair of Shoes* Company. He claimed to be 42 but had, he explained, registered as being 38 because he was an actor and liked to appear as young as possible. He was given bail for a week to produce a birth certificate. The company had meantime moved on to Northampton where he was due to appear in court on the Saturday. The question of his age was not then resolved, however, because he had meantime shot himself at his lodgings in Kerr Street and died the day after he was due back in Court. Another actor in the company, Ernest Lester, had a different story to tell the magistrates. He had registered as being 46 but found on checking his birth certificate that he was really 38. He was now willing to report and was ordered to do so. At the same court a variety artist from the New Theatre was charged with being an absentee.

War-time staffing problems do not seem to have affected the Harrison Frewin Opera Company which paid its first visit in September, 1916. It carried its own orchestra making the total strength up to over 100. Similar numbers were claimed by the Empire Grand Opera Company in September, 1917.

The prosperity of places of amusement frequently depends upon two factors— how much money the public have in their pockets at the time and to what degree they require to be diverted. At home, wars abroad have frequently been periods of great prosperity while at the same time of great anxiety, when the public have sought relaxation from the cares of the day and the problematical question of the nation's survival. The Northampton New Theatre had its two great periods of heyday during the times of the two World Wars. While I have no direct evidence on the point it appears that the first war also solved the problems of the Opera House. Certainly the standard of theatrical fare was markedly improved.

At the first war-time Christmas, of 1914, it was decided not to take the usual house-to-house collection for the Northampton Poor Children's Christmas Dinner Fund, because, as the Press noted, "Northampton people are enjoying a period of unexampled prosperity so that fewer hampers will be required." Therefore the fund-raising would be restricted to the usual appeal sent out by the treasurer, shoe manufacturer Sir Henry Randall. The spending of the funds raised would also be varied: in place of toys and dolls children in every household where a man was away at the war would be given a "medal commemorative of the great struggle."

From August, 1914, to August, 1916, the Opera House manager was Mr. William Ritchie King, who was succeeded by Mr. Knight-Pearse, who moved here from the Reading theatre.

The Boxing Day attraction of 1914 was the touring version of *The Pearl Girl,* which Robert Courtneidge had presented at the Shaftesbury Theatre, London, and in which Fay Compton had become a star as a replacement member of the cast. The Northampton company was among three touring the show in Britain and it was stated that the production was shortly to tour in America, Africa, Australia and India.

That December the proceeds of a performance at the Opera House of Mrs. Irene Osgood's play *The Menace* were divided between the Red Cross and the Good Samaritan Society.

At the end of January, 1915, came *Dick Whittington* produced by Mr. Edward Graham-Falcon, proprietor of the theatre at Bedford. It was followed by a touring version of *The Cinema Star,* despite the Germanic origins of that piece, which Jack Hulbert had adapted from *Kino Konigen.*

Then came *The Dancing Mistress* and *The Glad Eye,* a revival of *The Gay Parisienne,* after 1,000 nights at Drury Lane, *A Message from Mars,* and two plays with war-time themes—*Officer 66* and *Sealed Orders,* the latter including the destruction of Zeppelins by gunfire, a flower show at Chelsea, a sale at Christie's and a raid on a West End gaming den. It was claimed that "each performance means work in and out of the theatre for 250 people."

Seymour Hicks, who appeared with full London company from the Prince of Wales and Lyceum theatres in the screaming farce *Broadway Jones,* had just met his creditors. Through theatrical speculations some years earlier he had lost heavily but by means of theatre and musichall engagements had managed to pay back £45,000 of his debts leaving only a little over £1,000 owing. "If war had not come I should have been all right by now," he told them. "I hope to pay 10s. in the £ now and the rest as soon as I can."

In the latter half of 1915 there were *The Flag Lieutenant, Brewster's Millions, The Quaker Girl, Oh Oh Delphine, Diplomacy, The Dollar Princess* and *Tonight's The Night.*

January, 1916, brought the death of a former conductor of the Opera House orchestra, James Jackson, of 135 Whitworth Road, who was leader of the New Theatre orchestra at the time of his death. After the second house on Saturday night he had walked home but collapsed and died soon afterwards. Mr. Jackson was also a former conductor of the Whitworth Road Conservative Working Men's Club and leader of the St. Cecilia Orchestra which later became Northampton Symphony Orchestra. Eight months later another former player at both theatres died—former Colour Sergeant W. Corby who had also officiated for many years as trumpeter at Northamptonshire Assizes.

There were wounded soldiers in a number of hospitals in the district and companies at the Opera House sent entertainers to the Weston Favell Hospital (St. John's). Members of the Turner Opera Company went along and so did a party from Leslie Morton and Guyton Heath's *The Geisha* company. Among the patients was Private G. Aubrey, son of the company's advance manager, and upon him Miss Gertrude Newson bestowed a kiss and a wrist watch.

Noel Coward appeared at the Opera House in March, 1916, in *Charley's Aunt* "to good advantage" according to the Independent. "He entered thoroughly into the fun of the part and kept the audience in roars of laughter." The same month the former Compton company actress Haidee Gunn was with a Martin Harvey company in *Mr. Wu*. Martin Harvey himself appeared in the revival of Robertson's version of *David Garrick* the following January. April, 1916, brought the touring version of *The Follies* for the second time (the first had been in May, 1914) in the charge of Dan Everard, lieutenant of the show's late founder Pelissier. It was in burlesque style, taking off modern drama, grand opera, musichall etc.

That month Alfred Ewen, the District Official Receiver who wrote under the pen-name of Alfred England, gave a lantern talk as part of the local Shakespeare Tercentenary Celebrations. Some 18 months later he left the town to enter the priesthood. The legal circles of Northampton also concealed another playwright. The full name of George Pleydell, author of *The Ware Case,* which came to the Opera House in April, 1916, was George Pleydell Bancroft, who was the Clerk of Northamptonshire Assizes. This son of the famous actor-manager Squire Bancroft had written the mystery as a novel but as a play it was equally successful, having been first produced at Wyndham's Theatre the previous September, and was later made into a film. The principal scene in the play was in an Assize court where Sir Hubert Ware, Bart, was on trial for murder. At Northampton the cast was headed by Frank Fenton.

May 15, 1916, was a fateful day for the entertainment industry bringing the introduction of amusement (or entertainment) tax ranging from a halfpenny on a twopenny ticket to 2s. on a 12s. 6d. one. It was introduced as a war-time measure but was to last much longer than "the duration."

Two of the great patriotic songs of the war were reflected in Opera House titles of June, 1916,—*It's a Long Way To Tipperary* and *Keep The Home Fires Burning.*

The J. W. Turner Opera Company were back in February, 1917, followed by Cecil Barth's Company in the old favourite *The Private Secretary.* Gervase Elwes, the internationally famous singing squire of Great Billing Hall, filled the house for a Sunday concert, 400 being left outside. George Edwardes presented *Betty* that same month. Seymour Hicks was the author of *The Happy Day* which a George Edwardes company performed in March, 1917. George Dance presentations that year included *Potash and Perlmutter in Society* and *Manhattan.* Robertson Hare and Edith Evans were among the Charles Macdona Company in *Her Husband's Wife* in April, 1917.

An artist might appear at the theatre one week and at one of the town's cinemas the next. In July, 1917, Albert Chevalier was on the screen of the County Electric Pavilion, on the north side of Gold Street, in *My Old Dutch,* and on stage at the Opera House as Eccles in T. W. Robertson's *Caste.* He had previously appeared at the Corn Exchange and the Town Hall and returned to the Opera House in June, 1918, in *My Old Dutch* of which he was co-author.

Plays with a war theme included *The Munition Girl's Love Story,* given by John F. Carlyle's Company in July, 1917; *Inside the Lines* in February, 1918; and *By Pigeon Post,* August, 1918.

When the inhabitants held a Town Hall meeting to demand reprisals for German Zeppelin raids, news of which had filled the headlines of the local papers, a bloodthirsty letter was read from the former Opera House manager Isaac Tarry, of Richmond, Surrey, demanding that German cities be bombed and Cologne laid in ruins—sparing only the cathedral.

"The play which was banned for over 20 years" was the billing for Ibsen's *Ghosts* in August, 1917, and the following April the author had a two play week, with *The Doll's House* from Monday to Wednesday and *Ghosts* the rest of the week.

A significant increase in the competition to the Opera House came in May, 1918, when the Watch Committee unanimously granted a stage play licence to the New Theatre, widening the range of entertainment which it could provide. After five-and-a-half years it had presumably established its respectability.

Edward Compton died on July 16, 1918, aged 64.

In August, 1918, Tom A. Evans left the managerial seat at the Opera House after nearly two years, being replaced by William Ritchie King, who had been here previously and who now returned from the Kennington Theatre.

In October, 1918, Robert Courtneidge's *The Lilac Domino* returned and so did the reformed Compton Comedy Company, now managed by Mrs. Edward Compton and with Nell Compton, but not yet her sister Viola, among the cast. Bernard Shaw's *You Never Can Tell* was now included along with the old classics, and with *The Importance Of Being Earnest.*

On stage as the war ended in November, 1918, was *The Better 'Ole,* the Bairnsfather play presented by Charles B. Cochran—"this is the play, not the picture" pointed out the advertisement. The phrase was significant because as soon as the nation had recovered from the peace celebrations cinema building began in earnest.

In March, 1919, the Independent noted: "Several schemes are in the air for picture palaces in Northampton, one of which will be on a palatial scale both in size and splendour." This referred to the old Corn Exchange which was to be degutted and converted on luxurious lines, to provide a cinema seating 2,500. But there were also plans for an even more splendiferous picture house on the site of the George Hotel which had stood derelict for some years. This was to be a 2,610 seater (1,906 in the pit and 704 in the balcony) with six shops, two cafes and a restaurant. The Independent claimed, however, that what the town required much more than another cinema, was the replacement of the hotel and it cited the case of the Frank Benson Company who, after a long journey from Torquay, had spend the night motoring round Northampton until 11 p.m. looking for lodgings. The George Hotel project was to remain on paper and so was a suggestion for a new Opera House to be constructed in St. Giles Street as part of a war memorial for the town. The abortive proposal, put forward in the Independent, also involved an extended Town Hall seating over 3,000.

There was a great shortage of houses in Northampton so that people were offering £5 key money and this situation led to a demand for the restriction of luxury building, into which category "super cinemas" quite naturally fell. Under new powers the Town Council could prevent luxury building and appears in the case of the George to have done so, for in due course a plan to build a new bank for Lloyds on the site was substituted. The council also considered halting work on erecting a cinema in the Kingsthorpe Road (the Coliseum) but the situation proved to be Gilbertian. By the time any appeal against a ban had been heard, building carrying on the meanwhile, the place would be finished and open! So opposition to this one was not proceeded with and the cinema opened in August, 1920, on the same day as the Exchange.

A new cinema was also being erected, and duly opened in March, 1920, in Grove Road, with two bioscopes made by the local firm of Bassett-Lowke Ltd., best-known for model construction. This was the Vaudeville, which later became in turn the Regal, Essoldo and now the Plaza Bingo Hall. A former skating rink and picture house just beyond West Bridge was reopened as the St. James Electric Cinema, after being rescued from the derelict state to which it had been reduced by military occupation.

What was the cause of the great rise in cinema attendances which was to bring such a rich harvest for the speculator? In the opinion of the Independent it was due "not only to the higher wages and more leisure for the working classes but also from the production of pictures being lifted above mere sensationalism and becoming an educative force." Daily there were people in rows waiting to book seats while at night long queues formed outside. Be that as it may what cash was spent at the cinema could not be spent at the live theatre, although many continued to be amazed at the amount of money which the public did manage to find to spend on entertaining themselves.

Apart from the competition in general from "the pictures" there was increasing competition in particular from the screen versions of plays and the appearance in films of leading stars of the stage, many of whom jumped on the silent screen bandwagon, taking advantage of the easy money available in the film studios. Even the top line ones did so such as Ellen Terry and Sir John Hare, who appeared in *Caste* at the St. James Cinema. At the Opera House in August, 1919, Graham Pockett presented Eugene Walter's play *The Knife,* direct from the Queen's and Comedy Theatres and dealing with the question of whether condemned criminals should be used for medical experiments. The following week the film of the play was screened for three days at Northampton's Picturedrome Cinema. And although the screen was still silent there was some unlikely competition in the translations of stage musicals to the screen, such as *The Belle Of New York* which came to the same cinema during the month that it was given at the Opera House by J. Bannister Howard's company, presented by Comic Operas (1915) Ltd.

Mr. C. G. Colley-Grattan who took over the Opera House management in February, 1919, was a former manager of the Compton Comedy Company having then joined Milton Bode. Theatres he had managed included the Grand at Wolverhampton where his two children died in infancy and were buried, and the Royal County Theatre, Reading. He was described in the Independent as a highly educated man with great courtesy of manner. On his father's side he was said to be a direct descendant of the Irish statesman Henry Grattan and on his mother's side of the ill-fated Sir George Colley who was in charge of the British Forces, including a Northamptonshire Battalion, at the Battle of Majuba Hill, in the Boer War. After seven months at Northampton the Irishwoman he had married in 1913 was left a widow when he died of pneumonia at the age of 33 and was buried in Wolverhampton. The wreaths included those of Milton Bode and Edward Compton, the orchestra, stage staff, front of house staff and Mr. W. H. Holloway, editor of the Independent.

In November, 1919, the Compton Comedy Company paid what was to be a final visit. The very last play they presented in the theatre they had opened 35 years earlier was the one which had been the favourite of the late Edward Compton—*Davy Garrick*. Nell Compton led the revived company at this time, her sister Viola not joining until the Spring of 1920.

About this time the Independent suggested the setting up of a theatrical hostel for the large number of artistes who each week visited the town's two theatres. This would also "reduce the danger of young girls being tempted into undesirable company."

In May, 1920, Opera House patrons were asked to sign a petition protesting against a bit of bureaucracy forbidding the sale of chocolates in theatres after 8 p.m.

Frank Benson, who appeared in person with his company in March, 1920, had driven a motor ambulance in France during the war, his wife taking charge of a canteen. For 30 years he had organised the Stratford festivals. But, reported the Independent, the Northampton public appeared to prefer trashy pantomimes to Benson's Shakespeare, judging by the numbers in the audiences for *The Merchant of Venice, The Merry Wives of Windsor, The Taming of the Shrew,* and *Hamlet.* Interviewed by a Northampton reporter Benson was clearly undismayed. He said that there were ever increasing signs that the plays that were prevalent nowadays did not express the spirit or satisfy the desires of a nation which had emerged victoriously through the greatest ordeal in its history. He forecast that Shakespeare would soon come into his own again—"for he embodies the spirit of the nation,"

Mixed in with the Bard were musicals such as *The Southern Maid, The Arcadians* and *The Powder Girl;* plays such as *The Female Hun, A Pair of Silk Stockings,* and farces such as *Be Careful Baby;* visits by the D'Oyly Carte and other opera companies; and the occasional revue such as *Odds On* which was given twice nightly in May, 1920.

The Press was usually very adulatory about the "attractions" at the various entertainment houses but occasionally there was a peppery outburst, as for example during the D'Oyly Carte visit of October, 1920. "What a contrast," said the Independent, "these productions afford with the wretched rubbish which has been put on the boards during the last decade. To listen to the Sullivan music and the wholesome Gilbert humour is to slide back 20 years to a time before the theatre had debased itself by incorporating the mere frivolities of vaudeville. One can only regret that such opportunities for genuine enjoyment are few and far between." I find this inexplicable. It was not even fair comment.

Was the editor ageing? Did he have a hangover that morning? A couple of weeks later *Chu Chin Chow* visited the theatre—"the costliest production being toured." Scarcely a "vaudeville frivolity". And soon after that came the Birmingham Repertory Company in *Abraham Lincoln*. Was this "wretched rubbish"?

In 1920 Milton Bode was advertising for attractions for his "Milton Bode and Edward Compton" theatres at Northampton, Reading, Chester and two at Leicester.

Today, through the medium of advertising, almost every facet of life is subject to glamourisation or puffing. It is difficult for the ordinary housewife, even though she be intelligent, to be able to divine her own motives in buying dairy fresh butter instead of super-spread margarine (or vice-versa); to know whether she is buying it because she and the family like it, because one is cheaper than the other (as I write Euro-bureaucrats are seeking to cure that by a levelling-up in price) or because it promotes her to Super-Mum, as the adverts tell her. And similar nonsense.

In the world of showbiz the task of the historian has been made more difficult because puffing has for so long been part of the art of promotion—of fetching the audience into the theatre, a very vital part of the operation. My theatre belief is simply expressed "Get them in and entertain them." Without doing the first you cannot achieve the second.

Puffing has certainly been going on since the 18th century and may have been invented or at any rate developed by that great managerial character Jemmy Whitley.

The difficulty of separating fact from fiction applies equally to takings as to talent. Just what, for instance, does "Enormous Success!!!" represent in terms of cash takings? Private entrepreneurs of the theatre world have not been in the habit of publishing their receipts and sometimes their wills are the only firm evidence—fairly convincing evidence, one way or the other, in many cases.

The discovery of a set of hard facts in the form of the actual nightly accounts of a theatre, both at box office and bar, is therefore a great find, especially if the outgoings are also included. Such a vital piece of evidence was for many years used as a prop at the Opera House. A well-bound and impressive looking book it was handed about by members of the Repertory Players in the era which followed the one dealt with in the book. It seems likely that there was originally a number of account books which could have told the full financial story and which were left behind when the old management sold out in 1925 but all the others have disappeared. The one that survives covers the years 1920-3, a period of decline which is reflected in abysmally low takings for some of the presentations.

Repertory actors using the book as a prop would sometimes be called upon to write in it as part of the action and at other times they penned comments while waiting in the wings. Thus we find, in contrast from the neat clerical hand of the manager of the 20's, some scrawly and artistic writing by an actor of the 40's. While waiting in the wings to appear in *The Sparks Fly Upwards* in April, 1948, the Wellingborough-born actor Arnold Peters (Peter Gadd) wrote a few comments on an empty page of the account book, which was presumably used as a prop for the production. Here are two of the entries: "Wednesday: June dried—had a prompt now. Things are going wrong tonight. A flood slide fell off just now outside the window" and "Thursday matinee: Very good house. We are taking it fairly fast to get out to tea early. Beth just came on, got a laugh on her entrance, got a round on her exit. Alan was just off." Alan was Alan Bromly, later the head of B.B.C. Television Drama. June was June Ellis, whom he married. Beth was Beth Hawkes who married Essex cricketer Roy Smith. An entry on the Saturday night was: "I heard that the authoress is in front again—hope all goes well." The authoress was Doreen Simpson.

The actual accounts run from *Lilac Domino* in the week commencing February 7, 1920, to *The Sign of the Cross* in the week of September 17, 1923, though there are gaps, caused by actors tearing out sheets and using them for other purposes.

Considerable variations in annual income were shown in the books. The financial period ended in June, along with the season. In June 1920, the year's income of £10,065 exceeded outgoings of £9,497 by £568 but twelve months later there was a deficit of £42 on an income almost halved, at £5746 (expenses, £5788). The following year saw a swing back to income of £7,474 and expenses of £7,201 so that the theatre was again in surplus, by £272. Then came a slight falling-off, to June, 1923, with an income of £6,975 and expenses of £6,773, leaving £202 to carry forward. The accounts for the following period covered only nine weeks before petering out with the end of the book but at that stage income of £1,363 was again exceeding outgoings of £1,227.

The book began during the management of Mr. Knight-Pearse and his accounts are slightly more detailed than some of the later ones. Outgoings in those early pages included payments to two "money takers", Johnson, pit, 10s 6d; and Martin, gallery, 9s; and eight "checkers", A. Wilson, 17s 6d; Thomason 10s 6d; Aris and M. Wilson, 10s; Dean 9s; and Crick, Elliott and Wright, 7s. These are weekly figures! In the circle bar F. Richards got 12s 3d (again per week) while in the pit bar C. Richards got 10s 6d.

The orchestra payments were very clearly defined and show the instrumental composition, though this would vary with the type of show with augmentation for grand opera, for instance. As conductor and violinist Rudge received 12s 2d for each of seven performances, making £4 5s 2d in all. The others were leader, Harris, 9s 7d, £3 7s 1d; second violin, Tomlin, 8s 4d, £2 18s 4d, and the same amount for cello (Care), bass (R. Clarke), cornet (A. Clarke) and clarinet (Brewster). The rest got 10s 5d per performance, a total of £3 12s 11d a week—second cornet (Kingston), flute (J. C. Law), trombone (G. Edwards) and drums (Tebbutt). Payments also varied for once- and twice-nightly.

A payment in April, 1920, was of £275 to Milton Bode "on account of expenses" and £225 to the executors of Edward Compton. The following October £3 7s 6d was paid for a stage play licence.

Theatres had a percentage arrangement with each of the managements bringing companies to the house. What percentage the touring company could command would vary with their drawing power. The *Lilac Domino* company got as much as 65% and as the takings that week were £626 they received £407, leaving the theatre with £219 to pay all dues and demands. For *The Sign of The Cross* Mr. and Mrs. Maclaren got 50% and as it took a mere £110 they and the theatre each got £55. Among the few companies which could claim more than 65% were the D'Oyly Carte Opera Co. who received 66⅔ (two-thirds) of the £615 they aggregated in April 1920, with a selection of Gilbert and Sullivan

Operas; and the George Edwardes *A Southern Maid* company who got even more—70%, which as the take was £494 amounted to £346 (theatre £148).

Some of the lesser companies, such as the Ann Welfit-Cecil Gray Repertory Company, received less in percentage and much less in cash. This particular group were in for 40% of the first £100 and 45% above that for their two-week stay in July, 1920. Their plays included such passing pieces as *Toys of Fate, Remembered Kiss* and *A Perfect Day*. Their takings for the weeks and share were £300 (£130) and £160 (£67). On a return visit 12 months later they fared considerably worse with £76 (£30) in the first week and £50 (£20) in the second.

At this time the theatre had three bars, in the circle, pit and gallery and the accounts include the nightly takings in each of them. These bore no relation to the box office income, as for instance during the visit of Miss Leah Bateman's *A Peep Behind the Scenes* Company, twice nightly, in June, 1921, when the week's total ticket income of £181 (company share 40%, £72) included £15 on Monday and £55 on Saturday but corresponding bar takings of £4 3s 6d and £3 9s 8d respectively, so that though the Saturday ticket money was nearly four times that of the Monday the bar money was less. The £4 3s 6d taken on the Monday included £3 5s 6d circle, 15s pit and 3s gallery.

The Caesar's Wife company which followed *Lilac Domino* were contracted for 50% of the first £200, 55% of up to £400, and 60% of anything above that. In fact they took £247 and received £126, leaving £121 for the theatre. *The Purple Mask,* which came next, got 55% of the first £300 and 60% thereafter but took only £221 and did not therefore qualify for the upper bracket, receiving £121 (theatre £99).

Top money taken during the period included Grossmith and Laurillard's *Chu Chin Chow* in October, 1920 (takings £717, company £505, theatre £212). Companies came off worst when the theatre had a cash guarantee—such as the £150 guaranteed when Mr. Leon Vint's *Three Weeks* company performed in May, 1921: as they took only £170 they were left with a mere £20. They were worse off than Cecil Baillay's and Rupert Lister's Repertory Company despite the fact that the latter grossed a mere £47 13s. 1d. At 47½% their share came to £22 12s. 8d. leaving the theatre only £25. The worst actual house was that of the Welfit-Gray Repertory Company on their return in 1921—on Tuesday, June 21, the first house yielded only £1 4s. 5d. The company share at the end of the week was £20 2s. 7d.

Early shows of 1922 included Macdonald and Young's *Nothing But The Truth;* T. C. Wray's *The Blue Lagoon* and Alfred Ray's *Dick Whittington* and then came *The Arcadians* with Don Rolyat in his original part.

During the seven-week vacation of 1922 the manager, Mr. J. H. Turner, received £1 5s. 9d. expenses for travelling to Reading, no doubt to see "the boss". The same year a supply of chocolates left at the end of the season was sent on to the Leicester theatre, the carriage on £5 5s. 2d. worth being a mere 2s. 1d. Mr. Turner, who is shown receiving a wage of £5 a week, lived just around the corner at 20 Derngate which was owned by the theatre and for which he paid a rent of 10s. a week.

Taking in the musicians there were 21 named staff of whom only the manager received full pay during the summer vacation. Watson, whose wage was £1 15s a week, received 17s 6d for three days work during the 1922 summer break. Pratt, the stage manager, got £2 5s a week and Chambers £2 10s while other entries were anonymous casuals: 1 stage 10s 6d; 1 flies 12s 3d; 1 flies 10s 6d; 4 limes £2 2s; 1 props 10s 6d; 2 daymen 8s. Advertising outgoings were Daily Chronicle £3 8s; Daily Echo £4 4s; Northamptonshire Evening Telegraph £2 2s; and Independent 18s. The entry for the vacation week ending July 9, 1921, included "Deficit balance brought forward from old financial year £49 7s 1d" so that it would appear that the theatre actually lost money during the preceding 12 months, the figures being income £5,746 12s 2d and expenditure £5,788 19s 3d. At the start of the new financial year and season there was an entry on the income side "From M. Bode's Capital Account £250" from which it would appear that Bode had to send money to keep things afloat.

For 1922 the Northampton Amateur Operatic Company chose Les Cloches de Corneville which they presented at the New Theatre—their first show there. With ex-Mayor Harvey Reeves as The Baillie it was a considerable success and was visited by the ex-husband of Minnie Palmer, John R. Rogers, now aged 81 but still very young in heart (he claimed not to have touched a spoonful of neat water for 46 years, and no white bread for 51 years) and now operating as a talent scout, hoping to find some promising amateurs whom he could convert to professionals.

Of the Amateurs' takings, as of all theatrical takings at this time and for many years to come, a considerable proportion went in entertainment tax, that wartime measure which had stayed, as new taxes tend to do. Of each 4s. ticket the Government took 9d. Of total receipts of £829 11s. 6d. it appropriated £143. The Independent said that the tax was a millstone dragging down an industry essential to our social life. Full figures of the week were published in the Press. The hire of the theatre accounted for £265, performing rights £32, the coach, musical director and pianist £78, and the costumes, including carriage charges, £65. Nevertheless the company were able to show a £36 profit and this after paying off the £76 loss they had sustained the previous year with the Duchess of Dantzic at the Opera House. The company immediately chose La Mascotte for the following year (which was in due course attacked by the Independent for its "old fashioned artificiality") and remained at the New Theatre until the closure of that theatre in 1958.

March brought The Private Secretary (£198 total takings) again and another repeat visit was the March one of the Birmingham Repertory Company, with The Romantic Young Lady, The Importance of Being Earnest, Getting Married and Zola's Raquin. (£233)

Two Oscar Wilde plays came in September, the Kimberley and Clyde Repertoire Company staging A Woman Of No Importance from Monday to Wednesday and Lady Windermere'e Fan the second half of the week (£142).

As well as competing from the screen stage stars occasionally went along to cinemas for personal appearances. So that when Mrs. Patrick Campbell appeared at the Opera House that October in Ibsen's Hedda Gabler (£259) she had Norma Talmadge competing live on the stage of the Exchange Cinema as well as on the screen, in Smiling Thru'. Oddly enough the smallest house for the Ibsen play was on Saturday night when only £27 was taken.

As far as the Press were concerned Mrs. Patrick Campbell was a silent figure. The Independent cast her as "The Woman Who Wouldn't". The reason was that she utterly refused to give any Press interviews. The paper commented that this could not be due to any bashfulness on her part, judging by the startling character of her recently published memoirs. Determined to print something about the actress, preferably something to annoy her, the editor published a piece about a local man who was with her late husband in the trenches during the Boer War, on April 5, 1900, the very morning when Sgt. Patrick Campbell was killed. This was, no doubt, one in the eye for the Woman Who Wouldn't reflecting as it did upon her antiquity!

An unexpected appearance among the Opera House fare was *The Beggar's Opera,* which was being toured by Messrs. Taylor Platt and Wilfred Eaton following its successful revival by Nigel Playfair at the Lyric Theatre, Hammersmith, in 1920. It came to Northampton in October, 1922, taking £348.

The following month the D'Oyly Carte Company sent out a sporting challenge to Northampton teams. The secretaries of any clubs or teams desiring to challenge the company at tennis, golf, billiards, cricket, football or swimming were invited to write to the secretary of the D'Oyly Carte Sports Club at the theatre. Their line-up on stage included: Monday and Saturday matinee *The Mikado,* Tuesday and Friday *Yeomen of the Guard,* Wednesday and Saturday night *The Gondoliers;* Thursday *Trial By Jury* and *The Pirates of Penzance.* They received £508 of the takings of £763.

Two musicals in a week were given in November by J. A. E. Malone's Company—*The Merry Widow* the first half, and *Gipsy Love* the second. They aggregated £350.

George Bernard Shaw was in Northampton that autumn, not to visit the theatre but for a weekend stay at the Derngate home of Mr. and Mrs. W. J. Bassett-Lowke.

In December, 1922, Annie Hughes, of Northampton, sang from the early broadcasting station at Marconi House. "Stand By! Stand By!" from the announcer was heard by Mr. W. A. Tomlinson in the parlour of his shop at 60 Wellingborough Road, Northampton. With remarkable foresight he observed: "That will be the time when we can see the singer by wireless as well as hear, and it is assuredly coming." This was three years before the discovery of television, in 1926! A few weeks later Mr. Tomlinson heard the first broadcast of grand opera "live" from Covent Garden. He invited a reporter along to hear Mozart's The Magic Flute—"We heard the orchestra tuning up and salvoes of applause which at first sounded like an express train." All this was to provide much competition for the theatre and there were people who forecast that live entertainment would die when you could sit at home and listen to it, and, as Mr. Tomlinson forecast, watch it. As we know it was the onset of universal television which did put paid to scores of live theatres in the 1950s and 1960s.

When Tom Osborne Robinson, to whom this book is dedicated, died in January, 1976, his brother Colin found among a vast hoard of theatrical papers in his paint shop at Northampton Repertory Theatre (the former Opera House) a stained "voting slip" dated December, 1922. Headed "Opera House, Northampton" it read: "Milton Bode has been approached on the matter of smoking in the theatre during the season of first-class plays, with the exception of operas, Shakespearean and similar serious plays, and is anxious to meet the desires and convenience of the patrons as far as is possible. THEREFORE Milton Bode will be glad if patrons of the above house will please vote on the matter according to their wishes, stating both name and address as evidence of good faith and hand this in, or post it to him as soon as possible." Patrons were asked to vote in favour of smoking during performances or against it.

Colin Robinson, who has a fine collection of postcards, also looked out for me the publicity postcard of Nell Compton which is reproduced on Page 174 and which bears on the reverse side details of the plays presented by the Compton Comedy Company at Northampton in November, 1920—the company's last visit to the town.

Early in 1923 Robert Courtneidge paid a personal call to Northampton while presenting *Clothes And The Woman.* Herbert Marshall was in the cast and the show took £170.

In January that year there was nearly a birth on stage when Nora, one of the Shetland ponies pulling Cinderella's coach, foaled half-an-hour after the performance. The newcomer was named Cinderella. The following month there was a variety of livestock—camels, horses, mules, donkeys, sheep and goats, "as used at Drury Lane"—when Wylie Tate presented *The Garden Of Allah.* Prices were increased to meet the costs of this menagerie in miniature, the dress circle being 5s. 3d. In two weeks the takings totalled £1,443.

After *Paddy's The Next Best Thing* (£306) came a four week season by the Birmingham Repertory Company which included *The Romantic Age, The Importance of being Earnest, The New Morality, Advertising April,* and *The Rivals.* "Rarely has a touring company met with a more rapturous response" said the Independent. Rapturous it may have been but the hard facts of the accounts book do not indicate that the numbers in rapture were correspondingly large. Only £607 passed through the box office during the month's stay.

In April Prince Henry sat in the first row of the stalls—"a place he prefers as it prevents his being the cynosure of all eyes." In a London theatre just previously a young woman sitting taking notes behind him had her notebook confiscated. Whether she was taking down the pearls of Royal comment on the performance or taking down the show itself with plagiaristic intent is not clear.

After Dorothy Dickson in *Sally* for Easter Week (£646) came *The Rotters* (£105) and Nell Compton and Gerard A. Neville in *The Portrait* from Monday to Wednesday and *Too Much Money* (prior to London production) for the rest of the week. It is sad to note that the name of Compton did not hold sufficient magic or even nostalgia among the playgoers of the town to draw more than £68 of their money—£34 for the company and a similar sum for the theatre.

During a break from June 9 – July 21 the Opera House was renovated and redecorated with tapestry paper and white enamel and there were new tip-up seats for the upper circle and a new drop curtain.

To have seen Dot Stephens on stage in the reopening show *Sunshine Sally* (£176) you would scarcely have imagined that she had two artificial feet. She had fallen from a railway carriage en route from Wolverhampton to Glasgow, because of a door being insecurely fastened, and a passing train took off both her feet.

In August a short repertory season by the G. Carlton Wallace Company from the Theatre Royal, Norwich, did rather better than the Birmingham Rep. had done earlier in the year, with *The Two Orphans* (£134), *The Eternal City* (£139), *The Apple of Eden* (£134) and *East Lynne* (£213).

The book of accounts comes to an end in October, 1923, but for one week of the following year there are available a set of figures showing how the company part of the receipts might be allocated. This is for the week of December 8-13, 1924, when Sir Frank Benson's Company played in a different play at each performance—Monday, *A Midsummer Night's Dream;* Tuesday, *The School for Scandal;* Wednesday, *Romeo and Juliet;* Thursday matinee, *Twelfth Night;* Thursday, *Julius Caesar;* Friday, *She Stoops to Conquer;* Saturday matinee *As You Like It* and Saturday evening *The Merchant of Venice.* The figures are among a complete record of the Benson tour in the Shakespeare Library at Birmingham University. Not only are the takings given for each performance but also the numbers of people attending. On the outgoing side expenses are listed in detail down to £1 5s. for the hire of shrubs, 18s. 9d. for postage on circulars, and 26 fares at 2s. 6d. from Bedford, where the company had been the previous week. The first thing that emerges is that there was a loss of £144 12s. 4d. on the week, the expenditure totalling £252 7s. 9d. and the income (55 per cent of the takings) £107 15s. 5d. Gross receipts and attendances were: Monday (334) £20 16s. 9d.; Tuesday (248) £18 15s. 3d.; Wednesday (241) £18 8s. 4d.; Thursday matinee (263) £27 14s. 6d.; Thursday evening (334) £24 17s.; Friday (306) £24 18s. 6d.; Saturday matinee (446) £36 16s. 9d.; Saturday evening (316) £23 11s. 10d. The total attendance was 2,488; total takings, £195 18s. 11d. Company share (55%) £107 15s. 5d.

On the outgoing side salaries, at £155 7s. 6d., amounted to more than the company share of the receipts. The 26 fares from Bedford, at half-a-crown each totalled £3 5s. and other items were: Nairn's fare to London 6s. 1d.; advance agent 2s. 1d.; Truck, Bedford to Northampton 11s. 10d.; advance agent's costs 13s. 4d.; insurance 12s. 9d.; manager's petty cash £1 13s. 2d.; manager's commission £5 7s. 9d.; printing account £7 5s. 6d.; advertisements in newspapers in lieu of double crowns (posters) £2 10s.; postage on circulars 18s. 9d.; May's, hire wardrobe £14; Clarkson, hire wigs £2 10s.; carpenter's account £14 7s.; props account £1 1s. 1½d.; hire of shrubs etc. £1 5s.; wardrobe account 12s 8d.; 6d.; super account £1 7s.; stage gratuities, £1; cash for treasury £250. Finally: F. R. Benson £100.

After 40 years of operations prices of 1924 were identical with what they had been 40 years earlier, when the theatre first opened. A contrast indeed with the 1970s!

One of the London theatres which was closed for a long period at this difficult time was the Elephant and Castle but late in 1924 it was re-opened by A. H. and S. Barnard and N. Carter Slaughter. The last-named was to play an important part in the revival of the fortunes of the Northampton theatre.

In January, 1925, the Independent noted the golden jubilee in the profession of Mr. Alfred Watson, who had given up touring some 30 years previously to settle in Northampton and join the Opera House staff where he was then in charge of the saloon bar. Like all old pros he had many a yarn to tell about the stars with whom he had come into contact—Henry Irving, Shiel Barry, Wilson Barrett, Mrs. Bandmann-Palmer, Arthur Dacre and Amy Roselle. He had recently presented to Mrs. Frank Esmond, wife of the Opera House manager, a set of Harry Paulton programmes, she being a granddaughter of the family. While travelling with Wilson Barrett in *The Silver King* he had had the unusual experience of playing twice on Christmas Day at the Theatre Royal, Belfast.

In June, 1924, after a term of four years, Mr. J. H. Turner was succeeded as manager by Mr. Frank Esmond, who came from the Bode headquarters at the County Theatre, Reading, but had had at one time been assistant manager to Mr. Frank McClintock at the Cinema de Luxe in Campbell Street, Northampton. He had also toured with Moss Empires, been a prisoner of war from January to November, 1918, working on a German farm, and on demobilisation had joined Mr. Maclaren with Wilson's Barrett's Company and had played at Northampton four years earlier in *The Sign of the Cross*.

Shows of January, 1925, included *Lilies of the Field* and the musical comedies *Sally* and *The Merry Widow*. In February *Charley's Aunt* was followed by a new play by P. F. W. Ryan, *The Marlboroughs*, featuring Fred Terry as the Duke and his wife Julia Neilson as the Duchess. The 88-year-old Carter Edwards who was also in the cast was stated to be the oldest working actor. Then came the Birmingham Repertory Company, with Raymond Huntley, in Eden Philpott's *The Farmer's Wife*.

These were the terminal shows of the Bode regime—it was now solely his regime because Edward Compton's widow had found it impossible to get on with him and sold her share to him. Now he in turn sold the theatre to Northampton Theatre Syndicate, owners of the rival New Theatre. Their plan was to eliminate or control the opposition, if necessary by knocking down the theatre.

Bode lived at Reading. From 1912-19 his residence was at Westdene, Woodcote Road, Caversham; then he moved briefly to Charleville in the same road; until 1924 he had a house of the same name in The Warren before shifting finally to Cliffe House by the Thames. His direct links with Northampton were few, as with most of the towns of his other theatres. He seems only rarely to have visited the outposts of his theatrical empire although my Patron Harold Nash tells me that Bode did buy shoes from the Crick shoe factory in Northampton (wholesale?). As far as I can tell he seems to have been that typical man of business, whether running a cotton mill in Lancashire or a theatre empire from Berkshire, who managed to combine hardfaced tactics in the making of money, which is a sort of religion to them, with acts of kindness towards their fellow men and towards animals in other spheres or in particular cases.

Bode certainly had a soft spot for animals. He was a generous contributor to the Southern France branch of the Society for the Prevention of Cruelty to Animals (so the Reading Press stated) and from his villa in Monte Carlo he deprecated the local custom of shooting at pigeons released from traps. In his garden there he had a fountain built for the pigeons and to this liquid refreshment he would personally add the solid variety, taking pleasure in feeding them in the mornings, when resident. In later life he normally wintered abroad. Pigeons also provided him with a sporting interest; the lofts at Cliffe House housed some of the finest racing pigeons in Europe. When he gave a gold cup to the Reading Specialist Flying Club in 1930, for a race from Bordeaux, he won the trophy himself. Horse racing was another of his interests. He owned Page 1, Page II and Art Silk, his trainer being Lord Dundas, later Marquis of Zetland. He was also keen on poultry breeding and was a great lover of flowers, his carnation and orchid houses being well-known.

At Reading he played some part in the community life being at one time a member of the old Board of Guardians whose duties included supervision of the local workhouse and he was a founder member of Reading Chamber of Commerce. Besides the Wellington Club, Reading, he was a member of two London clubs, the Eccentric and the Constitutional.

Within a year of disposing of the Northampton theatre Bode was a key figure and witness in a sensational court case at Reading which put into gaol an ex-Mayor and an ex-Coroner. Having sold a property but not received the proceeds from his solicitors, Martin and Martin, Bode petitioned for their bankruptcy and the upshot was that the brothers, John Wessley Martin (74), three times Mayor of Reading, and Frederick William Martin (69), who had been acting Coroner during the 1914-18 War, were both sent down in January, 1926, for three years. Bode lost some £2,500 in the embezzlement.

At 65 when most people are thinking of retiring Bode took on a final theatre, the Theatre Royal, Bristol, in which his partners were Robert Courtneidge and Douglas Millar. By 1931, "crippled physically and artistically disheartened" Millar sold his share to William Ritchie King who had been Bode's manager and confidante at several theatres including Northampton Opera House, Leicester Opera House and the Dalston Theatre. King also acted as manager at Bristol. The "crippled" phase is that of Kathleen Barker who in 1974 wrote the history of the Bristol theatre. During her researches she came across some letters written by Bode and told me that they indicated that he was "a man of little education and less artistic integrity," adding, however, that they may have been typical only of the seventh age of man—"cranky old age."

After 1931, while shedding most of his other theatrical interests Bode retained his interest at Bristol, nominally at least, until his death at Cliffe House, after some months illness, on January 10, 1938, three days after his 78th birthday. His £45,000 will included a £500 bequest to King, whom he named as one of his executors. One of Bode's Miltonian idiosyncracies was to enclose appropriate quotations with his letters. One of the last he wrote was to George M. Slater, with which was enclosed: "Death is sweet—Death is rest—Think of it! To rest for ever. I promise you that whensoever and wheresoever Death comes to meet me I shall greet him with a smile."

As Bode had given up at Northampton two formidable competitors were on the horizon—radio drama and other entertainments, and the talking film. Advice about "always covering your earth plate in clay if you can possibly find it beneath the surface of the ground" prefaced the announcement in the Independent in 1925 that the "B.B.C. will transmit the first real broadcasting play on Sunday, August 9." It was a Mystery Play in modern style by a new author "with the underlying motive of the Christ running through it." That month saw the opening of the new Daventry Broadcasting Station, 5XX, situated only 14 miles from Northampton and described as "the finest station in the world . . . with two valves good results can be obtained in any part of the United Kingdom." The number of wireless licences issued on June 1 was 1,371,581, an increase of over half-a-million on the previous year. Real talkie films did not arrive in Northampton until August, 1929, by which time the Opera House had ended its private enterprise era, but in October, 1925, there was a form of sound film which reads rather amusingly. The Prince And the Maid, which came to the Exchange Cinema, was described as "the first musical comedy picture." The sound was achieved by travelling a quartet of singers and providing the orchestra with a proper score instead of their usual method of playing whatever the conductor thought appropriate.

My predecessor as editor of the Northampton and County Independent, Mr. Bernard G. Holloway, showed great leadership of opinion on the theatrical matter of the inauguration of Repertory, as we shall see, but he appears to have been less perspicacious in his comments on the purchase of the Opera House by the rival management, in March, 1925. In remarks made following the January announcement of the take-over bid he would seem to have disregarded the possibility that in business terms (and theatres were very much regarded in those terms) the logical thing for the "New", suffering its own share of the doldrums of the 20s, would be to eliminate the opposition, one way or another . . . by demolishing the rival house if necessary. A year or so later this is exactly what was proposed, though it did not happen.

Editor Holloway was almost certainly blinded by another admirable passion of his—a desire to keep Northampton business and enterprises in local hands, to keep at bay as long as possible the national syndicates and outsiders generally. Out of old world courtesy he said a pleasant thank you to Milton Bode but in truth he was glad to see the back of one who was an "outsider". In a leader he welcomed the change: "It is in our opinion a satisfactory circumstance that the important house of entertainment should be purchased by a local syndicate. It is a refreshing reflection that the Northampton Opera House was started by Northampton initiative. Now, after long years, it is restored to local gentlemen in whose hands we feel its continued success may be assured." The Independent understood that the administrative policy of the Opera House would remain the same for the present but "there is no doubt that in the near future many innovations may be introduced." Yes, indeed! Demolition.

It may be considered symptomatic of the way things were in the theatre world generally that during the month of the handover the staff and management of both theatres contributed to the funeral expenses of a 39-year-old actor Erno Astor (stage name Victor Antoine) who died in his lodgings in Northampton between weeks of playing The Beggar's Opera at Wolverton, Bucks, and Wigan, Lancs. They did so in order to save him from a pauper's grave.

In July, 1925, the Opera House announced that smoking was now allowed at all performances and another novelty that month was the appearance of the Savaloy Orpheans Burlesque Jazz Band, with "12 nippy dancers in an intoxicating revel of laughter and novelty." But immediately following the take-over there had been The Way of an Eagle, adapted from an Ethel M. Dell novel, with Colin Clive, who a few years later was to be the first Baron Frankenstein on sound film; Tons Of Money, one of the famous Aldwych farces presented by Tom Walls, Leslie Henson and Bannister Howard "as performed before the King'"; in June there was The Rat by David L'Estrange, presented by Fred Warden and Milton Bode, and starring F. V. Owen who had understudied the Ivor Novello role in London; and two three-day runs of plays "for adults only", The Flaming Passion and The Ruined Lives, played twice nightly. In August came the Frank Fortescue Famous Repertory Company for a season, of whom more later.

Audience participation was still being indulged in at the time. On August 25 the Daily Echo reported: "The second house at Northampton Opera House on Monday thoroughly enjoyed the presentation of a play which did not pretend to be highbrow. So absorbed were some members of the audience that they began to hiss the villain off the stage and had to be called to order. As the handsome hero was about to drink some drugged wine one languishing damsel called out 'Don't!' The hero did not take her advice for under the influence of the drug he was the central figure in a hectic love scene, and that could not be left out even to oblige a lady."

Meantime in July, 1925, Frank Esmond had been succeeded as manager by Captain James Dardie, late of the Worcestershire Regiment, who had retired after 35 years in the Army, including Boer War service. For several years he was with the Leinster Regiment under Col. Raynsford, who became commanding officer of the 1st. Battalion of the Northamptonshire Regiment.

When *The Arcadians* came to Northampton in the autumn of 1925 it was to the New Theatre, not the Opera House, which had seen so many previous versions. Later, in October, the Birmingham Repertory Company returned, with Raymond Huntley.

Though private enterprise theatre was to continue at the New Theatre until August, 1958, it was now on its way out down Guildhall Road.

Before passing on to the transformation this may be a suitable place to list some of the premieres which had taken place at the Opera House in those 42 years. Besides *The Lady Slavey* which had launched George Dance on his career of management, there was his *The Gay Parisienne*. Also there were *A Midnight Marriage, A Bad Lot, Two Johnnies, Best Intentions, From Shore To Shore, The Sensualist, The Crimson Mask, Ups and Downs Of Life, The Odds Are Even, Our Eldorado, A Country Dance, A Family Fix, Bilberry of Tilbury, The Menace, The Silver Stick, Simple Simon's Baby, Joan Of Arc, Nippy, The White Lady* and *Perdita Comes To Town.*

During the first 16 years of the reign of George V (1910-26) no fewer than 100 weeks had been devoted to musical pieces. There had been 12 weeks of Shakespeare, by the Florence Glossop Harris Company, the Alexander March Company, Sir Frank Benson's Company, Charles Dornton's Company and C. Bainton's Company. A total of 22 weeks of grand opera had been offered by the Moody-Manners Company, the J. W. Turner Company, Castellano's Company, the Harrison Frewin Company, the Empire Grand Opera Company, the H. P. Phillips Company, the Allington Charsley Company and, each seven times visitors, the Carl Rosa Opera Company and the D'Oyly Carte.

This era was now nearly over.

EPILOGUE

ADVENTURE IN REPERTORY

The New Theatre management, who now owned the Opera House, had notions of eliminating the opposition by demolition but the Northampton Independent and others had different ideas—why not form a repertory theatre? A meeting was called and on January 10, 1927, the great adventure began with Pinero's His House in Order. Today the company has just clocked up its half-century but there has been further talk of demolition.

286

Can Northampton Establish its Own Repertory Theatre?

WHAT BRISTOL AND BATH HAVE ACCOMPLISHED.

A CALL TO LOCAL PLAYGOERS.

By our Special Representative.

In last week's issue I endeavoured to prove that the long awaited re-birth of good drama in England was fast becoming an accomplished fact. I further sought to divine how far this welcome renaissance might be brought home to Northampton. It is gratifying to find that my confidence in the good taste of local playgoers and their willingness to support any effort to promote this desirable end is not misplaced. So numerous have been the assurances of appreciation of the suggestions provisionally thrown out in my previous article that I am encouraged to " carry on." During the week I have got into touch with the management of the Bristol and Bath Repertory Theatres, seeking information as to their establishment and administration. Their characteristically prompt and courteous replies are appended.

Bristol's theatre is, as I stated, run entirely by the Bristol Rotary Club. Their general honorary secretary, Mr. A. E. Stanley Hill, in the course of a cordial letter remarks : " If I can give you any further information even to the extent of seeing a few friends in Northampton who are interested, I shall be only too pleased." This . . . . . has given

when, for my sins, I managed the Abbey Theatre in Dublin. Those who are responsible for Bristol's Little Theatre have wisely ignored the austerely-minded person and have resolved that their theatre shall be one where all intelligent persons shall find intelligent recreation, rather than a place where melancholy men and misunderstood women may twiddle their souls. That, I think, is why Bristol's Little Theatre has done so well. That is why, I think, it will do better.

" I detect in this Little Theatre a note of enthusiasm which is the surest guarantee of its value. It is the misfortune of all institutions, however enthusiastically they may have been founded, that the enthusiasm begins to slacken. Much is taken for granted. Other interests grow up. I doubt if the enthusiasm in which the Little Theatre was founded will ever dwindle, for Mr. Stanley Hill surely has discovered the secret of perennial enthusiasm. I pray you all, who care for this Little Theatre that you keep your hearts up and your enthusiasm burning brightly. Do not behave like superior persons, but take a decent quiet pride in your work, for it is by such as you, ... intelligently . . . . un-

The first suggestion that a Repertory Theatre be formed in the town was made in the Northampton Independent in a series of articles in 1926.

Epilogue

ADVENTURE IN REPERTORY

It was as a direct result of comments and suggestions in the Northampton and County Independent that Northampton Repertory Company was formed and that Northampton Opera House became Northampton Repertory Theatre.

It all began in a fairly routine way with one of those articles in which the Press from time to time lay about them at members of the general public for not giving sufficient support to some facet of local activity. Sometimes it is sport which is suffering from the stay-at-homes, sometimes the arts. In this case it was a very plain-spoken piece, first attacking the general level of entertainment at the Opera House, then criticising the public for not supporting more adequately the few good shows which did come.

"Is Northampton's dramatic taste declining?" asked the magazine." Much ink has been spilt and discussions ensued in regard to the class of dramatic fare now being offered at Northampton Opera House. Criticism has been levelled which in effect describes the plays presented as an insult to the intelligence and dramatic taste of Northampton playgoers". The reference was to the appearance of the Frank Fortescue Famous Repertory Company. While not mentioning the company by name Aubrey Dyas describes their offerings in his book Adventure In Repertory, covering the first 21 years of the Repertory Company: "Drama lay in the doldrums in Northampton in the fateful year of 1926. A similar plight affected the majority of other towns and cities in England at that time. The theatre was at a low ebb, enfeebled, stale and moribund. Third-rate touring companies and tawdry stock companies were the chief purveyors of dramatic entertainment. Cheap plays were thrown on and badly acted. Small wonder that they often played to ruinous business. An apt example is provided by the season given at the Opera House, Northampton, from January to April, 1926, by an old-style touring-stock company. Playing twice nightly they put on two pieces a week for three nights each. Happily, the so-called plays in their repertoire have now been banished to the limbo of the past. The wonder is not that they are dead but that they were ever born. They were tuppenny paper tales adapted for the stage, cheap, crude, and, at the most, vulgarly diverting. The titles of the pieces billed during that season clearly indicate their class, *Her Life of Pleasure, The White Slaves of London,* and *The Plaything of an Hour.* In the main, they comprised three varieties; harrowing melodramas, like *The Face at the Window;* hackneyed sentimental stuff such as *When The Angelus is Ringing,* and *Back Home in Tennessee;*

and trite pieces with suggestive titles like *Soiled, The Unwanted Child, Not Fit to Marry, Shame* and *Should a Wife Refuse?*"

But, as the Independent revealed, when "good" shows had been put on some of them lost as much as £250 a week. "Before us as we write is a letter from the general manager of George Edwardes's (Daly's) Productions citing his experiences in Northampton with a previous play—one of the failures above referred to—and regretting on this score his disinclination to bring *Katza The Dancer* to Northampton. Thus has but one of London's finest shows given Northampton the go-by. Slowly but surely Northampton is being black-listed by leading producers. If the process is allowed to continue we may find ourselves unenviably isolated from the best in provincial dramatic art".

In April, 1926, an article by "a special representative" said that Britain needed a dramatic change. "Spectacular effects and lavish settings are fast failing to satisfy a dramatic appetite which craves for the food of thought and abiding impressions." London, declared the writer, had signified its desire for a change by emigrating to its suburban repertory theatres. "In the provinces repertory theatres are springing up like mushrooms in a night but unlike the mushroom have proved that they can endure." This came at the time when the Northampton theatre was starting a season by the Elephant Repertory Company whose productions were in complete and total contrast to those of the Fortescue establishment. By midsummer, when the theatre was normally closed altogether the "Elephant" was still doing excellent business and when the 200th performance took place on July 31 N. Carter Slaughter, its manager, travelled down from the Elephant and Castle Theatre to take part in a celebratory entertainment which included excerpts from previous productions, musical items etc. A special souvenir programme was printed and Percy Gallagher, manager of the New Theatre, went down Guildhall Road to mount the stage, pay a tribute to the company, and thank the audience for its support, on behalf of the owners, Northampton Theatre Syndicate.

At that moment, despite this temporary success, it must have seemed highly unlikely that the then 42-year-old theatre would still be standing many years after its then 14-year-old larger and more ornate competitor in Abington Street would be turned into rubble and replaced by a supermarket—especially as they were both in the same ownership.

The Independent arrived at the conclusion that a Repertory company should be formed, meetings to that end were held, and it was decided so to do. The Elephant Company carried on until December, moving to the New Theatre for the last fortnight to allow pantomime rehearsals to take place at the Opera House—the final production of its private enterprise era. The story is told in full in Adventure In Repertory, written by Aubrey Dyas Perkins under his pen-name of Aubrey Dyas, the signature for many years under the programme notes which he contributed to the theatre's programmes. He joined the Board of Directors in 1954 and served as chairman from 1961 to 1975, an era during which he firmly left his imprint on the theatre's activities. His insistence that the Board should take a part that was more than merely consultative in choosing the plays and supervising the budgets allowed the theatre to survive better than most and, compared with other theatres, without calling for extravagant hand-outs either from the Arts Council or from the local authorities. His book, the main part of which starts precisely where this one leaves off, on the night of Monday, January 10, 1927, with the new company on stage for Pinero's *His House In Order,* deals graphically with its ups and downs over 21 years. Unfortunately that volume is now out of print but I am pleased to say that Mr. Perkins is working on a fresh history of the theatre's Rep era, which will bring the story up to the golden jubilee of January, 1977.

In manner of which Edward Compton would assuredly approve, "birthdays" like the 21st are not ignored at the theatre. Perhaps the most memorable celebration came on May, 5, 1959, marking the 75th anniversary of the building, which was attended by two of Compton's children. Fay was there and so was Viola, along with her younger son John Crocker who had, as it happened, written two recent pantomimes for the company. Fay also brought a message from her brother Compton Mackenzie apologising for his absence but saying that he was proud to think that he was in some small way in at the beginning—asleep in his cot in a dressing room. Also present were Sir Emrys Williams, Secretary-General of the Arts Council, and Mr. Robert Digby, Secretary of the Council of Repertory Theatres. Introduced by Sir Gyles Isham, Bart., Fay made a short speech from the stage and was presented with a bouquet by the theatre's most regular customer—81-year-old Mr. William Frederick Wright, of 21 Ivy Road, Northampton, who had first attended the theatre at the age of 10 in the late 1880s, when he had seen *Falka,* and who had missed only three productions in the 31 years of Repertory. He was given a ticket for life, for his regular seat in

---

NORTHAMPTON REPERTORY PLAYERS

will open their First Season at the

Opera House on January 10th, 1927

by presenting :

" *His House in Order* "

By Sir ARTHUR PINERO.

Included in the Cast will be

BLUEBELL GLAID,   MARGOT LISTER,   J. DREW-CARRAN,
C GRAHAM-CAMERON,   C. T. DOE,   C. HARCOURT-BROOKE,

ETC., ETC.

BOOKING PLANS TO BE OPENED ON TUESDAY NEXT.

"Who knows but that from these modest foundations may arise a dramatic edifice in Northampton resembling those in Bristol, Bath and possibly even Birmingham? The venture will assuredly be watched and, we confidently anticipate, supported with the keenest enthusiasm on the part of all local playgoers in town and county alike"—the Northampton Independent, December, 1926.

the Upper Circle, No. 12 A. Even Mr. Wright was not the oldest customer, for 87-year-old Mrs. Annie Eccles, of 79 Gloucester Avenue, Northampton, could recall visiting the theatre in 1890 to see *The Village Ford,* and after the show walking the five miles back to her then home in the village of Pattishall. For that anniversary night the circle was "dressed" and the play was *Twelfth Night.* The part of Malvolio, which had been Edward Compton's on the opening night in 1884, was taken by Lionel Hamilton. Mrs. Compton had been Viola in 1884; in 1959 the role was taken by Jennie Goossens, daughter of Leon Goossens, the famous oboist. Ruth Trouncer was the 1959 Olivia and Charles Workman was Sir Toby Belch. Also present in the audience was the late Earl Spencer, who is, so to speak, a Patron of this volume from the grave, having subscribed only a fortnight before his death in the summer of 1975, and who pointed out to Sir Gyles Isham that night that his father had attended the opening in 1884.

The firm which built the Opera House is, sadly, no longer with us. The demise of Henry Martin Ltd. merited the main Page One headline in the Chronicle and Echo on Saturday, April 19, 1975: "Building Firm Closing Down," over a story of redundancy notices being issued to the workers of the firm established in 1872 which had become "another casualty of the depressed state of the building industry." Mr. Hugh Finnimore, great-grandson of Henry Martin, was the managing director at the time of dissolution, after 103 years: he described it as a very sad day.

The final lines of Adventure in Repertory looked forward 29 years to the golden jubilee: "After varying changes of fortune, the Northampton Repertory Theatre has successfully reached the twenty-first milestone in its exciting and adventurous journey. There is no reason why it should not continue to perform an indispensable service to the town. There is no reason why it should not continue to be honourably spoken of all over the world for its worthy representation of our rich dramatic heritage. There is no reason whatever why it should not go forward with confidence towards its golden jubilee, provided it believes in the past, trusts the present, and plans for the future." The author of these prophetic words, Aubrey Dyas (Perkins), was (and is) a most kindly man but for occasions when it was required to serve what he saw to be the best interests of the "Rep." he reserved a most acid tongue.

On the morning of Sunday, January 18, 1976, Mr. Perkins received a farewell presentation from the theatre at the Harlestone Road, Northampton, home of his successor as chairman, Mr. John Bennett. It was to be a happily informal get-together, with wives of the Board members present, but the first item on the agenda turned out to be the announcement that news had been received of the death a few hours earlier of Tom Robinson who had personally chosen the volume which was to be the farewell gift. In an impromptu tribute Mr. Bennett described Tom as "The person more than anyone else who has made the theatre what it is." Then he made the presentation to Mr. Perkins who, he said, had made it his aim above all other things to balance the books of the theatre. Acknowledging, Mr. Perkins paid his own tribute both to Mr. Robinson and to Mr. Bill Bland Wood, the recently retired general manager of whom he said: "I would not have carried on so long without him. He stopped me doing unwise things and suggested some things which it would be wise to do." For the future Mr. Perkins urged the Board to follow the maxim that "The Play's the Thing"

An early picture of the Northampton Repertory Company. In rear Robert Young (producer) and T. Osborne Robinson (scenic designer); centre row Errol Flynn, Julian Clay, Peter Rosser, Oswald Dale Roberts, Donald Gordon, John Stobart, Kenneth Grinling; front row, Zillah Grey, Doris Littell, Sheila Millar, Dorothy Galbraith, Elizabeth Inglis, Veronica Rose and Freda Jackson.

Members of the Compton family attended the 75th anniversary of the theatre in Guildhall Road, Northampton, in May, 1959. Pictured are Viola Compton (Mrs. Crocker), Freda Jackson, Fay Compton, Alderman Ewart Marlow and Sir Gyles Isham, Bart. *(Chronicle & Echo)*.

and to exercise great care in the choice of plays. Finally he pleaded with us not to let enemies demolish "this delightful, beautiful compact theatre"—"Keep it alive! Keep it open!"

A third generation connection with the theatre which is still surviving is represented by Dennis Richards in the circle bar. Such people as he epitomise long-term, reliable, steadfast service to the theatre, so much in contrast with the fly-by-night variety, but in his case it is a family connection going back much further than his own starting date of 1934. It was in 1890 that his grandmother, Mrs. Emma Richards, began at the theatre as cleaner and dresser, at the age of 24. The highlight of her 30 years at the Opera House was dressing Lily Langtry for *The Degenerates* in 1911. But Milton Bode was a poor payer—she got 6s a week—and when the Exchange Cinema opened in 1920 she took the chance of better money and moved there. Dennis's mother, Mrs. Florence Barratt, began at the theatre in 1900, as an usherette of 17. After a spell in the circle bar she too left in 1920, to work at the Fish Inn. Her brother and two sisters also worked at the Opera House so that the family service tots up to over 100 years. Dennis himself reaches retiring age in March, 1977.

This volume is timed to be published on April 1, anniversary of the fall of the New Theatre proscenium, and between the golden jubilee of repertory at the former Opera House on January 10, 1977, and the retrospective exhibition at Northampton Art Gallery of the work of T. Osborne Robinson, to whom the book is dedicated. This is not, however, the appropriate place to make any lengthy reference to the theatre's completion of half-a-century, especially as that task is being undertaken by Mr. Perkins. But it would be too blinkered altogether not to mention that the company's 49th year has for a variety of reasons been the most traumatic and difficult in its existence. In addition to that universal enemy of the 70s, Inflation, there have been all sorts of problems on which history will in due course pass its judgment: I have been rather too close to them, as a member of the (unpaid) Board, to do so at present. But as Mr. John Bennett put it in his latest annual report, "It is time to put our house in order"—a rather apposite phrase quoting the title of the Pinero play with which the company commenced its "adventure in repertory" in 1927.

But it is not inappropriate to move a vote of thanks to those other long service stalwarts who, like Osborne Robinson, have served the theatre steadfastly through thick and thin. People like Betty Reynolds, assistan manager, whose 42 years service was second only to that of Tom Robinson; Bryan J. Douglas, who has for a long period combined the roles of stage carpenter and theatre photographer; Dennis the barman, already referred to; and Phyllis Norman who was a familiar face in the box office for many years. These people tend to be taken for granted but their real life roles are equally as vital to the proper functioning of a theatre as the make-believe ones of the actors and actresses.

Now it is time for me to quit the subject of the Northampton stage, having told in four books, within the limitations of time and ability, much of the story of theatre in Northampton and hereabouts. Moved by the sight of the disappearance of the New Theatre under the hammers of demolition men in 1960 I wrote Death of a Theatre. Prompted by Cecil Madden, M.B.E., the man who produced the world's first television programme, I followed this up in 1974 with Theatre Un-Royal, an account of the tatty old theatre in Marefair, of 1806-1884.

The following year came a move further back in time with Drama That Smelled, covering the years prior to 1806, for some of which the drama was performed in the town's Riding House.

Now The Mackenzies Called Compton has emerged and it is time to ring down the curtain on "Northampton Theatre History." But not before resolving that if anyone ever tries to knock down our charming Victorian playhouse—the idea has been mooted by "progressives"—it will be over our dead bodies. Already far too much of our dear old town has been knocked down and we simply will not stand for the death of another theatre . . .

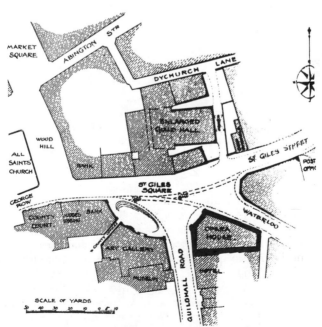

In 1919 the Independent reported on a plan to build a new Opera House as part of a War Memorial scheme.

This treasured souvenir presented to Betty Reynolds, assistant manageress, after 42 years service to Northampton Repertory Theatre, was the work of Tom Robinson. It is his drawing of her as she was when she joined the staff, three months after he did, in 1928. The "handbag" flap lifts and there unfolds a sheet of paper bearing the signatures of staff and others who wished her well on her retirement in 1970. All the names are not visible here, the flaps being only party unfolded. The invisible ones include M. Rilings, G. Tallett, P. White, B. Lilley, N. Farmer, Audrey Douglas, Bryan J. Douglas, L. Twiselton, D. Kingston, A. C. W. Wood, Jim Fisher, K. Worley, D. Dickens, Roger Gartland, Michael Foulkes, David Beale, Clare Ballantyne, C. W. Gamble, Emily Tuckley, Wendy Wilson, I. Wallis, G. Endersby, Dennis Richards, Jill Evans and Doris Hunting. *(Photo-copy, Patrick Wilson).*

Patrons

To me all the Patrons who have so far made four books possible are equal, and equally deserving of gratitude. But the rest must in this case forgive me if I single out for special mention Miss Betty Reynolds. I do so because her length of service to Northampton Repertory Theatre is second only to that of the man to whom this volume is dedicated. Sending her subscription Miss Reynolds stated: "I am delighted that you are dedicating your book on Northampton Theatre Royal and Opera House to Tom. We worked together for my 42½ years and remained great friends until his death last year. I look forward very much indeed to renewing old memories of our lovely little theatre." She also told me of times when they wondered whether the money would be there to pay their wages at the end of the week . . . but that is another story.

Here is the full list of those who, by pre-subscribing, made it possible to publish this book. Their financing the project does not, of course, imply agreement with all or any of the opinions expressed in the text:

B. J. ADAMS (Miss)
(Farthingstone)
CAROLYN ADAMS (Miss)
(Stony Stratford)
H. T. ADAMS
(Trentham, Stoke-on-Trent)
JOHN ADRIAN
(Stanstead Abbotts, Herts)
CHRIS AGER
IIILARY R. ALFORD
(Corby)
D. B. ANDERSON
LEONARD D. ANDREWS
WILLIAM ARNOLD
R. STERRY ASHBY
R. W. ASHBY
(Muscott, Flore)
CAPT. W. ASHBY
(Aynho, Banbury)
GRAHAM ASHLEY
(London)
MR. and MRS. PETER J. ASHTON
(Sao Paulo, Brazil, & New Duston)
LEONARD ATLEY
(Aylesbury)
G. L. ATTERBURY (Mrs.)
(West Haddon)
MARY ATTERBURY (Mrs.)
(West Haddon)
ROBERT J. AYERS
(Stony Stratford)
DR. RONALD AYLING
(Edmonton, Canada)

BOB BAKER
(Market Harborough)

RICHMOND BAKER
(Hardingstone)
ANDRÉ BALDÉT
DEREK BARBER
KATHLEEN BARKER (Miss)
(Wembley)
COUNCILLOR JOHN BARNES and
MRS. BARNES
(Mayor and Mayoress of Northampton,
1976-7)
DENNIS BARRATT
E. G. BARTH
GILBERT BATES
RUSSELL and SUSAN BAXTER
(New Duston)
ROGER BEACHAM
(Cheltenham)
G. H. BELGION (Mrs.)
(Titchmarsh)
HILDA M. BENHAM
(Greens Norton)
JOHN BENNETT
D. K. BERESFORD (Mrs.)
(Oundle)
BRIAN BERRILL
JOAN BETTS
HENRY BIRD
(Hardingstone)
R. T. BODILEY
GORDON BOSWELL
(Hardingstone)
TED BOTTLE
(Coalville, Leic.)
G. W. BRADBURY
(Whiston)

J. E. BRASSINGTON (Mrs.)
(Lowick)
PETER BRINSON
(London)
J. FRANCIS BROWN
(London)
LT.-COL. K. C. BROWN
(Ashton)
DUKE OF BUCCLEUCH and
QUEENSBERRY
H. BULLARD
(Duston)
ALAN MILLER BUNFORD
ALAN BURMAN
E. M. BURR
(Greens Norton)
I.D. BUTLIN (Mrs.)
(Kettering)
J. A. BYRNES
(Elizabeth, New Jersey, U.S.A.)

E. G. CADMAN (Mrs.)
JEREMY H. CALDERWOOD
(Harpole)
J. A. CALLOW, B.A.
(Redditch)
JOHN and MOLLY CAMPION
(Milton Malsor)
HAZEL & STANLEY CARR
(New York, U.S.A.)
BRIAN CARTER
(Milton Malsor)
CANON J. L. CARTWRIGHT
(Peterborough)
I. M. CHAMBERLAIN (Mrs.)
M. CHAMBERS (Mrs.)
JENNY CHANDLER
R. J. CHAPMAN
(Abthorpe, Towcester)
PHILIP CHARLETON
(Walton-on-Thames)
RICHARD C. CHATBURN
DAVID F. CHESHIRE
(London)
CYRIL A. CHOWN
DIANA CHUDLEY (Mrs.)
(Creaton)
MR. and MRS. V. S. CHURCH
MR. and MRS. W. V. CHURCH
THOMAS J. CLARKE
(Hackleton)

MR. and MRS. S. E. CLAYSON
FRANK and PEGGY CLOWES
DR. R. B. COLES
H. A. VICTOR COLLIN
(Lubenham)
HAROLD K. COLMAN
FRANCIS COLTON COMPTON
(Chicago, U.S.A.)
DR. L. W. CONNOLLY
(University of Alberta, Canada)
E. H. COOPER
HORACE COPSON
J. B. CORRIN
BRIAN COX
(Higham Ferrers)
THE REV. R. E. COX
NICHOLAS CROCKER
(Portishead, Bristol)
MRS. LOUIS D. CULLINGS
(Langton Hall, Leic.)
D. R. CUMMINGS
(Church Brampton)
L. and A. B. CURTIS
(Boughton)

GLADYS DAVIES (Mrs.)
(Little Brington)
C. M. DELANEY (Miss)
CHRISTOPHER DENYS
(Pitlochry, Scotland)
PETER DESBOROUGH
(Great Billing)
CYRIL E. DIAMOND
(Thrapston)
PHILIP DICKENS
(Great Houghton)
W. A. DICKENS (Mrs.)
COUNCILLOR JOHN DICKIE
D. WEEDON DODWELL
(Silverstone)
J. E. DOLBY
C. F. O'BRIEN DONAGHEY
(Poringland, Norwich)
Lt.-Col. D. M. DORR, O.B.E.,T.D.
(Wellingborough)
BRYAN J. DOUGLAS
PETER A. DOUGLAS
(Troy, Albany, New York, U.S.A.)
DR. GEORGE BRENDAN DOWELL
(Baltimore, Maryland, U.S.A.)
MONA DRAKE (Mrs.)
(Wellingborough)

MAURICE L. DUNMORE
D. DURHAM
(Hardingstone)
A. DWYER (Mrs.), (Mollie Mayhew)
(Milton Malsor)

GERALD EELE
OLIVE ELLIOTT (Miss)
(Harpole)
JAMES ELLIS
(South Hadley, Mass., U.S.A.)

E. M. FACER (Miss)
C. J. FARROW
(Great Houghton)
REV. J. W. H. FAULKNER
(Bedford)
ARTHUR FAWCETT
(Manchester)
DR. & MRS. E. FINLAY
(Walgrave)
ARTHUR and ELLEN FISHER
(Girard, Ohio, U.S.A.)
THE EARL FITZWILLIAM
(Milton, Peterborough)
LEN & RENE FLOYER
(Flore)
MARGARET FOOT
(Pinner, Middx.)
DEREK FORBES
(Hertford)
JOHN FORD
MICHAEL FORSYTH
RICHARD FOULKES
(Nether Heyford)
WILFRED H. FOX
(Pattishall)
G. B. FREEMAN
(Horton)
SIR GEOFFREY DE FREITAS, K.C.M.G.,
M.P.
H. C. R. FROST
MR. and MRS. H. M. FROST
(Little Oakley)

COUNCILLOR J. J. GARDNER and
MRS. GARDNER
(Mayor and Mayoress of Northampton,
1975-6)
PHYLLIS M. GASCOYNE
H. W. GEARY
(Kettering)
A. GEOFFREY GEE

NORMAN E. GIBBS
(Harlestone)
MARGARET GLADYS GILBERT
L. J. GILES
C. J. GLAZEBROOK, L.G.H.
D. R. GLENN
SIR GERALD GLOVER
(Pytchley)
SADIE GOODMAN (Miss)
MADGE GOSLING (Mrs.)
(Moulton)
MERVYN GOULD
(Boston, Lincs)
JULIE GRAHAM
(Nethercote, Rugby)
HARRY N. GREATOREX
(Swanwick, Derbyshire)
DAVID M. GREEN
(Staverton)
GEORGE GREEN
PAT GREEN (Mrs.)
LT.-COL. T. R. L. GREENHALGH
(Overstone)
PHILIP M. L. DE GROUCHY
(Southampton)
LELAND L. GRUBB Junior
(Milton Malsor)
MR. and MRS. ROBIN GUINNESS
(Hardingstone)

TREVOR HADLAND
(Horton)
JACK HALE
(Brixworth)
BRIAN G. HALL
V.S. HALTON
LIONEL HAMILTON
RAE HAMMOND
(Cheltenham)
ALEX HANCOCK
A. J. HARGRAVE
SIR WILLIAM HART, C.M.G.
(Turweston)
RONALD HARTE
ROGER HASDELL
(Little Houghton)
A. HASTIE
VICTOR A. HATLEY
ALFRED HAWTIN
P. G. HAYWARD
(Largs, Ayrshire)
M. G. HEGGS (Mrs.)

IRIS HENSON
(Manchester)
LADY HESKETH
(Easton Neston)
LORD HESKETH
(Easton Neston)
P. M. HEYGATE (Mrs.)
(Litchborough)
COUNCILLOR PETER HIAMS
BARRY A. HILLMAN
GEORGE HOARE
(Boughton)
MR. and MRS. J. HOCKENHULL
(Great Doddington)
CHERRY HOLLOWAY
(Pitsford)
ALAN MACKENZIE HOWARD
(London)
ARTHUR HOWARD
(London)
WINSTON HUGHES F.B.R.I.S.T. and
ELLEN HUGHES
LYSBETH A. HUMFREY
(Dallington)

TONY IRESON
(Kettering)
ERIC IRVIN
(Normanhurst, Sydney. N.S.W.)

VERNON W. JACKSON
(Wellingborough)
MR. and MRS. A. JACKSON-STOPS
(Wood Burcote, Towcester)
LOUIS JAMES
(University of Kent)
MARCUS JELLEY
ARTHUR JONES M.P.
(Pavenham, Beds)
PROFESSOR H. A. JONES
(Great Bowden, Leic.)
IVOR WYNNE JONES
(Llandudno)
MICHAEL JONES
JACK JOSEPH

DAVID KELSEY
(Hull)
GERALD KENDALL
(Scaldwell)
PAUL KERTI
(Gedney Hill, Lincs)

SYDNEY KILSBY
E. R. KNAPP
(Duston)
ELIZABETH L. KNIGHT
(Ecton)
JESSIE P. KNIGHT (Mrs.)

ERIC LAWE, F.I.I.P., A.R.P.S.
MARGARET E. LEASK
(Lane Cove, Australia)
MARGARET C. LEWIS (Miss)
(Moreton Pinkney)
SANDRA LEY
JOAN LIGHTWOOD (Miss)
N. LINE
COL. P. H. (PEN) LLOYD
(Blaston, Leic.)
PROFESSOR WILLIAM B. LONG
(New York, U.S.A.)
KEITH LOVELL
(Wollaston)
PHIL LYMAN
(Nether Heyford)
W. LYTH
(N.O.D.A., North Western Area)

ANGUS MACKAY
(London)
DR. DONALD M. MACKAY
(Colliers Wood, London)
EDWARD M. C. MACKENZIE
(London)
LILIAN COMPTON MACKENZIE
(Edinburgh)
MARY FAY C. MACKENZIE
(New York, U.S.A.)
JOSEPH MACLEOD
(Florence, Italy)
CECIL MADDEN, M.B.E.
PAUL MANN
(Sherington, Bucks)
CYRIL MARSTON
(Milton Malsor)
A. C. MASON
(Deene)
MASAHIKO MASUMOTO
(Nagoya, Japan)
IAN MAYES
(Hardingstone)
STEPHEN MEAKINS
RON MEARS
(Kettering)

GEOFF MELLOR
(Bradford)
MARTIN MERRITT
(Little Houghton)
MR. and MRS. JAMES R. MERTES
(Milton Malsor and Canton, Ohio,
U.S.A.)
DAVID O. MICHEL
(Milton Malsor)
BILL MIDDLETON
BERNARD J. MILES
(Earls Barton)
MARY MILLBURN, M.A. (Miss)
MR. and MRS. A. J. MINNEY
(Kettering)
W. ROWAN MITCHELL
(Brixworth)
DR. J. MOLONEY
FREDERICK A. MOORE
(Kettering)
VERNE MORGAN
(London)
IN MEMORY OF MALCOLM MORLEY
(London)
NANCY MUNKS (Mrs.)
(Rottingdean)
J. A. J. MUNRO

HAROLD NASH
JOHN F. NASH
(Burton Latimer)
MARGARET V. NASH
CLIFFORD N. NEEDLE
PETER NEWCOMBE
(Blisworth)
GERALD G. NEWELL
(Northampton, Mass., U.S.A.)
FRANK NIGHTINGALE
KEN and JULIA NUTT

BRENDAN O'BRIEN
(Athlone, Ireland)
EVA ONLEY
(Wellingborough)
L. C. ONLEY
CHRISTOPHER OXFORD
(Southport)

BERNARD W. PAINE
(Pershore, Worcs)
MR. & MRS. A. PALFREYMAN
(Maidwell)

PANACHE (TONY & ROSEMARY
SHERIDAN)
(Burton Latimer)
W. E. PARKER
(Church Brampton)
COMMANDER and MRS.
PASLEY-TYLER
(Coton Manor Wildlife Garden)
COUNCILLOR KENNETH R.
PEARSON, M.B.E., A.E.
DR. ALICIA C. PERCIVAL
(London)
A. DYAS PERKINS
A. E. PERKINS
JOHN R. PHILLIPS
W. E. PIGOTT
(Eastbourne)
RAYMOND P. POOLE
J. A. H. PORCH
(Maidwell)
DAVID POWELL
CYRIL PRESCOTT
(Scarborough)
NANCY B. PRINGLE
(Charlton Kings, Cheltenham)
DAVID J. PRIOR
(Thrapston)
LORD PRITCHARD
(West Haddon)
JIM PURVIS
ALMA PYKE
(Great Houghton)

GEORGE RALPH
(Holland, Michigan, U.S.A.)
MR. and MRS. JOHN RAWLINGS
(Mayor and Mayoress of Northampton,
1974-5)
JACK READING
(London)
HYLDA REECE (Mrs.)
(Grafton Regis)
BETTY REYNOLDS (Miss)
ERNEST REYNOLDS
JOHN RICHARDS
(Cardiff)
K. H. RISDALE
(Rushden)
LT.-COL. EVAN ROBERTS
(Deal, Kent)
GRACE E. ROBERTS

COLIN ROBINSON
(Whiston)
MR. and MRS. NICHOLAS ROBINSON
MR. and MRS. SIMON ROBINSON
(East Grafton, Wilts.)
WILLIAM ROGERS
(Nether Heyford)
SYBIL ROSENFELD
(London)
MR. and MRS. J. E. ROWLATT
(Wellingborough)

MOLLIE SANDS
(London)
P. M. SAPPER & CO.
MARGARET SAULL (Miss)
(Edgbaston)
PETER SAUNDERS
(London)
C. B. SAVAGE
RICHARD SAVAGE
(Australia)
H. JILLIAN SELLERS
(U.S.A.)
ANN SHORE
(Barton Seagrave, Kettering)
VALERIE SKARDON
(Harrogate, Yorks)
VIDA SLINN (Mrs. Eric Slinn)
KONRAD SMIGIELSKI
(Cold Ashby)
MR. and MRS. JOHN F. SMITH
(Towcester)
KENNETH A. J. SMITH
(Pitsford)
IVOR SPENCER
(President, Guild of Professional
Toastmasters)
HENRY G. SPOKES
(Church Langton, Leic.)
VICTORIA SQUIRES
(Duston)
T. R. STAUGHTON
NINA STEANE
(Kettering)
GRACE M. STURGIS (Mrs.)
(Overstone)
W. D. SUMMERLY
(Kettering)
J. O. L. SWANN

D. NORMAN TAYLOR

MARIE P. ALLINGTON TAYLOR (Mrs.)
(Long Buckby)
WILFRID TEBBUTT
(Kettering)
W. N. TERRY
PHIL THOMAS
PROFESSOR PETER THOMSON
(Exeter)
JOHN H. THORNTON
ANNE TIBBLE
(Guilsborough)
ERIC TIMS
(Wellingborough)
FRANK TOULSON
(Holcot)
MEG TOYER
VALERIE TRAVIS
BRIAN TRELIVING
KAY TREMBLAY
(Flore)

DR. F. WADDY
(Great Brington)
SIR HEREWARD WAKE, Bart., M.C., D.L.
(Courteenhall)
H. C. WAKE
(Courteenhall)
PETER WAKE
(Hambleden, Herts)
CHARLES WILLIAM WAKERLEY
(Hambleton, Rutland)
DAVID A. WALMSLEY
OSWALD BARRETT WARD
H. J. WATKINSON
ETHEL WHITTINGHAM (Miss)
QUEENIE WIBBERLY
(Wollaston)
DOROTHY WIGGINS (Mrs.)
PETER A. WILCOX
(London)
CYRIL B. WILSON
(Finedon)
KITTY WILSON
(Clipston)
MR. & MRS. S. WILSON
COUNCILLOR ROGER WINTER
PETER WOOD
(Great Shelford, Camb.)
W. BLAND WOOD
PROFESSOR JOSEPH E. WRIGHT
(Nashville, Tennessee, U.S.A.)

KIM A. C. YARDLEY
JOHN REGINALD YATES
  (Old Swinford, Stourbridge)

MOLLIE YATES (Mrs.)
  (Moulton)
WILL YEOMANS
W. H. YORK

PATRONS DECEASED

F. DRIVER (Mrs.)
  (Rhyl)
SIR GYLES ISHAM, Bart.
  (Lamport).
ALLARDYCE NICOLL
  (Colwall, Malvern).
EARL SPENCER
FRED TUCKLEY

Libraries and other organisations

ABINGTON VALE SCHOOL

UNIVERSITY OF AUCKLAND
(New Zealand)

BEDFORDSHIRE COUNTY LIBRARY

BERRY BROS. & LEGGE

BIRMINGHAM PUBLIC LIBRARY

BRIGHTS HARDWARE LTD.

BUCKINGHAMSHIRE COUNTY
LIBRARY

THE BRAMPTON DISCUSSION
GROUP

BRIGHTON PUBLIC LIBRARIES

BRITISH LIBRARY LENDING
DIVISION
(Boston Spa, Yorks)

CHESHIRE PUBLIC LIBRARIES

LEICESTER UNIVERSITY CENTRE,
NORTHAMPTON

UNIVERSITY OF CHICAGO

DALHOUSIE UNIVERSITY LIBRARY
(Halifax, Nova Scotia, Canada)

DERBYSHIRE COUNTY LIBRARY

UNIVERSITY OF DURHAM

UNIVERSITY OF EDINBURGH

FRANKFURT-AM-MAIN TOWN
& UNIVERSITY LIBRARY

HARVARD COLLEGE, CAMBRIDGE,
MASS., U.S.A.

HARVARD THEATRE COLLECTION,
CAMBRIDGE, MASS., U.S.A.

UNIVERSITY OF ESSEX

LEICESTERSHIRE LIBRARIES

LINCOLNSHIRE LIBRARY SERVICE

GARRICK CLUB, LONDON

LEICESTER UNIVERSITY LIBRARY

THE LONDON LIBRARY

RAYMOND MANDER and JOE
MITCHENSON THEATRE
COLLECTION, LONDON

MARC FITCH FUND

MOTLEY BOOKS
(Romsey, Hants)

ENGLISCHES SEMINAR, MUNSTER
UNIVERSITY, WEST GERMANY

OVERSTONE SCHOOL FOR GIRLS

CHRONICLE & ECHO, NORTHAMP-
TON

MERCURY & HERALD, NORTHAMP-
TON

UNIVERSITY OF READING

ROCHDALE LIBRARIES & ARTS
SERVICES

JOHN RYLANDS UNIVERSITY
LIBRARY OF MANCHESTER

NENE COLLEGE, NORTHAMPTON,
PARK CAMPUS

NENE COLLEGE, NORTHAMPTON,
AVENUE CAMPUS

NORTHAMPTON & COUNTY
INDEPENDENT

NORTHAMPTON AMATEUR
OPERATIC COMPANY

NORTHAMPTON COLLEGE OF
FURTHER EDUCATION

NORTHAMPTON HIGH SCHOOL FOR
GIRLS

NORTHAMPTON SCHOOL FOR BOYS

NORTHAMPTONSHIRE RECORD
OFFICE

NORTHAMPTON PLAYGOERS' CLUB

NORTHAMPTON REPERTORY
THEATRE

NORTHAMPTONSHIRE PUBLIC
LIBRARIES

NORTHAMPTON THEATRE GUILD

NORTHAMPTONSHIRE RECORD
SOCIETY

PENNSYLVANIA STATE UNIVERSITY
LIBRARY

CORPS H.Q. ROYAL PIONEER CORPS,
WOOTTON, NORTHAMPTON

UNIVERSITY OF ST. ANDREW'S,
SCOTLAND

SAN DIEGO STATE UNIVERSITY,
CALIFORNIA

SCOTT BADER COMMONWEALTH
(Wollaston)

SHAKESPEARE BIRTHPLACE TRUST,
STRATFORD-UPON-AVON

SHAKESPEARE INSTITUTE,
UNIVERSITY OF BIRMINGHAM

SEFTON LIBRARY SERVICES

SHEFFIELD CITY LIBRARIES

UNIVERSITY OF SHEFFIELD

SMITH COLLEGE LIBRARY,
NORTHAMPTON, MASS., U.S.A.

SOCIETY FOR THEATRE RESEARCH

SOUTHLANDS COLLEGE,
WIMBLEDON
SPINNEY HILL(E) TOWNSWOMEN'S
GUILD, NORTHAMPTON
DOUGLAS MACARTHUR ACADEMY OF
FREEDOM, HOWARD PAYNE
UNIVERSITY, TEXAS, U.S.A.
HUMANITIES RESEARCH CENTRE
UNIVERSITY OF TEXAS IN AUSTIN,
U.S.A.
VICTORIA & ALBERT MUSEUM
METROPOLITAN TORONTO
CENTRAL LIBRARY
MAURICE WHITING PHOTOGRAPHY
READING PUBLIC LIBRARIES
CITY OF NOTTINGHAM PUBLIC
LIBRARIES

UNIVERSITY OF LONDON LIBRARY
UNIVERSITY OF LUND, SWEDEN
UNIVERSITY COLLEGE OF SWANSEA
UNIVERSITY OF LEICESTER
UNIVERSITY OF NOTTINGHAM
TRENT PARK COLLEGE OF
EDUCATION
ROYAL LIBRARY OF COPENHAGEN
MINNEAPOLIS PUBLIC LIBRARY
WESTMINSTER CITY LIBRARIES
LIVERPOOL CITY LIBRARIES
THEATRE MUSEUM, VICTORIA &
ALBERT MUSEUM, LONDON
FOUR PILLARS RESTAURANT, OLNEY,
BUCKS.
FRIENDS OF NORTHAMPTON
MUSEUMS & ART GALLERY

Theatre being sold up—drawing by Osborne Robinson on September 17, 1959, the day the contents of the New Theatre, Abington Street, were auctioned from the stage. *(Photo-copy Bryan J. Douglas).*

ENCORE . . . . . . By Special Request(?)

"One could perhaps be churlish and say that Lou Warwick's book could well serve as a model of how NOT to write theatre history."

I hope I will not be considered churlish in turn in thus launching a little sales talk about three books "by the same author" as they say.

The usual practice in quoting from reviews, whether of books or of dramatic productions, is to pick out the nice bits and ignore the less complimentary phrases. Always aiming to be a little different (and that includes my theatre books) I have instead chosen the above introductory extract from a review of Theatre Un-Royal in the Educational Theatre Journal, published by the American Theatre Association. The reviewer, L. W. Conolly, of the University of Alberta, did in fact, in a later passage, say that the book was "a well illustrated, amiably rambling labour of love." With which I am more than content (especially as L. W. C. has been a Patron of my two subsequent books).

Apart from Death of a Theatre which was published in 1960, a time when it was possible to make profits on ventures like this (the profit of £335 was given to the surviving Northampton Repertory Theatre) my three further efforts have left me financially out of pocket, but a wiser man (which is much more important). Nevertheless, I am keen to sell a few more of the remaining stocks of those books, so as, perhaps around the year 2,000, to break even.

Accordingly I quote below some of the other remarks which have been made, some by reviewers, but others by Patrons. But first here is what one worthy Patron has had to say about the scheme of subscription patronage in general: "Since I first heard (or rather read) of your work into the Northampton theatres in 1974 I have been pleased to think that I could play a small part in the publication of a work of theatre history. Since I first received and read your Theatre Un-Royal that feeling of pleasure has been more than doubled . . . I am deeply interested in your work and hope that the example you have set will be followed by other local historians and that the system of 'patronage' will be greater used to bring to the public the glories of the past." The writer was John Adrian, of Stanstead Abbots, Hertfordshire, who was for 20 years a performer but is now in administration and at the time he wrote this had recently formed the Theatre Research Group of the London Borough of Camden.

Whatever degree of satisfaction the four books have brought to various sections of the readers, it has certainly been most absorbing to act as a one-man band in producing them – to think of them, sell them to people before they had been written, research and write the text, meet and make contact with lots of wonderful people who helped with information, choose the pictures, design the dustcover, select a printer, read the proofs, help the driver unload the books off the delivery lorry, inscribe names on the flyleaf, stagger round delivering them, and finally to pay the bill.

But this Pooh-Bah role means that I must also act as public relations and advertising consultant. If I do not quote the "nice bits" (all entirely unsolicited!) no-one else will so here goes, with suitable blushes and cringes of embarrassment:

Peter Wilcox: "You are, I feel, the natural successor to W. Macqueen-Pope, whose books I also adore. You both have a delightfully theatrical style of writing."

Joseph Macleod, of Florence, Italy: "I would like to congratulate you on Drama That Smelled, a most informative and entertaining work. Especially I admire 'The Dodges

Around the Law' part of the Interlude, which is one of the best accounts I know of the results of the Patent Act and full of things, like the rest of the book, which I did not know about at all."

Mr. George Attewell, of Northampton: "In addition to its history of the New Theatre, in Death of a Theatre, I greatly enjoyed its accurate and quite enthralling portrayal of the social and economic period through which the theatre was born, flourished, and ultimately died. It is, indeed, a complete history of these times."

Daily Telegraph: (of Death of a Theatre): "An unusual record . . . has the historical importance of being equally true of 50 or 100 theatres outside the West End."

The Stage (of Death of a Theatre): "Carried out with skill and care . . . if the reading of this story makes people put up a better fight for future threatened theatres, this cogent, objective analysis must take much of the credit. This book should awaken a new resolve."

Louis James, of the University of Kent: "I was delighted to get Theatre Un-Royal which I am using in the course I teach here on melodrama, I find it a fascinating book both for its theatrical and its general detail."

Paul Scofield (about Drama That Smelled): "Very fascinating indeed."

The Rev. J. W. H. Faulkner, of Bedford: "I was delighted to receive Drama That Smelled . . . heartiest congratulations on another really splendid volume."

Professor Allardyce Nicoll: "I found all the chapters of Theatre Un-Royal of very real interest and value, with numerous pieces of theatrical information which previously had not come my way."

Cecil Madden: "Theatre Un-Royal is splendidly and beautifully got up and presented . . . a masterpiece of research . . . great bargain by any standards."

Anonymous: (of Death of a Theatre); " . . . rather turgid in the middle."

Whether they are "models of how not to write theatre books," worthy of W. Macqueen-Pope, or "turgid in the middle" I shall be very pleased to dispose of the remaining copies of Theatre Un-Royal, Drama That Smelled, and The Mackenzies Called Compton to anyone who has the wherewithal, which is £3.50 for Theatre Un-Royal, or £5 for either of the other two. Plus postage, of course, and as that is a rising as well as scandalous factor I will leave anyone ordering a book to consult their friendly postmaster as to the amount required, merely remarking that if they want the volume to be sent to Australia it will be cheaper than sending it 10 miles in my native country.

There is also the chance to help to republish Death of a Theatre which has been out of print for about 15 years. This arises because there have been a number of inquiries as to the availability of this first book, for which I received invaluable editorial assistance from Miss Meg Toyer. Now that the set of four books has been completed quite a few Patrons have the last three, but not the first. In January, 1976, Mr. Brian G. Hall, a leading light of Northampton's musical scene, asked me: "How can I complete my set of four?" adding that he was not asked the first time. My reply was that I would endeavour to reprint the book if there was sufficient demand. Would he care to send me the money? He did and the scheme was thus in being. Whether it goes ahead depends entirely how many people write to me on reading these lines. It is planned that the new book shall include the whole of the previous one, with revised illustrations, plus some up-to-date comments and an index, which, through my lack of experience, the original lacked, and was therefore useless as a book of reference. It is hoped to be able to re-create the striking original dustcover which was designed by the late Mr. Harold Bagley, manager of the now defunct Mercury Press which printed the book. To make the project possible in these days of soaring costs it is likely that facsimile reproduction will be used, though this would have the merit of being an exact copy of the original, warts and all.

To proceed, with the project around 150 subscriptions are needed, of which 20 have already been received. As usual the names of all patrons will be listed in the book and there will be the customary "thanks" panel on the flyleaf. The cost will be £6.50 including postage. It is hoped that these few lines will produce the necessary 130 further subscribers. If not then all funds will, as usual, be held in trust for return in the (un-precedented) case of failure to go ahead.

Death of a Theatre is the story of the New Theatre, Abington Street, Northampton, opened in 1912 and demolished in 1960, when it was replaced by a supermarket sur-mounted by an income tax office (there's progress for you!). One of the last musichalls to be erected it was unusual in that it was for many years independent, not linked to any circuit. Later it was leased by S. H. Newsome who ran it in conjunction with his Coventry Hippodrome. Finally it become a "nude" theatre in the F. J. Butterworth group. Its story is traced in detail and then an inquest is held on how it came to be knocked down—a story duplicated in the case of dozens of other theatres throughout the country during the 1950s and 60s.

There is also the possibility of producing a further, entirely new, theatre book on the life of James Augustus Whitley, one of the great theatrical characters of the 18th century whose story has not yet been collated in its entirety between the covers of one book. "Jemmy", as he was known, was a decidedly eccentric Irishman who came to England after marrying a widowed actress-manager and built up an extensive empire of provincial theatres which formed the basis of the Nottingham and Derby circuit. Readers of the Northampton Theatre History series will already have encountered him briefly in Theatre Un-Royal and Drama That Smelled.

Whitley died in September, 1781, and the book is planned as a bicentennial tribute to him, though its appearance can be arranged at any prior date when sufficient patrons have been persuaded to part with their money. How much money? These days it is inviting insolvency to set a price on an article up to four years ahead. If the British Post Office continues its present downward path, by 1981 it may cost a fiver to post a book, let alone print it. However it is essential to fix a sum so as to get started and I therefore nominate £10, without many clues as to whether it is too much or too little. The object is to cover costs.

Whatever happens to either of these projects I am loth to disband abruptly the splendid group of Patrons who have gathered around me over a period of 16 years, many in Northampton and the county, others in Australia and Japan etc. I would love, some day, to do a book called The Art of Coarse Music, dealing with that worthy member of the community, the musician, with all his lovable eccentricities.

So if you fancy neither of the above projects but would still like me to carry on pro-ducing some sort of books do, please, write and tell me. But don't forget to enclose some money. . . .

The demolition of the New Theatre, Northampton (picture taken by S. Day on January 28, 1960) and the book about its history, published the following November. Now a reprint is planned of *Death of a Theatre*.

REP MAY HAVE TO COME DOWN

By John Sharpe

NORTHAMPTON'S Royal Theatre could be knocked down and replaced with a completely new theatre if a suggestion by some members of the Town Council is followed.

The building is over 80-years-old and lacks many of the facilities of a modern theatre.

It would be so difficult to modernise and enlarge this building that the supporters of the scheme think a completely new theatre is the only answer.

If a new theatre is built, then the old building would become redundant, and possibly would go to make way for new buildings planned for the Arts Complex in Guildhall Road.

The plan has been discussed by the Leisure and Recreation Advisory Committee of the Town Council, which was set up to advise on plans for an arts complex, probably at Guildhall Road, and a sports complex at Delapre Park.

Different

Alderman Ron Dilleigh, the man who put forward the idea said: "A new theatre would be different, it would not be just a place where you see a play. There would be a proper restaurant for example."

He said a new theatre need not seat many more people than the present one, some 600, "It is not so much the number of seats, it is the facilities provided, the type of stage, dressing accommodation, and restaurant."

There are difficulties with enlarging the present building, he said. There is little room backstage, the dressing rooms are through a tunnel at the other side of Swan Lane, and there is little room in the front booking office.

But Mr. Dilleigh suggested that a new building would make the old Repertory Theatre redundant "It would not be economic to have two theatres," he said.

The advisory committee has discussed the suggestion, and will report its advice on this matter, and on the whole of the sports and arts complex plans to the Town Expansion Committee of the council soon.

Complex

Members of this committee have visited modern theatres at Bristol, Leicester, Nottingham, and Dusseldorf to get ideas.

They are looking at plans for a concert hall, library, art gallery, museum, perhaps an experimental theatre and other facilities which could be sited in a complex of buildings in Guildhall Road.

The committee reports just before the old Town Council gives way to the new District Council, and the suggestions will go to the new council's Leisure and Recreation committee.

This new committee does not have to pay any attention to the report, but as some people sit on both of these committees, for example Mr. Dilleigh, it is likely to carry some weight.

A report in the Northampton Chronicle and Echo on February 13, 1976. February 13 does not appear to be a fortunate date for the theatre in Guildhall Road—it was on that date in 1887 that it burned down.

Index

Looking to the Future . . .

On the last page we step into the Time Machine kindly brought to the Northampton Repertory Theatre by Dr. Who (Tom Baker), of the currently highly successful B.B.C. Television Series, January 10, 1977, the actual 50th anniversary of the "Rep", found him at the theatre, filming for a future episode. He also replied, in highly individual style, to the Toast to "The Profession" proposed by Lady Hesketh, for some years a member of the Board of Directors, at the golden jubilee dinner, at the Saxon Inn Hotel, Northampton. It was at this dinner, at which other speakers included the Minister for the Arts, Lord Donaldson, that Mr. John Bennett, chairman, announced the appointment as Director of productions of Mr. David Kelsey, who is pictured on right with George Bernard Shaw. I am sure that Patrons and other readers of *The Mackenzies Called Compton* will wish him well in his endeavours at the theatre, one of only three to have passed their half-centuries the others being at Liverpool (1911) and Birmingham (1913). *(Photo on left by Barry Roberts, on right by Patrick Wilson)*